# Reassessing Russia's Security

This book provides a detailed analysis of the evolution of Russia's security policy. Based on extensive original research, including an analysis of official documents, political and military elite speeches, interviews, and reports, and considering the subject from the early 20th century onward, the book evaluates how far Russia's security policy is underpinned by "strategic asymmetry"—the acceptance by Russia of its inferior military position, and the pursuit of its strategic aims through the application of a variety of methods, military and non-military, including the manipulation of public opinion, the use of economic leverage, and external security approaches—known as Russia's "hybrid war operations"—to gain the advantage over a militarily and economically superior adversary. The book discusses how Russia's security policy has been and is being applied in specific cases, including the present war in Ukraine, the Russian anti-satellite program, and Russia's contemporary Afghan policy. The aim of the book is to explain how and why Russia uses different security strategies and methods using these three cases.

**Nurlan Aliyev** is a lecturer in the University of Economics and Human Sciences in Warsaw, Poland.

# Routledge Contemporary Russia and Eastern Europe Series

105 **The Nagorno-Karabakh Conflict**
Historical and Political Perspectives
*Edited by M. Hakan Yavuz and Michael Gunter*

106 **Innovation and Modernization in Contemporary Russia**
Science Towns, Technology Parks and Very Limited Success
*Imogen Sophie Kristin Wade*

107 **Ukraine, Russia and the West**
When Value Promotion met Hard Power
*Stefan Hedlund*

108 **Regional Leadership in Post-Soviet Eurasia**
The Strategies of Russia, China, and the European Union
*Edited by Irina Busygina and Svetlana Krivokhizh*

109 **Dagestan – History, Culture, Identity**
*Robert Chenciner and Magomedkhan Magomedkhanov*

110 **Media and Masculinities in Contemporary Russia**
Constructing Non-heteronormativity
*Olga Andreevskikh*

111 **Russia and Latvia**
A Case of Sharp Power
*Andis Kudors*

112 **Reassessing Russia's Security Policy**
*Nurlan Aliyev*

For more information about this series, please visit: www.routledge.com/Routledge-Contemporary-Russia-and-Eastern-Europe-Series/book-series/SE0766

# Reassessing Russia's Security Policy

Nurlan Aliyev

Routledge
Taylor & Francis Group
LONDON AND NEW YORK

First published 2024
by Routledge
4 Park Square, Milton Park, Abingdon, Oxon OX14 4RN

and by Routledge
605 Third Avenue, New York, NY 10158

*Routledge is an imprint of the Taylor & Francis Group, an informa business*

© 2024 Nurlan Aliyev

The right of Nurlan Aliyev to be identified as author of this work has been asserted in accordance with sections 77 and 78 of the Copyright, Designs and Patents Act 1988.

All rights reserved. No part of this book may be reprinted or reproduced or utilised in any form or by any electronic, mechanical, or other means, now known or hereafter invented, including photocopying and recording, or in any information storage or retrieval system, without permission in writing from the publishers.

*Trademark notice*: Product or corporate names may be trademarks or registered trademarks, and are used only for identification and explanation without intent to infringe.

*British Library Cataloguing-in-Publication Data*
A catalogue record for this book is available from the British Library

*Library of Congress Cataloging-in-Publication Data*
Names: Aliyev, Nurlan, author.
Title: Reassessing Russia's security policy / Nurlan Aliyev.
Description: Abingdon, Oxon ; New York, NY : Routledge, 2024. | Series: Routledge contemporary Russia and Eastern Europe series | Includes bibliographical references and index.
Identifiers: LCCN 2023032077 (print) | LCCN 2023032078 (ebook) | ISBN 9781032382968 (hardback) | ISBN 9781032382999 (paperback) | ISBN 9781003344391 (ebook)
Subjects: LCSH: National security--Russia (Federation)--21st century. | Russia (Federation)--Military policy. | Soviet Union--Military policy. | Russia (Federation)--Foreign relations--1991- | Hybrid warfare--Russia (Federation)
Classification: LCC UA770 .A5864 2024 (print) | LCC UA770 (ebook) | DDC 355/.033547--dc23/eng/20230818
LC record available at https://lccn.loc.gov/2023032077
LC ebook record available at https://lccn.loc.gov/2023032078

ISBN: 978-1-032-38296-8 (hbk)
ISBN: 978-1-032-38299-9 (pbk)
ISBN: 978-1-003-34439-1 (ebk)

DOI: 10.4324/9781003344391

Typeset in Times New Roman
by KnowledgeWorks Global Ltd.

*In memory of my parents*

# Contents

| | | |
|---|---|---|
| *Acknowledgments* | | *viii* |
| | Introduction | 1 |
| 1 | The evolution of Russian security thought | 7 |
| 2 | Determinants of Russia's security policy | 41 |
| 3 | The Soviet legacy of Russia's security policy | 81 |
| 4 | Evolution of the Russian Federation's security concept | 116 |
| 5 | Functions of Russia's foreign security policy: New approaches | 147 |
| 6 | The implementation of Russia's foreign policy and the role of its security policy | 192 |
| 7 | Russia's security and foreign policy approaches: Ukraine, star wars, and Afghanistan | 229 |
| | Why does Russia prefer strategic asymmetry? | 280 |
| | *Index* | *288* |

# Acknowledgments

This book emerged from a research project realized at the Faculty of Political Science and International Studies of the University of Warsaw and was financially supported by the Visegrad Scholarship Program in 2018–2023. I am grateful to the faculty and the Visegrad Fund for this amazing opportunity. I would like to thank Dr. Maciej Raś, Dr. Alicja Curanovic, Dean Prof. Daniel Przastek, Prof. Ryszard Zięba, Mr. Alexander Parmee, Mr. Matthew Nieniewski-Mello (the language editor of this book), and Mr. Jiří Sýkora from the Visegrad Fund for all their support. I very much appreciated the helpful comments and support from this book's editor Mr. Peter Sowden as well as the anonymous academic reviewer. Special thanks to Ambassador Jerzy Koźmiński and Professor Ali Abasov for their support during the research. I am especially grateful to the scholars and experts whose works I used as well as all the interviewees for their contributions.

# Introduction

The topic of this book was chosen for its significance to one of the main issues of contemporary international security, namely the evolution and function of Russia's security policy. The book covers several of the main theories and methods of the Russian external security policy. It discusses the tactics, operational and strategic-level developments, and focuses on Russian security and foreign policy postures. The book studies how these methods contribute to the implementation of Russia's security and foreign policies. It emphasizes the necessity of asymmetry in the Russian security strategy. This is the book's main argument, and it runs through every chapter. It aims to guide the reader through the main arguments with an introduction that focuses on the contexts in which asymmetry applies. *A secondary argument states that asymmetric approaches are preferable for Russia mainly because of its own weaknesses and shortcomings, specifically as its military issues (such as a lack of troop preparations, logistical nightmares, and shortcomings in armament supplies) have been revealed following the start of the war in Ukraine.*

The book covers several important issues including the evolution of Russia's security thought since the beginning of the 20th century; general security thoughts and their asymmetric approaches; a thorough analysis of official security documents of the Russian Federation and how asymmetric approaches are reflected in them; recent developments in Russian security thinking as well as the tools of the security policy including the cyber and information spheres of that policy. The book further addresses how Russia used, and uses, proxy forces (counterinsurgents, insurgents, political groups, etc.) in addition to how insurgency or semi-official coordinated military groups are used in the security policy. It discusses the security thinking and threat perceptions of Russia's current political and military elites while analyzing how those perceptions were formed. At the same time, it looks at the role of the security elite in high-level decision-making, especially as it relates to foreign policy concerns.

In discussing foreign policy, the book looks at the role Russia's security policy plays and concludes that there are no "hybrid" or "asymmetric" strategies to be found, but that it is the foreign policy of a relatively weaker power using appropriate diplomatic tactics. It looks at Russia's vision for the world order and the main foreign policy concepts, specifically "Primakov's doctrine" and Chubais' "Liberal

DOI: 10.4324/9781003344391-1

Empire." The book also explains how and why Russian foreign policy has been affected by the current war in Ukraine.

The book argues that carryover from the Soviet period influences the development of contemporary Russian security strategy. As such, the strategy and approaches, including the asymmetric ones, of the Soviet Union are analyzed and compared. It goes on to compare the opinions on external security and foreign policy issues, of the general public and the elite, using several surveys conducted in Russia between 1990 and 2023. Moreover, the economic facets of security developments are discussed.

The determinants and instruments of Russia's foreign and security policy, problems such as NATO enlargement, and color revolutions are explained. An examination of what these mean and why they matter for Russia is done through an analysis of three cases—Russia's external security approaches in Ukraine and Afghanistan and the anti-satellite program.

Russia's offensive military activities in Ukraine in 2022 are considered throughout the book including when theorizing how the lessons learned will be incorporated in the future. In this analysis, the book argues that the Ukrainian forces have more than capably used strategic asymmetry against Russia. Russia has also used asymmetric approaches including using Iranian UAVs and heavy airstrikes due to Ukraine's shortcomings in air defense capabilities.

The book explains the theoretical and practical bases for the main concepts and methods of Russian, historical and contemporary, security policy. It argues that Russia's external security strategies are not new but the asymmetric approach of a relatively weaker global power in the face of stronger competitors. In such a confrontation, the weaker party uses several, but not necessarily military, means and methods to overthrow a militarily and economically superior adversary. One of the main distinguishing facets of the book is its intention to explain how Russia uses asymmetric approaches in the strategic interaction of its conventional military.

*The main finding of the research is that the primary issue in Russia's contemporary security policy is not the asymmetric approaches themselves but the strategic asymmetry which applies to almost all areas of Russia's external security policy.*

The results of several surveys on the Russian elite and the general public's security thinking, which date between 1990 and 2023, and works of Russian and Western authors (the Soviet and contemporary periods) are used in the book. Moreover, to analyze why Russia prefers asymmetric approaches, the research uses the results of several surveys from international and Russian institutions. In this respect, the techniques of data collection and analysis have been used. To explain Russia's possibilities in several areas, data comparisons of Russia, world, and regional powers are considered. In this respect, military expenditures, the total number of nuclear weapons, world development indicators, and human development index data are compared.

Primary and secondary Russian and other sources are used. The book reviews Russia's official security documents and explains how asymmetric warfare approaches are reflected. Historical and contemporary sources (books, research, journals, reports, official documents, and newspapers) are used as well as Russian primary sources, such as speeches, interviews, and archive materials. The study covers the security policy in the Soviet Union and contemporary Russia.

The book consists of seven chapters that describe and analyze various facets of the main warfare methods, approaches, concepts, theoretical basis, history, and functions of Russia's security policy.

The first chapter, *"The evolution of Russian security thought,"* discusses the development and implementation of Russia's warfare theories and concepts since the beginning of the 20th century.

Russia's non-linear warfare theory and Evgeny Messner's mutiny warfare theory [*myatezh voina*] are analyzed, and how they are utilized by contemporary Russia is explained. The chapter studies how the necessity of using asymmetric warfare methods, and especially asymmetry of strategic interaction, in contemporary Russian military thought emerged. It reviews Russian military scholars' thoughts on warfare and their understanding of asymmetric warfare, its strategies, and techniques. The chapter analyzes how these thoughts influenced the formation of Russia's external security policy.

The first chapter is a guiding map for the rest of the book. It discusses the thoughts of Russian and Soviet theorists. In this respect, the works of Mikhail I. Dragomirov, Dmitrii A. Milutin, Aleksandr A. Neznamov, Nikolai P. Mikhnevich, Arseny A. Gulevich, Lev Trotsky; the Soviet non-linear warfare theorists: Vladimir K. Triandafillov, Georgii S. Isserson, Mikhail N. Tukhachevskii; and Evgenii Messner's mutiny warfare theory are discussed. In the last part of the chapter, I examine, and try to explain, why asymmetric approaches and the role of asymmetry in strategic interaction are emphasized in contemporary Russian military science. To do this, I refer to military thinkers including Makhmud A. Gareev and Dmitrii G. Baluev, and representatives of the military elite such as Valerii Gerasimov and others.

The second chapter, *"Determinants of Russia's security policy,"* tries to explain how a weaker geographical position in terms of security, economic shortcomings, and historical political turmoil strengthened the "fortress under siege" thinking in Russia. This became the mind-set not only of the political elite but in other segments of Russian society. The chapter examines Russia's understanding of its actual conditions. It mainly compares Russia's and other global and regional powers' indicators, which are essential in security perspectives. The chapter studies how the experiences of the Russian Empire and the Soviet Union exert influence on threat perceptions in contemporary Russia's security policy and in the political elite's security thinking. Characteristics such as fears based on environmental, economic, and socio-political weaknesses; the geographical size of the country, which creates concerns regarding the management and prevention of separatism or decentralization; and problems of the Russian Empire and the Soviet Union's colonization policies in the former Soviet republics are discussed. It is emphasized that, as the economy of the country is primarily based on natural resources, it is a popular thought among the elites that another great power or powers might desire to destroy or destabilize Russia for the purpose of controlling those resources.

The chapter explains why the avoidance of a surprise attack and the creation and maintenance of geopolitical buffer zones, as a guarantee against such an attack (which were basic facets of the Soviet military and political elite's threat perceptions after WWII) are the underlying characteristics of the security thinking of Russia's contemporary elites. It analyzes Russia's main external and internal threats, as perceived by the elites. In this respect, NATO enlargement is considered the main external threat, while color revolutions are seen not only as an internal threat but also as an external one and are analyzed as such.

The third chapter, "*The Soviet legacy of Russia's security policy*," analyzes how similar non-military methods and approaches were used during the Soviet Union. The chapter presents the functions of similar warfare methods in the Soviet Union's security policy. It explains why asymmetries in strategic approaches were preferable for the Soviet Union even in its most powerful periods when it had its nuclear weapons arsenal between the 1960s and 1980s. It discusses how and why Moscow and Washington used proxy wars to weaken or diminish the influence of the other in several regions during the Cold War. The chapter emphasizes information warfare, cryptography or codebreaking, insurgency or guerrilla warfare, and the use of asymmetric strategies in conventional military deterrence, such as the developments in weapons programs during the USSR. It compares similar security cases of the Soviet Union and the Russian Federation. For instance, the case of medical scholars in 1947 was dubbed a "fight against 'sycophancy' and cosmopolitanism" and the contemporary Russian security organizations witch-hunt against "spies of hostile states" are compared. Another comparison considers arms control-related issues of the Soviet Union and contemporary Russia.

The chapter argues that since the formulation of post-Soviet Russia's security policy in the 1990s, the Soviet legacy has played a key role, especially during Putin's presidency. Simultaneously, with the strengthening of the positions of former Soviet security organizations officers within the upper echelons of the political elite, the revitalization of Soviet practices in Russia's security policies has increased.

The fourth chapter, "*Evolution of the Russian Federation's security concept*," reviews and outlines Russia's security documents. It analyzes facets of Russia's security policy documents and explains how and why facets of the official documents have been changed since 1990s. It focuses on the asymmetric approaches within Russia's security policy documents. The chapter also discusses the role of the security institutions and their influence on the formation of the state's security policies. This chapter explains how Russia's political elite threat perceptions, which are influenced by the Soviet past, processes in international relations, and Russian domestic politics, are depicted in security documents. Using existing social survey data and qualitative analyses, the chapter explains that since 1999 the participation of security institution representatives in high-level political positions has been strengthening. It argues that political elites play a model role for the public in contemporary Russia and the latter has only a minor impact on the former's security thinking. After comparing the security documents of Russia, the United States, China, and the European Union, it discusses what differentiates Russia's security documents from the other world powers.

The fifth chapter, "*Functions of Russia's foreign security policy: new approaches*," analyzes the instruments of Russia's security policy and how they function. The chapter covers how Russia approaches its external security operations. In this respect, information and cyber warfare approaches are discussed. Russia's use of asymmetric strategies in a purely conventional military sense is examined. Other warfare methods are discussed, specifically the insurgency and guerrilla warfare strategies in Russia's security policy. It explains how Russia uses private military companies in its military conflicts as part of an asymmetric warfare approach. It examines how, in the Russian view, the United States and its allies use conventional and non-conventional, non-military methods with the aim of forcing regime change in Russia with the help of internal opposition groups, NGOs, and the media. This understanding is perceived by the Russian elite as justification for Moscow to use similar methods as countermeasures. Moreover, the book explains whether that approach might be one of the excuses for the invasion of Ukraine.

The chapter includes the continuing discussion among experts, since Russia's intervention in Ukraine in 2014, regarding how Russia's security activities and strategy can best be explained. The chapter explains that the best way to understand Russia's security approach is that they will use any possible and affordable method in their confrontation with a stronger adversary or adversaries. But Russia with its goals, threat perceptions, and possibilities must use mostly asymmetric strategies and instruments rather than symmetric ones.

It explains that Russia uses any available means against stronger adversaries. This approach can make Russia perceivably stronger in a particular niche including the information sphere, the Internet, cyber tools, social media, etc. The use of these non-kinetic warfare instruments does not mean that Russia eschews conventional military force, just that Russia prefers asymmetric strategies in this as well.

The sixth chapter, "*The implementation of Russia's foreign policy and the role of its security policy*," is devoted to the role of security approaches in Russia's foreign policy. It analyzes the confrontation between Russia and the West. It tries to explain the form of that confrontation and answer whether it is a second Cold War or only an asymmetric confrontation between Russia and the West over the world order or Russia's "sphere of influence."

It states that the drivers of Russia's vision of the international system are based on factors such as historical legacy, self-determination and sovereignty in international relations, and regime survival. It explains why Russia prefers a multipolar world order. It argues that despite confrontations between the West and Russia, the current situation cannot be called a second or new Cold War. It explains the differences between the Cold War and the current state of relations. The chapter discusses the main foreign policy concepts in contemporary Russia: "Primakov's doctrine" and Chubais' "Liberal Empire" concept. Russia's foreign policy activities are also reviewed.

The chapter explains that asymmetry in the strategy of its external security policy might be a primary means for Russia to maintain its role as a great power or achieve certain goals on the international stage. It analyzes the impacts of the security policy on the implementation of Russia's foreign policy. The chapter also explores the influence of the security policy on the relations between Russia and the post-Soviet countries, while also considering the implications of using asymmetric methods for Russia's position in the international system. Based on the research, it is emphasized that there are no asymmetric or hybrid strategies in Russia's foreign policy, but that the asymmetric strategies and methods of Russia's external security policy exert influence on the implementation of Moscow's foreign policy.

The seventh chapter, "*Russia's security and foreign policy approaches: Ukraine, star wars, and Afghanistan*," discusses three of the more relevant cases of Russia's contemporary security policy. In discussing the war in Ukraine, the Russian anti-satellite program, and Russia's contemporary Afghan policy the chapter aims to explain how and why Russia uses different security strategies and methods.

In the conclusion, "Why does Russia prefer strategic asymmetry?" the asymmetric warfare concept is discussed and explains that the main facet of Russia's security policy is not the asymmetric approaches themselves but rather the strategic asymmetry, which applies to almost all areas of Russia's external security policy. The chapter explains asymmetric warfare theory, its formation, and how it classifies the methods and actors of asymmetric war. In this part, the asymmetric warfare theory is presented by using several historical explanations and approaches. The modern research on the subject is reviewed and from this, the most essential findings applicable to Russia's case are discussed. This part of the book explains why asymmetric approaches, and especially asymmetry in strategic interactions, can be considered important tools in Russia's security policy.

As the book covers the main aspects of Russian security policy, it would be of interest to several audiences. In general, the research results can help facilitate a better understanding of Russian thinking and approaches to its security policy and forecast security-related events in Russia, its neighboring regions, and globally, given Russia's involvement in several parts of the contemporary world. The book is prepared for scholars, students, and journalists interested in Russian security and foreign policy, as well as for a general audience.

# 1 The evolution of Russian security thought

### The development of Russian military thinking

Military thinking and affairs played a historically important role in Russia. Economic, political, social, and even educational reforms were, in many cases, triggered by the military problems—preparation for wars or following unsuccessful military campaigns (for instance, defeat in the Crimean War of the middle of 19th century and the Russian-Japanese war at the beginning of 20th century) in the Russian Empire. It should be noted that reforms during the reigns of Peter the Great and Catherine II—as well as 19th-century reforms—were made during military and external security challenges. Moreover, since the Muscovite period, the military has been a main component of Russian statehood. Despite these facts, the Russian Army was weaker than Western militaries in relation to forms of army, tactics, and technical innovations. This was a central reason for Peter's, and others, reforms. According to Pipes, the establishment of a large standing army, initiated by Peter the Great, is one of the critical events in Russian history.[1]

However, despite the military's prominent role, Russian military thinkers had few famous works or any major influence on the development of military thought in the wider world. Even though several major military thinkers of the 19th century, such as Carl von Clausewitz and Antoine-Henri Jomini, were in the service of the Russian Army, Russia could not succeed in realizing large and significant military reforms. As Walter Pintner notes, Russia entered the 19th century with the practical experience of military success, in part because of its backwardness, or at least because of the distinctive characteristics of their social and political order. But nothing in the cultural or intellectual efforts of their countries compared to their political and military achievements. "They were the winners, but they had to look to the West, in a sense to the losers, represented by Clausewitz and Jomini, to instruct them in strategic thought," writes Pintner.[2]

Since the 17th century, Western military thought has had a huge influence on the formation of the Russian military school. But Western and Russian military schools had significant differences, and the Soviet Union and contemporary Russia would maintain the legacy of the Russian Empire's military thinking. Key among them is the so-called Suvorov's legacy, the crucial importance of moral or spiritual factors, specifically the role of human will in war. Prominent supporters of this theory were

DOI: 10.4324/9781003344391-2

M.I. Dragomirov and G.A. Leer. Dmitrii Miliutin, Minister of War from 1861 to 1881, was clearly struck by Suvorov's emphasis on the crucial importance of moral or spiritual factors in war. He noted that there are two sides in military art—the material and the spiritual.[3]

Despite a conservative attitude in Russian military thinking, new ideas circulated among the military elite regarding the waging of war at the beginning of the 20th century. A main trigger of this was defeat. As Walter Pintner put it, "the defeat in the Russo-Japanese war brought forth a wave of self-criticism and for some this meant, as it always had throughout Russian history, looking west for solutions."[4] Foremost among them was Colonel Aleksandr A. Neznamov, lecturer on tactics at the General Staff Academy and Nikolai P. Mikhnevich. The former's thoughts were close to the *blitzkrieg* while the latter's ideas were similar to attrition and had some elements of asymmetric warfare. Neznamov discussed the problems of dealing with mass armies on extended forms. Neznamov stressed that the goal of war remained the destruction of the enemy army in a quick decisive battle, but he realized that such an outcome was unlikely in the future war he attempted to describe. "However, he did not foresee the stalemate of trench warfare, but expected the continued deployment of large forces over wide areas with considerable movement as each side tried to outflank the other, a scenario that presumably could not last for more than some months, so that the war would be short," stressed Walter Pintner.[5] Another interesting thought of Neznamov focused on a historical (and contemporary) problem of the Russian Army—strikingly felt in Ukraine—command and control.[6]

General Nikolai Petrovich Mikhnevich's thoughts regarding his preferred methods of waging war are quite interesting. General Mikhnevich was one of the rare Russian military thinkers who also occupied a decision-making position within the Army. Between 1904 and 1917, he was director of the General Staff Academy and chief of the general staff. In contrast to Neznamov and many European military writers of the time, Mikhnevich rejected the notion of a "lightning war" and argued that Russia had an advantage over the more developed European industrial states, whose economies would be disrupted by the mobilization of labor[7] stating "thus time is the best ally of our military forces, and for that reason it is not dangerous for us to follow 'a strategy of attrition and exhaustion,' initially avoiding decisive engagements with enemy on the border when the superiority of forces may be on its side."[8] According to Pintner, this opinion "which recalls Gulevich, was something of a departure from the usual national view that discounted economic backwardness as an advantage, despite the possible example of Kutuzov's defeat of Napoleon."[9]

At the end of the 19th century, Lt. Colonel A.A. Gulevich of the General Staff Academy recognized the intimate connection of modern war and the national economy. He would predict that the next war in Europe would be exhausting rather than quick and decisive. He also, like Mikhnevich, considered Russia's economic weaknesses and poor social conditions as factors that would enable it to withstand the strain of such a war. According to him, a smaller proportion of Russia's large labor force would be mobilized than in the well-developed industrial economies of France and Germany, which were much more fragile, easily disrupted, and would suffer more because of greater withdrawals of manpower caused by a mobilization.[10]

In fact, Gurevich and Mikhnevich argued for the use of an indirect strategy rather than a direct one, which is a main factor in a weaker side's victory in an asymmetric war.

The Soviet period saw several changes in security thinking. They generally lined up with the official state ideology and several tremendous, non-natural elite changes resulting from the 1917 revolutions. The official ideology of the Soviets—Marxism-Leninism—largely dealt with warfare. War was one of its basic ideological elements. The founding fathers of the ideology fully appreciated Carl von Clausewitz's contributions not only to military thought but also to social thought in general, and it is from him that they drew some of their most interesting approaches. According to Walter Gallie, "Marx himself, despite his many other heavy intellectual preoccupations, but more particularly Engels and Lenin," explored Clausewitz's work. Their special interest in "was only one expression of a more general facet of their thought: their ever-increasing concern, after 1849, with the relevance of war and of military force, military preparation and military threats, to their own revolutionary predictions, plans, and projects," writes Gallie.[11] However, after the Bolsheviks took power, they faced a cold reality that often contradicted Marxist visions of waging war. Although Marxism provided a framework, it did not provide an exact plan or strategy. According to Condoleezza Rice, "the Bolsheviks tried to take seriously Engels's promise that 'freeing the proletariat will create its special and entirely new military method.'"[12] The first years of the Bolshevik government, following the revolution and the creation of the new socialist society, took place under complex and hazardous circumstances. The recently won victory was threatened by internal and external enemies, and it seemed as though the Bolshevik government would last no more than a matter of months.[13] In those first years, there were discussions about military and external security problems and what future strategic direction would be taken by the political and military elites.

> The main issue was the need to create a standing army whereas Lenin, Engels, and Marx all preferred a militia (the concept of a citizen's volunteer army—an armed working class).[14] According to Engels, "in the communist society, no one will think of a regular army."[15] The concept "no war, no peace" was put forth by Lev Trotsky who aimed to threaten Germany by allowing internal instability to halt the German advance while the Soviets would refuse to make war.[16] Trotsky's thoughts are interesting for their asymmetric nature: (1) Down with the war of the imperialists against the workers' state and proletarian dictatorship; (2) Transformation of the imperialist war into a civil war in all states attacking the Soviet Union; (3) Defeat of all the bourgeois states making war on the Soviet Union. Every honest proletarian of the capitalist countries ought actively to work for the defeat of "his" government; (4) Coming over to the side of the Red Army of every foreign soldier who does not want to help the labor exploiters of "his" country. The Soviet Union is the fatherland of all workers; (5) The slogan "Defend the Fatherland" will be a false disguise of the interests of imperialism in all bourgeois countries, except the colonial and semi-colonial countries who are carrying on a national revolutionary war against the imperialists.[17]

Although Trotsky may have initially been seen as the winner of this debate with Lenin—who had insisted on an immediate peace with Germany—following Germany's massive offensive response, Trotsky lost the argument.

Fighting simultaneously with internal (white forces) and external (Japan, France, Britain, the United States, and units of Czechoslovak soldiers of the former Austrian Army) enemies pushed the Soviets to establish a strong, centralized army. They faced a difficult choice. Centralized, disciplined, and trained forces were critical for victory, but it sounded to some like the resurrection of the standing army that they had recently helped to destroy. A new army needed specialists and high-ranking officers, which was not possible to find among the proletariats and peasants. By the end of November 1918, following Trotsky's initiative, 22,315 former Empire officers had entered the Red Army, and by the middle of August 1920, that number had grown to 48,409.[18]

There were regular discussions among the military leadership regarding the future of the army. Most of the sharpest divisions took place between the so-called Frunze and Trotsky groups and centered around a unified military doctrine and forms of waging war. In his article "A Unified Military Doctrine and the Red Army," Frunze wrote that a unified doctrine was important to all countries as it expressed the system of life and the class character of a state. According to him, European countries—such as Germany, England, and France—had unified doctrines, but Russia did not, owing to the pathetic state of military affairs under the Tsar.[19] Trotsky was against the formulation of such a doctrine and heavily criticized its proponents.[20] Trotsky stated that the thesis about the unified doctrine was "theoretically incorrect, practically non-productive." The Ukraine thesis of Frunze and other commanders in the [Soviet] Ukraine Army was considered by Trotsky as "dangerous and harmful."[21] It should be noted that the importance of a unified military doctrine was an old subject within Russian military thought and had been hotly debated by the Russian Empire's military staff since the end of the Russo-Japanese War and until the outbreak of World War I.[22] One of the interesting points in these discussions focused on the forms of waging future wars. Frunze laid huge on importance on maneuvering, but Trotsky preferred positioning operations. More interestingly, Frunze's 1922 report mentioned the importance of aspects of operations in future wars that would become basic elements of the Soviet's non-linear warfare theory, which would also be actively used by the Russian military elite following the collapse of the Soviet Union. In part of his speech, "Maneuver—a feature of future revolutionary wars" Frunze stated that there can be no stability of the frontline as during the "imperial wars," since each country will have "allies on the other side of the front, and this fact will kill the immobility."[23]

Another question was whether the Red Army should be prepared for offensive or defensive military operations. Marxism, as a dynamic theory of historical progress based on dialectical approaches, saw defense only as a temporary condition until the offensive could be seized. The debate on this question survived both Frunze and Trotsky. However, those debates influenced Russian military thinking during the Soviet Union. As Rice put it, there was "a peculiar wedding of a defensive political doctrine and an offensive military strategy that would seek to gain the upper hand by initiating attack." [24]

It was also the military discussions of that period to which the Soviet Union owes the legacy of an entire country prepared for war—a garrison state which Russia was before the revolution. At that time, one of the main proponents of whole-country war was Frunze, who argued for the militarization of key industries and the centralization of authority in military decision-making.[25] Similar developments can be followed in contemporary Russia as well. The developments in Russia after the start of the invasion of Ukraine in 2022 strengthen this argument.

In analyzing the links between the ruling elite's security thinking and Marxism, George Kennan emphasized that after the establishment of the Bolshevik regime, Marxist dogma—rendered even more truculent and intolerant by Lenin's interpretation—became a perfect vehicle for the sense of insecurity with which the Bolsheviks, even more than previous Russian rulers, were afflicted.[26] "Without Marxism," Kennan wrote, "ruling elite stand before history, at best, as only the last of that long succession of cruel and wasteful Russian rulers who have relentlessly forced country on to ever new heights of military power in order to guarantee external security of their internally weak regimes."[27] Interestingly, Kennan writes in his memoirs that during the war in the Korean Peninsula in 1950–1953, he urged the American leadership that it was not appropriate to view the Soviet leaders as absorbed in the pursuit of something called a "grand design"—a design for the early destruction of American power and for world conquest. He defined this vision as a chimera and emphasized Russia's weaknesses.[28]

One of the most important tasks for the Soviet political and military elites— from the end of the World War II (WWII) until the collapse of the USSR—was the avoidance of a decisive surprise attack in the first phase, or "initial period," of war. A repeat of the disastrous Soviet experience against Nazi Germany in the early stages of WWII, the invasion of Russia in June 1941, could not be tolerated. According to Cimbala, "Soviet military theorists also wrestled later with the problem of avoiding defeat and ensuring victory in the initial period of war under Cold War conditions: bipolarity, and the availability of nuclear weapons to the US, NATO, and Soviet militaries."[29] In such conditions, the two adversaries of the Cold War tried to avoid direct military confrontations. Instead, they used proxy wars and other indirect methods of asymmetric warfare.

In the USSR, every official document in all spheres, including security, was based on, or linked to, the ideology of the Communist Party of the Soviet Union (CPSU)—Marxism-Leninism. In the 1960s, the authors of "Military Strategy," a collective work of Soviet military thinkers, explained military problems and the responses to them from the vantage point of the Marxist-Leninist concept. Throughout nearly all the chapters, military questions or security developments are analyzed in connection with Soviet ideology.[30]

It should be noted that security thoughts from the last period of the Russian Empire and especially the Soviet Union are basic elements of contemporary Russia's security policy. Currently, several warfare theory approaches of these periods are actively utilized in Russian security strategies. They are adapted and modified based on the realities and challenges of the present period. Main among them are "Deep Operations" (operations in depth), or non-linear warfare and mutiny warfare theories. These approaches are appropriate for the waging of asymmetric warfare operations on large scales. If the former is useful for conventional means of waging war, the latter considers using unconventional methods. We are going to briefly discuss them in the next subchapters.

**Russia's non-linear warfare theory**

One of the distinguishing characteristics of the 1920s and early 1930s was the freedom of debate that existed within the army. Discussions regarding the future of military affairs and war following the Russian Revolution provided the stimulus for theorists to attack the old approaches and historical experience. The result of these debates was an understanding regarding a new type of warfare. This was the non-linear (operations in depth, or deep operations in Russian parlance) warfare theory.[31]

The founders of the deep operations theory (V. K. Triandafillov, G. S. Isserson, N. M. Tukhachevskii, K.B. Kalinovskii, and others) can be considered major theorists in the field of the Soviet military art of that period. Before analyzing the theory itself, it is important to research developments of the late 1920s, which influenced or even created the conditions for the development of the non-linear warfare theory.

There was a significant need for military reform in the 1920s, mainly resulting from the continuation of Soviet political strife. The inner-party discussions, opened by Trotsky in the fall of 1923, forced his opponents to search for effective countermeasures. The army, the former patrimony of Trotsky, inspired the greatest fear in I. V. Stalin, L. B. Kamenev, and G. E. Zinoviev, the then ruling triumvirate. The attack on the Red Army had two goals: to weaken Trotsky's military and party authority by discrediting the institution and conducting a "purge" among the troops, masking it with pragmatic arguments. Both of these tasks were successful. On the other hand, the army really did need change. By the end of 1923, it still bore the imprint of the Russian civil strife of 1918–20, in which the army grew up. Widespread breakdowns were feared, as they alternately awaited either inner calm in the country or revolutionary chaos beyond its borders. Trotsky's frequent illness was also hampered by the inevitable reform in 1923–1924 and the power vacuum in Russia during the many-month illness of Lenin. In such conditions, when the party split occurred, it was, paradoxically, the element that not only strengthened the modernization of the Red Army but also made it possible in the shortest time.[32]

However, the development of the non-linear warfare theory did not take place in a vacuum. Foreign military thinking was studied by the Soviets and played an important role in the formulation of the theory. A key facet of this was the period of collaboration with Germany, which existed following the Treaty of Rapallo in 1922.

Józef Unszlicht, a Deputy Chief of the People's Commissars for Military and Naval Affairs, correctly explained this cooperation in a report to the Politburo of the Central Committee of the CPSU (b) and to Stalin on December 31, 1926. He summed up the military and, in a certain sense, the political cooperation of the USSR with Germany. Regarding the changes in foreign policy of Germany, he stressed that "until now, the main idea of cooperation for us has relied on the usefulness of attracting foreign capital to the matter of increasing the country's defense capability, for them, it stemmed from the need to have a completely concealed base of illegal weapons."[33] Despite this, however, the Soviet military actively followed developments in military thinking in other Western countries and carefully read foreign literature on new developments in military affairs. For instance, Georgii Isserson stressed that the British military theorist John Fuller was the creator of the operations in depth. According to Isserson, the theory of deep operations was not created instantaneously, and later modifications prevented the reconstruction of its early core.[34]

The first work on the Soviet's non-linear warfare theory was written around 1928 by Vladimir Triandafillov, a head of the Red Army's operations administration staff, and Konstantin Kalinovskii, a chief inspector of the tank forces. Their work, "The theory of the offensive of modern armies in modern warfare," demonstrated enormous potential of the armored troops in conducting offensive operations. The essence of this theory centered on achieving two main tasks during an operation: breaking the frontline of the enemy's defense with a simultaneous strike on his entire tactical depth; and mechanized armored troops immediate entry into the breakthrough operation, in which they should launch their rapid attack on the entire depth of operational defense of the enemy before the defeat of his entire group.[35]

In 1929, Triandafillov published his new book on the theory, "The character of the operations of modern armies." He continued developing theory and presented a new concept of operations in depth. It emphasized the need to break through the defenses of the enemy toward their full depth and involving a mass of mobile troops—tanks, motorized infantry, and cavalry—which went to the operational scale. Their actions should be supported by aviation, and with the purpose of crushing enemy reserves, the landing of airborne forces in the rear was planned. At the same time, several simultaneous breakthroughs had to be carried out along the frontline, which would lead to the complete collapse of the enemy's entire defensive systems. He gave detailed plans of the first stage of the deep operations, but only for the starting period.[36] He stressed that a decisive victory could only be achieved if the enemy did not have an opportunity to regroup its forces. He emphasized not just breaking through the enemy lines but utilizing preparation to deliver a decisive and annihilating strike. His formulation recognized the importance of operating in depth against the enemy's supporting units and lines of communication.[37] It was the first theoretical book in the field of operational issues from which it was possible to learn, and it changed the usual way of thinking of many operational militaries.[38]

Triandafillov's ideas were further developed by Tukhachevskii, Isserson, Berzin, Nikokov, and others. Although they had understood that Triandafillov's ideas were too optimistic regarding the state of the Soviets existing potential for encircling and crashing the enemy, they developed the theory further in such a way that would enable the army to conduct operations for breakthrough, encirclement, and the decisive defeat of an enemy. Mikhail Tukhachevskii emphasized that the creation of a deep battle—the simultaneous defeat of the enemy's battle formation at its entire depth—requires tanks to push forward or accompany infantry, while on the other hand, penetrating the enemy's rear lines to simultaneously disorganize the latter and cut off the main forces from their reserves:

> this deep tank breakthrough should create a barrier in the rear of the enemy, to which they should be locked and where their main forces should be destroyed. At the same time, this breakthrough should destroy enemy artillery, disrupt communications, and seize its headquarters.[39] According to Georgii Isserson, emerging technologies "made it possible to abandon the 'sticky old tactics' of successive destruction of the enemy piecemeal, and to go over to a new form of simultaneous deep strike."[40]

Isserson further developed the Soviets non-linear theory and, on the eve of WWII, published a book, "New forms of struggles." This book further developed the theory, and it justified the concept with practical explanations from wars and battles (the Spanish Civil War and Nazi Germany's occupations of Czechoslovakia and Poland) of the period. One of Isserson's thoughts is applicable not only for that period but also for Russia's recent military interventions in Georgia and Ukraine, especially the invasion of 2022. According to Isserson, war is not declared, and it simply begins with pre-deployed armed forces. Even mobilization and concentration do not refer to the period following the onset of a state of war, as was the case in 1914, but are gradually, and imperceptibly, carried out long before that. It is impossible to completely hide it, and the concentration of forces inevitably becomes known:

> However, there is always a step from the threat of war to entry into war. It gives rise to doubt whether a real military action is being prepared or whether it is only a threat. And while one side remains in this state, the other, firmly resolved to act, continues to concentrate until, at last, a huge armed force is deployed on the border. After that, it remains only to give a signal, and the war immediately breaks out in full.[41]

Thoughts about non-linear warfare were, however, strongly opposed by so-called old-school proponents. Strangely, the alliance between Voroshilov and former imperial officer Svechin promoted an opposing view, in which operations in depth used to achieve decisive victory were questioned. Aleksandr Svechin stressed in his book "*Strategiya*" that attrition, not rapid victory, would be the strategy in the next war. In such a war, a country's economy would be the decisive factor. Svechin emphasized that any war would be long and protracted. The country had to prepare for a war of attrition, that defensive operations would also be a key factor, and total victory could not be achieved rapidly as was being supported by Svechin's opponents.[42]

During the purges between 1937 and 1938, almost all the main designers of the theory were arrested or executed. Even their opponent Aleksandr Svechin was executed in 1938. The purges hit the Soviet Army's professional staff hard. According to John Erickson, by the end of 1938, "only some 39% of the officers at a level running from divisional commander to Marshal of the Soviet Union remained as compared with the position in May 1937."[43] Erickson estimates that the strength of the "Soviet officer corps as a whole could be set reasonably at a maximum of 75–80,000 (which would include naval officers)." [44] He notes that the extent of the loss estimates varies. The highest figure set for the losses reaches 30,000, and the lowest is half of that figure. However, Erickson highlights that the purges were by no means a minor operation carried out on the Soviet officer corps and that they left terrible scars.[45] Few commanders would survive the purges. As Erickson precisely put it, "the best brains of the Red Army had been removed."[46]

More of the pre-war theory of non-linear, mechanized, and motorized operations that had been pioneered in Soviet military theorists' writings was forgotten in the aftermath of the military purges and had to be relearned in the hasty reorganization of Soviet defenses following the start of WWII. Although there were attempts to make changes after the Finnish War, it was only fully begun on the eve of the war with Germany. However, it should be noted that the Soviet victory in WWII was primarily a win for the concepts and theories that were formulated in the 1920s and 1930s, such as Frunze's concept of a whole-country war and the non-linear theory played key strategic roles.

It should also be noted that the methods used in asymmetric war were successfully utilized by the Soviets in WWII. With the tremendous propaganda campaign by the state, the battle against Germany became a struggle for "Mother Russia;" a struggle that had been waged many times in Russia's history. On the other hand, partisan warfare was successfully conducted in both urban and rural areas. The Bolshevist government, which had to that point strictly persecuted religions, closed sacred places, arrested and executed clergymen, reopened churches, mosques, and temples to gather support among priests and believers.

It happened during WWII that the Soviet Army for the first time utilized operations in depth and defending in depth. According to the field regulations [*Boevoi ustav pexoty Krasnoi Armii*] of 1942, defense was finally accepted explicitly as a "normal form of combat," although offense was to be maintained as the "fundamental aspect of combat action for the Red Army."[47]

Isserson, Tukhachevskii, and others like them were founding members of military reforms whose goal was to change the way armies and leaders thought about war. Unlike their contemporaries, such as B.H. Liddell Hart or Billy Mitchell, they had the opportunity to build their ideas into the modern Red Army and see their doctrine survive despite the existential challenges of Stalin's purges and the German invasion.[48] In the 1920s and 1930s, Russian military theorists started to grasp the operational potential of maturing "second wave" technologies like mechanization and radio communications. According to Sean B. Mackfarland, Russian military theorists "saw them as means of expending less energy resisting the natural non-linearity of warfare, thus allowing them to work more efficiently within war's natural framework," and this insight enabled them to achieve a high degree of operational simultaneity.[49]

It should be noted that since the 1990s, the work of Soviet non-linear warfare theory authors has been actively studied by the foremost research centers in the West.[50]

After WWII despite practical limitations, the Soviets continued with their vision of non-linear warfare as a method of achieving the simultaneous destruction of enemy forces. As a result, they quickly understood the military implications of the beginning of the information age.[51] The Soviet military realized in the mid-1980s that the new information technology would allow for far greater non-linear possibilities and would increase the simultaneity of actions. Lester W. Grau draws analogies between the Russians vision of non-linear future warfare and a soccer game:

> Linear warfare is roughly analogous to US football. An attacking and defending side face one another on line. After a short period of concerted effort to gain or deny ground or advantage, both sides regroup and reform to try again. Nonlinear warfare, as the Soviets envision it, is roughly analogous to soccer. There is constant activity with players on the same team simultaneously defending, attacking, or making the transition between the two. Team members rapidly coalesce into temporary attack or defensive groups and then disperse again.[52]

These analogies are interesting because the strategic interaction in asymmetric warfare uses similar approaches. The key factor for victory in asymmetric wars is strategic formulas (indirect-direct or direct-indirect).

In the 1980s, the Russians forecasted that future non-linear operations would possess the following characteristics[53]:

- No well-defined spatial limits
- Combination of offense and defense
- Proliferation of operational and tactical maneuvers (ground and vertical)
- Increased requirement for mobility, maneuverability, and flexibility
- Decentralized conduct of maneuvers
- Requirement for centralized command and control to coordinate operations
- Increased lethality

Summing up, we can say that the Soviet non-linear warfare theory is actively explored and exploited in modern-day Russia's security policy but with modifications. As in the 1980s, Soviet military scholars understood that the information revolution would give new possibilities for the implementation of non-linear warfare. Since the collapse of the Soviet Union—which resulted in economic shortcomings and general weakness for the country—Russia's military and political elites have been exploring additional possible tools and methods for successively utilizing the theory. As theorists of the 1920s argued that victory in the next war would depend on an offensive blow that would shock the weakened "capitalist countries" suffering from deep class divisions, and each country would have allies on the other side of the frontline, Russia's current military thinkers have considered utilizing high-precision strikes and unconventional approaches for success in any possible confrontation with stronger adversaries. It should be noted that Russia's current military elites and military scholars emphasize the use of non-military means in contemporary wars. According to them, contemporary wars are non-linear and unconventional methods are necessary.

The article by General Valerii Gerasimov, a head of Russia's General Staff, released in 2013, largely used non-linear warfare approaches with an emphasis on the importance of using unconventional methods. Gerasimov mentioned Isserson and even used a quotation from his work:

> Our country paid a great deal of blood for not listening to the conclusions of the professor [Isserson] at the Academy of the General Staff. Thus, to neglect new ideas, unconventional approaches, a different point of view in military science are unacceptable. And the more unacceptable is the scornful attitude towards science from the side of practitioners.[54]

Gerasimov stresses that even a stronger adversary has vulnerabilities, and they should be used:

> Summing up, I want to say that no matter how strong the enemy may be, no matter how perfect his forces and means of warfare are, the forms and methods of their implementations are, he will always have vulnerabilities. Therefore, there is the possibility of adequate resistance. At the same time, we should not copy someone else's experience and catch up with leading countries, but to get ahead of the curve and take leading positions. And here military science plays an important role.[55]

Gerasimov stressed the role of "non-military" unconventional methods in "resolving conflicts between states."

Such attitudes about contemporary military conflicts are typical of post-Soviet Russia's military thinking. The main Russian methodical and theoretical basis for using unconventional methods in military conflicts was designed by Russian military theorist Yevgenii Messner between the 1950s and 1960s. His thoughts will be analyzed further in the next subchapter.

## Mutiny warfare theory

Yevgenii Messner was an officer of the Imperial Russian Army and served as a colonel of the General Staff of the Kornilov Division of the Wrangel Army during the civil war. He was one of the preeminent Russian military theorists of the 20th century as an émigré. He participated in the First World War and fought on the side of the Whites against the Bolshevists in the Civil War. After the defeat of the Whites, he emigrated to Yugoslavia and at the end of WWII to Argentina. His works were predominantly published in several journals and newspapers of the Russian émigré community. Messner was an anti-communist and a Russian nationalist, and during WWII he was sympathetic to the Nazis.[56]

Messner closely followed developments in the Soviet military. Chief among his works was a tetralogy under the general name "Problems of War and Peace," which included: "The face of modern war" (1959), "Mutiny – the name of the Third World(war)" (1960), "Modern officers" (1961), and "the World Mutiny

War" (1971). It is in these books that the idea of a new form of warfare ("struggle against rebellion") had been formulated. His works contained a thorough analysis of the issues such as the roles of unconventional, asymmetric warfare methods in war. Mainly referring to his experiences in the Russian Civil War and guerrilla warfare in the Balkans, he also studied unconventional methods in the smaller wars after WWII (the Korean War, insurgency and counterinsurgency in Algeria, military conflicts in the Middle East, and the Vietnam War). Adam Klus stresses that Messner's thoughts were very much shaped by the trauma of defeat during the Russian Civil War, where he experienced first-hand fighting against an enemy using irregular warfare, terror, and propaganda on a massive scale. "Later, during the Second World War, he saw up-close intense guerrilla and anti-guerrilla warfare in the Balkan cauldron."[57] During the Cold War, Messner focused on peripheral and covert conflicts, seeing them as the primary arena of confrontation between the superpowers. Messner tried to explain the strategic logic behind various seemingly disparate events, believing that they were all elements of a grand design crafted and executed by the Communists.[58]

Throughout the 1960s and the beginning of the 1970s, Messner persistently tried to convince political and military leaders in the West to make public his works on the threats and destructiveness of a new form of war, namely the Soviets targeting public opinion, and why appropriate countermeasures had to be taken. He even gave military-political reviews in the "Russian Word" and other outlets under the heading "On the Fronts of the World Mutiny War," but rarely found a sympathetic audience. However, his works received numerous critical accolades, and they, especially the aforementioned tetralogy, found the support of several military scholars among émigrés.[59]

The main facet of Messner's works is his mutiny warfare concept. Interestingly, in the period when world superpowers were preparing for nuclear war and their armies were prepared for linear operations, Messner urged that "traditional notions of war are outdated" and had been replaced by a new form of warfare. As he put it, "Clausewitz's war is replaced by Engels's war" and he insisted that the next world war would not happen in "the army style, but in the style of insurrection." Guerrilla and insurgency, unrest and unlimited terror, destruction of the foundations and beliefs of societies, and attacks on the consciousness of the population will be the battlefields. and the lines between peace and war will be permanently blurred. But all of them will be part of the mutiny war. It should be noted that it is possible to find aspects of Messner's mutiny warfare theory in contemporary Russia's security activities. It is also possible to find Messner's thoughts in the speeches and articles of Russia's political and military elites and scholars as they discuss contemporary forms of warfare or external security affairs.

According to Messner, contemporary wars have four dimensions (land, sea, air, and influences on souls of adversary's army and people). Messner stressed the role of the fourth dimension in contemporary wars:

> ... the soul of the enemy army, the soul of the enemy's civilians became the most important strategic objects; the mobilization of the spirit of one's own

people has become the most important task of the supreme strategist. To decompose the spirit of the enemy and protecting one's own from decay— this is the point of fighting in the fourth dimension, which has become more important than the other three dimensions.[60]

Today, Messner's fourth dimension analogy can easily be defined as information warfare.

Messner argued that there are no exact lines between armed forces and civilians, and he emphasized the role of insurgent groups in contemporary wars. He argued that there is no dividing line between the territories of one's adversaries and the theater of war, between legal and illegal ways of war, or between army and civilians. "Now the regular army lost its military monopoly: An irregular army is fighting along with it (and maybe even more than it), and the irregular army was supported by underground organizations," he wrote.[61]

Messner called such situations a state of "war and semi-war." He also mentioned "aggressive diplomacy" as a form of confrontation that uses covert operations. According to Messner, the differences between semi-war and aggressive diplomacy are obvious: "In the first one, the weapons, troops, partisans, sabotage groups are used, and in the second one political methods prevail, although pistol shootings and bombings happen for high effects."[62]

More than 50 years ago, Messner accurately explained the main forms of subversive activities present in the confrontation between states of which contemporary Russia has been accused since 2014. Messner emphasized the role of propaganda in subversive, covert operations during peacetime. "In modern conditions, diplomacy is easily converted into aggressive diplomacy: By continuously (supposedly peaceful) coexistence with a tough state, it mobilizes oppositionists and revolutionaries through propaganda and bribery. Radio propaganda has become [a] powerful means of aggressive diplomatic activities."[63] He also mentioned the use of diplomacy as a tool of propaganda or to influence the public opinion of a targeted state: "During a semi-war diplomats are, on the one hand advisers of strategists [military leaders] in aim of the latter's activities would not affect the main diplomatic intentions, and on the other hand, diplomats continue to lead the oppositional public in the enemy camp in conformity with the strategists."[64] Messner recognized the role of psychology and psychological operations in war, arguing that psychological influences in propaganda activities are a main facet of mutiny war.

More interestingly, Messner suggested to use relevant approaches and professionally designed information interventions. He argued that propaganda—both offensive and defensive—is doomed to fail if it looks like propaganda. "The tone of propaganda," he wrote, "should be chosen with respect to the flavor and the psyche of each people." "Propaganda fights for the benefit of strategy and is guided by the instructions of psychology."[65] "Agitation should be considered one of the main means of waging the mutiny war," he wrote. He stressed that offensive agitation helps weaken the enemy while defensive agitation strengthens "our spirit."[66] According to Messner, the defensive does not mean defending, justifying, or apologizing. It must actively strengthen the emotions and thoughts of soldiers, fighters, and civilians. He emphasized the importance of using appropriate approaches in information confrontation, "We must remember that the mass absorbs a meaning of an idea with difficulty—an appearance of the idea is more accessible to them. Therefore, the secret of the success of agitation is not so much what to present, but rather how to present."[67]

Messner emphasized the role of internal confrontations within a target country in a mutiny war. "People with their growl, disobedience, resistance and finally, with insurrection can fight against the [our] enemy and their own government, the value of which may be no less, rather than the clashes of millions of armies." According to Messner, the center of gravity of war is therefore relocated from the battlefield to the people's struggles within the national, political, social, and economic arenas and the psychology of popular movements. This is the difference between war and mutiny war.[68]

Messner recognized future wars non-linear operations. His vision on non-linear operations differs from the non-linear warfare theory of the Soviet military theorists of the 1930s. Messner's version of non-linear warfare does not so much deal with mechanized military operations in depth; it relies more on using the means of mutiny warfare. According to Messner, in WWII, the frontline separating enemies was vague and could basically be erased by partisans on one side or the other. But a future war will not happen on the line; it will be on the entire surface of the territories of both opponents because behind military fronts there will be political, social, and economic ones. Adversaries will not fight on two domains as in the old days; they will not fight in three domains, as was the case since the birth of military aviation, but rather in four domains. The fourth domain, as it is mentioned above, is the "psyche of the warring nations." He emphasized that the belligerent will primarily act within the territory of the opposing side by creating and fostering a guerrilla movement. It will provide ideological, logistical, informational, and financial support to favorable opposition, "defeatist" or pacifist parties there. They will promote disobedience, sabotage, and terror by all means. Using those groups will create a mutiny within the territory of the enemy. The government and troops of the belligerents will then involve their entire population in the occupied regions in their struggle against enemy agents of insurrection.[69]

As a participant in the civil war in Russia, Messner observed how the Soviets used guerrilla and irregular approaches. Messner explained that participation in the Civil War was the beginning of his study. Observing from the very beginning the formation of the Soviet military doctrine, he was convinced that some elements of guerrilla warfare would be applied by the Soviets in a future war.[70] Messner noted that after WWII, the Soviets mainly used NGOs, newspapers, and even youth organizations as underground forces for their subversive or mutiny war operations in the West.[71]

Other methods, not solely guerilla warfare, could be used in a mutiny war: terror, banditry, uprising, riots, and even demonstrations and rallies. The key rules of that warfare are to set feasible goals, take the enemy by surprise, mislead them, and always take the initiative. Messner emphasized that the West was not "trying to seize the initiative" in the mutiny war.[72]

Messner considered the democratic systems of Western countries vulnerable to adversarial meddling in the 1970s. He called liberal democracies an "individualistic world" and emphasized that the West was prepared for conventional war but not for unconventional attacks: "The individualistic world considers military dangers through the conventional type of warfare and has some protection (the conventional army and armaments) against conventional attacks, but it cannot defend itself from covered attacks on the unprotected side of its organism; it does not have an eye on this side to see the danger."[73] He called such a conflict situation a doubly one-sided war: "The attacker is at war, and the defender has no information for defense; the attacker is fighting according to the plan, according to the doctrine developed by him, and the defender does not even see the waging war against him."[74]

In recent years, Messner's works have been popularized in Russia. It is possible to find Messner's thoughts in the speeches of Russia's political and military elites and in the works of military and security scholars. In analyzing Messner's works, we find several similarities between his visions and the contemporary thoughts of the Russian elite and expert classes regarding security and forms of modern warfare. Having established that the similarity in thought exists, it is important to review and explain why Messner's works are so attractive to the current Russian political regime.

First, it should be noted that Messner was an officer in the Russian Empire Army and, after its collapse, joined the White Movement and fought against the Bolsheviks. He was a determined anti-communist, monarchist, and supported classic conservative visions. He tried to warn Western political leaders and the public about the threats from the Soviet Union and China and considered the "Reds" as humanity's, and the world's, main danger. But he was also a supporter of tough preventive activities against social and political protests and liberal freedoms. He vehemently supported the idea of a strong state, and as with many conservative thinkers in pre-revolutionary Russia, Messner was a proponent of maintaining order within the state and society. His visions are shared by the contemporary regime as well. Even though the political regime in Russia selectively promotes the Soviet legacy, it also uses conservative visions of the pre-revolutionary period. Such a mixture is acceptable within contemporary Russian security thinking as well. In this respect, Messner's thoughts on the mutiny war attract Russian political and military elites.

Simply put, Messner's works were about how the Soviets used asymmetric methods and approaches in confrontation with the stronger West and how to prevent such attacks. He noted that the Kremlin could easily spread mutiny everywhere without fear that it would boomerang back because of the tough controls in the USSR. He also analyzed social clashes in the Soviet Union and the Soviet bloc countries and noted that mutinies did occur within Moscow's sphere of influence and inside the USSR itself. His conclusion might be interesting to contemporary Russian elites, who also consider social clashes or "color revolutions" as major threats to regime security. He pointed to the social protests in Berlin in 1953, in Poland, Hungary, and Czechoslovakia and to the uprisings in the USSR itself: in Vorkuta, Rostov, and Novocherkassk. He concluded that

> Maybe this was the result of self-seeding, or perhaps Soviet propaganda is right when it accuses the capitalist world of sowing these insurrections. But sending agents, provocateurs, and instructors there from the West is not possible. It might be possible if the insurrections could be realized by radio propaganda (Radio Liberty, Free America, etc.) or by launching balloons with propaganda literature to the communist countries. It also might be that anti-communism could infect the Soviet people while they are on business or tourist trips in the West.[75]

Messner emphasized that in a mutiny war, the hierarchy of leadership and strategic unity must be strong. According to him, the red side was always carefully prepared:

> By propaganda and political maneuvers, it creates an opportunity for itself [to] swim, "like a fish in friendly water." Under the "friendly water" there lies confusion and flabbiness as well as an inability to resist among the attacked people. Therefore, the "weapons" used in mutiny war "weapon-pornography," "weapon-drugs," "weapon-brainwashing" have never been conceived in this century.[76]

These types of thoughts are similar to the language of the political and military leadership in contemporary Russia. Messner argued that by spreading mutiny, the USSR did not provoke a larger war, which would have been a disaster for Moscow. It did not want to get itself into trouble with something such as a large military campaign against the West.[77] He was convinced that the peaceful coexistence concept used by the Soviets was solely for misleading the West:

> The West sees only the superficial. It took years for them to see the war under the surface of coexistence. Then the East came up with a new camouflage of warfare—the détente. The surface of this concept would have meant the elimination of the danger of war. But there is no danger of war: who is going under the rain is not at risk to be outside in the rain. Under the surface of "the détente" lies the continuation of war.[78]

Considering contemporary relations between Russia and the West, Messner's thoughts about the Soviets real attitudes toward détente and NATO seem to remain applicable today.

Messner was also a strong proponent of decisive and drastic measures for maintaining state security, which are appreciated by the contemporary Russian political regime as well. For instance, he was against negotiations with terrorists who captured politicians, public figures, or ordinary civilians, and he called for decisive actions, without hesitation and consideration for civilian causalities, when the situation warranted it.[79]

*The evolution of Russian security thought* 23

Most interestingly, Vladislav Surkov, who is famous as an author of "the sovereign democracy" concept and who was involved in the creation of the Donbas and Luhansk separatist republics in Ukraine, also mentions similar warfare methods in his paper. Surkov published, under his pseudonym Dubrovski, a short fiction story "Without Sky," where he talks about an ambiguous future after the Fifth World War. His narrative about the future of war reminds some of Messner's thoughts. Moreover, he calls that war "the first non-linear war," and it is strikingly similar to Messner's explanation rather than Isserson's one.[80] Surkov also shares his vision about the duration of the war, and it is very similar to Messner's thought about "no peace, no war" relations between states and "war without victory," writing that "... naive commanders of the past sought a victory. Now they did not act so stupidly. But some, of course, still use the old habits and tried to get old murky spells from the archives, like that: victory will be ours. Sometimes it worked, but mostly, war was understood as a process. More precisely, part of the process, its acute phase. But, maybe, not its most important part."[81]

It should be noted that several days after the publication of Surkov's story, Russia annexed Crimea. The timing of the publication was probably no coincidence. That period of mobilization for war was the official political model that Kremlin political strategists and technologists used to set the stage for intervention in Ukraine. Russian television was full of propaganda about "enemies of Russia, fascists taking over Ukraine" which was artificially associated with the Second World War, the great conflict with the "hostile" West. "Psycho war" narratives were used during the 2022 Russian invasion of Ukraine.

Since the collapse of the Soviet Union, Russian military experts have been actively exploring Messner's works. At the end of the 1990s, during the discussions on Military Doctrine 2000, several experts referred to Messner's works and argued the necessity of preventative measures against the mutiny warfare methods in contemporary doctrines. According to those arguments, the draft of the new military doctrine, which was actively discussed in the media, gave the following classification for possible modern wars: world, regional, local, and armed conflict. In one such article, Messner's concept is analyzed by Igor Dominin, who studied Messner's works. The author argued that among the common features of modern war is a wide use of indirect activities: information confrontation, participation by regular forces together with irregular armed formations, including illegal groups. According to the author, behind these characteristics, and including peacekeeping, humanitarian, counterterrorism, and other special operations, economic and information wars, criminals' offensive, terrorist acts, and high-profile assassinations; the true face of modern warfare appears, and it is mutiny war. The author regretfully stressed that mutiny warfare has not been doctrinally clarified. But under its control are not only the peripheries of Russia but almost the entire territory of the country: "To combat this threat, which is now clearly manifested in the North Caucasus, it is necessary to revive the military art, a professional army, and a special political-military strategy are required," he urged.[82] These thoughts about Messner and his works show the importance of his ideas in contemporary Russia.

Some key elements and ideas in contemporary Russian warfare strategies resemble concepts from Messner's thoughts on the evolution of military conflicts. In this regard, the head of Russia's General Staff, General Valerii Gerasimov, did not reveal anything new when he wrote about the blurred line between war and peace. Gerasimov writes that in the 21st century, there is a tendency to erase the differences between states of war and peace. "Wars are no longer declared, but when they start, they do not follow the pattern we are used to," Gerasimov notes, "roles of non-military means in achieving political and strategic goals greatly exceed weapons power."[83] Although Gerasimov points to the West, which might use such methods, such thoughts are similar to Messner's mutiny war explanations mentioned above.

According to Russian military expert and journalist Igor Plekhanov, Russia's interventions in Ukraine and Syria, dubbed "hybrid war," should not be considered something new. "A theoretician of this type of war was a colonel and professor Yevgenii E. Messner," Plekhanov writes, "who comprehensively developed the theory and predicted the development of this type of war in his books."[84]

### The important emergence of asymmetric warfare methods in contemporary Russian military thinking

Discussions about possible military reforms and future wars started during the past years of the Soviet Union. The Soviet military and international security experts tried to forecast the characteristics of future wars by considering the revolution in military affairs and developments in the military industry, such as high-precision weapons. During the political, social, and economic turmoil at the end of the 1980s, the Soviet General Staff was faced with a series of complex problems: the direction of Soviet doctrine; the shape, size, and manning of the Soviet armed forces; the function and future of the Warsaw Pact; the complete redrafting of war plans; and the use of military forces for civil control.[85] The military elites' view of future war envisaged dynamic, high-tempo, high-intensity land-air operations that would extend over vast expanses and include new areas such as space. According to their vision, tactical combat would be even more destructive than in the past and would be characterized by fragmented [*ochagovy*] or non-linear combat.

> The frontline will disappear and terms such as "zones of combat" will replace the outdated concepts such as FEBA (the forward edge of the battle area) and FLOT (the forward line of own troops). There will not exist safe havens or "deep rear" and nuclear war must be avoided at all costs, as it may heighten to strategic exchange and the "destruction of the entire world's people."[86]

The Soviet's strategic planners believed that it would be possible to achieve the requisite superiority of forces on the main axes of offensives and counteroffensives by exploiting qualitative improvements in firepower, mobility, and the effects of surprise.[87] This surprise, accompanied by strong and intensive air and artillery fire strikes, would allow for the rapid insertion of ground units, air-assault forces, and other specially trained forces into the depths of its opponents' territory while covering its own flanks with long-range fire. Aviation and long-range and high-precision fire would attack reserve forces and support bases, which could influence the operation.[88]

According to General Vladimir Slipchenko, high-precision weapons, strong air, and cosmic forces will play leading roles in future wars. Although he emphasized the role of nuclear forces in deterrence, he noted that "now there is not a single civilized state with a developed economic base and infrastructure which is able to survive even in a fourth-generation past war using conventional means of destruction, much less nuclear ones."[89] Therefore, in the wars of the new generation, the values of military supremacy in aerospace with high-precision missiles sharply increase. The combat capability of the country's air and military space forces, as well as its aerospace defense, will be the determining factor necessary for victory in a 21st-century war, wrote Slipchenko. He emphasized the importance of high-precision airspace and cruise missiles, electron warfare, and appropriate offensive and defensive strategies in future wars. Slipchenko called this new generation of warfare the 6th-generation warfare.[90]

Immediately following the dissolution of the Soviet Union, the need to reform or reorganize the army around the use of new or appropriate warfare approaches strengthened. Since then, discussions have continued, but it was between 2000 and 2005 that the commonly accepted thought—using several methods and approaches appropriate to Russia's contemporary economic and military possibilities—was formulated. It should be noted that an influential number of contemporary Russian military scholars are carriers of the Soviet military school legacy, having studied or been in service, during the Soviet Union. And that legacy had a huge influence on the development of contemporary Russian military thinking. Although they accept the realities and experiences of military conflicts during the Soviet Union, the collapse of the USSR frames their mindset.

One of the key elements of the Soviet military school—which exists through to the present—is the consideration of military problems not only in purely military means, but also as a political or in Russian parlance as a "military-political" problem. According to the Russian academic point of view, when comparing the thoughts and approaches of contemporary Russian and the foreign scholars on the evolution of nature and the essence of war at the present time, the following differences can be noted: First, Russians are driven by the violence theory regarding the problems of war, whereas foreign theorists tend to view the problem from the point of conflict research. Another important difference in their approaches, as seen by Russian scholars, is that representatives of Russian military thought give priority to highlighting the socio-political, while Western thinkers focus on the military-technical and geopolitical foundations. The common character of both is a statement about the changes that have taken place in recent decades that have radically reflected on the phenomenon of war itself. This applies primarily to the transformation of the causes of war and attitudes toward them, the emergence of new war actors such as supranational and regional entities, interstate economic, political, and military alliances, transnational economic and financial corporations, and other non-state actors, and also to the emergence of new means and methods of warfare.[91] Moreover, Russian experts think that Western studies on the nature and essence of modern war lack unity in interpretation. This is also common in Russian contemporary war studies.[92]

In the works of leading Russian military scholars such as M.A. Gareev, V.V. Serebryannikov, M.N. Shakhov, and others, military and social sciences define "war" and "peace" as a global system of interrelated social relations, which owing to the adaptive ability of war are reviewed and updated based on the ever-changing conditions of modernity.[93] According to them, this leads to the emergence of new forms of war and new subjects of military violence. At the same time, the authors believe that armed struggle continues to remain the main sign of war.[94] Gareev wrote that the essence of war, its main feature, is the use of armed violence. According to Gareev, war in its true sense is connected with military activities, and it is not a war when using solely non-military means.[95] At the same time, Gareev did not deny the influence of such forms of struggle as economic, ideological, psychological, informational, etc. Below, we will analyze Gareev's thoughts on asymmetric approaches in more detail.

Opponents of Gareev, such as M.A. Borchev, V.P. Gulin, and A. Kapitanetz, argue that war and armed struggle are independent means of politics, and therefore war can proceed without armed struggle. These authors agree with the thesis that the bloody ones are replaced by "bloodless," "non-painful," and "civilized" wars, in which the goals are achieved not as a result of direct armed intervention but through the use of alternative forms of violence: economic, informational, psychological, and diplomatic.[96] According to Gulin, "the war is distinguished not by a form of violence, but by its main essential features: an uncompromising struggle with the use of means of violence for a certain time, the victory of one of the parties and the defeat of the other, a significant change in the balance of power, and as a result, their different disposition."[97] He believes that the concept of total war, which sits at the heart of the strategic attitudes of many states, including Russia, has become obsolete and anachronistic. Gulin argues that the world is entering a new generation of war, which is not aimed at deliberately destroying the enemy but at achieving political goals without battles between massive armies. Another military scholar Mikhael Borchev wrote that "wars as an independent social and historical phenomenon are not always associated with armed struggle, they are diverse in their goals, types of violence and struggle, but they are always exclusive means of achieving outlined plans."[98]

Dmitrii Baluev writes that war, at the beginning of the 21st century, again returned to the political arsenal of opposing states in the international arena. It again began to occupy much of international relations, more than was typical during the decades of "confrontational stability" in the bipolar era. "The view on the war was revived, above all, as a political act, and not just a simple clash of the armed forces of adversaries."[99] Baluev argues that the war moves (or rather, returns) from the sphere of military planning itself to the sphere of politics. The process of (re)integration of military instruments in the foreign policy arsenal of leading states and non-state actors of international politics is noticeable. In this regard, the author considers four groups of factors to understand the changes in the nature of war and its place in current world politics: technological, informational, psychological, and the actual political aspects of war. More interestingly, the author offers to clarify ideas regarding the features of modern warfare by using the factor of asymmetry.[100]

A prominent military thinker and one of the key influential military scholars in Russia, Army General (ret.) Mahmud Gareev considered modern military problems in conjunction with political or geopolitical conditions in the world. Gareev, who was also head of the Academy of Military Science—the organization that plays a key role as a platform for high-level discussions on military affairs in Russia—emphasized the necessity of considering military problems amid the international political situation in almost all his works. Gareev's works are important for understanding contemporary Russia's military and security thinking because almost all of the Russian military and non-military conflict approaches are reflected. Moreover, Gareev, who was in key military positions from the 1950s until the collapse of the USSR, was considered a respectful and reliable military theorist by the Russian political and military elite.

In his article on future wars in 2003, Gareev stresses that the study of the characteristics of future wars is a fundamental issue in military science because "only in the basis of a correct assessment of the shape of the future armed struggle give possibility to determine scientifically what defense tasks the Russian state will have to solve and what kind of armed forces are needed for this."[101] And the characters of threats and wars of the 21st century largely depend on what the world will be, the balance of power in international relations, and the place and role of Russia in the new geopolitical system. As for the fundamental circumstances that determine these factors, Gareev considers globalization at all levels: political, socio-economic, scientific, cultural, technological, and information processes.

> They have great potential: both positive and negative. To isolate or to stay away from them is impossible. This might be the same as someone trying to get off the globe ... The only real way for Russia is to integrate into these global processes, while trying to get everything that is useful for it and, if it is possible, to neutralize the negative manifestations of globalization.[102]

Gareev stresses the balance of power as the second circumstance. He writes that the military-political situation will be determined by the desire of the United States and leading Western countries to dominate the world while—at the same time—objectively developing the current tendency toward the multipolar world. Such trends do not suit everyone. He believed that many leading states, and above all China, India, and Europe, which is "partly squeezed within the framework of NATO," will be unlikely to be fully satisfied with the one superpower monopoly position. Gareev stressed that through its "reliance mainly on the use of force, the United States under the guise of fighting terrorism implements narrowly selfish national interests, takes little other countries interests into account."[103]

Gareev recognized the Russian political elite's main fear. He emphasized that the theory of "limited sovereignty" and "unceremonious" forceful invasion on the territory of other "undesirable" states seems to be especially dangerous. "Thus, they kind of make it clear to us that under certain conditions, such a fate can also befall Russia. But, how really events will develop in the world depends largely on the position and policy of Russia. First of all, it will depend on how its relations with the USA and China will develop."[104]

According to Gareev, the third main circumstance is the sources of contradictions between states and nations; conflicts and wars are still the same—territorial claims, the struggle for raw materials, and interethnic, social, and political antagonisms. But the main issue in the 21st century will be competition and the struggle for energy resources, primarily oil because its reserves are decreasing more and more rapidly at the current level of consumption. Gareev emphasized that this is why the United States is seeking to take control of the world's major oil reserve areas.[105] He believed that in the foreseeable future, not only would it be unlikely that a world war would happen, but that the danger of large-scale aggression against Russia would decrease. And it is not because "someone arbitrarily cancelled world wars ... They are not foreseen, on the one hand, because of the threat of the use of nuclear weapons with disastrous consequences; on the other hand, new forms and ways of achieving political and strategic goals were found by waging local wars, conflicts, political, economic, informational pressure, and subversive actions within the opposing countries," Gareev suggested.[106]

Gareev, who was known as the conventional warfare adherent, emphasized using asymmetric strategies and methods, mostly non-military ones, for dealing with external threats in future conflicts.

He suggested that the prevention, localization, and neutralization of threats by political-diplomatic, economic, information, and other non-military means are a top priority.[107] He explains his thought with the popular claim among the Russian elite that it witnessed how the USSR and the Warsaw bloc collapsed without the direct use of armed force on the international stage. According to Gareev, the main reason for this was that the crises in certain countries, along with their internal instability, were compounded by the influence of external factors. He noted that the ratio of political-diplomatic, economic, informational, psychological, and military means of struggle on the international stage has changed significantly, and the value and proportion of non-military means has increased as well. He believes that "in the context of globalization, they have acquired a more purposeful and coordinated characters, their technological advancement, scale and effectiveness have increased."[108]

Gareev noted that the ratio of direct and indirect actions in strategy changes based on the methods of conducting military activities. According to him, indirect activities are related to the political, economic, and moral-psychological impact on the enemy; they are also dependent on "the methods of disinformation against enemy and its undermining from the inside." Such activities have always played a huge role. But in the current conditions, when global confrontation is curtailed and nuclear weapons deter strategic goals, the role of indirect actions increases significantly. "It is about greater flexibility in the art of war, more complete use of the whole variety of means and methods of activities, including non-military and

*The evolution of Russian security thought* 29

non-traditional ones."[109] He calls such asymmetric methods "non-direct activities in military strategy."[110]

Gareev suggests using indirect strategy in military confrontations and not using the preferred methods of an adversary. In his opinion, Russia must take urgent measures to build its long-range, high-precision weapons to avoid, in the event of a fight, being led by an adversary into what it wishes to avoid, namely, contact battles. According to him, Iraq and Yugoslavia had such opportunities, but they did not dare. "Remember how in 1941 our aviation, being in a difficult situation in the first days of the war, still managed to strike at Berlin and Königsberg," he stressed.[111]

Gareev calls for remembering that the war between technologically well-equipped opponents cannot be limited to contactless activities. To support his argument, he pointed to the operations in Iraq in 1991 and in Afghanistan beginning in 2001. "Contactless operations," he wrote, "must be followed sooner or later by contact ones."[112]

Gareev noted in his 2008 report, issued immediately after the five-day war in Georgia, that the primary task of ensuring Russian national security was to counter political, economic, ideological, psychological, informational, intelligence and counterintelligence, terrorist, and other activities of states that sought to undermine it. To counter those forces, the full use of all non-military means should be maximized.[113] Gareev stressed that Russia just amounted to directly counteract faced threats in the past. Excessive zeal often intensified and exacerbated those threats. To prove his argument, he referred to the Soviet efforts in the arms race with the West and noted that the Soviet strategy was not asymmetrical but that it straightforwardly answered every turn of the arms race:

> Nowadays, when Russia's economic and military powers are incomparable with the capabilities of the USSR and the US, and in order to achieve greater rationality of actions, we must respond to the emerging threats in a more flexible manner and, if possible, not with direct but rather asymmetric measures. All these measures should be united by a single goal and plan of action.[114]

To this end, he proposes the concept of "strategic deterrence" but not in the classic sense. According to Gareev, that term was not always equally understood, nor did it refer simply to strategic nuclear deterrence. In his explanation, strategic deterrence is a complex of interrelated political, diplomatic, information, economic, military, and other measures aimed at deterring, reducing, and preventing threats and aggressive actions by another state (alliance) and simultaneously, by responsive measures that would reduce the fears of the attacked side or by an adequate threat which would create unacceptable consequences for the adversary [attacker].[115] He emphasized that strategic deterrence is carried out by the efforts and defense power of the entire state. In this respect, Gareev suggested using asymmetric or non-military measures together with military ones. He urged the use of non-military and military activities for strategic deterrence and to ensure Russia's national interests. To achieve those goals, asymmetric strategies should be preferred.[116]

30  *The evolution of Russian security thought*

Even though Gareev emphasizes the role of non-military methods in contemporary wars, he does not diminish the role of military power. He urged using indirect strategies in military conflicts, preferably operations in depth, as it is the preferable strategy for a weaker side in asymmetric warfare. Given the extreme disadvantage and danger of passive, purely defensive actions, the battles in future military conflicts will—from the very beginning—require an active and decisive character. Following the firing of high-precision missiles and electronic strikes on the entire depth of the enemy's position, airborne assault forces will land, special forces will deploy their operations and then the ground forces will rapidly advance. He suggested that by avoiding frontal attacks and by using methods of operative maneuver groups, the military forces will be able to realize broad raid actions, and manage to get to the flanks and rear of the enemy. "In general, there is a tendency toward a convergence of methods of conducting offensive and defensive operations," he wrote.[117] If an adversary would prefer to avoid direct strikes or contactless battles (i.e., as in the US operations in Yugoslavia, Afghanistan, and Iraq), it should be drawn into battles. He stressed that the main task of defeating the enemy will be solved not during the collision of advance units but by the method of firing from a distance. Gareev also stresses the roles of psychological and information operations in such operations:

> The intensity of the fire impact on the participants in the war will sharply increase, causing unprecedented, possibly marginal neuro-psychological stress. Special place in the system of indirect activities will be occupied by special methods of warfare, starting with psychological operations, subversive activities, and ending with operations of special forces. All armed struggles will be permeated by the extensive informational confrontation.[118]

It is possible to find the eclectic approach in Gareev's writings and in the works of many other Russian military scholars. In this respect, he argues that several forms of warfare should be used in contemporary and future wars, but as components of a single war strategy. According to Gareev, three-dimensional, network, asymmetric, contactless, and information warfare elements will be used, but they reflect one of the characteristic features of a united strategy, whereas none of them separately can fully characterize the face of war.[119] However, Russia proved Gareev's eclectic approach in regards to forms of warfare through the manner of their involvement in recent conflicts.

A more detailed Russian vision and clarification of the appropriateness of asymmetric warfare in contemporary Russian military thought are given by General Andrei Kartapolov. By widely analyzing the US and NATO's sophisticated high-tech military and informational possibilities, their "non-direct" methods, and emphasizing the experiences of the military conflict in Syria, in which he was a participant, Kartapolov stressed the importance of Russia using asymmetric warfare methods. He notes that non-standard forms and methods are being developed for use by the Russian armed forces, which would reduce the technological superiority of the enemy. For this, Russia should prepare to wage new types of war and design asymmetric methods of confrontation. According to Kartapolov, asymmetric actions are inherent in any conflict situation in which an economically and diplomatically—and regarding its informational and directly military characteristics—weaker opponent implements an asymmetric strategy and tactics of armed struggle to reduce the military-technological advantages of the stronger side.[120]

He stresses that the exact identification of the most vulnerable and weakest points of the enemy is essential to the effectiveness of asymmetric measures. The impact which will give the maximum effect with minimum cost to weaker side's own forces and resources. Asymmetric measures may be the activities of special operation forces, foreign intelligence, various forms of information influence, as well as political, economic, and other non-military impacts. However, it is problematic to develop a universal set of asymmetric actions for all possible conflicts due to the nature of each. "Asymmetrical actions tend to have a fast-moving nature, as a stronger opponent is able to quickly adapt to the situation and provide effective resistance," he writes.[121] Kartapolov emphasizes that the effectiveness of the implementation of asymmetric activities depends on the completeness and timeliness of their fulfillment, which is achieved by coordinated action on the goals, place, and time by the state's various agencies.[122] It should be noted that Kartapolov occupied several high-level positions within the Russian military.

General Gerasimov, Chief of the Russian General Staff, also repeated Gareev's thoughts on conventional and non-conventional methods. His 2018 report emphasizes the multi-pronged nature of the threats to Russia's security, such as political-diplomatic, economic, informational, cybernetic, psychological, and other non-military forms and methods of confrontation. Referring to the Syrian conflict experience, he notes that there is a transition from consistent and focused activities to continuous and distributed ones that are carried out simultaneously in all areas of confrontation, as well as in the remote theaters of military operations. Gerasimov stresses that there is a transition to the "complex defeat" of an adversary based on the integration of all strike and fire powers in a single system. In such operations, the roles of electronic warfare and information technology as well as informational and psychological impacts are increasing. Based on the identified threats, new forms and methods of combat use by the armed forces, and the further transformation of the state's military organization, were proposed by the Russian Defense Ministry.[123]

Another important issue for using asymmetric approaches in military affairs is the human will to fight. In the age of revolution in military affairs, the United States and its coalition mainly relied on mechanics and technology. The United States military institutions tended to treat war as a fundamentally mechanical process, driven primarily by acquisitions and technology. In this regard, Russia maintains Suvorov's legacy—the role of will in war—intact. In 2018, the main political-military directorate of the army was reestablished. Colonel-General Andrei Kartapolov was assigned as the Deputy Minister of Defense and head of the main political-military directorate of the Russian armed forces. He stated that the main responsibility of the directorate was to create the necessary conditions so that "invincible spirit, convinced patriotism, and high spirituality will become hallmarks of the future Russian soldier."[124] However, Russia's 2022 invasion of Ukraine showed that the "invincible spirit" of the Russian military had serious problems.

## Summary

To understand the formation of Russia's security and military thinking and its basic facets, this chapter briefly reviews the history of Russian military thought since the end of the Russian Empire. It emphasized that some Russian military scholars had asymmetric warfare thoughts even before the revolutions of 1917. The conclusion is that 19th-century and Soviet-era military and security thoughts are basic elements in Russia's contemporary security policy.

Two major Russian warfare theories are analyzed, and it is shown that several approaches from those periods' warfare theories are actively utilized in current Russian security strategies, but that they are adapted and modified to the realities and challenges of the modern world. Main among them are non-linear warfare and mutiny warfare theories. The approaches of those theories are appropriate for the waging of asymmetric warfare operations on large scales. If the former is useful for conventional means of waging war, the latter considers the use of unconventional methods. In this respect, Soviet military theorists (Vladimir Triandafillov, Georgii Isserson, etc.) works on non-linear warfare theory, and the warfare concept of Yevgenii Messner on using non-military methods is analyzed in detail. By comparing the thoughts of the 20th century with those of Russia's contemporary scholars and security elites, it can be concluded that some key elements and ideas of contemporary Russian warfare strategies closely resemble concepts from the past century regarding the evolution of military conflicts.

It is noted that discussions about military reforms and future wars started in the final years of the Soviet Union. The Soviet military and international security experts tried to forecast the characteristics of future war in light of the revolution in military affairs and developments in the military industry, such as high-precision weapons. In that time of political, social, and economic turmoil, the Soviet General Staff faced a series of complex problems. Immediately after the Soviet Union's dissolution, the need for reform or reorganization of the army around the use of new or appropriate warfare approaches strengthened. Between 2000 and 2005, the commonly accepted thinking regarding the use of several methods and approaches appropriate to Russia's contemporary economic and military possibilities was formulated. In military means, it was emphasized that precision weapons, as well as strong air and cosmic forces, would play major roles in any future war. Although the role of nuclear forces in deterrence is emphasized, thoughts on using asymmetric strategies have been increasing since that period.

Differences and similarities between contemporary Russian and Western scholars' thoughts are also explained in the chapter from the point of view of Russian scholars.

Clarifying the ideas around the features of modern warfare with the help of asymmetry is popular in contemporary Russia. In accepting Russia's weaknesses, scholars stress the importance of using asymmetric approaches rather than symmetric ones. Even though many Russian scholars support the role of conventional military power in contemporary wars, they also emphasize the increasing role of non-military methods in conflicts. Even in purely military terms, most Russian scholars push for the use of asymmetric strategies in conflict with an adversary that has superior military power.

**Notes**

1 Pipes, Richard (1974) *Russia Under the Old Regime*. New York: Charles Scribner's Sons, p. 115.
2 Pintner, Walter (1986) "Russian Military Thought: The Western Model and the Shadow of Suvorov". Paret, Peter (ed.), *Makers of Modern Strategy – From Machiavelli to the Nuclear Age*, Princeton: Princeton University Press, p. 357.
3 Miliutin, Dmitrii A. (1822–1855) *Istoriia voiny s Frantssiu v Tarsstvovavnie Imperatora Pavla I, v 1799 godu*, 5 vols. St. Petersburg: Tipografiya Shtaba voyenno-uchebnykh zavedeniy; Translated in Pintner, pp. 361–362, online: http://militera.lib.ru/h/milyutin_da02/index.html.
4 Pintner, Walter (1986) "Russian Military Thought: The Western Model and the Shadow of Suvorov" …, p. 368.
5 Beskrovnyi, Lyubomir Grigor'yevich (ed.) (1960) *Russkaya voyenno-teoreticheskaya mysl' XIX i nachala XX vekov*, Moskva: Voyenizdat, pp. 557–561, 567, 624, 673–693; Translated in Pintner, Walter (1986) "Russian Military Thought: The Western Model and the Shadow of Suvorov…", p. 369.
6 Neznamov, Aleksandr A. (1912) "Sovremennoya voyna. Deystviya polevoy armii", Beskrovnyy, Lyubomir G., *Russkaya voyenno-teoreticheskaya mysl' XIX i nachala XX vekov*, Moskva: Voen. izd-vo, 1960, pp. 551–668.
7 Mikhnevich, Nikolai "Vliyaniye noveyshikh tekhnicheskikh izobreteniy na taktiku voysk"; "Taktika i yeye evolyutsiya v zavisomosti ot usloviy komlektovaniya voysk i tekhnicheskikh izobreteniy dannoy epokhi"; "Osnovy strategii", Beskrovnyy, Lyubomir G., *Russkaya voyenno-teoreticheskaya mysl' XIX i nachala XX vekov*, Moskva: Voen. izd-vo, 1960, pp. 415–440; 441–451 and 452–550.
8 Pintner, Walter (1986) "Russian Military Thought: The Western Model and the Shadow of Suvorov" …, p. 373.
9 Ibid.
10 Gurevich, Arsenii (1898) *Voina i narodnoe khoziaistvo*. St. Petersburg, pp. 15–16, 23–32. Cited in Pintner, Walter (1986) "Russian Military Thought: The Western Model and the Shadow of Suvorov…", p. 365.
11 Gallie, Walter Bryce (1989) *Philosophers of peace and war: Kant, Clausewitz, Marx, Engels and Tolstoy*, New York: Harcourt, Brace and Company, pp. 66–67.
12 Rice, Condoleezza (1986) "The Making of Soviet Strategy". Paret, Peter (ed.), *Makers of Modern Strategy – From Machiavelli to the Nuclear Age*, Princeton: Princeton University Press, p. 648.
13 Ibid.
14 Ibid., p. 649.
15 Engels, Friedrich (1957) *Izbrannye voennye proizvedenie*, Moscow: Voyennoye izdatel'stvo Ministerstva Oborony SSSR, p. xiv.
16 Rice, Condoleezza (1986) "The Making of Soviet Strategy" …, p. 649.
17 Trotsky, Leon (1928) *The real situation in Russia*, Transl. by Max Eastman, New York: Harcourt, Brace and Company, p. 145.
18 Erickson, John (1962) *The Soviet High Command*, New York and London: Macmillan, p. 33.
19 Frunze, Mikhail V. (1921) "Edinaia voennaia doktrina i krasnaia armia", *"Voennaia nauka i revolutsia"*, Iyul-avgust 1921, Moskva, 1921. Perepechatana v *Voennaia Mysl*, № 5/2008, http://militaryarticle.ru/voennaya-mysl/2008-vm/10112-edinaja-voennaja-doktrina-i-krasnaja-armija.

20 Trotsky, Lev Davidovich (1925) *Kak voruzhalas revoliutsia*, Moskva: Vissh. Voen. red. sovet. T.3: Tysiacha deviatsot dvatsatyi pervyi-tretii gody. Kniga 2, pp. 210–240.
21 Vysshii Voennyi Redaktsionnyi Sovet (1922) *Osnovnaya voennaya zadacha momenta. Diskussiyana temu o edinoi voennoi doctrine. Doklady t.t.Trotskogo, Frunze I preniya po nim*. Stenograficheskii otchet 2-go dnya soveshchaniya voennykh delegatov XI-go S"ezda R.K. P. 1-go aprelya 1922g, Moskva: Vysshii Voennyi Redaktsionnyi Sovet. http://rkka.ru/analys/doktrin/main.htm#s3.
22 Rice, Condoleezza (1986) "The Making of Soviet Strategy" ..., p. 655.
23 Vysshii Voennyi Redaktsionnyi Sovet (1922) *Osnovnaya voennaya zadacha momenta. Diskussiyana temu o edinoi voennoi doctrine. Doklady t.t.Trotskogo, Frunze I preniya po nim* ...
24 Rice, Condoleezza (1986) "The Making of Soviet Strategy…", pp. 657–658.
25 Ibid., p. 660.
26 Kennan, George Frost (1946) *The Chargé in the Soviet Union (Kennan) to the Secretary of State Moscow*, February 22, 1946, Part 2: Background of Outlook, Foreign relations of the United States, 1946, Eastern Europe, the Soviet Union, Volume VI, 861.00/2–2246: Telegram, 1969, https://history.state.gov/historicaldocuments/frus1946v06/d475.
27 Ibid.
28 Kennan, George Frost (1973) *Memories 1950–1963*, London: Hutchinson & CO (Publishers) LTD, p. 92.
29 Cimbala, Stephen J. (2013) "Russian Threat Perceptions and Security Policies: Soviet Shadows and Contemporary Challenges", *The Journal of Power Institutions in Post-Soviet Societies*, Issue 14/15: War Trauma in Post-Soviet Russia & Military Reform in Russia and the CIS-Russian Military Reform. http://journals.openedition.org/pipss/4000.
30 Sokolovskiy, Vasili Danilovich (ed.) (1962) *Voennaya strategia*, the second edition, Moscow: Voenizdat, pp. 129–193, 194–239.
31 Differences between linear and non-linear military operations are well explained by Sean Mackfarland: Absolute non-linearity consists of small numbers of highly dynamic forces operating in a large space, with a thorough intermingling of friendly and enemy forces throughout the theatre. Absolute linearity consists of 100% of all forces within a theatre occupying continuous and static positions within range of enemy weapons systems. In this state, enemy and friendly forces would be completely segregated; there would be no intermingling, gaps, or flanks. (Mackfarland, B. Sean (1994) Non-Linear Operations: A new doctrine for a new era, Monograph, DTIC, School of Advanced Military Studies United States Army Command and General Staff College ~Second Fort Leavenworth, Term AY 93–94 Kansas, p. 15.)
32 Yarov, Sergey (2009) *Istoriya dlya izucheniya obshchestvennykh nastroenii I kul'tury Rosii XX veka*, Sankt-Peterburg: Nestor-Istoriya, pp. 304–305.
33 Gorlov, Sergey (2001) *Sovershenno sekretno: Al'yans Moskva-Berlin, 1920–1933 gg*, Moskva: OLMA-PRESS, http://militera.lib.ru/research/gorlov1/04.html, accessed 21 September 2018.
34 Isserson, Georgii (1937) *Evoloutsia operativnogo iskustva*, Moskva: Voenizdat, pp. I32–I33.
35 Raevskii V. and Yarukhin U. (2015) "Teoriiaglubokoioperatsii", "Yazaveriauvas, tovarish Stalin ...", Fondveteranovvoennoirazvedki, Kiev, p. 18, http://vrazvedka.com/book/ilnickij/il-3.pdf, accessed 30 October 2019.
36 Triandafillov, Vladimir (1936) *Kharakter operatsii sovremennykh armii*. 3-e izd., Moskva: Gosvoenizdat, http://militera.lib.ru/science/triandafillov1/index.html, accessed 30 September 2018.
37 Rice, Condoleezza (1986) "The Making of Soviet Strategy" ..., p. 664.
38 Triandafillov Vladimir (1932) *Kharakter operatsii sovremennykh armii*. Izdanie vtoroe, Moskva: Gosvoenizdat, p. 3.

39 Tukhachevskii, Mikhail N. (1964) *Novyye voprosy voyny, Izbrannyye proizvedeniya v 2-kh t.*, Tom I (1919–1927 gg.); Tom II (1928–1937 gg.), Moscow: Voenizdat, http://militera.lib.ru/science/tuhachevsky/35.html#.
40 Simpkin, Richard, E. (1987) *Deep Battle: The Brainchild of Marshal Tukhachevskii*, New York: Brassey's, p. 38; Cited in Mackfarland, B. Sean (1994) *Non-Linear Operations: A new doctrine for a new era*. Monograph. DTIC. School of Advanced Military Studies United States Army Command and General Staff College ~Second Fort Leavenworth, Term AY 93–94 Kansas, p. 11.
41 Isserson, Georgii Samoilovich (1940) *Novie Formy borby*, Moscow: Voengiz, http://militera.lib.ru/science/isserson/index.html.
42 Svechin, Aleksandr A. (1927) *Strategiia*, Moscow: Voennyi Vestnik, Glavlit, p. 42.
43 Erickson, John (2001) *The Soviet High Command – A Military-Political History 1918–1941*, the third edition, London: Frank Cass Publishers, p. 506.
44 Ibid.
45 Ibid.
46 Ibid., p.507.
47 *Boevoi ustav pekhoty Krasnoi Armii* (1942), Moskva: Voenizdat NKO SSSR.
48 Isserson, Georgii (2013) *The evolution of operational art/brigade commander Georgii Samoilovich Isserson*, translated by Bruce W. Menning. The first edition. Combat Studies Institute Press US Army Combined Arms Centre Fort Leavenworth, Kansas, p. iii.
49 Mackfarland, B. Sean (1994) *Non-Linear Operations: A new doctrine for a new era* …, p. 11.
50 Isserson, Georgii (2013) *The evolution of operational art/brigade commander Georgii Samoilovich Isserson* … p. iii.
51 U.S. Army Combined Arms Command (1992) *The Non-Linear Nature of Future War. A Soviet/Commonwealth View*, Foreign Military Studies Office, Soviets Study, 4 March, p. 1; Cited in Mackfarland, B. Sean (1994) *Non-Linear Operations: A new doctrine for a new era* …, p. 12.
52 Grau, Lester W. (1990) *Soviet Non-Linear Combat: The Challenge of the 90s*, Soviet Army Studies Office, U.S. Army Combined Arms Centre Fort Leavenworth, Kansas, September 1990, p. 2.
53 Mackfarland, B. Sean (1994) *Non-Linear Operations: A new doctrine for a new era* …, p. 12.
54 Gerasimov, Valerii (2013) "Tsennost nauki v predvidenii", 26 February 2013, *Voenno-Promishlenniy Kurer*, https://www.vpk-news.ru/articles/14632.
55 Ibid.
56 Dominin, Igor (2005) "Ot Pervoi mirovoi do 'Tret'ei Vsemirnoi'". *Khochesh' mira, pobedi myatezhvoinu!*. Ed. DomininI V., Moskva: Voennyi universitet, Russkii put', T. 21, pp. 18—51.
57 Klus, Adam (2016) "Myatezh Voina: The Russian Grandfather of Western Hybrid Warfare", http://smallwarsjournal.com/jrnl/art/myatezh-voina-the-russian-grandfather-of-western-hybrid-warfare.
58 Ibid.
59 Russkoe Slovo (1971) "The World Mutiny War", Vol. 453.
60 Messner, Evgenii (1959) *Lik sovremennoi voiny*, Buenos Aires, p. 4; Cited in Dominin I.V. (ed.) (2005) *Khochesh' mira, pobedi myatezhvoinu!*, Moskva: Voennyi universitet, Russkii put', T. 21, p. 52.
61 Dominin I.V. (ed.) (2005) *Khochesh' mira, pobedi myatezhvoinu!*, Moskva: Voennyi universitet, Russkii put', T. 21, p. 58.
62 Ibid., p. 59.
63 Messner, Evgenii (1959) *Lik sovremennoi voiny* …, p. 61.
64 Ibid.
65 Ibid., p. 24; Cited in Dominin I.V. (ed.) (2005) *Khochesh' mira, pobedi myatezhvoinu!* …, p. 72.

36  *The evolution of Russian security thought*

66 Messner, Evgenii (1960) *Myatezh –imya Tret'ey Vsemirnoi*, Buenos Aires: Buenos Aires, p. 34; Cited in Dominin I.V. (ed.) (2005) *Khochesh' mira, pobedi myatezhvoinu!* ..., p. 122.
67 Ibid.
68 Messner, Evgenii (1960) *Myatezh –imya Tret'ey Vsemirnoi* ..., p. 14; Cited in Dominin I.V. (ed.) (2005) *Khochesh' mira, pobedi myatezhvoinu!* ..., p. 102.
69 Messner, Evgenii (1960) *Myatezh –imya Tret'ey Vsemirnoi* ..., pp. 9–10; Cited in Dominin I.V. (ed.) (2005) *Khochesh' mira, pobedi myatezhvoinu!* ..., pp. 97–98.
70 Messner, Evgenii (1971) *Vsemirnaya Myatezhvoina*, Buenos-Aires, p. 1; Cited in Cited in Dominin I.V. (ed.) (2005) *Khochesh' mira, pobedi myatezhvoinu!* ..., p. 130.
71 Ibid., p. 2; Cited in Dominin I.V. (ed.) (2005) *Khochesh' mira, pobedi myatezhvoinu!* ..., p. 131.
72 Messner, Evgenii (1971) *Vsemirnaya Myatezhvoina* ..., p. 20; Cited in Dominin I.V. (ed.) (2005) *Khochesh' mira, pobedi myatezhvoinu!* ..., p. 149.
73 Messner, Evgenii (1971) *Vsemirnaya Myatezhvoina* ..., p. 23; Cited in Dominin I.V. (ed.) (2005) *Khochesh' mira, pobedi myatezhvoinu!*, Moskva: Voennyi universitet, Russkii put', T. 21, p. 152.
74 Ibid., p. 24; Cited in Dominin I.V. (ed.) (2005) *Khochesh' mira, pobedi myatezhvoinu!* ..., p. 153.
75 Messner, Evgenii (1971) *Vsemirnaya Myatezhvoina* ..., p. 12; Cited in Dominin I.V. (ed.) (2005) *Khochesh' mira, pobedi myatezhvoinu!* ..., p. 141.
76 Ibid., p. 18; Cited in Dominin I.V. (ed.) (2005) *Khochesh' mira, pobedi myatezhvoinu!*, Moskva: Voennyi universitet, Russkii put', T. 21, p. 147.
77 Ibid., p.12; Cited in Dominin I.V. (ed.) (2005) *Khochesh' mira, pobedi myatezhvoinu!* ..., p. 141.
78 Ibid, p.20; Cited in Dominin I.V. (ed.) (2005) *Khochesh' mira, pobedi myatezhvoinu!* ..., p. 149.
79 Ibid., p.19; Cited in Dominin I.V. (ed.) (2005) *Khochesh' mira, pobedi myatezhvoinu!* ..., p. 148.
80 Dubrovitskii, Natan (Vladislav Surkov) (2014) *Bez neba*, 12 March, http://ruspioner.ru/honest/m/single/4131; Translation of the Bewilderingstories.com was used with the additional edition by Nurlan Aliyev, http://www.bewilderingstories.com/issue582/without_sky.html#.
81 Ibid.
82 Dominin, Igor (1999) "Myateezhvoina", November 5, http://nvo.ng.ru/history/1999-11-05/7_rebelwar.html.
83 Gerasimov, Valerii (2013) "Tsennost nauki v predvidenii", 26 February 2013, *Voenno-Promishlenniy Kurer*, https://www.vpk-news.ru/articles/14632.
84 Plekhanov, Igor (2017) ""Doktrina Gerasimova" I pugalo "gidridnoi voiny" Rossii", 28 June, https://ria.ru/analytics/20170628/1497445931.html.
85 Grau, Lester W. (1990) *Soviet Non-Linear Combat: The Challenge of the 90s*, Soviet Army Studies Office, U. S. Army Combined Arms Centre Fort Leavenworth, Kansas, September 1990, p. 1.
86 Reznichenko, Vasilii G. (ed.) (1987) *Taktika*, Moskva. Voenizdat, pp. 63, 181, 194; Translated in Grau, Lester W. (1990) *Soviet Non-Linear Combat: The Challenge of the 90s* ..., p. 1.
87 Salmanov, Grigorii I. (1988) "Sovetskaya voennaya doktrina i nekotorye vzglyady na kharakter voiny v zashchitu sotsializma", *Voyennaya mysl'*, Vol. 12, dekabr 1988, p. 9. Cited in Grau, Lester W. (1990) *Soviet Non-Linear Combat: The Challenge of the 90s* ..., p. 1.
88 Ibid., pp. 9–10.
89 Slipchenko, Vladimir (2002) *Voiny shestogo pokoleniya: oruzhie i voennoe iskusstvo budushzhego*, Moskva: Veche, pp. 365–366.
90 Ibid., p. 146.
91 Bocharnikov, I.V., Lemeshev, S.V., Liutkene G.V. (2013) *Sovremennye kontseptsii voin I praktika voennogo stroitel'stvo*, Moskva: Ekon-inform, pp. 75–76.
92 Ibid., p. 72.

93 Gareev, Makhmud A. (1995). *Esli zavtra voina*, Moskva: VLADAR.
94 Serebrryannikov V.V. (2002) "Otvoinstvennostikmiroliubiu". *Sotsiologicheskie issledovaniya*, Vol. 5, pp. 81–88.
95 Gareev, Makhmud (2003a) "Kharakter budushzhix voin", *Pravo I bezopasnost'* Vol. 1–2 (6–7), June, http://dpr.ru/pravo/pravo_5_4.htm.
96 Bocharnikov, I.V., Lemeshev, S.V., Liutkene G.V. (2013) *Sovremennye kontseptsii voin I praktika voennogo stroitel'stvo* ..., p. 73.
97 Gulin, V.P. (1997) "O novoi kontseptsii voiny", *Voennaya mysl'*, Vol. 2 (3–4), p. 14.
98 Borchev, M.A. (1993) "Voennaya nauka: razvitie I sovremennaya struktura", *Voennaya mysl'*, 1993, Vol. 12, p. 38.
99 Baluev, Dmitri G. (2005) "Politika v voine postindustrial'noi epokhi", *Mezhdunarodnye protsesy*, 2005, Vol. 3 (9), pp. 18–32; Cited in Bocharnikov, I.V., Lemeshev, S.V., Liutkene G.V. (2013) *Sovremennye kontseptsii voin i praktika voennogo stroitel'stvo* ..., p. 74.
100 Ibid.
101 Gareev, Makhmud (2003b) "O kharaktereioblikevooruzhennoibor'bybudushchego", *"Armeiskii sbornik"*, Vol. 4, http://www.soldiering.ru/war/war.php.
102 Ibid.
103 Ibid.
104 Gareev, Makhmud (2003b) "O kharaktere i oblike vooruzhennoi bor'by budushchego" ...
105 Ibid.
106 Gareev, Makhmud (2005a) "O kharaktere vooruzhennoi bor'by budushchego", *Vestnik Akademii voennykh nauk*, Vol. 2, p. 2.
107 Gareev, Makhmud (2003a) "Kharakter budushzhix voin"...
108 Gareev, Makhmud (2003b) "O kharaktere i oblike vooruzhennoi bor'by budushchego", *"Armeiskii sbornik"*, Vol. 4, http://www.soldiering.ru/war/war.php.
109 Gareev, Makhmud (2005a) "O kharaktere vooruzhennoi bor'by budushchego" ..., p. 12.
110 Gareev, Makhmud (2005b) "Uroki i vivody iz velikoi otechestvennoi voiny, lokalnykh voin i perspektivy razvitiia sovremennoi voennoi nauki i voennogo iskustva". *Vestnik Akademii voennykh nauk*, Vol. 2, 2005, p. 23.
111 Gareev, Makhmud (2003a) "Kharakter budushzhix voin", *Pravo I bezopasnost'* Vol. 1–2 (6–7), June, http://dpr.ru/pravo/pravo_5_4.htm.
112 Gareev, Makhmud (2003a) "Kharakter budushzhix voin" ...
113 Gareev, Makhmud A. (2008) "Strategicheskoe sderzhivanie: problemy i resheniya", gazeta *"Krasnaya Zvezda"*, October 8, http://old.redstar.ru/2008/10/08_10/2_04.html.
114 Ibid.
115 Ibid.
116 Gareev, Makhmud A. (2009) "Strategicheskogoe sderzhivanie v sovremennykh usloviyakh", *Vestnik Akademii voennykh nauk*, Vol. 2(27), http://militaryarticle.ru/voenno-promishlennii-kurer/2009-vpk/10908-problemy-strategicheskogo-sderzhivanija-v.
117 Gareev, Makhmud (2005a) "O kharaktere vooruzhennoi bor'by budushchego", Vestnik Akademii voennykh nauk, Vol. 2, p. 13.
118 Gareev, Makhmud (2003b) "O kharaktere i oblike vooruzhennoi bor'by budushchego", "Armeiskii sbornik", Vol. 4, http://www.soldiering.ru/war/war.php, accessed 28 November 2018.
119 Gareev, Makhmud (2003b) "O kharaktere i oblike vooruzhennoi bor'by budushchego" ...
120 Kartapolov, Andrei V. (2015) "Uroki voennykh konfliktov, perspektivy razvitiya sredstv i sposobov ikh vedenniya. Pryamye i nepryamye deistviya v sovremennykh mezhdunarodnykh konfliktakh", *Vestnik Akademii voennykh nauk*, Vol. 2 (51), p. 35.
121 Ibid., p. 36.
122 Ibid.
123 Khudoleev, Viktor (2018) "Voennaya nauka smotrit v budushchee", "Krasnaya zvezda", March 26, http://archive.redstar.ru/index.php/mohov/item/36626-voennaya-nauka-smotrit-v-budushchee.
124 Dzhordzhevich, Aleksandra (2018) "Minoborony vzyalos' za soldatskii dukh", *"Kommersant'"*, September 5, https://www.kommersant.ru/doc/3732686.

## Bibliography

Baluev, Dmitri G. (2005) "Politika v voine postindustrial'noi epokhi", *Mezhdunarodnye protsesy*, Vol. 3, No. 9, pp. 18–32.
Beskrovnyi, Lyubomir Grigor'yevich (ed.) (1960) *Russkaya voyenno-teoreticheskaya mysl' XIX i nachala XX vekov*, Moskva: Voyenizdat.
Bocharnikov, I.V., S.V. Lemeshev, and G.V. Liutkene (2013) *Sovremennye kontseptsii voin I praktika voennogo stroitel'stvo*, Moskva: Ekon-inform.
Borchev, M.A. (1993) "Voennaya nauka: razvitie I sovremennaya struktura", *Voennaya mysl*, Vol. 12, pp. 35–44.
Cimbala, Stephen J. (2013) "Russian Threat Perceptions and Security Policies: Soviet Shadows and Contemporary Challenges", *The Journal of Power Institutions in Post-Soviet Societies*, Issue 14/15: War Trauma in Post-Soviet Russia & Military Reform in Russia and the CIS-Russian Military Reform. http://journals.openedition.org/pipss/4000, accessed 20 November 2018.
Dominin, Igor (1999) "Myateezhvoina", 5 November, available at: http://nvo.ng.ru/history/1999-11-05/7_rebelwar.html, accessed 27 November 2018.
Dominin, Igor (ed.) (2005) *Khochesh' mira, pobedi myatezhvoinu!*, Moskva: Voennyi universitet, Russkii put', T. 21.
Dubrovitskii, Natan (Vladislav Surkov) (2014) *Bez neba*, 12 March, available at: http://ruspioner.ru/honest/m/single/4131, accessed 19 November 2018.
Dzhordzhevich, Aleksandra (2018) "Minoborony vzyalos' za soldatskii dukh", *"Kommersant"*, 5 September 2018, available at: https://www.kommersant.ru/doc/3732686?utm_source=facebook.com&utm_medium=social&utm_campaign=amplifr_social, accessed 20 December 2018.
Engels, Friedrich (1957) *Izbrannye voennye proizvedenie*, Moscow: Voyennoye izdatel'stvo Ministerstva Oborony SSSR.
Erickson, John (1962) *The Soviet High Command*, New York and London: Macmillan.
_____ (2001) *The Soviet High Command – A Military-Political History 1918–1941*, the third edition, London: Frank Cass Publishers.
Frunze, Mikhail V. (1921) "Edinaia voennaia doktrina i krasnaia armia", *"Voennaia nauka i revolutsia"*, Iyul-avgust 1921. Moskva, 1921. Perepechatana v *Voennaia Mysl*, № 5/2008, http://militaryarticle.ru/voennaya-mysl/2008-vm/10112-edinaja-voennaja-doktrina-i-krasnaja-armija, accessed 1 November 2018.
Gallie, Walter Bryce (1989) *Philosophers of Peace and War: Kant, Clausewitz, Marx, Engels and Tolstoy*, New York: Harcourt, Brace and Company.
Gareev, Makhmud A. (1995) *Esli zavtra voina*, Moskva: VLADAR.
_____ (2003a) "Kharakter budushzhix voin", *Pravo I bezopasnost*, Vol. 1–2, No. 6–7, June, available at: http://dpr.ru/pravo/pravo_5_4.htm, accessed 30 November 2019.
_____ (2003b) "O kharaktere i oblike vooruzhennoi bor'by budushchego", *Armeiskii sbornik*, Vol. 4, available at: http://www.soldiering.ru/war/war.php, accessed 28 November 2018.
_____ (2005a) "O kharaktere vooruzhennoi bor'by budushchego", *Vestnik Akademii voennykh nauk*, Vol. 2, pp. 11–14.
_____ (2005b) "Uroki i vivody iz velikoi otechestvennoi voiny, lokalnykh voin i perspektivy razvitiia sovremennoi voennoi nauki i voennogo iskustva", *Vestnik Akademii voennykh nauk*, Vol. 2, pp. 15–27.
_____ (2008) "Strategicheskoe sderzhivanie: problemy i resheniya", gazeta *"Krasnaya Zvezda"*, October 8, available at: http://old.redstar.ru/2008/10/08_10/2_04.html, accessed 30 November 2018.

_____ (2009) "Strategicheskogoe sderzhivanie v sovremennykh usloviyakh", *Vestnik Akademii voennykh nauk*, Vol. 2 (No. 27), available at: http://militaryarticle.ru/voenno-promishlennii-kurer/2009-vpk/10908-problemy-strategicheskogo-sderzhivanija-v, accessed 26 November 2018.

Gerasimov, Valerii (2013) "Tsennost nauki v predvidenii", 26 February 2013, *Voenno-Promishlenniy Kurer*, https://www.vpk-news.ru/articles/14632. Accessed 10 June 2018.

Gorlov, Sergey (2001) *Sovershenno sekretno: Al'yans Moskva-Berlin, 1920–1933 gg*. Moskva: OLMA-PRESS, available at: http://militera.lib.ru/research/gorlov1/04.html, accessed 21 September 2018.

Grau, Lester W. (1990) *Soviet Non-Linear Combat: The Challenge of the 90s*, Soviet Army Studies Office, U.S. Army Combined Arms Centre Fort Leavenworth, Kansas, September 1990.

Gulin, V.P. (1997) "O novoi kontseptsii voiny", *Voennaya mysl*, Vol. 2, No. 3–4.

Gurevich, Arsenii (1898) *Voina i narodnoe khoziaistvo*, St. Petersburg: Tipografiya Glavnogo Upravleniya Udělov.

Isserson, Georgii (1937) *Evoloutsia operativnogo iskustva*, Moskva: Voenizdat.

_____ (1940) *Novie Formy borby*, Moscow: Voengiz, available at: http://militera.lib.ru/science/isserson/index.html, accessed 28 January 2018.

_____ (2013) *The evolution of operational art/brigade commander Georgii Samoilovich Isserson*, translated by Menning, Bruce W. The first edition. Combat Studies Institute Press US Army Combined Arms Centre Fort Leavenworth, Kansas.

Kartapolov, Andrei V. (2015) "Uroki voennykh konfliktov, perspektivy razvitiya sredstv i sposobov ikh vedenniya. Pryamye i nepryamye deistviya v sovremennykh mezhdunarod-nykh konfliktakh", *Vestnik Akademii voennykh nauk*, Vol. 2, No. 51, pp. 26–36.

Kennan, George Frost (1946) *The Chargé in the Soviet Union (Kennan) to the Secretary of State Moscow*, February 22, 1946, Part 2: Background of Outlook, Foreign relations of the United States, 1946, Eastern Europe, the Soviet Union, Volume VI, 861.00/2-2246: Telegram, 1969, https://history.state.gov/historicaldocuments/frus1946v06/d475, accessed 27 November 2018.

_____ (1973) *Memories 1950–1963*, London: Hutchinson & CO (Publishers) LTD.

Khudoleev, Viktor (2018) "Voennaya nauka smotrit v budushchee", "Krasnaya zvezda", 26 March 2018, available at: http://archive.redstar.ru/index.php/mohov/item/36626-voennaya-nauka-smotrit-v-budushchee, accessed 7 December 2018.

Klus, Adam (2016) "Myatezh Voina: The Russian Grandfather of Western Hybrid Warfare", *Small Wars Journal*, available at: http://smallwarsjournal.com/jrnl/art/myatezh-voina-the-russian-grandfather-of-western-hybrid-warfare, accessed 25 November 2022.

Mackfarland, B. Sean (1994) *Non-Linear Operations: A new doctrine for a new era*, Monograph, DTIC, School of Advanced Military Studies United States Army Command and General Staff College ~Second Fort Leavenworth, Term AY 93–94 Kansas.

Messner, Yevgenii (1959) *Lik sovremennoi voiny*, Buenos Aires: Izdaniye Yuzhnoamerikan-skogo otdela Instituta po issledovaniyu problem voyny i mira imeni generala Golovina.

_____ (1960) *Myatezh –imya Tret'ey Vsemirnoi*, Buenos Aires: Izdaniye Yuzhnoameri-kanskogo otdela Instituta po issledovaniyu problem voyny i mira imeni prof., generala Golovina.

_____ (1971) *Vsemirnaya Myatezhvoina*, Buenos Aires: Izdaniye Yuzhnoamerikanskogo otdela Instituta po issledovaniyu problem voyny i mira imeni prof., generala Golovina.

Miliutin, Dmitrii A. (1822–1855) *Istoriia voiny s Frantssiu v Tarsstvovavnie Imperatora Pavla I, v 1799 godu*, 5 vols. St. Peterburg: Tipografiya Shtaba voyenno-uchebnykh zavedeniy; online available at: http://militera.lib.ru/h/milyutin_da02/index.html, accessed on July 31, 2022.

Paret, Peter (ed.) (1986) *Makers of Modern Strategy – From Machiavelli to the Nuclear Age*, Princeton: Princeton University Press.
Pipes, Richard (1974) *Russia Under the Old Regime*. New York: Charles Scribner's Sons.
Plekhanov, Igor (2017) '"DoktrinaGerasimova" I pugalo "gidridnoi voiny" Rossii", 28 June, https://ria.ru/analytics/20170628/1497445931.html, accessed 27 November 2018.
Raevskii, V., and U. Yarukhin (2015) "Teoriia glubokoi operatsii", *"Ya zaveriau vas, tovarish Stalin …"*, Fond veteranov voennoi razvedki. Kiev, available at: http://vrazvedka.com/book/ilnickij/il-3.pdf, accessed 30 October 2019.
Reznichenko, Vasilii G. (ed.) (1987) *Taktika*, Moskva: Voenizdat.
Russkoe Slovo (1971) "The World Mutiny War", Vol. 453, pp. 2–3.
Salmanov, Grigorii I. (1988) "Sovetskaya voennaya doktrina i nekotorye vzglyady na kharakter voiny v zashchitu sotsializma", *Voyennaya mysl*, Vol. 12, dekabr.
Serebrryannikov, V.V. (2002) "Ot voinstvennosti k miroliubiu". *Sotsiologicheskie issledovaniya*, Vol. 5, pp. 81–88.
Simpkin, Richard (1987) *Deep Battle: The Brainchild of Marshal Tukhachevskii*, New York: Brassey's.
Slipchenko, Vladimir (2002) *Voiny shestogo pokoleniya: oruzhie i voennoe iskusstvo budushzhego*, Moskva: Veche.
Sokolovskiy, Vasili Danilovich (ed.) (1962) *Voennaya strategia*, the second edition, Moscow: Voenizdat.
Svechin, Aleksandr A. (1927) *Strategiia*, Moscow: Voennyi Vestnik, Glavlit.
Triandafillov Vladimir (1932) *Kharakter operatsii sovremennykh armii*, Izdanie vtoroe, Moskva: Gosvoenizdat.
_____ (1936) *Kharakter operatsii sovremennykh armii*, 3-e izd., Moskva: Gosvoenizdat, available at: http://militera.lib.ru/science/triandafillov1/index.html, accessed 30 September 2018.
Trotsky, Lev Davidovich (1925) *Kak voruzhalas revoliutsia*, Moskva: Vissh. Voen. red. sovet. T.3: Tysiacha deviatsot dvatsatyi pervyi-tretii gody. Kniga 2.
_____ (1928) *The real situation in Russia*, Transl. by Max Eastman, New York: Harcourt, Brace and Company.
Tukhachevskii, Mikhail N. (1964) *Novyye voprosy voyny, Izbrannyye proizvedeniya v 2-kh t.*, Tom I (1919–1927 gg.); Tom II (1928–1937 gg.), Moscow: Voenizdat, available at: http://militera.lib.ru/science/tuhachevsky/35.html#, accessed 23 November 2018.
U. S. Army Combined Arms Command (1992) *The Non-Linear Nature of Future War. A Soviet/Commonwealth View*, Foreign Military Studies Office, Soviets Study, 4 March.
Vechnoi, P.L. (Major General) (ed.) (1942) *Boevoi ustav pekhoty Krasnoi Armii*, Moskva: Voenizdat NKO SSSR.
Vysshii Voennyi Redaktsionnyi Sovet (1922) *Osnovnaya voennaya zadacha momenta. Diskussiyana temu o edinoi voennoi doctrine. Doklady t.t.Trotskogo, Frunze I preniya po nim*. Stenograficheskii otchet 2-go dnya soveshchaniya voennykh delegatov XI-go S"ezda R.K. P. 1-go aprelya 1922g, Moskva: Vysshii Voennyi Redaktsionnyi Sovet, available at:. http://rkka.ru/analys/doktrin/main.htm#s3, accessed 28 October 2018.
Yarov, Sergey (2009) *Istoriya dlya izucheniya obshchestvennykh nastroenii I kul'tury Rosii XX veka*, Sankt-Peterburg: Nestor-Istoriya.

# 2 Determinants of Russia's security policy

**Weaknesses as the foundational elements of Russia's security policy**

A weaker geographical position in terms of security, economic shortcomings, and political turmoil historically strengthened the "fortress under siege" thinking, not only within the political elite but also Russian society at large. Here we examine Russia's main power indicators to understand the real conditions of its capabilities. It is appropriate to compare Russia's indicators against those of other powerful states as they are essential from a security perspective.

*Military-arms spending*

According to the Stockholm International Peace Research Institute (SIPRI) data analysis, at $66.3 billion, Russia's military spending in 2017 was 20% lower than in 2016, the first annual decrease since 1998. SIPRI expert Siemon Wezeman noted that although military modernization remains a priority in Russia, the military budget has been restricted by economic problems since 2014. At the same time, triggered by the perception of a growing Russian threat, military spending in both Central and Western Europe increased in 2017 by 12% and 1.7%, respectively. According to SIPRI, many of NATO's European members have agreed to increase their military spending. "Total military spending by all 29 NATO members was $900 billion in 2017, accounting for 52% of world spending."[1] Moreover, unlike Russia, several global, rising, and regional powers increased their spending during the same period. China increased its military spending by 5.6% to $228 billion in 2017. China's spending as a share of world military expenditure has risen from 5.8% in 2008 to 13% in 2017. It should be noted that China made the largest absolute increase in spending ($12 billion) in 2017 (in constant 2016 prices), while Russia made the largest decrease (–$13.9 billion). India spent $63.9 billion on its military in 2017, an increase of 5.5% compared with 2016. In 2017, the United States spent more on its military than the next seven highest-spending countries combined. At $610 billion, US military spending was unchanged between 2016 and 2017.[2]

Russia's advanced fielded capabilities mostly represent late-generation Soviet designs, which were finished and deployed across the force thanks to an initial

DOI: 10.4324/9781003344391-3

$670 billion modernization program. Michael Kofman notes that questions remain about the defense industry's (and the wider economy's) capacity to sustain research and development into the 2030s. He explains that future procurement (2018–2022) will focus less on platforms, except in the growing ground force, and more on new families of weapon systems, writing that "Russia has demonstrated the capability of new or modernized weapon systems, but what it currently lacks is capacity."[3]

According to Kofman, although military spending achieved its peak in 2015, with perhaps 4.2% of GDP, it remained well above 3% in 2017. However, he stresses that the problem is more about whether the country's economy "can provide the resources required to sustain it, given the prolonged impact of sanctions on access to defense technologies."[4]

In 2021, according to data on global military spending published by SIPRI, the five largest spenders were the United States, China, India, the United Kingdom, and Russia, together accounting for 62% of expenditure. Russia's military expenditure increased by 2.9% in 2021 to $65.9 billion, at a time when it was building up its forces along the Ukrainian border. This was the third consecutive year of growth, and Russia's military spending reached 4.1% of GDP in 2021.[5] Lucie Béraud-Sudreau, Director of SIPRI's Military Expenditure and Arms Production Programme, explains that high oil and gas revenues helped Russia boost its military spending in 2021, but Russian military expenditure had been in decline from 2016 to 2019 as a result of low energy prices combined with sanctions in response to Russia's 2014 annexation of Crimea.[6] According to SIPRI's report, because it has strengthened its defenses against Russia, Ukraine's military spending has risen by 72% since the annexation of Crimea in 2014. And while spending fell in 2021 to $5.9 billion, it still accounted for 3.2% of the country's GDP.[7]

For comparison, US military spending amounted to $801 billion in 2021, a drop of 1.4% from 2020. The US military burden decreased slightly from 3.7% of GDP in 2020 to 3.5% in 2021. China allocated an estimated $293 billion to its military in 2021, an increase of 4.7% compared to 2020. China's military spending has grown for 27 consecutive years, according to the SIPRI report. India's military spending was up by 0.9% from 2020 and, at $76.6 billion, ranked third highest in the world.[8]

Several years ago, an alternative method of measuring Russian military expenditures was put forward by Richard Connolly. He used a purchasing power parity (PPP) calculation instead of market exchange rates. According to Connolly, exchange rate volatility was the most important issue when using market exchange rate-based measures of military expenditure because many goods and services have different relative prices within a country, with non-traded goods and services being relatively less expensive in poorer countries. He explains that this has important implications for assessing the relative level of Russian military expenditure. "Because a ruble buys relatively more military output in Russia than a dollar does in the US, Russia's real level of military expenditure is likely to be considerably higher than a market exchange rate-based estimate would suggest."[9] Connolly notes that the most important difference between Russian military expenditure appears using market exchange rates and PPP exchange rates, and argues that the level of expenditure is around 2.5 times higher using PPP exchange rates.[10]

Connolly's key research conclusion is that after adjusting PPP-based estimates of total military expenditure for imported military equipment, Russia has held a steady position as the world's fourth largest military spender, behind the United States, China, and India.[11]

Despite tangible differences from market-exchange-rate-based calculations, the PPP-based military expenditure estimation also shows that Russia's financial support for its military is much less than the United States and China, and even less than India. Moreover, Connolly concludes that although the level of Russian military expenditure is clearly much higher regarding PPP-based calculations than indicated by market-exchange-rate-based estimates, "this should not necessarily be cause for serious alarm." He highlights that Russia has to spread its military budget across a wide range of different needs, "these range from R&D on new hypersonic weapons to maintaining a large strategic nuclear deterrent and the world's largest arsenal of tactical nuclear weapons. It must also be used to maintain, equip, and train one of the world's largest conventional militaries, tasked with dealing with threats spanning vast borders and oceans."[12]

However, answering how significant the differences would be if the military budgets of NATO countries and Russia were compared using purchasing power parity, the Russian deputy foreign minister Alexander Grushko said that the calculation methods may be different, but the essence of this will not change, "the numbers are still not comparable."[13]

*Nuclear power*

Strictly based on the number of their nuclear weapons, Russia is the leading nuclear power in the world, ahead of the other eight nuclear weapons states: the United States, the United Kingdom, France, China, Israel, India, Pakistan, and North Korea. As of early 2022, Hans M. Kristensen and Matt Korda of the Federation of American Scientists estimated that Russia's nuclear arsenal includes a stockpile of approximately 4,477 warheads. Of these, about 1,588 strategic warheads are deployed on ballistic missiles and at heavy bomber bases, while an approximate additional 977 strategic warheads, along with 1,912 non-strategic warheads, are held in reserve. Russia is continuing a comprehensive modernization program that is intended to replace most Soviet-era weapons by the mid- to late-2020s while also introducing new types of weapons.[14]

According to Kristensen and Korda, as of February 23, 2022, some of the Russian delivery vehicles that are deployed near Ukraine are considered to be dual-capable, meaning they can be used to launch either conventional or nuclear weapons. However, they note that "at the time of publication, we have not seen any indication that Russia has deployed nuclear weapons or nuclear custodial units along with those delivery vehicles."[15]

Russia has spent decades modernizing its strategic and non-strategic nuclear forces to replace Soviet-era weapons with newer systems. "These modernizations, combined with an increase in the number and size of military exercises and occasional explicit nuclear threats against other countries," Hans M. Kristensen and

Robert S. Norris write, "contribute to uncertainty about Russia's long-term intentions and growing international debate about the nature of its nuclear strategy."[16] Such concerns drive increased defense spending, nuclear modernization programs, and political opposition to further nuclear weapon reductions in Western Europe and the United States. "But Russia's financial crisis represents a significant challenge to maintaining even that force level, as exemplified by the delays of several major weapon systems, like the small ICBM (SS-28) and the rail-based ICBM," write Kristensen and Robert S. Norrisin 2018.[17]

However, Russia began to improve the capabilities of its strategic missile forces, after the United States withdrew from the anti-ballistic missile treaty in 2002, in order to expand its missile deterrence. Russia's recently developed hypersonic missile system, which is reportedly capable of carrying a nuclear warhead, may be a short-term game changer in the strategic arms deterrence between Russia and the United States. On December 27, 2019, Russia's defense minister, Sergei Shoigu, stated that the first missile regiment armed with the glide vehicle "Avangard" missile systems was operational.[18] Colonel General Sergei Karakayev, the chief of the Russian strategic missile forces, said that the new missile system was deployed with a military unit in the town of Yasny of the Orenburg region on the border with Kazakhstan in 2019.[19] Russia claims that its hypersonic glide vehicle can fly lower in the atmosphere, thereby avoiding ballistic missile defense radars. It is mounted on an intercontinental ballistic missile, allowing the warhead to be initially carried toward a target on a traditional piece of technology. But as it gets closer to the target, it flies at hypersonic speeds in an unpredictable path—making detection, tracking, and interception extremely difficult.

Diplomats mentioned to the New York Times that the Russian announcement may be as much about spurring a new round of diplomatic talks as it is about reviving an arms race, "Moscow is eager for President Donald Trump to renew the last remaining arms control treaty between the United States and Russia, called New START, which limits strategic nuclear missile launchers and deployed warheads for both nations."[20] The treaty expired in February 2021. In his annual address to the Federal Assembly in February, 2019, Putin called the "Avangard" missile system one of the "mirror and asymmetric responses" to the United States missile defense system program.[21] After President Joe Biden started his presidency, in February 2021, Russia and the United States extended the New START Treaty until February 5, 2026.[22] President Putin, who in 2019 threatened "asymmetric responses" praised the extension, saying that he had suggested this to "our US partners a long time ago ... I am pleased to note that the new US administration has fulfilled its campaign promises in this sphere. We praise this decision."[23]

Russia is in the later stages of a modernization campaign to replace its Soviet-era strategic and non-strategic nuclear forces with newer systems.[24] In December 2021, Russian Defense Minister Sergei Shoigu reported that modern weapons and equipment now make up 89% of Russia's strategic nuclear forces.[25]

Approximately 90% of all nuclear warheads in the world are owned by Russia and the United States, which each have around 4,000 warheads in their military stockpiles; no other nuclear-armed state sees a need for more than a few hundred nuclear weapons to maintain national security.[26] According to the Federation of American Scientists approximate estimates for early 2022, the status of deployed strategic warheads in Russia's nuclear arsenal is lower (1,588) than that of the United States (1,644).[27]

It should be noted that their nuclear arsenal is considered by Russian political and military elites mainly as a deterrence tool and not as a means for offensive military operations, especially with peer powers. However, at the very beginning of the 2022 invasion of Ukraine, President Putin ordered the strategic forces to be put on a special alert ("a special mode of service"). During the meeting with his defense minister and the Russian Chief of General Staff, he explained the reasoning for his decision by pointing out the "aggressive statements" against Russia made by the leadership of "the leading NATO countries."[28] Most likely, it was a Kremlin information move to deter the United States and its allies from becoming directly involved in the war since strategic forces in any nuclear weapons country should be on high alert on any given day.

Russian political and military leadership emphasizes the need for Russia's nuclear forces to keep balance with Russia's competitors.[29] In recent years, Russian leadership has regularly expressed concerns about the deployment of elements of the US global missile defense system near Russia, stating that they may target the Russian strategic forces and threaten their strategic deterrence capabilities. For instance, in his 2021 end-of-year speech, Putin noted that he is "extremely concerned that elements of the US global missile defense system are being deployed near Russia." He particularly accused the United States of using the missile defense deployments as a guise to deploy offensive systems targeted at Russia stating, "located in Romania and planned for deployment in Poland, the Mk 41 launchers are adapted to the use of Tomahawk strike systems. If this infrastructure moves forward, if US and NATO missile systems appear in Ukraine, then their flight time to Moscow will be reduced to seven to ten minutes, and if hypersonic weapons are deployed, to five."[30] Putin stressed that for Russia, this is a major challenge to its security.[31] Officials from the United States and NATO deny that the launchers have been adapted for use of Tomahawk missiles.[32] Now looking back, Putin's stressing of Ukraine as a possible strategic threat can be seen as a justification for the eventual invasion of Ukraine just two months after the speech.

During the invasion of 2022, Russia and Ukraine accused one another of nuclear terrorism. Ukraine accused the Russian military of having mined the Zaporizhzhia nuclear power plant. For its part, the Russian Defense Ministry claimed that Ukrainian military formations continue to strike the Zaporizhzhya nuclear power plant (NPP), which could lead to a humanitarian disaster.[33] Insider sources at the Zaporizhzhia nuclear power plant in Energodar—occupied by Russia since March—reported suspicious activity of Russian soldiers at the plant. The publication also has video of Russian military trucks pulling onto the plant site and unloading cargoes and that the turbine room of the NPP was mined.[34]

Moreover, in August 2022, Russia announced that it would refuse to let the United States inspect its facilities under the START treaty. The Russian Foreign Ministry announced that Russia was temporarily withdrawing its facilities from inspection activities under the START Treaty. The ministry explained that Moscow's decision was a result of "Washington's persistent desire to implicitly achieve a restart of inspection activities on conditions that do not take into account existing realities, create unilateral advantages for the United States, and effectively deprive the Russian Federation of the right to carry out inspections on American soil." Moscow stressed what it perceived as "an unacceptable situation" such as "a result of anti-Russian unilateral restrictive measures taken at the suggestion of Washington, normal air traffic between Russia and the United States was interrupted, and the airspace of states that are allies and partners of the United States is closed to Russian aircraft delivering Russian inspection teams to points of entry on American territory."[35] The difficulties for Russian inspectors in the United States were because of the interrupted air traffic and the restricted airspace of EU countries, which were closed to Russian aircrafts. Moscow seemingly tried to use the START Treaty to respond to the United States and its allies "restrictive measures" following Russia's invasion of Ukraine.

However, the Russian leadership believed its threat of nuclear war to be a guarantee that Russia's invasion of Ukraine would be reliably protected from outside encroachments, which has demonstrated its insufficiency. The warnings of President Putin regarding "the most serious consequences" for Western countries in the event of their intervention in the Ukrainian conflict did not prevent the active and effective participation of the United States and NATO in arming and training the Ukrainian Army, the transfer of intelligence information to Kyiv in real time, large-scale financial, economic, and technical assistance to Ukraine. Moreover, the statements of Russian officials referring to Russia's nuclear potential, and specifically the exercises of the Russian strategic nuclear forces, were seen by the West as evidence of Moscow's preparations for unleashing a nuclear war.

In this respect, Russian expert Dmitry Trenin complains that "this information campaign, did not lead to public outcry in the West against the nuclear threat and in favour of ending military support for Ukraine."[36] However, amid the poor performance of the Russian conventional military in the war, Russia, most probably, will even hugely rely on its nuclear weapons arsenal for deterrence and also to secure or promote its interests in the upcoming years. Moreover, there are calls among pro-government experts to reconsider the attitude toward strategic stability and the non-proliferation of nuclear weapons. For instance, Trenin writes that the key to strategic stability for Russia is to develop its own potential in various areas, and agreements with the United States, if any, can only be an addition to this potential—very conditional, given the high degree of distrust between the parties. "There is also a need for careful consideration of the problem of non-proliferation of nuclear weapons," Trenin suggests.[37] He believes that Russia cannot act in line with "American non-proliferation" approaches to Iran and North Korea.[38] All of this suggests that Russia will increasingly use the threat of nuclear weapons as a tool in its foreign security policy. Although it is difficult, if not impossible, to predict what could happen in Putin's brain, the use of non-strategic nuclear weapons by Russia—in the event of strategic losses in the war—remains high. Russia is likely to continue threaten and challenge the West with nuclear weapons-related issues. In February 2023, Putin declared that Russia was suspending Moscow's participation in New START, a strategic nuclear arms reductions treaty between the United States and Russia.[39] Dmitry Peskov justified the decision by declaring that "the involvement of NATO in the conflict in Ukraine" was a main factor and that "Russia will resume the implementation of the provisions of the treaty with the United States if the West listens to Russia's position."[40]

*Economy*

In June 2022, the World Bank's Global Economic Prospects report stated that following the COVID-19 pandemic, spillover from Russia's invasion of Ukraine was set to sharply hasten the deceleration of global economic activity, leading to high commodity prices, adding to supply disruptions, increasing food insecurity and poverty, exacerbating inflation, contributing to tighter financial conditions, magnifying financial vulnerability, and heightening policy uncertainty. The report stressed that it has magnified the slowdown of the global economy, in what could become a protracted period of feeble growth and elevated inflation.[41] Moreover, the report notes that Russia's invasion of Ukraine disrupted global energy markets and damaged the global economy.[42]

Even before the invasion, Russia's GDP compared to other global and regional powers in 2010 and 2020 was low and declining.[43] According to the World Bank World Development Indicators, Russia had 1,524.9 (2010) and 1,488.3 (2020). Other powers, such as the United States had 15,049.0 (2010) and 20,893.7 (2020); China 6,087.2 (2010) and 14,687.7 (2020); India 1,675.6 (2010) and 2,667.7 (2020); the United Kingdom 2,491.1 (2010) and 2,756.9 (2020); Germany 3,399.7 (2010) and 3,846.4 (2020); France 2,645.2 (2010) and 2,630.3 (2020).[44] After the release of international sanctions following the invasion of Ukraine, in early 2022, Russia's GDP had decreased to 1,306.[45]

The economic implications of the war hit an already stagnating economy. Russia's GDP per capita in early 2022 was only slightly higher than before the onset of the financial crisis in 2008 and, since 2009, its economy has grown at an average rate of less than 1% per year, a growth rate far too low for a country of Russia's economic potential and natural resources.[46]

According to the Russian Ministry of Economy, in June 2022, GDP contracted by 4.9% in annual terms after a decline of 4.3% in May and 2.8% in April 2022, and in the first half of the year, the economy shrank by 0.5%. The output of products and services by basic types of economic activity decreased by 4.5% in June (after 3.2% in May and 2.4% in April 2022), and the financial sector made an additional negative contribution to the economic dynamics. The issue is supported only by mining and agriculture, and the unknown duration of the intervention in Ukraine is the main factor of uncertainty for companies.[47]

According to the World Bank's Global Economic Prospects June 2022 report, in Russia, the Purchasing Managers' Index (PMI) shrank in March and April of 2022 and the manufacturing PMI for new export orders had also contracted, reaching its lowest reading since mid-2020. The invasion also affected Russia's banking sector, with several Russian banks cut off from the SWIFT network. "About half of Russia's international reserves are frozen due to restrictions on the Central Bank of the Russian Federation (CBR)," the report says.[48] Additionally, a sharp fall in domestic demand and declining exports occurred because of the war. GDP is expected to contract in 2023 by 2%, as the impact of the partial embargo on Russia's oil exports to the EU takes effect. Moreover, private consumption is expected to remain depressed as income losses and supply shortages mount.[49]

The report noted that the ban of key high-tech goods, including software, semiconductors, and avionics, to Russia by many countries will deprive Russian industries of critical inputs and exacerbate regional supply chain disruptions. The report paints a gloomy picture regarding the future of the Russian economy stating that "oil production will be curtailed due to the exit of foreign oil companies, investment will weaken, and access to foreign technology will shrink."[50]

However, the World Bank's Global Economic Prospects report of January 2023 stated that in 2022, the Russian economy contracted by 3.5%, in 2023 it is expected to decline by 3.3%, and in 2024 it will grow by 1.6%. Sanctions, reduced investment, and increased emigration affect GDP dynamics, according to the report.[51]

According to the World Bank annual report 2018, Russian demographic trends were worse than those found in other Emerging Markets and Developing Economies (EMDEs) as the country's low total fertility rate in the early 1990's accelerated population aging. Russia's total fertility rate remained low until the mid-2000s. The decline in the total fertility began to take its toll on the working-age population after 15 years, with potential labor force growth peaking in 2007 at 0.7% before declining to −0.7% in 2017. [52]

According to United Nations Development Programme (UNDP) Human Development Index (HDI), Russia's rank is 52, less than all Western countries.[53] Moreover, since the start of the invasion and following the Russian government's measures at tightening control over society, brain drain from the country has accelerated.

Russia's economy has already been affected by the invasion of Ukraine. Besides the burden of waging the war, the Russian economy faces an unexpected and extraordinarily broad-based spiral of sanctions. The sanctions included previously unthinkable measures: blocking sanctions on Russian banks, freezing the assets of the country's central bank, and disconnecting several financial institutions from SWIFT.[54] Gunter Deuber argues that although Russia has been preparing for years for measured Western economic and financial sanctions some measures, specifically the freezing of substantial public and private funds, were deployed quickly while "private" voluntary sanctioning (company withdrawals, supply stops in non-sanctioned sectors, etc.) were unexpectedly comprehensive.[55] It even seems likely that sanctions and company withdrawals will remain in place for a long time, even after the end of the war. Alexey Yusupov suggests that the era of prosperity that began with Putin's first presidency in 2000 is now over and that Russia's technological decline will be felt by everyone in the country.[56] He believes that although the sanctions haven't ended Russia's war on Ukraine, they might set the country's economic development back by 30 years.[57]

However, Maria Shagina believes that drastic measures lack conditionality because a clear endgame is missing. She points out that disruption for disruption's sake will be received with resentment and antagonism. Therefore, the burden of choice must lie with the Kremlin. "The US and allies should use their measures of massive consequences to table strong demands," Shagina stresses.[58]

## The Russian Empire and the Soviet Union legacies' influences on threat perception in contemporary Russia's security policy

To understand the security thinking of the Russian elite during the Soviet and contemporary periods, it is important to analyze the main pillars which were formulated in the Muscovite epoch. Since the Middle Ages, the security thinking of Russia's political elite has been influenced by its natural shortcomings: disadvantages of geographical location regarding security, source limitations, and being surrounded by stronger, sometimes hostile powers. These weaknesses affected public life and the development of public institutions in a country where peasants were a major social group. Patrimonialism was another factor and, as Richard Pipes wrote, was rooted in the failure of Russian statehood to evolve from a private into a public institution and was accompanied by rapid territorial expansions. Pipes noted that the overwhelming military might first of Muscovy and then of imperial Russia, as well as the absence of natural obstacles to conquest, enabled their rulers to expand to all points of the compass, creating a vast empire contiguous to the Russian heartland and indistinguishable from it. "During the 150 years that elapsed between the reigns of Ivan I and that of Ivan III," Pipes wrote, "Muscovy grew more than 30 times." "And it kept on expanding: From the middle of the sixteenth century to the end of the seventeenth, it acquired year after year territory equivalent to that of modern Holland."[59] Ironically, such territorial expansions, which were realized mainly to maintain the security and economic prosperity of the Empire's heartland, would turn into one of the main challenges to security in subsequent centuries. The immense size of their realm, as well as dispersal and ethnic diversity of its population, imbued Russia's rulers with permanent anxiety about the stability and the very survival of their empire.

> Fear was the principal reason why the tsars adamantly refused to concede any of their absolute authority until forced to do so in 1905–06 by countrywide revolution. They were convinced—and not without reason as the events 1917–20 were to show—that lacking strong central authority acting for the benefit of the whole and independently of the particular wants of the diffuse populations, the country would promptly disintegrate.[60]

Fears based on environmental, economic, and socio-political weaknesses have been reflected in Russia's political culture since the Muscovite period. Edward Keenan argues that during the Muscovite period, Russia's political culture was based on three rather distinct political cultures: the court, the bureaucracy, the village. According to him, the general tendency of policy in all three cultures was to strive for stability and risk avoidance, rather than change, including progress.[61]

Colonization was another key factor, which played an important role in the formation of threat perception behavior, security thinking, and generally in establishing relations between the state and people of Russia. This factor was initiated by the need for ever fresh land, and compelled Russian peasants to continuously push outward. Colonization was so fundamental a characteristic of Russian life that Kluchevskii considered the history of the country, "the history of a country which colonizes itself."[62] Until their colonization expanded in the direction of the taiga, the process unrolled spontaneously and did not need military protection. But when they moved toward the rich and desirable soil that lay in the steppe, they faced nomadic Turkic and Mongol tribes who not only controlled those lands but also did not tolerate any agricultural settlements on their territories and frequently carried out raids in search of slaves and loot. After Russia's superior political and military had started to protect and encourage colonization, in the 16th and 17th centuries, there was scarcely a year when Russians did not fight along their southern and southeastern borders. Pipes explained that although Soviet historians tended to depict these wars as defensive in nature, they were as often as not instigated by Russian colonist pressure.[63] The colonization continued until the collapse of the Russian Empire. Several colonies were established in all directions of the Empire and in regions where the Indigenous populations had other cultures. Moreover, the Soviet period changed almost nothing in this respect. But the Soviet period colonization, in contrast with that of the past, was mostly urban. Although the reverse process started after the collapse of the Soviet Union as ethnic Russians, or Russian speakers, moved back from former ethnic regions to Russia. And in the early 2000s, a new strategy of Moscow—Russia's official policy of compatriots—was launched. According to the official position, which is also reflected in official security documents, Russia protects Russian and Russian speakers who mainly live in the former colonies or Soviet republics. As witnessed during the military conflicts in Georgia and Ukraine, Russia is ready to protect them or to use "the protection of compatriots" as reasons for military interventions.

The Soviet period is an important phase for understanding the security thinking of Russia's political elite in the 20th century and today. It played a bridge role between pre-revolutionary and contemporary Russian elite thinking. It also has a huge influence on the contemporary political and military elites' threat perception. In this regard, we are going to deeply explore the security thinking characteristics of the elites during this period.

During the Soviet period, some developments took place within the security thinking of the political elites. Mainly these linked official state ideology and several tremendous, non-natural elite change processes which were the results of the 1917 revolutions. These changes, which began with the February Revolution, were forced by the October Revolution or the Bolshevik's coup d'état, and were accomplished during Stalin's regime in the 1930s. As a result of these developments, a new political culture based on several traditional characteristics was created. In the 19th and early 20th centuries, the modernization of the country helped expand the group of Western thinkers into a large and articulate body of public opinion. "Russia's gradual cultural Westernization," Pipes writes, "produced a social group distinguished from the mass of the population by its education, its way of life, and a general sense of affinity with the Western cultural community," but as a consequence of dramatic social and political changes in the early 20th century, this group "intelligentsia" experienced "a deep crisis that for most of it ended either in exile or physical annihilation."[64] Consequently, they played an unimportant role in the political apparatus. As a result, the traditional elements again became the basic pillars of the elites' new political culture.

According to Edward Keenan, at least three factors strengthened the role of traditional elements in this new political culture, which were to the exclusion of other notions that had played so visible a role in the previous period of revolutions: First, a hegemonic political power, the Bolshevik Party, whose creed of centralism, elitism, and conspiratorial rule was most compatible with traditional patterns, became the principal agent and beneficiary of the reestablishment of political stability. Second, the processes of social revolution and intraparty struggle had selectively eliminated from political life almost all representatives of those classes and groups that had, in the revolutionary period, become most profoundly committed to a non-traditional political culture. Third, and most importantly, was the fact that "in a process that mirrored changes in the society at large, the new political elite that emerged by the end of the thirties was dominated by individuals of proletarian or peasant background, whose political culture was formed on the base of what we have called the village political culture, and strongly reinforced by the experience of the chaotic and risk-laden environment in which they had risen to power."[65]

Newcomers learned the skills required for playing these new roles, and they did not thoroughly refuse their original attitudes and even brought them with them to their new positions. Indeed, in that period for one to survive or even prosper in politics, practicing the traditional habits of risk avoidance and the subjection of individual will and impulse—including one's own—to the interests of the group was vital. As put by Keenan, "they took control of an increasingly stable state and society whose traditional patterns of centralization, bureaucratization, and pragmatism, whose objectives of security and control, all based upon a fear of uncontrollable situations, were newly reinforced by the experiences of the preceding decades of insecurity and chaos."[66] The previously mentioned characteristics were the main determinants of Soviet political culture, and they played a direct role in the formation of security thinking for the Soviet and current Russian elites, having determined Russian political culture for centuries.

George Kennan, in his "Long Telegram" to the State Secretary, George Marshall, in 1946, wrote that the USSR still lives in antagonist "capitalist encirclement" with which in the long run there can be no permanent peaceful coexistence.[67] Kennan explained that at the bottom of the Kremlin's neurotic view of world affairs was the traditional and instinctive Russian sense of insecurity. Kennan differentiated threat perceptions between the Soviet political leadership and its people. According to him, that particular type of insecurity was one which afflicted Russian rulers rather than the Russian people:

> ... For Russian rulers have invariably sensed that their rule was relatively archaic in form, fragile and artificial in its psychological foundation, unable to stand comparison or contact with political systems of Western countries. For this reason they have always feared foreign penetration, feared direct contact between the Western world and their own, feared what would happen if Russians learned the truth about the world without or if foreigners learned the truth about the world within.[68]

Interestingly, during the Cold War, both adversaries usually perceived each other's military activities as offensive, often mistakenly. And such perceptions created security dilemmas in relations between the two. Typically, discussions around security dilemmas are best illustrated by the armaments game: "The arms race is seen as the epitome of competition for illusory security. Sometimes, at least implicitly, the security dilemma is seen operating in the adversary game (competition other than armaments), as in explanations that ascribe the cold war to the United States and the Soviet Union misperceiving each other's 'defensive' actions in Europe as 'aggressive.'"[69] Moreover, during that period, Soviet preparations for large-scale warfare were widely accepted as offensive in nature. But according to some scholars, such preparations were related to the Soviet elites' fears and experiences from WWII and their Marxist-Leninist ideology.

According to the military thinking of that period, one of the most important tasks for the Soviet political and military elites, from the end of WWII until the collapse of the USSR, was the avoidance of a decisive surprise attack in the "initial period" of a war. A repeat of the disastrous Soviet experience against Nazi Germany, in the early stages of WWII, could not be tolerated.

The Soviet analysis of their experiences in the Spanish Civil War and the Soviet-Finnish War of 1939–1940, together with a study of earlier experiences, produced minor changes in operational art and tactics. Assessment of the experiences of Soviet tank specialists in the Spanish Civil War cast doubt on the feasibility of using large tank units in combat because of the difficulty in controlling theater and because of their vulnerability to artillery fire.[70] Soviet occupation of eastern Poland in September 1939 highlighted the command and control and logistical difficulties involved in employing large motor-mechanized forces. The 15th and 25th Tank Corps, which participated in that operation, suffered greatly from mechanical breakdowns and logistical shortages.[71] Only after disappointments in their war against Finland, and after having observed the successes of the Germans against Poland and France did the Soviet High Command turn to the practical reequipping and retraining of the armed forces for large-scale, mobile offensive and defensive operations. But they were caught in the midst of reorganization and re-equipment, and their concepts of the strategic defensive had not been carefully thought out.[72]

After the war, Soviet military academics carefully studied the commencement of the war. They referred to this period as the "initial period of war." For instance, the authoritative study under the editorship of General of the Army S. P. Ivanov was devoted to this subject.[73] Those studies revealed the strengths and weaknesses of the Soviet conduct of campaigns at the operational and operational strategic levels in the early period of the war and subsequently. Future Soviet commanders would have to apply those lessons to a different technological and policy context after World War II, and special account would have to be taken of the "revolution in military affairs" that had been brought about by the development and deployment of nuclear weapons.[74] Generally, the avoidance of a surprise attack was part of a broader interest within the Soviet military and political elites. Moreover, the tradition in Russia's security thinking—to create and maintain geopolitical buffer zones (i.e., socialist countries in Central and Eastern Europe) as a guarantor against a sudden attack—was strengthened after WWII.

The growth of Soviet military power in the Brezhnev years was not accompanied by commensurate gains in foreign policy objectives. Far from making the Soviet Union more secure, its growth merely provoked the United States and its allies into building up their own forces. According to David Holloway, this in turn "created new threats to Soviet security and imposed new military requirements on the Soviet Union."[75]

Although Gorbachev's foreign security policy considered cooperation and promoted the establishment of a new security situation in Europe, even Gorbachev's Perestroika and new thinking policies could not change historically established determinants of Russia's security thought. Understanding of threat perceptions happened in the same way. After the collapse of Brezhniev's détente policy and economic shortcomings, Gorbachev's new thinking did not indicate that the Soviet Union wished to abandon its role as a world power, but it provided a different picture of the world and redefined the Soviet role in it. "It assigns a less important role to conflict in international relations," Holloway writes, "and calls for the Soviet Union to base its world role not on military power and the search for unilateral advantage, but on a more cooperative-more normal-involvement in the international system."[76] It should be noted that the deteriorating economic situation and the possibility of deployments of American missiles to Europe primarily triggered Gorbachev's new thinking policy.[77]

During Gorbachev's leadership, agreements on eliminating all nuclear and conventional missiles as well as their launchers (the Intermediate-Range Nuclear Forces Treaty—INF) and the reduction and limitation of strategic offensive arms (the Strategic Arms Reduction Treaty—START I) were signed by the leaders of the Soviet Union and the United States. These agreements, together with Gorbachev's decisions on the reduction of troop numbers and his thoughts about changing the military strategy from offensive to defensive in Europe and actions taken in this direction (reductions of numbers of amazements and military equipment in the Warsaw Pact countries), created the rifts of estrangement and distrust between him and the military and security establishment.[78] The Soviets have always maintained that their military doctrine was "defensive" which meant that the Soviet Union would only resort to military force when the "gains of socialism" were threatened. Its only goal in war would be defending the socialist world.[79] To support that defensive doctrine, however, the Soviet Union had a decidedly offensive military strategy. According to Stephen M. Meyer, "the new concept of "defensive defense" represented a significant departure from this formula, and Gorbachev's new thinking policy crosses from the realm of doctrine to the realm of military strategy."[80]

However, as Gorbachev was launching his "new thinking policy," Soviet military academics actively discussed the importance of preparing for non-linear combat in future wars. In the book "*Taktika*" ("Tactic"), published under the editorship of General Reznichenko in 1987, the role of depth strikes and high-precision weapons in future wars was emphasized.[81] Moreover, projects for several contemporary Russian high-precision weapons were designed in the last years of the Soviet Union. For instance, the INF Treaty was the beginning of the creation of a short-range ballistic missile system—the 9K720 Iskander-M (known in NATO parlance as the SS-26 Stone).[82] Although Gorbachev was a vocal opponent of missile defenses, Soviet military leadership Supported anti-ballistic missile (ABM) defense capabilities. According to Jennifer G. Mathers, the persistent interest in missile defenses within the Soviet, and now Russian armed forces, seems to stem from widely shared views about future war and "the optimum strategy for it which recommends a combination of offensive and defensive weapons and emphasizes the importance of territorial protection." "The need to protect the country's territory, industrial capacity, population, political leadership, military command structure, and essential elements of the armed forces appears to be deeply embedded in the mindset of the Soviet and Russian military," writes Mathers, "going beyond the furthering of personal or institutional interests and undoubtedly shaped by the experience of the invasion of Nazi forces in 1941."[83]

## NATO enlargement as the main external threat

Since the 1990s being "misled" by Western leaders on assurances regarding NATO non-enlargement toward the Russian border has been the primary reason for subsequent Soviet and Russian complaints. And it is specifically this issue, the possibility of Ukrainian membership in the unspecified future that was used by the Kremlin to justify the interventions in 2022.

The Soviet leadership emphasized the importance of maintaining buffer zones in the negotiations with Western leaders on the reunification of Germany in 1990 and 1991. Soviet leader Mikhail Gorbachev and his supporters in the political elite were also against the enlargement of NATO, and they considered post-Warsaw Pact countries a neutral zone between the Soviet Union and the Alliance.[84] According to Shevardnadze, then the minister of foreign affairs, those countries were considered part of the Soviet Union's sphere of influence. Moreover, Gorbachev even had the idea of the Soviet Union joining NATO in 1990, but Shevardnadze stressed that "he never took any realistic steps towards achieving this and that is why it was never really discussed amongst the Soviet leaders."[85]

According to declassified documents, the first concrete assurances by Western leaders on NATO began on January 31, 1990, when West German Foreign Minister Hans-Dietrich Genscher opened the bidding with a major public speech, at Tutzing, in Bavaria, on German unification. According to these documents, the US Embassy in Bonn informed Washington that Genscher made it clear "that the changes in Eastern Europe and the German unification process must not lead to an 'impairment of Soviet security interests.'" "Therefore, NATO should rule out an expansion of its territory towards the east, i.e., moving it closer to the Soviet borders." The Bonn cable also noted Genscher's proposal to leave East German territory out of NATO military structures even if a unified Germany was in NATO.[86] The problem was that neither Western leaders nor the Soviet political elite believed that the dissolution of the Warsaw bloc and the USSR would happen any time soon. The new reality following the collapse of the Soviet Union dictated other decisions, which—since 1994—have been seen by the majority of Russia's political elite as misleading.

Despite critical comments on the West's "misleading" and noncompliance regarding NATO enlargement made by Soviet and contemporary Russian elite representatives, a question one may ask is: Why didn't either Gorbachev and his elite, or Yeltsin and his team, insist on any legal obligations from the West? The main explanation for this tends to be that the Soviet Union and Russia's economic shortcomings and hazardous social conditions required financial support for the survival of their political regimes. And both Gorbachev's and Yeltsin's elites most probably understood that in such conditions, Russia was incapable of insisting on its geopolitical interests. Afterward, the issue would be used by political regimes and their opponents in internal political relations. Since the middle of the 2000s, the issue has been used by the Kremlin as justification for its interests in the former Soviet and socialist-bloc countries, its "sphere of interests."

Moreover, recently declassified documents show that despite Yeltsin's requests, Bill Clinton—then president of the United States—refused to make even a verbal, non-public "gentlemen's agreement" that NATO enlargement would not embrace the former Soviet republics.[87] According to documents, Yeltsin asked Clinton to tell him what he wanted to hear "one-to-one—without even our closest aides present—that you won't take the new republics in the near future; I need to hear that. I understand that maybe in ten years or so, the situation might change, but not now," asked Yeltsin for the survival of his presidency. Clinton shot back negatively and mentioned that a private commitment would be the same as a public one, "... I know what a terrible problem this is for you, but I can't make the specific commitment you are asking for. It would violate the whole spirit of NATO."[88]

Vladimir Denisov, a Russian veteran of military intelligence and ex-deputy secretary of the Security Council of the Russian Federation who directly participated in the negotiations with NATO in the 1990s, explains that by the mid-1990s, the Russian armed forces had lost their ability to conduct military operations on an operational scale.[89] According to him, the presence of more or less modern equipment by the end of the 90s was from 12% to 15%, the most prosperous were the Strategic Missile Forces, and for the ground forces this figure was only 3%–5%. There were then 2.1 million military personal in the armed forces. Of this number, and with great difficulty, they managed to find 85 thousand for operations in Chechnya and, with grief, provided them with half.[90] Denisov stresses that this was the real situation facing Russia during negotiations with NATO. And its leaders, of course, saw and understood all this, he notes.[91]

Most probably, the main reasons for the lack of acceptance regarding the Kremlin's interests were its policies and activities in Central and Eastern Europe following WWII and its weaknesses. Both of these were mainly the results of foreign and external security policy mismanagement by the Russian elites, both during the Soviet Union and after its collapse. Historical experiences dictated that Western leaders push NATO toward an eastward enlargement. The experiences of WWII and the Cold War taught the Western and Eastern European political establishments that Russia pursues more constructive policies in international relations when it is weaker rather than stronger. However, the NATO eastward enlargement would be the main subject of grievances and the primary source of distrust among Russia's political elite regarding the West in the years after the breakup of the Soviet Union.

It should be noted here that some developments following the collapse of the USSR, and perceived as threats by the post-Soviet Russian elite, are also based on their traditional historical threat perception. NATO enlargement is first among them. The eastward enlargement of NATO is an important facet, which heavily influenced the security thinking of the political elite and public since the 1990s. Available survey data shows how this problem played a significant role in changing external security attitudes in Russia between 1993 and 1999. In this regard, William Zimmerman's research explaining the changing threat perception of the elites and general public—based on the data of that period—is incredibly valuable.

Between 1993 and 1995, the proportion of Russian foreign policy elites that viewed the United States as more powerful than Russia remained essentially unchanged. Twice as many termed the United States a threat in 1995 as they had in 1993. Half the elites categorized the growth of US military power as a great or the greatest danger in 1995; a fifth had assessed the United States as a great or the greatest threat in 1993. According to Zimmermann, there was no statistical relationship between the assessment of the elites regarding the distribution of power between the United States and Russia and their perceptions regarding the threat of NATO expansion into Eastern Europe. "Russian foreign policy elites balance perceived threat not power."[92]

Zimmermann presents the mean responses to a battery of questions asked of foreign policy elites and a national sample of ordinary Russians in the fall of 1995 and again in the fall of 1999 concerning perceived security threats to Russia. As the survey results revealed, NATO expansion was both far more salient and a greater source of concern for Russian elites than it was for the mass public in 1995.[93] "With all the elite utterances," Zimmerman writes, "the outpouring of media about Kosovo, demonstrations at the American embassy in Moscow, and the like, a case could be made that NATO expansion had achieved by 1999 a level of mass public awareness that bought it in line with other major foreign policy concerns."[94]

According to Zimmerman's data, slightly less than half of both the foreign policy elite and the mass public termed US military power a great or the greatest danger in 1993. Almost five in six of the foreign policy elites and three-quarters of the mass sample did so in 1999, and only 10% of the market democratic elites and a quarter of the liberal democratic mass public answered that US military power constituted a danger or the greatest danger in 1993. "In 1999 almost half the liberal democratic elites and two-thirds of the liberal democratic mass publics said the growth of US power was a great or the greatest danger," notes Zimmerman.[95] "There are elites," concludes Zimmerman, "who under some circumstances would restore the Soviet bloc and the Soviet Union or at least reunify the Slavic nations and persons in the mass public exist who would respond to calls for action from such leaders":

> NATO expansion constitutes a genuine, the word is inescapable, deterrent to these people and such actions as NATO expansions have had effects on Russians regardless of their orientation to, for instance, the domestic political economy or their predispositions as to whether Russia should follow its own path or seek to emulate the West.[96]

At the end of the 2000s, when Russia was more powerful than it was in the 1990s, Moscow started to demonstrate its willingness to secure, at least how the political and military elites perceived it, Russia's "legitimate sphere of interests." The military interventions in Georgia in 2008 and Ukraine, first in 2014–2015 and once again in 2022, were perceived or justified by the Russian political and military elite as necessary for preventing the US and NATO's military presence on Russia's border and securing their sphere of interests.

However, since the middle of the 2000s, Russia's grievances on NATO enlargement have been increasing amid the deteriorations of Russia's relations with the United States, the European Union, and NATO. The suspension of political relations between Russia and NATO in October 2021 signaled the official end of the heyday between them. The freezing of the Russian Permanent Representation to NATO and the NATO Military Liaison Mission in Moscow, as well as the closing of the NATO Information Office, demonstrated that interaction and, most importantly, mutual trust had decreased year by year.[97]

In December 2021, the Russian President proposed to start "substantive negotiations" with the United States and NATO on the "non-expansion of NATO to the East." He explained that Russia, in dialogue with the West, would try to reach agreements on the refusal of the North Atlantic Alliance to expand to the east and deploy weapons near its country's borders.[98] According to him, it will be about providing "legal, legal guarantees" since the Western countries refused to fulfill the corresponding verbal obligations.[99]

On December 7, Presidents Putin and Biden discussed Ukraine on a video call. According to the Washington Post, Putin claimed that the eastward expansion of the Western alliance was a major factor in his decision to send troops to Ukraine's border and that Russia was simply protecting its own interests and territorial integrity. Biden responded that Ukraine was unlikely to join NATO any time soon and that the United States and Russia could come to agreements on other concerns Russia had about the placement of US weapons systems in Europe.[100]

Several days later, the Russian Foreign Ministry published drafts of the treaty between Russia and the United States on security guarantees as well as the agreement on measures to ensure the security of the Russian Federation and NATO member states.[101] The documents contained some theses that the United States and NATO could theoretically subscribe to, such as the "primary responsibility" of the UN Security Council for the "maintenance of international peace and security" as well as the "need to combine efforts to effectively respond to modern challenges and threats to security." But, it was obvious that the West would not agree with the key theses of the documents.[102] Moscow proposed that the West legally guarantee that they would not admit former Soviet republics to NATO and that Washington would not develop "bilateral military cooperation" with these countries.[103] The draft agreement with NATO also proposed that "the member states of the North Atlantic Treaty Organization renounce any military activity on the territory of Ukraine, as well as other states of Eastern Europe, the South Caucasus and Central Asia."[104]

Such a formulation regarding the subjects for the negotiations was against the basic principles of NATO, and moreover, it meant the capitulation of the Northern Alliance without defeat in a war. Russian expert Dmitri Trenin called Moscow's tactic "forcing for negotiations." He explains that after the spring of 2021, when Russian troops began large-scale military exercises along the Ukrainian border, the United States suspected the drills could be cover for preparations to invade Ukraine. "Unable to ignore Russia's actions," writes Trenin, "US President Joe Biden invited Putin to meet with him in Geneva, even though Russia had not previously been among the White House's priorities."[105] Alexander Baunov noted that with the understanding that the West's aim is to avoid war, Russia can exploit Western fears of war without actually using force.[106]

This was likely Moscow's strategy to achieve its main goals and then demand more. About a month after the Russian proposed draft agreement was published, the Russian Deputy Foreign Minister Sergei Ryabkov stated that as an alternative to a guarantee of NATO non-expansion to the east, Russia may consider a legal obligation of the United States not to vote for Ukraine's entry into the alliance. Ryabkov explained that following "the formula of the Bucharest summit in 2008," Ukraine and Georgia becoming NATO members should be ruled out and should be replaced by the understanding that this will never happen or "alternatively, if the US makes a unilateral commitment in a legally binding manner that it will never vote for Ukraine and other countries to join NATO, we are ready to consider this option." According to him, Moscow's priority is clear and legally binding guarantees from the United States that Ukraine and other countries, whose membership Russia opposes, will not join NATO.[107]

The United States dismissed Russia's demands as non-starters, demanding Russia pull back its forces from the border with Ukraine and instead offering dialogue on issues including military exercises and transparency, as well as the placement of missiles.[108] US Secretary of State Antony Blinken explained that the document Washington delivered included the concerns of the United States and its allies and partners about Russia's actions that undermine security, a principled and pragmatic evaluation of the concerns that Russia had raised, and the United States' own proposals for areas where two countries might be able to find common ground. "We make clear that there are core principles that we are committed to uphold and defend—including Ukraine's sovereignty and territorial integrity and the right of states to choose their own security arrangements and alliances," Blinken said.[109] According to him, the United States addressed the possibility of reciprocal transparency measures regarding force posture in Ukraine as well as measures to increase confidence regarding military exercises and maneuvers in Europe: "And we address other areas where we see potential for progress, including arms control related to missiles in Europe, our interest in a follow-on agreement to the New START treaty that covers all nuclear weapons, and ways to increase transparency and stability."[110] Regarding the US response Russian Foreign Minister Lavrov said that it offered grounds for serious talks only on matters of secondary importance stating that "there is no positive response to the main issue, which is our clear stand on the continued NATO enlargement towards the east and the deployment of strike weapons that can pose a threat to the territory of the Russian Federation."[111]

However, despite debates and high-level meetings between officials of Russia and the United States in December and January, no agreement was brokered, and Moscow did not achieve what it proposed. Seemingly, Moscow's demands led to the war or, at least, served as a pretext for Russia's invasion of Ukraine.

On the eve of war, several Russian experts and scholars warned about the security implications for Russia because of the ever-increasing confrontation with NATO as a result of large-scale operations in Ukraine. For instance, Vladimir Denisov suggested it is not NATO that is "against" Russia but 30 states of Europe and America, including Switzerland, Austria, Sweden, and Finland. "We will go through humiliations, hurtful compromises, weakening," Denisov warned. He suggested that the situation will be defused, but with the deterioration of the Russian position. He believed that either the further expansion of NATO or Russia's search for and implementation of military-technical answers, is a road to nowhere.[112] Russian scholar Aleksey Arbatov suggested that Germany will pursue the same policy, and perhaps become more skeptical about the admission of Ukraine to NATO, if there would be no large-scale military conflict between Russia and Ukraine.[113]

It seems an agreement between Russia's current political leadership and NATO is not on the horizon. As a veteran of the negotiations, Vladimir Denisov put it, "when we [Russia and NATO] had the opportunity to agree, we did not agree." "With all the weakness then we [Russia] had the main capital—we were trusted. Now this is no longer the case."[114] For sure, that trust would be further affected by Russia's invasion of Ukraine in 2022.

**Color revolutions and regime change as external threats**

Historically, regime security has been a key facet of Russia's security policy. This is mainly related to confrontations in society, in which high levels of injustice resulted in several social clashes and revolutionary situations. "To maintain order" has been historically more important than political reform and human freedoms in Russia. Moreover, considering its multiethnicity and the existence of ethnic republics and autonomies, sovereignty for those national regions is considered by Moscow a threat to Russia's territorial integrity. In this respect, Russia's main internal security concerns are revolutions or civil disobediences, separatism, and demands for more independence for national regions. The aforementioned concerns are reflected as threats in Russia's security documents and have a huge influence on Russia's external security policy.

Revolutions and social clashes have played a tremendous role throughout Russia's history. The collapses of the Russian Empire and the Soviet Union were accompanied by revolutions, protests, and social clashes. The legacy of these historical cases exerts influence on Russia's political elite and mass public consciences, which mainly remember them as negative experiences.

Since the breakup of the USSR, ethnic and language problems—specifically the importance of strengthening Russian statehood and language in the ethnic regions—have circulated in expert, statist, and nationalist circles. The problem is complicated because of the multilingual and multiethnic makeup of the country. Understanding the complications of this problem led Putin to demonstrate more careful policies toward nationality and language. Moreover, one of the main goals of Putin's first presidency was to reach unity among Russia's nationalities around the narratives of Russia and citizenship to avoid or prevent schism ["*rasskol*"] in society and recentralization of governance in Russia. In his first program article as head of state in 1999, Putin appealed to citizens using the word "people of Russia" ["*rossiyskiy narod*" or "*rossiyan*"], not "nation" ["*natsiya*" or "*russkie*"]. According to him, "the acceptance by our people supranational, universal human values, towering above social, group and ethnic interests."[115]

It must be emphasized that historically, the language question and Russification strategies toward national regions gave impetus to rising national consciousness and movements in the Russian Empire and the Soviet Union.[116] Despite the popularization of nationalistic ideas in society in recent years, Putin, at least publicly, has kept a relatively pluralistic attitude. But furthering the confrontation with the West and increasing economic shortcomings and social dissatisfactions could lead Putin's current presidency to enhance control with the aim of preventing possible separatism in the ethnic regions.

Since the breakup of the Soviet Union, the threat of revolution has been the main challenge for Russia's governing elite. During Yeltsin's presidency, the source of such threats was mainly the far-left and far-right political groups, whose narratives were strengthened by the social dissatisfaction of the majority. After the Rose Revolution in Georgia in 2003 and especially after the Orange Revolution in Ukraine in 2004, the source of such "threats" became the political groups known as liberals. Putin's presidency, which began with a defense of liberal values and liberal markets, has, year by year, turned authoritarian. Putin's governing elite fought against schism, and for a united Russia, in their first years. Since regime changes in some former Soviet republics in 2003–2005 as a result of public protests, Russia's political elite have considered color revolutions as social engineering projects whose aim is, according to the Kremlin, to realize political regime changes first in the former republics and then in Russia.

In this respect, new political narratives about Russia's sovereignty regarding political freedoms and democratic developments, such as "Russia has its own way

## Determinants of Russia's security policy 61

of political development," were created. Partly the legacy of the Soviet Union's collapse, partly the increasing roles of former security servicemen who brought with them the threat perception culture of the KGB and other Soviet intelligence organizations' institutional attitudes to political elites, influenced and strengthened "the fortress under siege" thinking in the Kremlin.

As a starting point, the Kremlin ideologists chose the sovereignty projection. It should be noted that in the early 2000s, several new subjects and problems were added to the government's ideological projects. According to Aglaya Snetkov, in practice, many of the themes that became central to the mid-2000s were nowhere to be seen in the early stages of this period, such as sovereignty projection, growing concerns over regime security, and increasing tensions with the West. "Hence, rather than developing along a teleological path, from a 'weak' to a 'strong' state, this political project developed along its own trajectory and in response to shifting domestic and external circumstances."[117]

President Vladimir Putin's chief strategist of that period, Vladislav Surkov, is the main architect of the "sovereign democracy" concept. Simply put, sovereign democracy means to privatize or coordinate the Russian political system from the Kremlin. According to this concept, democratic institutions are maintained with semi-democratic freedoms, and democratic processes, e.g., elections, freedom of demonstrations, etc., are the internal issues of Russia, and no one can involve themselves in or influence "Russia's sovereignty" from the outside.

According to Surkov, there wasn't anything wrong with the Kremlin supporting political parties (pro-government and opposition). In 2005, he stated that the instability of Russia's multiparty system is one of the Russian political system's greatest defects. But Surkov indirectly confirmed that this was done for regime security and he pointed to the communists and nationalists as sources of threats:

> The current balance of power in the parliament makes it difficult to imagine a trouble-free transfer of power. Just look at the Communists or the Rodina Party nationalists. With all due respect, I cannot imagine what would happen to the country if they came to power.[118]

He considered the revolutions in Georgia, Kyrgyzstan, and Ukraine in his 2005 interview and stated that there would be no chance for such a revolution in Russia:

> There will be no uprisings here. We realize, of course, that these events have made an impression on many local politicians in Russia and on various foreign non-governmental organizations that would like to see the scenario repeated in Russia. We understand this. By now there are even technologies for overthrowing governments and schools where the craft can be learned.[119]

After the first public announcement of the concept in the summer of 2006, several leaders of the governing political group commented on it from different points of view. For the first time, the thesis on "sovereign democracy" was voiced by Vladislav Surkov on June 28 of that year at a briefing in Moscow. According to him, the Russian model of democracy is called sovereign democracy: "We are building an open society ... We want to be an open nation among other open nations and cooperate with them according to fair rules, and not be controlled from the outside."[120] He contrasted the new term with a certain "managed democracy" denoting it as "imposed by certain centers of global influence on all nations indiscriminately—by force and slyness—a model of ineffectiveness and, therefore, controlled from outside economic and political regimes."[121] Surkov used "sovereign democracy" as a confronted terminology to "manageable democracy," which was used in the West for an explanation of the political system under Putin. On July 13, then Russian Defense Minister Sergei Ivanov, who was also named one of Putin's possible successors, published a program article in the newspaper Izvestia in which he declared that society should rally around the "new triad" of national values, which were, in his opinion, sovereign democracy, strong economy, and military power. At the same time, he explained the meaning of the notorious concept as follows: "Sovereign democracy is the quintessence of our internal structure, implying the right of citizens to decide the policy in their own country and protect this right from external pressure in any way, including by military means."[122]

Gleb Pavlovskii, then one of the Kremlin's main political campaign experts—or political technologist in the Russian parlance—tried to explain the new concept in comparison with "sovereign" western democracies. "Discussions about democracy are going on in all states. In the European Union, the official concept has become 'social democracy' in the United States—the 'market' one which is mysterious for Europeans. In each case, the historical and momentary context of this discussion is important. Therefore, our 'sovereign democracy' should not be interpreted as something 'local' or 'limited.' It needs to be developed as a universal concept."[123] Pavlovskii indirectly explained the exact significance of the concept. He postulates that the Westphalian sovereignty regime (with the Vienna and Yalta amendments) is the basis of international tolerance. "Attempting to get away from it leads to a renewed risk of war, to the revival of invasion-oriented regimes, to the construction of nations from the outside. This is not appropriate for Russia for sure."

The words of the Kremlin's key expert could be seen as the aim of the Russian political regime—do not allow external influences over democratic changes, which could threaten the reach of Putin's governmental authority. This has remained a topical problem in Russia since the color revolutions in Georgia and Ukraine.

Surkov conveyed the concept of integration through the strengthening of military and police roles in Russia:

> What I agree with our liberal comrades is that sovereignty, especially in the Russian tradition, in our ideological matrix is always associated with our few allies as the army and navy. That is, it [the concept] has a sort of military-police color. I think that in modern societies this also does not go anywhere and it is still needed. Still, the question is no longer only in the narrow sense of defense—but rather in an integrated way, forcing us to talk about the country's competitiveness. This important feature reminds us that it is still not about the sovereignty of any state, but about the sovereignty of a democratic state.[124]

## Determinants of Russia's security policy 63

According to Mikhail Zygar, the new ideological concept developed by Surkov essentially replaced the "managed democracy" of Alexander Voloshin, who, as the Kremlin's liberal-minded policy strategist during Putin's first term, "had believed in the need for economic and political reforms-democracy would not simply grow by itself but needed external assistance."[125]

Surkov's concept was that the problem would not be solved through simple internal adjustments since Russia's problems were not solely internal and possibly not internal at all. Rather, Russia was hampered by an external enemy forever encroaching on its sovereignty. Therefore, Russian democracy had to be unique, and ready to defend itself against external threats.[126]

Surkov was also responsible for the creation of youth organizations, which, according to the Kremlin strategy, would fight against revolutionary youth organizations and, if needed, defend the governing regime's interests in the streets. Such a pro-government, anti-revolutionary organization was established in 2005, immediately after the success of the opposition in Ukraine's Orange Revolution. It was called Nashi [Ours]. Zygar notes that Surkov "artfully copied the external trappings of rebellious youth organizations to turn the movement into a powerful state structure."[127]

There was also a "power sector," on the basis of which organizers planned to create "youth squads of law and order." In addition to this strategic supertask, the movement pursued tactical goals, among which was "preventing the Ukrainian version of the change of power in Russia." Vasilii Yakemenko, Surkov's protégé and the leader of Nashi, said that "as result of coups, external controls were utilized in Georgia, Serbia, and Ukraine, which cannot be allowed in Russia." And at one of the first meetings with the organization's members, he noted that a branch of the "Pora!" [It's time] (a youth organization that played a significant role in the Orange Revolution in Ukraine) had already been created in Moscow. The Nashi was created as a counterweight to such organizations.[128] Yakemenko previously worked in the presidential administration and, in the early 2000s, was a leader of a pro-government youth organization "Walking Together." That organization was known for its several extraordinary activities, including the "damned liberal books" or destruction of the books of the "wrong" writers, which led Western observers to mention historical associations that the Kremlin did not like.[129]

Gleb Pavlovskii, in the meeting with Nashi's activists ("commissars"), stated that European civilization is so arranged that it constantly needs an enemy, especially during periods when everything is fine:

So it was with the Jews in the late 19th – early 20th century, as it is now happening with the Russians. Russians for the West today are objectively the main outcasts, no matter how good we are. Russians are the Jews of the 21st century, and this must be taken into account. You must be tougher, learn to hold a rifle in your hands, to answer your opponents toughly. Nashi, I think, is such a fist that society should show to fascists.[130]

Later, the "fight against fascists" accusations developed and popularized in the mid-2000s by Kremlin experts would be used by the state-affiliated media against Ukraine. Such narratives, defining internal and external opponents as "fascists," have been strengthened year by year and were actively used by Kremlin strategists during the intervention in Ukraine. In this respect, Surkov and other Kremlin strategists were "openers" of "the Pandora's box" in Russia's contemporary history. According to Mikhail Zygar, Surkov was aware that at the heart of any revolution lies a negative agenda—it is much easier to mobilize the masses to fight against something than to fight for something. Zygar notes that the fear of an external threat/enemy, especially a historically formulated one, is always the best mobilizing agent. "He selected the most active and enterprising young people and then leaded them with ideology—the idea of uprising and rebellion against external enemies, which in this case were the United States and the global conspiracy against Russia."[131] Starting with the threat of a possible revolution in Russia and beginning in 2005, the government has been escalating its promotion of the external enemy. This is generally based on the regime's fears about its own security but became even more sophisticated following public demonstrations over the parliamentary and presidential elections in 2011 and 2012.

It should be noted that color revolutions are not only considered internal social and political threats, but they are also considered external military threats by the Russian military leadership. It has been common in recent years for Russian military thought to depict the multi-vector nature of the threats to Russia's security. According to Ieva Berzina, the legitimation of Russia's reactions to "color revolutions" is rooted in the way that Russian political leaders, military officers, and pro-government academics define "color revolutions." "Russian views are centered on two interrelated elements that allow a 'color revolution' to be treated as an undesirable phenomenon: It is considered to be a coup d'état and a foreign intervention."[132]

Color revolutions are considered part of the non-direct and non-military forms of confrontation on the international stage. The color revolutions, according to the Russian official political and military thought, together with political-diplomatic, economic, informational, cybernetic, psychological, and other non-military forms, are methods of confrontation conducted against adversaries in the contemporary world. The Russians argue that the West (mainly the United States) realizes color revolutions in their "hybrid war strategies" against targeted countries.

According to Russian military scholar Aleksandr Bartosh, hybrid wars create conditions for coups and color revolutions, as has already happened in Ukraine and several countries in the Middle East. He notes that such approaches represent a development of Western strategy during the Cold War, when the West used ideological means to undermine the Soviets. But tools of "hybridization" of world politics are new factors and phenomena that include hybrid war, color revolutions, and non-state actors, for example, international terrorism, PMCs: "The existing of nuclear and conventional precision weapons in the arsenal of tools of warfare stimulates the development of new modern technologies of warfare, allowing to prevent the direct military-power influence characteristic of past conflicts," Bartosh believes.[133] He notes that the hybrid war strategy acquires a complex character and combines elements of attrition and crushing strategies:

> The first is designed for a long period and forms a kind of shell within which the strategy of destruction can be used in the presence of conditions that allow the protest potential of the population to be used to decisively destroy the state. Such conditions can be created by the critical state of the economy, which causes impoverishment of the masses, corruption, and ill-considered actions of the authorities in the social sphere.[134]

According to Bartosh, color revolution strategies are more aligned with the crushing strategy. He stresses that the strategy of the color revolution is one of indirect actions and includes a system of political, socio-economic, informational, ideological, and psychological measures to influence the population of the country, the staff of law enforcement agencies, and the armed forces to undermine the power of a targeted state:

> This method of activities is based on non-military technologies of organizing coups by provoking actions of mass civil disobedience in order to overthrow the government and transfer the country to external control. The high dynamics of the stages of the implementation of this strategy and its relatively short time frame allows us to classify it as a strategy of crushing.[135]

It is very difficult to achieve a decisive victory, especially in relation to stable, large states. Bartosh notes that it is not always possible that the color revolution method will achieve its desired goal. Therefore, subversive work against such states provides for the development of a hybrid warfare strategy designed as a kind of strategy of attrition.

Bartosh concludes that the combination of crushing and attrition strategies in organizing color revolutions and hybrid wars "forms a kind of destructive tandem that purposefully uses the global critical features of the modern world to undermine the fundamentals of the existing world order and to destabilize individual countries in order to achieve their surrender and subjugate them."[136]

Bartosh also gives his explanation of the color revolution implementation process and its actors, which is similar to the Russian political and military elite's perceptions. Bartosh notes that the subsequent stages of the strategy are implemented within a relatively short period of time (several weeks) and provide for the delivery of a powerful ram attack on the authorities with the aim of overthrowing the government and placing the country under external control.[137]

Russia's military leadership also understands color revolutions as methods of modern warfare. According to Chief of the Russian General Staff Valerii Gerasimov, the main components of hybrid methods are the falsification of events and the restriction of media activities. He believes that these are becoming the most effective asymmetric methods of contemporary warfare and that their effects can be comparable to the results of large-scale use of troops and forces. Illustrative examples of which, according to General Gerasimov, are "the incitement of nationalism" in Ukraine and revolutionary unrest in the Arab world. "The massive impact on people's minds contributed to the growth of the protest potential of the population, the spread of "color movement" in the states of North Africa, which led to a change of political regimes in some of them."[138] For confronting such threats, Gerasimov suggests organizing interdepartmental activities "to neutralize the negative impact on the consciousness of the population, especially young citizens of the country, which undermines the historical, spiritual, and patriotic traditions of the defense of the Motherland acquires great importance."[139] Moreover, he emphasizes the role of armored forces in resisting the aforementioned threats. According to him, the growth of hybrid threats necessitates improving the effectiveness of territorial defense. In this regard, several nationwide measures have been taken. He notes that according to the legislation, along with the armed forces, other troops, and military formations, the forces and resources of all federal executive bodies, regional administrations, and local self-government are involved in territorial defense. "This will make it possible, in the period of an immediate threat of aggression, to strengthen measures to counter foreign private military companies, sabotage groups, and terrorist organizations," notes Gerasimov.[140] But now, he continues, scientific research is needed regarding the forms and methods for using multi-departmental groups (for coordination of the military and non-military components of territorial defense) in cases of crisis situations within a matter of days or even hours. "This, in turn, requires an almost immediate response from the leadership of the country, involving not only the armed forces, but also the resources of almost all ministries and departments."[141]

**Summary**

From the analysis above, we can conclude that the main determinants of Russia's political elite's security thoughts and threat perceptions are based on, or related to, historical experiences. These determinants are characterized by the fears of environmental, economic, and socio-political weaknesses; the size of the country, which thereby creates concerns regarding the management and prevention of separatism or de-centralization; and the problems of the Russian Empire and the Soviet Union's colonization policies such as the Russian diaspora or Russian speakers in the former Soviet republics. Moreover, as the economy of the country is based mainly on natural resources, it is a popular thought among elites that another great power or powers might have as their goal the destruction or destabilization of Russia to acquire its resources. For instance, Russia's Security Council Secretary Nikolai Patrushev stated that the United States government has a goal to dominate the world and "it's possible that they want to achieve this goal through Russia's collapse, which will allow the US access to its rich resources, which, in their opinion, Russia does not deserve to possess."[142]

There are also security characteristics which are influenced by the Soviet past. The avoidance of surprise attacks and the creation and maintenance of geopolitical buffer zones as a guarantee against a sudden attack were basic facets of Soviet military and political elite policies after WWII and are prerogative characteristics of the contemporary elite's security thoughts too. According to this security thought, the primary importance of the buffer zone is to prevent the deployment of NATO tactical nuclear forces and high-precision missiles near Russia's borders. As put by former Russian President and Prime Minister Dmitri Medvedev, when "the ring around our country begins to contract—and the number of countries that are members of NATO is increasing—this cannot but worry us." "Because in this case we are talking not only about strategic nuclear forces, but also about tactical nuclear weapons," Medvedev states, "which when approaching the borders of the Russian Federation acquires the quality of strategic nuclear weapons, as well as about non-nuclear weapons, which at the moment, taking into account that that they are of a high-precision nature, are capable of causing enormous damage." According to Medvedev, NATO enlargement is an absolute threat to the Russian Federation and this is an unconditional challenge.[143]

Historically, the creation of buffer zones was one of the key characteristics of Russia's security thinking. According to this, Russia must have buffer zones or keep a geographical distance from its real and potential adversaries. Now, instead of Soviet republics and socialist states, Russia has created or uses gray buffer zones such as Nagorno-Karabakh, Abkhazia, South Ossetia, Donetsk, Lugansk, and Transnistria separatist republics. Russia uses these conflicts to keep former Soviet republics under its control, mainly prevent them from joining the West's alliances or projects, and especially to prevent NATO enlargement. As Benn Steil puts it, "the combined separatist territories, under effective Russian control, now form a valuable protective arc along Russia's western and south-western border." "Just as Stalin strengthened the Soviet Union's buffer zone in response to the Marshall Plan, which he expected Washington to supplement with military force," he writes, "Putin has strengthened Russia's buffer zone in response to NATO expansion."[144]

It should be noted that the main difference between Soviet and contemporary Russian elite security thoughts is ideological content. If the Soviet political elite mainly tried to explain or justify military developments based on Marxist-Leninist ideology, ideology is seemingly absent in the contemporary elite's security thought. Although Soviet inheritances have a huge influence on Russia's security thinking and behavior, and even as Putin's regime tries to position itself as a defender of conservative values for political purposes, an official ideology as found during the Soviet Union does not currently exist. The primary aim of Russia's current external security policy is to maintain Moscow's "sphere of influences," keep former Soviet republics—which are not yet members of the EU and NATO—under its control or prevent their membership in these organizations in an effort to keep the buffer zone between Russia and its stronger adversaries.[145] At the same time, they seek to economically bind these former Soviet republics to Russia.

Largely by using the media, the political elite guides the population's attitudes on external security, and the public is inclined to see themselves surrounded by foes. In the conclusion of surveys of Russian opinion between the end of the 1990s and the beginning of the 2000s, Richard Pipes argued that the majority of Russians approve of Putin's actions and that Putin is popular "precisely because he has reinstated Russia's traditional model of government: an autocratic state in which citizens are relieved of responsibility for politics and in which imaginary foreign enemies are invoked to forge an artificial unity."[146] Analyzing the results of opinion surveys, he concluded that "the only desire that Putin has not yet satisfied is restoring Russia's status as a great military power," and he wrote in 2004, "but if his response to other public demands offers a model, then this wish, too, is likely to be provided in good time."[147] Such "good times" were witnessed later, in 2014, when Crimea was occupied, and when Russia began the invasion of Ukraine in 2022. And, in both cases, the invasions had an influence on increasing Putin's popularity throughout Russia. Although the state's information monopoly and subsequent media campaign also played huge roles. Moreover, tough controls over society, and a fear of being punished for resisting official policy, might deter large protests in Russia and exert some influence on the results of opinion surveys.

Recent developments in Russia's foreign policy reflect the country's struggle to preserve its status as a "great power" and its sphere of influence. This is supported by its security policy. Contemporary Russia remains unsatisfied with its current position in the world's power posture but is seeking to rectify the situation. Russia's political elite is confident that the NATO enlargement projects are threats to its national interests and is looking for ways to counter their influence. Since 2003, following the second Gulf War, Russia has embarked on a course of active resistance to what it perceives as dominance by the United States and NATO. It launched a massive media campaign against the purported Western threat, which included alleged designs to gain control of Russia's natural resources, the possible enlargement of NATO to Ukraine and Georgia, and plans to deploy ballistic missile defense and conventional prompt global strike systems.[148] In this realm, Russia very often uses offensive measures under the justification of defensive efforts, following the Soviet tradition.

Since Ukraine's Orange Revolution of 2004, the Russian government has been strengthening preventive measures with the aim of deterring similar social and political processes in Russia. Since then, the political regime has seen any sign of such a possibility as one of the main threats to regime security. Given the strong social dissatisfaction of the populace, high levels of corruption, and the mismanagement of central and regional governments, the Kremlin understands that such conditions could make the regime's position particularly fragile in the face of social and political protests. To prevent such undesired results, the strategists of the regime created manageable democracy while adding the attractive "sovereign" term. It should be noted that since 2005 such "sovereignty" has covered almost all spheres of Russia. By the end of 2018, even the Internet was considered "sovereign" by the political regime.[149] Since the 2022 invasion of Ukraine, the tightening of control over society has increased. Triggered by revolutions in several former Soviet republics and mainly because of the respective political regime's own weaknesses, the threat of color revolutions is perceived by the Russian governing elite not only as an internal political challenge for regime security but also as an external threat, and in the parlance of the military elite, "a new form of waging war" against Russia.

To sum up, Russia's political elite security thinking and threat perceptions are influenced by the past, by Russian domestic politics—specifically regime security by its weaknesses, and by the developments of West-Russian, especially US-Russian, affairs. These pose burdens for Russian elites in developing a pragmatic assessment of Russia's foreign and security policy interests.[150]

**Notes**

1 SIPRI (2018) *Global military spending remains high at $1.7 trillion*, May 2, https://www.sipri.org/media/press-release/2018/global-military-spending-remains-high-17-trillion.
2 Ibid.
3 Kofman, Michael (2018) "From Hammer to Rapier: Russian Military Transformation in Perspective", Russia Brief, Issue I, January, http://www.ccw.ox.ac.uk/russia-brief-issue-i/.
4 Ibid.
5 SIPRI (2022) *World military expenditure passes $2 trillion for first time*, April 22, https://sipri.org/media/press-release/2022/world-military-expenditure-passes-2-trillion-first-time.
6 Ibid.
7 Ibid.
8 Ibid.
9 Connolly, Richard (2019) "Russian Military Expenditure in Comparative Perspective: A Purchasing Power Parity Estimate", Report, CAN, October 9, p. 13, https://www.cna.org/CNA_files/PDF/IOP-2019-U-021955-Final.pdf.
10 Ibid., p. 14.
11 Ibid.
12 Ibid.
13 Chernenko, Yelena (2019) «NATO navyazyvayet nam skhemu obespecheniya bezopasnosti vremen kholodnoy voiny», *Gazeta "Kommersant"* 239, December 26, p. 5, https://www.kommersant.ru/doc/4207094?from=doc_vrez.
14 Kristensen, Hans M. and Korda, Matt (2022) "Nuclear Notebook: How many nuclear weapons does Russia have in 2022?" *The Bulletin of the Atomic Scientists*, February 23, https://thebulletin.org/premium/2022-02/nuclear-notebook-how-many-nuclear-weapons-does-russia-have-in-2022/.
15 Kristensen, Hans M. and Korda, Matt (2022) "Nuclear Notebook: How many nuclear weapons does Russia have in 2022?" …
16 Kristensen, Hans M. and Norris, Robert S. (2018) "Russian nuclear forces, 2018", *Nuclear Notebook, the Bulletin of the Atomic Scientists,* Vol. 74, No. 3, pp. 185–195, p. 185. DOI: 10.1080/00963402.2018.1462912.
17 Ibid.
18 *Krasnaya Zvezda* (2019) "Byt' vsegda v avangarde", December 28, http://redstar.ru/byt-vsegda-v-avangarde/.
19 Ibid.
20 Barnes, Julian E. and Sanger, David E. (2019) "Russia Deploys Hypersonic Weapon, Potentially Renewing Arms Race", *The New York Times*, December 27, https://www.nytimes.com/2019/12/27/us/politics/russia-hypersonic-weapon.html.
21 Putin, Vladimir (2019) "Poslaniye Prezidenta Federal'nomu Sobraniyu", February 20, http://kremlin.ru/events/president/transcripts/messages/59863.
22 US Department of State (2021) "On the Extension of the New START Treaty with the Russian Federation, Press Statement, Antony J. Blinken, Secretary of State, February 3, https://www.state.gov/on-the-extension-of-the-new-start-treaty-with-the-russian-federation/.
23 The Kremlin (2021a) "Meeting with permanent members of the Security Council", February 11, http://en.kremlin.ru/events/president/news/64985?utm_source=pocket_mylist.

24 Kristensen, Hans M. and Korda, Matt (2022) "Russian nuclear weapons, 2022", *Nuclear Notebook, the Bulletin of the Atomic Scientists,* Vol. 78, No. 2, pp. 98–121, DOI: 10.1080/00963402.2022.2038907.
25 The Kremlin (2021c) "Rasshirennoye zasedaniye kollegii Minoborony", December 21, http://kremlin.ru/events/president/news/67402.
26 Federation of American Scientists (2022) "Status of World Nuclear Forces", https://fas.org/issues/nuclear-weapons/status-world-nuclear-forces/.
27 Ibid.
28 TASS (2022) "Putin prikazal perevesti sily sderzhivaniya armii RF v osobyy rezhim neseniya sluzhby", February 27, https://tass.ru/politika/13885447.
29 The Kremlin (2020) "Expanded Meeting of the Defence Ministry Board". December 21, http://en.kremlin.ru/events/president/news/64684.
30 The Kremlin (2021) "Rasshirennoye zasedaniye kollegii Minoborony"…
31 Ibid.
32 Kristensen, Hans M. and Korda, Matt (2022) "Russian nuclear weapons, 2022"…, p. 98.
33 The Insider (2022a) "Ukraine and Russia accuse each other of nuclear terrorism", August 8, https://theins.ru/en/news/253938.
34 The Insider (2022b) "Russian troops deliver unknown cargo to Zaporizhzhia NPP, sources say power plant is mined (video)", August 5, https://theins.ru/en/news/253868.
35 The Ministry of Foreign Affairs of the Russian Federation (2022b) "Zayavleniye MID Rossii o situatsii s Dogovorom o merakh po dal′neyshemu sokrashcheniyu i ogranicheniyu strategicheskikh nastupatel′nykh vooruzheniy (DSNV)", August 8, https://www.mid.ru/ru/foreign_policy/news/1825525/.
36 Trenin, Dmitriy (2022b) "Spetsial′naya voyennaya operatsiya na Ukraine kak perelomnaya tochka vneshney politiki sovremennoy", Rossii, Rossiya v global′noy politike, November 30, https://globalaffairs.ru/articles/perelomnaya-tochka/.
37 Ibid.
38 Ibid.
39 Putin, Vladimir (2023) "Poslaniye Prezidenta Federal′nomu Sobraniyu", 21 February 2023, http://kremlin.ru/events/president/news/70565.
40 Nekhoroshkin, Semen and Denis Voroshilov (2023) "V Kremle svyazali vozvrat k SNV s vospriimchivost′yu Zapada k pozitsii Moskvy", RBK, February 22: https://www.rbc.ru/politics/22/02/2023/63f5dfc19a7947461cc3b49f?from=from_main_1.
41 World Bank (2022a) *Global Economic Prospects, June 2022,* Washington, DC: World Bank, DOI: 10.1596/978-1-4648-1843-1.
42 World Bank (2022a) "Russia's invasion of Ukraine: Implications for Energy Markets and Activity", *Global Economic Prospects, June 2022.* Washington, DC: World Bank, DOI: 10.1596/978-1-4648-1843-1, pp. 79–90.
43 GDPs are calculated in USD billions. Reasons why those countries were selected for the comparison are their involvement level in international security and international relations, and their relations with Russia in recent years.
44 World Bank (2022b) Table 4.2 – World Development Indicators: Structure of value added, http://wdi.worldbank.org/table/4.2#.
45 Russian Analytical Digest (2022) "Russian Financial and Economic Indicators, Figure 1: GDP Russia in Foreign Currency (USD bn)", *Sanctions Against Russia,* No. 280, 21 March, p. 8.
46 Rochlitz, Michael (2022) "Is Russia Becoming a Second North Korea?", Russian Analytical Digest, *Sanctions Against Russia,* No. 280, 21 March, pp. 10–13, DOI: 10.3929/ethz-b-000538061.
47 Shapovalov, Aleksey (2022) "Operatsionnyy spad", 28 July, https://www.kommersant.ru/doc/5482363?from=main.
48 World Bank (2022a) Global Economic Prospects, June 2022…, p. 99.
49 Ibid., p. 101.
50 World Bank (2022a) Global Economic Prospects, June 2022…, p. 102.

51 World Bank (2023) Global Economic Prospects, January 2023, Washington, DC: World Bank, DOI: 10.1586/978-1-4648-1906-3. pp. 59–62.
52 World Bank (2018) Russia's Economy: Preserving Stability, Doubling Growth, Halving Poverty – How?, 40th issue of the Russia Economic Report, December 4, p. 55, http://pubdocs.worldbank.org/en/673631543924406524/RER-40-English.pdf.
53 United Nations Development Programme (UNDP) (2022) *Latest Human Development Index (HDI) Ranking,* https://hdr.undp.org/data-center/human-development-index#/indicies/HDI.
54 Shagina, Maria (2022) "An unprecedented response to Russia's war in Ukraine", *Riddle,* March 7, https://ridl.io/an-unprecedented-response-to-russia-s-war-in-ukraine/.
55 Deuber, Gunter (2022) "Fortress Russia: Completely Lost in (Financial) Sanctions Warfare, A Deep Economic Crisis Is Unavoidable", *Russian Analytical Digest*, Sanctions Against Russia, No. 280, 21 March, pp. 2–7, DOI: 10.3929/ethz-b-000538061.
56 Yusupov, Alexey (2022) "What did Western sanctions on Russia achieve?", *IPS*, July 20, https://www.ips-journal.eu/topics/foreign-and-security-policy/what-did-western-sanctions-on-russia-achieve-6076/.
57 Ibid.
58 Shagina, Maria (2022) "An unprecedented response to Russia's war in Ukraine"…
59 Pipes, Richard (2005) *Russian conservatism and its critics: a study in political culture.* New Haven; London: Yale University Press, p. 181.
60 Ibid, p. 183.
61 Keenan, Edward L. (1986) "Muscovite Political Folkways". *The Russian Review*, Vol. 45, No. 2 (April), pp. 115–181, p. 158. Wiley on behalf of The Editors and Board of Trustees of the Russian Review, http://www.jstor.org/stable/130423.
62 Kliuchevskii, Vasilii Osipovoch (1937) *Kurs Russkoi istorii.* Moscow, I, p. 20, cited in Pipes, Richard (1974) *Russia under the old regime.* New York: Charles Scribner's Sons, p. 14.
63 Pipes, Richard (1974) *Russia under the old regime.* New York: Charles Scribner's Sons, p. 20.
64 Pipes, Richard (1961) "The Historical Evolution of the Russian Intelligentsia", Richard Pipes (ed.), *The Russian Intelligentsia.* New York: Columbia University Press, pp. 48–49.
65 Keenan, Edward L. (1986) "Muscovite Political Folkways"…, pp. 168–169.
66 Ibid., p. 169.
67 Kennan, George Frost (1946) *The Chargé in the Soviet Union (Kennan) to the Secretary of State Moscow,* 22 February 1946, Part 2: Background of Outlook, Foreign relations of the United States, 1946, Eastern Europe, the Soviet Union, Volume VI, 861.00/2–2246: Telegram, 1969, https://history.state.gov/historicaldocuments/frus1946v06/d475.
68 Ibid.
69 Snyder, Glenn H. (1984) "The Security Dilemma in Alliance Politics", *World Politics*, Vol. 36, no. 4(July), p. 461, Published by: Cambridge University Press Stable. http://www.jstor.org/stable/2010183.
70 Glantz, Col. D. M. (1990) *Soviet Operational Art and Tactics in the 1930s.* Ft. Leavenworth, KS: Soviet Army Studies Office, http://www.dtic.mil/dtic/tr/fulltext/u2/a232954.pdf.
71 Ryzhakov, A. (1968) "K voprosu o stroitelstve bronetankovykx voisk Krasnoi Armii v 30-e gody". VIZH, M9 8; Cited in Glantz, Col. D. M. (1990) *Soviet Operational Art and Tactics in the 1930s …*, p. 21.
72 Cimbala, Stephen J. (2013) "Russian Threat Perceptions and Security Policies: Soviet Shadows and Contemporary Challenges", *The Journal of Power Institutions in Post-Soviet Societies,* Issue 14/15: War Trauma in Post-Soviet Russia & Military Reform in Russia and the CIS-Russian Military Reform, http://journals.openedition.org/pipss/4000.
73 Ivanov, S.P. (ed.) (1974) *Nachalniy period voiny(Po opytu pervikh kompanii i operatsii vtoroi mirovoi voiny).* Moscow: Voenizdat, http://militera.lib.ru/science/npv/index.html.

74 Cimbala, Stephen J. (2013) "Russian Threat Perceptions and Security Policies: Soviet Shadows and Contemporary Challenges"...
75 Holloway, David (1988) "Gorbachev's New Thinking". *Foreign Affairs*, Essay, America and the World, 1988 Issue, https://www.foreignaffairs.com/articles/russia-fsu/1989-02-01/gorbachevs-new-thinking.
76 Ibid.
77 Adamishin, Anatoliy (2016) *V raznyye gody.Vneshnepoliticheskiye ocherki*, Moskva: Izdatel'stvo "Ves' Mir".
78 For more details about those developments see: Adamishin, Anatoliy (2016) V raznyye gody.Vneshnepoliticheskiye ocherki…, pp. 109–226.
79 Zhilin, P.A. (ed.) (1986) *Istoria voennogo iskustva*, Moscow: Voenizdat, p. 406; Cited in Meyer, Stephen M. (1988) "The Sources and Prospects of Gorbachev's New Political Thinking on Security"…, p. 150.
80 Meyer, Stephen M. (1988) "The Sources and Prospects of Gorbachev's New Political Thinking on Security". *International Security*, Vol. 13, No. 2 (Fall, 1988), p. 150.
81 Reznichenko, V.G. (ed.) (1987) *Taktika*. The second edition, Moscow: Voenizdat, http://militera.lib.ru/science/tactic/02.html.
82 VPK name (2018) "Operativno-takticheskii komleks 9K720 "Iskander" (NATO: SS-26 Stone)", https://vpk.name/library/f/iskander.html.
83 Mathers, Jennifer G. (2000) *The Russian nuclear shield from Stalin to Yeltsin: The Cold War and beyond*. Basingstoke: Macmillan Press; Oxford: St Antony's College, St. Antony's Series, p. 176.
84 Klussmann, Uwe (2009a) "Did the West Break Its Promise to Moscow?", November 26, http://www.spiegel.de/international/world/nato-s-eastward-expansion-did-the-west-break-its-promise-to-moscow-a-663315.html.
85 Klussmann, Uwe (2009b) "We Couldn't Believe that the Warsaw Pact Could Be Dissolved", Interview with Eduard Shevardnadze, November 26, http://www.spiegel.de/international/europe/interview-with-eduard-shevardnadze-we-couldn-t-believe-that-the-warsaw-pact-could-be-dissolved-a-663595.html.
86 Savranskaya, Svetlana and Blanton, Tom (2017) "NATO Expansion: What Gorbachev Heard". National Security Archive, George Washington University, December 12, https://nsarchive.gwu.edu/briefing-book/russia-programs/2017-12-12/nato-expansion-what-gorbachev-heard-western-leaders-early.
87 *Memorandum of Conversation*, "Morning Meeting with Russian President Yeltsin: NATO-Russia, START, ABM/TMD", Helsinki, 21 March 1997, pp. 106–110,: https://clinton.presidentiallibraries.us/items/show/57569.
88 Goldgeier, James (2018) "Bill and Boris: A Window Into a Most Important Post-Cold War Relationship", *Texas National Review*, Vol. 1, Iss 4. August, https://tnsr.org/2018/08/bill-and-boris-a-window-into-a-most-important-post-cold-war-relationship/#_ftn31.
89 Shiryayev, Valeriy (2022) "Chuvstvuyu, kak NATO prevrashchayut v monstra", *Novaya Gazeta,* February 2, https://novayagazeta.ru/articles/2022/02/02/natokatstvo.
90 Ibid.
91 Ibid.
92 Zimmerman, William (2002) *The Russian people and foreign policy: Russian elite and mass perspectives*, 1993–2000. Princeton, NJ: Princeton University Press, p. 219.
93 Zimmerman, William (2002) The Russian people and foreign policy…, p. 195.
94 Ibid., p. 197.
95 Zimmerman, William (2002) *The Russian people and foreign policy: Russian elite and mass perspectives, 1993–2000*…, p. 224.
96 Ibid., p. 225.
97 The Ministry of Foreign Affairs of the Russian Federation (2021a) "Zayavleniye MID Rossii ob otvetnykh merakh na resheniya Severoatlanticheskogo al'yansa v otnoshenii Postoyannogo predstavitel'stva Rossii pri NATO v Bryussele", October 18, https://www.mid.ru/ru/press_service/spokesman/official_statement/-/asset_publisher/t2GCdmD8RNIr/content/id/4907931.

## Determinants of Russia's security policy 73

98 The Kremlin (2021b) "Tseremoniya vrucheniya veritel′nykh gramot", December 1, http://kremlin.ru/events/president/news/67250.
99 Ibid.
100 Harris, Shane, Karen DeYoung, Isabelle Khurshudyan, Ashley Parker and Liz Sly (2022) "Road to war: US struggled to convince allies, and Zelensky, of risk of invasion", *The Washington Post*, August 16 https://www.washingtonpost.com/national-security/interactive/2022/ukraine-road-to-war/?itid=ap_shaneharris.
101 The Ministry of Foreign Affairs of the Russian Federation (2021b) "O rossiyskikh proyektakh dokumentov po obespecheniyu pravovykh garantiy bezopasnosti so storony SSHA i NATO", December 17, https://www.mid.ru/ru/foreign_policy/news/1790809/.
102 Tarasenko, Pavel and Chernenko, Elena (2021) "Rasshireniye smerti podobno", *Kommersant*, December 17, https://www.kommersant.ru/doc/5139102.
103 The Ministry of Foreign Affairs of the Russian Federation (2021c) "Dogovor mezhdu Rossiyskoy Federatsiyey i Soyedinennymi Shtatami Ameriki o garantiyakh bezopasnosti", December 17, https://mid.ru/ru/foreign_policy/rso/nato/1790818/.
104 The Ministry of Foreign Affairs of the Russian Federation (2021d) "Soglasheniye o merakh obespecheniya bezopasnosti Rossiyskoy Federatsii i gosudarstv-chlenov Organizatsii Severoatlanticheskogo dogovora", December 17, https://mid.ru/ru/foreign_policy/rso/nato/1790803/.
105 Trenin, Dmitri (2022a) "What a Week of Talks Between Russia and the West Revealed", *Carnegie Moscow Center*, January 20, https://carnegiemoscow.org/commentary/86222.
106 Baunov, Alexander(2022) "The West Has Responded to Russia's Ultimatum. Is It Enough?", *Carnegie Moscow Center*, February 1, https://carnegiemoscow.org/commentary/86326.
107 Lisitsyna, Maria and Veronika Vishniakova (2022) "Ryabkov predlozhil SSHA yeshche odnu «optsiyu» po Ukraine i Gruzii v NATO", *RBK*, January 19, https://www.rbc.ru/politics/19/01/2022/61e803519a79471ac69e59b9?from=from_main_2.
108 Ching, Nike (2022) "US Responds to Russia's Security Demands, Renewing Call for Diplomacy", *Voice of America*, January 26, https://www.voanews.com/a/us-responds-to-russia-s-security-demands-renewing-call-for-diplomacy-/6413910.html.
109 U.S Department of State (2022) "Secretary Antony J. Blinken at a Press Availability", January 26, https://www.state.gov/secretary-antony-j-blinken-at-a-press-availability-13/.
110 Ibid.
111 The Ministry of Foreign Affairs of the Russian Federation (2022a) "Foreign Minister Sergey Lavrov's answer to a media question", January 27, https://www.mid.ru/ru/foreign_policy/news/1796041/?lang=en.
112 Shiryayev, Valeriy "Chuvstvuyu, kak NATO prevrashchayut v monstra", *Novaya Gazeta*, February 2, https://novayagazeta.ru/articles/2022/02/02/natokatstvo.
113 Interfax-AVN (2022) "Aleksey Arbatov: v voprose ne rasshireniya NATO nuzhen memorandum o namereniyakh", February 2, https://www.militarynews.ru/story.asp?rid=2&nid=565883&lang=RU.
114 Shiryayev, Valeriy (2022) "Chuvstvuyu, kak NATO prevrashchayut v monstra", *Novaya Gazeta*, February 2, https://novayagazeta.ru/articles/2022/02/02/natokatstvo.
115 Putin, Vladimir (1999) "Rossiyanarubezhetysyacheletii", December 30, http://www.ng.ru/politics/1999-12-30/4_millenium.html.
116 Belikov, V.I. and Krysin, L.P. (2001) *Sotsiolingvistika*, Moskva: Rossiyskiy gosudarstvennyi gumanitarnyi universitet, pp. 264–297, https://studfiles.net/preview/5458437/.
117 Snetkov, Aglaya (2005) *Russia's security policy under Putin: a critical perspective*. London; New York: Routledge, p. 72.
118 Maner V. and Kussman N. (2005) "The West Doesn't Have to Love Us", Spiegel, June 20, http://www.spiegel.de/international/spiegel/spiegel-interview-with-kremlin-boss-vladislav-surkov-the-west-doesn-t-have-to-love-us-a-361236.html.
119 Ibid.
120 Newsru.com (2006) "Surkov rasskazal o prezidente I istinnoi rossiiskoi demokratii", June 28, https://www.newsru.com/russia/28jun2006/surkov.html.

121 Ibid.
122 Ivanov, Sergei (2006) "Triada natsional'nykh tsennostei", *Izvestia*, July 13, https://iz.ru/news/315377.
123 Dobrynina, Yekaterina (2006) "Prishli k soglasiyu", *Rossiyskaya gazeta* – Federal'nyy vypusk, № 4163 (0), September 6, https://rg.ru/2006/09/06/diskussia.html.
124 Dobrynina, Yekaterina (2006) "Prishli k soglasiyu"…
125 Zygar, Mikhail (2016) *All the Kremlin's men*, New York: Public Affairs, p. 102.
126 Ibid.
127 Ibid., p. 98.
128 Shevchuk, Mikhail and Kamyshev, Dmitrii (2018) "Obyknovennyi 'Nashizm' Kreml' sozdayet novoye molodezhnoye dvizheniye", February 21, https://www.kommersant.ru/doc/549170.
129 Cecil, Clem (2002) "Pro-Putin cult urges return to Soviet 'glory'", January 27, https://www.telegraph.co.uk/news/worldnews/europe/russia/1382860/Pro-Putin-cult-urges-return-to-Soviet-glory.html.
130 Kashin, Oleg and Mel'nikov, Valerii (2005) "Otryad vlastonogikh", July 25, https://www.kommersant.ru/doc/595759.
131 Zygar, Mikhail (2016) *All the Kremlin's men*…, p. 100.
132 Bērziņa, Ieva (2019) "Weaponization of 'Colour Revolutions'", *Journal of Political Marketing*, p. 4, DOI: 10.1080/15377857.2019.1678905.
133 Bartosh, Aleksandr (2018a) "Rossii ne izbezhat' gibridnykh voin", Nezavisimoe voennoe obozrenie, March 9, http://nvo.ng.ru/concepts/2018-03-09/1_987_hybridwar.html.
134 Ibid.
135 Bartosh, Aleksandr (2018b) "Gibridnoia voina- novyi vyzov natsional'noi bezopasnosti Rossii", *Natsional'noya oborona*, 9, September, 2018, http://www.oborona.ru/includes/periodics/maintheme/2017/1016/154222573/detail.shtml.
136 Ibid.
137 Ibid.
138 Gerasimov, Valerii (2016) "Po opytu Sirii", *Voenno-Promyshlennyi Kur'er(VPK)*, 9 (624) March 7, https://vpk-news.ru/articles/29579.
139 Ibid.
140 Ibid.
141 Ibid.
142 Rostovskiy, Mikhael (2016) "Nikolay Patrushev: "Mirovoe soobshestvo dolzhno skazat nam spasibo za Krym". Interview with Nikolay Patrushev, January 26, Mk.ru, http://www.mk.ru/politics/2016/01/26/nikolay-patrushev-mirovoe-soobshhestvo-dolzhno-skazat-nam-spasibo-za-krym.html.
143 Solovev, Vladimir (2018) "Rossia poluchila glavnoe – mir". *Kommersant*. August 7, https://www.kommersant.ru/doc/3707031?from=doc_vrez.
144 Steil, Benn (2018) *The Marshall Plan: Dawn of the Cold War.* New York: Simon and Schuster, p. 398.
145 Aliyev, Nurlan (2019) "Determinants of Russia's Political Elite Security Thought: Similarities and Differences between the Soviet Union and Contemporary Russia", *Problems of Post-Communism*, Published online: December 17, p. 8, https://doi.org/10.1080/10758216.2019.1689827.
146 Pipes, Richard (2004) "Flight From Freedom: What Russians Think and Want", *Foreign Affairs*, May/June 2004 Issue, https://www.foreignaffairs.com/articles/russia-fsu/2004-05-01/flight-freedom-what-russians-think-and-want.
147 Ibid.
148 Arbatov, Alexey (2016) "Russian Foreign and Security Policy", Carnegie Moscow Centre, June 21, http://carnegie.ru/2016/06/21/russian-foreign-and-security-policy-pub-63860.
149 Shestoperov, Dmitrii; Korchenkova, Natal'ya and Tishina Yuliya (2018) "S suverennost'u v zavtrashnem dne", *Gazeta "Kommersant"*, 238, December 25, p. 1, https://www.kommersant.ru/doc/3842329?from=main_1.

150 Aliyev, Nurlan (2019) "Determinants of Russia's Political Elite Security Thought: Similarities and Differences between the Soviet Union and Contemporary Russia"…, p. 9.

## Bibliography

Adamishin, Anatoliy (2016) *V raznyye gody. Vneshnepoliticheskiye ocherki*, Moskva: Izdatel′stvo "Ves′ Mir.

Aliyev, Nurlan (2019) "Determinants of Russia's Political Elite Security Thought: Similarities and Differences between the Soviet Union and Contemporary Russia", *Problems of Post-Communism*, Published online: 17 December 2019, DOI: 10.1080/10758216. 2019.1689827.

Arbatov, Alexey (2016) "Russian Foreign and Security Policy", Carnegie Moscow Centre, 21 June 2016, available at: http://carnegie.ru/2016/06/21/russian-foreign-and-security-policy-pub-63860, accessed 25 December 2018.

Barnes, Julian E., and David E. Sanger (2019) "Russia Deploys Hypersonic Weapon, Potentially Renewing Arms Race", *The New York Times*, 27 December 2019, available at: https://www.nytimes.com/2019/12/27/us/politics/russia-hypersonic-weapon.html, accessed 2 August 2022.

Bartosh, Aleksandr (2018a) "Rossii ne izbezhat' gibridnykh voin", Nezavisimoe voennoe obozrenie, 9 March 2018, available at: http://nvo.ng.ru/concepts/2018-03-09/1_987_hybridwar.html, accessed 25 December 2018.

Bartosh, Aleksandr (2018b) "Gibridnoia voina- novyi vyzov natsional'noi bezopasnosti Rossii", *Natsional'noya oborona*, 9, September, 2018, available at: http://www.oborona.ru/includes/periodics/maintheme/2017/1016/154222573/detail.shtml, accessed 25 December 2018.

Baunov, Alexander (2022) "The West Has Responded to Russia's Ultimatum. Is It Enough?", *Carnegie Moscow Center*, February 1, available at: https://carnegiemoscow.org/commentary/86326, accessed 9 August 2022.

Belikov, V.I., and L.P. Krysin (2001) *Sotsiolingvistika*, Moskva: Rossiyskiy gosudarstvennyi gumanitarnyi universitet, pp. 264–297, available at: https://studfiles.net/preview/5458437/, accessed 15 December 2018.

Bērziņa, Ieva (2019) "Weaponization of 'Colour Revolutions'", *Journal of Political Marketing* (online publication), p. 4, DOI: 10.1080/15377857.2019.1678905.

Cecil, Clem (2002) "Pro-Putin cult urges return to Soviet 'glory'", 27 January 2002, available at: https://www.telegraph.co.uk/news/worldnews/europe/russia/1382860/Pro-Putin-cult-urges-return-to-Soviet-glory.html, accessed 28 December 2018.

Chernenko, Yelena (2019) «NATO navyazyvayet nam skhemu obespecheniya bezopasnosti vremen kholodnoy voiny», *Gazeta "Kommersant"* 239, 26 December 2019, p. 5, available at: https://www.kommersant.ru/doc/4207094?from=doc_vrez, accessed 26 December 2019.

Cimbala, Stephen J. (2013) "Russian Threat Perceptions and Security Policies: Soviet Shadows and Contemporary Challenges", *The Journal of Power Institutions in Post-Soviet Societies*, Issue 14/15: War Trauma in Post-Soviet Russia & Military Reform in Russia and the CIS-Russian Military Reform, available at: http://journals.openedition.org/pipss/4000, accessed 20 April 2018.

Ching, Nike (2022) "US Responds to Russia's Security Demands, Renewing Call for Diplomacy", *Voice of America*, January 26, available: https://www.voanews.com/a/us-responds-to-russia-s-security-demands-renewing-call-for-diplomacy-/6413910.html, accessed 9 August 2022.

Connolly, Richard (2019) "Russian Military Expenditure in Comparative Perspective: A Purchasing Power Parity Estimate", Report, CAN, 9 October 2019, p. 13, https://www.cna.org/CNA_files/PDF/IOP-2019-U-021955-Final.pdf, accessed 18 December 2019.

Deuber, Gunter (2022) "Fortress Russia: Completely Lost in (Financial) Sanctions Warfare, A Deep Economic Crisis Is Unavoidable", *Russian Analytical Digest*, Sanctions Against Russia, No. 280, 21 March, pp. 2–7, DOI: 10.3929/ethz-b-000538061.

Dobrynina, Yekaterina (2006) "Prishli k soglasiyu", *Rossiyskaya gazeta*, Federal'nyy vypusk, 4163 (0), 6 September 2006, available at: https://rg.ru/2006/09/06/diskussia.html, accessed 24 December 2018.

Federation of American Scientists (2022) "Status of World Nuclear Forces", available at: https://fas.org/issues/nuclear-weapons/status-world-nuclear-forces/, accessed 11 August 2022.

Gerasimov, Valerii (2016) "Po opytu Sirii", *Voenno-Promyshlennyi Kur'er (VPK)*, 9 (624) 7 March 2016, available at: https://vpk-news.ru/articles/29579, accessed 25 December 2018.

Glantz, Col. D. M. (1990) *Soviet Operational Art and Tactics in the 1930s*, Ft. Leavenworth, KS: Soviet Army Studies Office, https://apps.dtic.mil/sti/tr/pdf/ADA232954.pdf, accessed 28 May 2018.

Goldgeier, James (2018) "Bill and Boris: A Window Into a Most Important Post-Cold War Relationship", *Texas National Review*, Vol 1, Iss 4. August, available: https://tnsr.org/2018/08/bill-and-boris-a-window-into-a-most-important-post-cold-war-relationship/#_ftn31, accessed 20 August 2018.

Harris, Shane, Karen DeYoung, Isabelle Khurshudyan, Ashley Parker, and Liz Sly (2022) "Road to war: U.S. struggled to convince allies, and Zelensky, of risk of invasion", *The Washington Post*, August 16, available at: https://www.washingtonpost.com/national-security/interactive/2022/ukraine-road-to-war/?itid=ap_shaneharris, accessed 17 August 2022.

Holloway, David (1988) "Gorbachev's New Thinking". *Foreign Affairs*, Essay, America and the World, 1988 Issue, available at: https://www.foreignaffairs.com/articles/russia-fsu/1989-02-01/gorbachevs-new-thinking, accessed 31 May 2018.

Interfax-AVN (2022) "Aleksey Arbatov: v voprose ne rasshireniya NATO nuzhen memorandum o namereniyakh", February 2, available at: https://www.militarynews.ru/story.asp?rid=2&nid=565883&lang=RU, accessed 9 August 2022.

Ivanov, S.P. (ed.) (1974) *Nachalniy period voiny (Po opytu pervikh kompanii i operatsii vtoroi mirovoi voiny)*, Moscow: Voenizdat, available at: http://militera.lib.ru/science/npv/index.html, accessed 1 June 2018.

Ivanov, Sergei (2006) "Triada natsional'nykh tsennostei", *Izvestia*, 13 July 2006, available at: https://iz.ru/news/315377, accessed 11 December 2018.

Kashin, Oleg, and Valerii Mel'nikov (2005) "Otryad vlastonogikh", 25 July 2005, available at: https://www.kommersant.ru/doc/595759, accessed 28 December 2018.

Keenan, Edward L. (1986) "Muscovite Political Folkways". *The Russian Review*, Vol. 45, No. 2 (April), pp. 115–181, p. 158. Wiley on behalf of The Editors and Board of Trustees of the Russian Review, http://www.jstor.org/stable/130423, accessed 05 February 2018.

Kennan, George Frost (1946) *The Chargé in the Soviet Union (Kennan) to the Secretary of State Moscow*, 22 February 1946, Part 2: Background of Outlook, Foreign relations of the United States, 1946, Eastern Europe, the Soviet Union, Volume VI, 861.00/2–2246: Telegram, 1969, https://history.state.gov/historicaldocuments/frus1946v06/d475, accessed 27 November 2018.

Kliuchevskii, Vasilii Osipovoch (1937) *Kurs Russkoi istorii*, Part 1, Moscow: Gos. sots.-ekon. izd-vo.

Klussmann, Uwe (2009a) "Did the West Break Its Promise to Moscow?", 26 November 2009, http://www.spiegel.de/international/world/nato-s-eastward-expansion-did-the-west-break-its-promise-to-moscow-a-663315.html, accessed 10 June 2018.

―――― (2009b) 'We Couldn't Believe that the Warsaw Pact Could Be Dissolved', Interview with Eduard Shevardnadze, 26 November 2009, http://www.spiegel.de/international/europe/interview-with-eduard-shevardnadze-we-couldn-t-believe-that-the-warsaw-pact-could-be-dissolved-a-663595.html, accessed 10 June 2018.

*Krasnaya Zvezda* (2019) "Byt' vsegda v avangarde", 28 December 2019, http://redstar.ru/byt-vsegda-v-avangarde/, accessed 28 December 2019.

Kristensen, Hans M., and Robert S. Norris (2018) "Russian nuclear forces, 2018", *Nuclear Notebook, the Bulletin of the Atomic Scientists'*, Vol. 74, No. 3, pp. 185–195, DOI: 10.1080/00963402.2018.1462912.

Kristensen, Hans M., and Matt Korda (2022) "Nuclear Notebook: How many nuclear weapons does Russia have in 2022?" *The Bulletin of the Atomic Scientists*, February 23, available at: https://thebulletin.org/premium/2022-02/nuclear-notebook-how-many-nuclear-weapons-does-russia-have-in-2022/, accessed 11 August, 2022.

Kristensen, Hans M., and Matt Korda (2022) "Russian nuclear weapons, 2022", *Nuclear Notebook, the Bulletin of the Atomic Scientists'*, Vol. 78, No. 2, pp. 98–121. DOI: 10.1080/00963402.2022.2038907.

Kofman, Michael (2018) "From Hammer to Rapier: Russian Military Transformation in Perspective", Russia Brief, Issue I, January, 2018, available at: http://www.ccw.ox.ac.uk/russia-brief-issue-i/, accessed 12 July 2022.

Lisitsyna, Maria, and Veronika Vishniakova (2022) "Ryabkov predlozhil SSHA yeshche odnu «optsiyu» po Ukraine i Gruzii v NATO", *RBK*, January 19, available at: https://www.rbc.ru/politics/19/01/2022/61e803519a79471ac69e59b9?from=from_main_2, accessed 9 August 2022.

Maner, V., and N. Kussman (2005) "The West Doesn't Have to Love Us", *Spiegel*, 20 June 2005, available at: http://www.spiegel.de/international/spiegel/spiegel-interview-with-kremlin-boss-vladislav-surkov-the-west-doesn-t-have-to-love-us-a-361236.html, accessed 11 December 2018.

Mathers, Jennifer G. (2000) *The Russian nuclear shield from Stalin to Yeltsin: the Cold War and beyond*, Basingstoke: Macmillan Press; Oxford: St Antony's College, St. Antony's Series.

*Memorandum of Conversation*, "Morning Meeting with Russian President Yeltsin: NATO-Russia, START, ABM/TMD," Helsinki, 21 March 1997, pp. 106–110, available at: https://clinton.presidentiallibraries.us/items/show/57569, accessed 20 August 2018.

Meyer, Stephen M. (1988) "The Sources and Prospects of Gorbachev's New Political Thinking on Security", *International Security'*, Vol. 13, No. 2 (Fall, 1988).

Nekhoroshkin, Semen, and Denis Voroshilov (2023) "V Kremle svyazali vozvrat k SNV s vospriimchivost'yu Zapada k pozitsii Moskvy", *RBK*, February 22, available at: https://www.rbc.ru/politics/22/02/2023/63f5dfc19a7947461cc3b49f?from=from_main_1, accessed 22 February 2023.

Newsru.com (2006) "Surkov rasskazal o prezidente I istinnoi rossiiskoi demokratii", 28 June 2006, available at: https://www.newsru.com/russia/28jun2006/surkov.html, accessed 11 December 2018.

Pipes, Richard (ed.) (1961) *The Russian Intelligentsia*, New York: Columbia University Press.

Pipes, Richard (1974) *Russia under the old regime*, New York: Charles Scribner's Sons.

――― (2004) "Flight From Freedom: What Russians Think and Want", *Foreign Affairs*, May/June 2004 Issue, available at: https://www.foreignaffairs.com/articles/russia-fsu/2004-05-01/flight-freedom-what-russians-think-and-want, accessed 2 May 2018.

――― (2005) *Russian conservatism and its critics: a study in political culture*, New Haven; London: Yale University Press.

Putin, Vladimir (1999) "Rossiya na rubezhe tysyacheletii", 30 December 1999, available at: http://www.ng.ru/politics/1999-12-30/4_millenium.html, accessed 15 December 2018.

――― (2019) "Poslaniye Prezidenta Federal'nomu Sobraniyu", 20 February 2019, available at: http://kremlin.ru/events/president/transcripts/messages/59863, accessed 29 December 2019.

――― (2023) "Poslaniye Prezidenta Federal'nomu Sobraniyu", 21 February 2023, available at: http://kremlin.ru/events/president/news/70565, accessed 22 February 2023.

Reznichenko, V.G. (ed.) (1987) *Taktika*. The second edition, Moscow: Voenizdat, available at: http://militera.lib.ru/science/tactic/02.html, accessed 25 May 2018.

Rochlitz, Michael (2022) "Is Russia Becoming a Second North Korea?", Russian Analytical Digest, *Sanctions Against Russia*, No. 280, 21 March, pp. 10–13, DOI: 10.3929/ethz-b-000538061.

Rostovskiy, Mikhael (2016) "Nikolay Patrushev: "Mirovoe soobshestvo dolzhno skazat nam spasibo za Krym". Interview with Nikolay Patrushev, 26 January 2016, Mk.ru, available at: http://www.mk.ru/politics/2016/01/26/nikolay-patrushev-mirovoe-soobshhestvo-dolzhno-skazat-nam-spasibo-za-krym.html, accessed 5 June 2018.

Russian Analytical Digest (2022) "Russian Financial and Economic Indicators, Figure 1: GDP Russia in Foreign Currency (USD bn)", *Sanctions Against Russia*, No. 280, 21 March.

Ryzhakov, A. (1968) "K voprosu o stroitelstve bronetankovykx voisk Krasnoi Armii v 30-e gody". VIZH, M9 8.

Savranskaya, Svetlana, and Tom Blanton (2017) "NATO Expansion: What Gorbachev Heard". National Security Archive, George Washington University, 12 December 2017, available at: https://nsarchive.gwu.edu/briefing-book/russia-programs/2017-12-12/nato-expansion-what-gorbachev-heard-western-leaders-early, accessed 10 June 2018.

Shagina, Maria (2022) "An unprecedented response to Russia's war in Ukraine", *Riddle*, March 7, available at: https://ridl.io/an-unprecedented-response-to-russia-s-war-in-ukraine/, accessed 8 August 2022.

Shapovalov, Aleksey (2022) "Operatsionnyy spad", 28 July, available at: https://www.kommersant.ru/doc/5482363?from=main, accessed 4 August 2022.

Shestoperov, Dmitrii, Natal'ya Korchenkova, and Tishina Yuliya (2018) "S suverennost'u v zavtrashnem dne", *Gazeta "Kommersant"*, 238, 25 December 2018, available at: https://www.kommersant.ru/doc/3842329?from=main_1, accessed 26 December 2018.

Shevchuk, Mikhail, and Dmitrii Kamyshev (2018) "Obyknovennyi 'Nashizm' Kreml' sozdayet novoye molodezhnoye dvizheniye", 21 February 2005, available at: https://www.kommersant.ru/doc/549170, accessed 28 December 2018.

Shiryayev, Valeriy (2022) "Chuvstvuyu, kak NATO prevrashchayut v monstra", *Novaya Gazeta*, February 2, available at: https://novayagazeta.ru/articles/2022/02/02/natokatstvo, accessed 9 August 2022.

SIPRI (2018) *Global military spending remains high at $1.7 trillion*, 2 May 2018, available at: https://www.sipri.org/media/press-release/2018/global-military-spending-remains-high-17-trillion, accessed 12 July 2022.

SIPRI (2022) *World military expenditure passes $2 trillion for first time*, 22 April, available at: https://sipri.org/media/press-release/2022/world-military-expenditure-passes-2-trillion-first-time, accessed 12 July 2022.

Snetkov, Aglaya (2005) *Russia's security policy under Putin: a critical perspective*, London; New York: Routledge.

Snyder, Glenn H. (1984) "The Security Dilemma in Alliance Politics". *World Politics*, Vol. 36, no. 4(July), pp. 461–495, Published by: Cambridge University Press Stable, available at: http://www.jstor.org/stable/2010183, accessed 31 May 2018.

Solovev, Vladimir (2018) "Rossia poluchila glavnoe – mir". *Kommersant*. 7 August 2018, available at: https://www.kommersant.ru/doc/3707031?from=doc_vrez, accessed 9 August 2018.

Steil, Benn (2018) *The Marshall Plan: Dawn of the Cold War*, New York: Simon and Schuster.

Tarasenko, Pavel, and Elena Chernenko (2021) "Rasshireniye smerti podobno", *Kommersant*, December 17, available: https://www.kommersant.ru/doc/5139102, accessed 9 August 2022.

TASS (2022) "Putin prikazal perevesti sily sderzhivaniya armii RF v osobyy rezhim neseniya sluzhby", February 27, available at: https://tass.ru/politika/13885447, accessed 11 August 2022.

The Kremlin (2020) "Expanded Meeting of the Defence Ministry Board." December 21, available at: http://en.kremlin.ru/events/president/news/64684, accessed 11 August 2022.

―――― (2021a) "Meeting with permanent members of the Security Council", February 11, available at: http://en.kremlin.ru/events/president/news/64985?utm_source=pocket_mylist, accessed 2 August 2022.

―――― (2021b) "Tseremoniya vrucheniya veritel'nykh gramot", December 1, available: http://kremlin.ru/events/president/news/67250, accessed 9 August 2022.

―――― (2021c) "Rasshirennoye zasedaniye kollegii Minoborony", December 21, available at: http://kremlin.ru/events/president/news/67402, accessed 11 August 2022.

The Insider (2022a) "Ukraine and Russia accuse each other of nuclear terrorism", August 8, available at: https://theins.ru/en/news/253938, accessed 11 August 2022.

―――― (2022b) "Russian troops deliver unknown cargo to Zaporizhzhia NPP, sources say power plant is mined (video)", August 5, available at: https://theins.ru/en/news/253868, accessed 11 August 2022.

The Ministry of Foreign Affairs of the Russian Federation (2021a) "Zayavleniye MID Rossii ob otvetnykh merakh na resheniya Severoatlanticheskogo al'yansa v otnoshenii Postoyannogo predstavitel'stva Rossii pri NATO v Bryussele", October 18, available at: https://www.mid.ru/en/press_service/spokesman/official_statement/1783976/?lang=ru, accessed 9 August 2022.

―――― (2021b) "O rossiyskikh proyektakh dokumentov po obespecheniyu pravovykh garantiy bezopasnosti so storony SSHA i NATO", December 17, available: https://www.mid.ru/ru/foreign_policy/news/1790809/, accessed 9 August 2022.

―――― (2021c) "Dogovor mezhdu Rossiyskoy Federatsiyey i Soyedinennymi Shtatami Ameriki o garantiyakh bezopasnosti", December 17, available at: https://mid.ru/ru/foreign_policy/rso/nato/1790818/, accessed 9 August 2022.

―――― (2021d) "Soglasheniye o merakh obespecheniya bezopasnosti Rossiyskoy Federatsii i gosudarstv-chlenov Organizatsii Severoatlanticheskogo dogovora", December 17, available: https://mid.ru/ru/foreign_policy/rso/nato/1790803/, accessed 9 August 2022.

_____ (2022a) "Foreign Minister Sergey Lavrov's answer to a media question", January 27, available at: https://www.mid.ru/ru/foreign_policy/news/1796041/?lang=en, accessed 9 August 2022.

_____ (2022b) "Zayavleniye MID Rossii o situatsii s Dogovorom o merakh po dal'neyshemu sokrashcheniyu i ogranicheniyu strategicheskikh nastupatel'nykh vooruzheniy (DSNV)", August 8, available at: https://www.mid.ru/ru/foreign_policy/news/1825525/, accessed 11 August 2022.

Trenin, Dmitri (2022a) "What a Week of Talks Between Russia and the West Revealed", *Carnegie Moscow Center*, January 20, available at: https://carnegiemoscow.org/commentary/86222, accessed 9 August 2022.

_____ (2022b) "Spetsial'naya voyennaya operatsiya na Ukraine kak perelomnaya tochka vneshney politiki sovremennoy", Rossii, Rossiya v global'noy politike, November 30, https://globalaffairs.ru/articles/perelomnaya-tochka/.

U.S. Department of State (2021) "On the Extension of the New START Treaty with the Russian Federation, Press Statement, Antony J. Blinken, Secretary of State, available at: https://www.state.gov/on-the-extension-of-the-new-start-treaty-with-the-russian-federation/, accessed 2 August 2022.

U.S Department of State (2022) "Secretary Antony J. Blinken at a Press Availability", January 26, available at: https://www.state.gov/secretary-antony-j-blinken-at-a-press-availability-13/, accessed 9 August 2022.

United Nations Development Programme (UNDP) (2022) *Latest Human Development Index (HDI) Ranking*, available at: https://hdr.undp.org/data-center/human-development-index#/indicies/HDI, accessed 8 August 2022.

VPK.name (2018) "Operativno-takticheskii komleks 9K720 "Iskander" (NATO: SS-26 Stone)", https://vpk.name/library/f/iskander.html, accessed 9 June 2018.

World Bank (2018) Russia's Economy: Preserving Stability, Doubling Growth, Halving Poverty – How?, 40th issue of the Russia Economic Report, December 4, p. 55, available at: http://pubdocs.worldbank.org/en/673631543924406524/RER-40-English.pdf, accessed 14 July 2022.

_____ (2022a) *Global Economic Prospects, June 2022*, Washington, DC: World Bank, DOI: 10.1596/978-1-4648-1843-1.

_____ (2022b) Table 4.2 – World Development Indicators: Structure of value added, available at: http://wdi.worldbank.org/table/4.2#, accessed 4 August 2022.

_____ (2023) *Global Economic Prospects*, January 2023, Washington, DC: World Bank, DOI:10.1586/978-1-4648-1906-3. http://hdl.handle.net/10986/38030, accessed 4 February 2023.

Yusupov, Alexey (2022) "What did Western sanctions on Russia achieve?", *IPS*, July 20, available at: https://www.ips-journal.eu/topics/foreign-and-security-policy/what-did-western-sanctions-on-russia-achieve-6076/, accessed 8 August 2022.

Zhilin, P.A. (ed.) (1986) *Istoria voennogo iskustva*, Moscow: Voenizdat.

Zimmerman, William (2002) *The Russian people and foreign policy: Russian elite and mass perspectives*, 1993–2000, Princeton, NJ: Princeton University Press.

Zygar, Mikhail (2016) *All the Kremlin's men*, New York: Public Affairs.

# 3 The Soviet legacy of Russia's security policy

**Security policy in the Soviet Union**

The use of asymmetric approaches in the Soviet Union's security and foreign policy was initiated and justified by the official state ideology, Marxism-Leninism. Moreover, the economic weaknesses, which accompanied the USSR from its establishment until its breakup, also made asymmetric approaches preferable for Moscow. This was true even during the USSR's comparably strong periods between the 1960s and 1980s, as the existence of nuclear weapons on both sides deterred them from engaging in a direct war against each other, that is, conventional strategies.

The main distinguishing characteristics of the Soviet security strategy were the influences of the official ideology—Marxism-Leninism—on it, one of the pillars of which was the dialectics. If the security policies of the Soviets were analyzed in relation to the laws of the dialectical materialism, it is possible to find similarities between developments in the Soviet security policy and the laws. Dialectics defines that all things change, develop, and continue to do so in a definite and regular manner. Therefore, Soviet approaches could change, and such change was encouraged by the state ideology. Such a condition is suitable for the utilization of asymmetric approaches. Considering their adaptability, it should be noted that the Soviet strategies and tactics stressed infiltration, division, instigation of defection in order to amplify the enemy's internal contradictions, and "negate of the negation" as a solution of, and new unity for, such contradictions.[1]

These were some of the basic principles of dialectical materialism which the Soviets used when designing their security strategies. According to Wang Chueh-Yuan, the Soviets adopted Clausewitz's principle of unlimited war ["absolute war" in Clausewitz's work]. Yuan explained that in an unlimited war, the state of suspended operation is supposed to be longer than direct engagement. Yuan noted that in such a war, the weaker side might try to use the strengths of its adversary as its weaknesses, or vice versa, an adversary's weaknesses as its strengths:

> However, it does not mean end of all hostile activities. All of Clausewitz's political and psychological tactics is primarily used to change the balance between the two parties—to change the enemy's material and spiritual superiority into inferiority and to change one's own inferiority into superiority.[2]

DOI: 10.4324/9781003344391-4

Moreover, similarly to Evgeny Messner, he argued that the Soviet Union used "peaceful coexistence" as a tactic of unlimited war and that such a war does not know a time or space limit. The "battlefield can be changed and so can the method to conduct the war. Infiltrations, propaganda, organization, alienation, political stratagem, subversions, sabotage, and armed revolt are closely coordinated with the frontal political, economic, cultural, diplomatic, and psychological attack against the enemy," Yuan writes.[3]

Analyzing the influence of dialectical materialism's laws on the security thinking in Soviet Russia and China during those socialist states' first years, Wang Chueh-Yuan focused on the guerrilla tactics of both, as this is one of the means of asymmetric warfare. He notes that the Soviets and the Chinese considered guerrilla tactics as a means to attain "quantitative change," which is to lead, in turn, gradually to sudden, qualitative change. He explained that the "law of contradictions" is applied at different stages in order to create and amplify contradictions. Quantitative change will reach a certain point, and when qualitative change occurs in the strength ratio between the Communists and their enemy, the struggle will enter the phase of "negation of the negation."[4] This was how tactics were applied in the early period of the Soviet Russian Revolution, according to Yuan. Generally, since the Bolsheviks took power, the dialectical way of thinking has prevailed in Russia.

George Kennan also argued that the Soviet leaders thinking on warfare was based on Marxist-Leninist ideology and that it did not suggest that it was through a single grand military conflict between the world of communism and the world of capitalism that these aims were to be achieved. According to Kennan, "central to the Soviet view of how socialism was to triumph on a world scale has always been the operation of social and political forces within the capitalist countries ... While Moscow has always recognized that civil violence would have a legitimate place in the operation of these processes—while it has not hesitated in certain instances to promote or even to organize such civil violence," he wrote.[5] It has not, in other words, sought to obtain its objectives by the traditional processes of open and outright warfare, stressed Kennan.[6]

Such thinking is justified by the publications and public speeches of Soviet ideologists and leaders. Years before the Cold War, Josef Stalin, a leader of the ruling party and the state, emphasized the importance of using the weaknesses and internal confrontations of one's adversaries. For instance, in his speech at the Fourteenth Congress of the C.P.S.U.(B.) in 1925, Stalin stated that, "at the bottom of this weakness lie the contradictions which capitalism cannot overcome, and within the framework of which the entire international situation is taking shape—contradictions which the capitalist countries cannot overcome, and which can be overcome only in the course of development of the proletarian revolution in the West."[7]

Using confrontations between "the proletariat and the bourgeoisie in the capitalist countries," imperialism as well as the liberation movement and other weaker points of the West, as suggested by Stalin, were explored and largely used by the Soviet Union during the Cold War. The Soviet Union actively supported left and far-left political groups in Western countries and liberation movements in Third World countries. Later, such practices would be used in post-Soviet Russia during

Putin's presidency, but this time the far-right would be preferred to the far-left political groups. The KGB and Main Intelligence Directorate (the GRU) were the main institutions and often orchestrated the anti-government activities of the aforementioned groups between the 1950s right until the dissolution of the Soviet Union.[8] In post-Soviet Russia, the role of the KGB would be played by its successor agencies and the GRU, which would continue existing after the breakup of the USSR.

Differences in security thinking between the eras of Lenin, Stalin, and Khrushchev are, of course, relative, but they are not unimportant. After Khrushchev gained power, some political and cultural openness took place. Such changes, commonly dubbed Khrushchev's "Thaw" [*ottepel*], especially influenced internal security attitudes. After Stalin's repression policy and political purges, the government started to pursue a relatively moderate internal security policy. George Kennan evaluated these as having "deep and encouraging significance to some of the changes in the character and structure of the Soviet regime that have taken place since Stalin's death."[9] "The drastic alteration," he wrote, "in the role of the police has constituted a basic change in the nature and spirit of Soviet society."[10] According to him, it had somewhat altered the character of the political process, particularly in the senior echelons of the Party.[11] He also accepted as a fact that it was a reform, which could be reversed at any time. After Khrushchev was toppled, and even during his last years in power, the leadership of the Party began to strengthen restrictions in the country. It continued until 1987, but by then the government could not, and did not, make a U-turn.

Most importantly, a significant change was carried out in the Soviet leadership's security thinking during that period. It concerned contradictions and confrontations between the Soviet Union and its main adversary in the international system. According to the Soviet assessment, the main contradiction between socialism and imperialism shaped the nature of all other contradictions, and the intensity of the contradiction largely determined the global expectations of violence. "For Khrushchev and his successors," wrote William Zimmerman, "the assumption that there is a main contradiction symbolizes the centrality of Soviet-American relations in avoiding a third world war ... And this centrality underlies the thinking that led Soviet observers, in a striking departure from the Leninist theory of war, virtually to exclude the possibility of intra-imperialist war."[12]

Moreover, the Soviet Union and the United States reached nuclear power status during Khrushchev's period. Since then, Moscow and Washington accepted the fact that direct military confrontation would result in the tremendous military and civilian casualties and economic losses, if not outright Armageddon. Such possibilities pushed the Soviet Union and the United States to fight each other indirectly using asymmetric methods and strategies. In that competition, battle fields were in the territory of third-party countries, and the official fighters also had to be from other nations. Several military conflicts between the 1950s and the final years of the USSR saw Moscow and Washington use such proxy wars to weaken and diminish the influences of the other.

Following the death of Stalin, the main security institution—the Cheka, which was combined with the Ministry of Internal Affairs (*Ministerstvo Vnutrennyx*

*Del*—MVD) and enlarged as MVD between 1917 and 1953—was reorganized and divided into two divisions in 1954, the KGB (State Security Committee) and the MVD.[13] Consequently, by the time Yuri Andropov, the long-serving head of the KGB (1967–1982), was promoted to the CPSU Central Committee, the KGB reached the peak of its power and the number of its staff and non-staff personnel had multiplied many times. As estimated by Yevgenia Albats and other Russian publicists of the democratic movement in the early 1990s, the KGB had slightly more than half a million employees, of whom 220,000 were border troops. Moreover, dozens, maybe hundreds of thousands, of officers of the so-called active reserve sat in the first departments of enterprises, scientific and educational institutions, ministries, and departments "under the roof" of newspapers, magazines, publishing houses, foreign policy, and foreign trade institutions. In addition to the security servicemen and agents, Albats calculated that some 2.9 million "voluntary assistants" worked for the KGB, many of whom, like the keepers of detention or the most active agents, received "incentives" (payment) for their services.[14] Throughout the world, regular employees of the special services recruited agents in a variety of ways.

Most were told that they should inform the KGB about all dubious personalities, statements, violations of the secrecy regime, etc. It was believed that all party and non-party members should fulfill their civic duty in this way. Many people were helped in their careers by being promoted to better-paid or more interesting jobs. Others found the prospect of cooperation more attractive when they were caught committing a crime or some minor offense. According to Igor Sinitsin, who was an assistant to Andropov in the CPSU Central Committee, in the Soviet Union "almost every fact, scientific development or foreign newspapers and magazines in the library were considered as secret, all those hundreds of thousands of officers of the 'operational reserve,' or more simply the KGB men, 'under the roof' (under the protection) had a fairly well-paid job."[15]

According to Soviet dissident and publicist Andrei Amalrik, a part of society, mostly peasants and their urbanized heirs, were inclined to denouncing. The reason for this was a misunderstanding of the meaning of justice among Soviet society:

> Justice in practice turns into desire, "that no one is better than me.' This idea turns into hatred of everything from an extraordinary number that they try not to imitate, but on the contrary—to force oneself to be like them, to any initiative, to any higher, and the dynamic life than we live. Of course, this psychology is most typical for the peasants and the least for the middle class. But peasants and yesterday's peasants make up the overwhelming majority of our country.[16]

Richard Pipes linked such behavior to the Russian Empire's policy of encouraging denunciation among the population. The tsarist government encouraged peasants and other social strata to denounce each other as a means of maintaining control over the country. In this regard, denunciation was the most effective and widely used tool. According to Pipes, the Code of 1649 made one exception to the rule forbidding peasants to complain against landlords, "and that was when the complaint concerned actions detrimental to the *gosudar* and his *gosudarstva.*"[17]

## Functions of asymmetric warfare methods during the Soviet period

The use of asymmetric warfare methods began in the first years of the Soviet Union. Any method which could help to achieve their intended goals was typical for the Bolsheviks even before they took over the government in Russia.

### *The Soviet intelligence services disinformation and propaganda*

In their years of fighting against the Czar regime—and during the revolutions—the Bolsheviks learned in practice the strength of information. Moreover, they practiced disinformation activities as strong tools in political battles. The Bolsheviks used disinformation as a tool of political struggle long before they captured power in Russia, but the creation of a government body responsible for deception operations within the state could only be realized in 1923. That same year, the Politburo of the Central Committee of the RCP(b) decided that in order to organize "the struggle against the enemy's propaganda," it was necessary to set up a special disinformation bureau for conducting active intelligence.[18]

The initiative for the implementation of similar activities at the state level was applied by the leadership of the State Political Directorate [*Gosudarstvennoe Politicheskoe Upravleniya–GPU*], the Soviet intelligence service. The administration of the GPU could not solve such issues on its own initiative because the coordination of work between various departments was required. Therefore, the leadership decided to seek permission from the highest party instance. On December 22, 1922, the deputy chairman of the GPU Józef Unszlicht sent a memorandum to two members of the Politburo, Iosif Stalin, and Lev Trotskii, about the need for disinformation activities. In that document, he wrote:

> The skillful, systematic circling of our opponents with a network of disinformation will allow us to exert some influence in the desired sense for us on their policies. It would allow us to force them to build practical conclusions based on incorrect information. In addition, disinformation helps our direct struggle against foreign intelligence services, facilitates the penetration of our agents into the intelligence agencies of the bourgeois states.[19]

He also proposed involving military intelligence officers and diplomats, that is, the GPU and the People Commissariat of Foreign Affairs [*Narodnyi Kommisariat Innostrannykh Del*] (NKID), to participate in this work and create a special bureau at the GPU consisting of representatives of all interested departments.[20]

According to Unszlicht, the main tasks of the newly created structure should be: an accounting of the information received by the GPU, Intelligence Agency [*Razvedovatelnoe Upravleniya-Razvedupra*], and other institutions about the level of awareness of foreign intelligence services about Russia; an accounting of the information which the enemy is interested in; and determining the degree of awareness of the enemy. Additionally, he suggested that "it was necessary to start the drafting and production of a number of false information and documents giving the wrong thought to the opponents about the internal situation in Russia; about the organization and condition of the Red Army; about the political work of the party and Soviet bodies and the work of the Commissariat of Foreign Affairs."[21]

According to Yevgenii A. Gorbunov, the main issue was supplying the enemy with materials and documents through the agents of the GPU and the Razvedupra. "For greater reliability of the information transmitted to the West, it was proposed to develop and publish a series of articles for the periodical press, which should have prepared the ground for putting into circulation all kinds of fictitious materials."[22] Józef Unszlicht's proposal was discussed at the next meeting of the Politburo on January 11, 1923, and adopted without any major changes or amendments.[23]

The only amendment was that all the articles that were developed for the periodical press had to be reviewed and approved by one of the secretaries of the party's Central Committee before publication.[24] The political leadership was scared to leave all disinformation measures at the mercy of the GPU and give general control to them.[25]

It should be noted that disinformation was also used by the Russian Empire and other countries in their external security practices before the Bolshevik disinformation bureau was organized. But the direct involvement of diplomats and the Ministry of Foreign Affairs as the institutional source for such activities was something new entirely. Before, Russian diplomats would, at least officially or at the institutional level, keep their distance from such activities, which were seen primarily as methods of the security institutions. But the party leadership and the GPU were not interested in their opinion and put the leadership of the Commissariat of Foreign Affairs in front of a fait accompli. The leadership of the Foreign Ministry was forced to submit to the highest party instance. Yevgenii Gorbunov argues that this was likely against the will of Maxim Litvinov, but as an old party member, he was bound by strict party discipline, and that former tsarist diplomat Georgy Chicherin was most probably in a difficult position.[26] However, after reviewing the document, the first deputy of the Foreign Affairs commissar, Litvinov, sent a letter to the secretary of the Central Committee of the Party (Stalin) in which he expressed the opinion of the diplomats regarding the disinformation issue. He wrote that the People's Commissariat of Foreign Affairs was aware of the need to circulate in certain cases "disorienting information" and often used this method. But he also stressed that by no means can the People's Commissariat of Foreign Affairs consider the GPU competent to decide when, and by what means, the disinformation should be put into circulation.

According to Gorbunov, the diplomats did not have a high opinion of the intellectual abilities of the GPU staff, who were supposed to be the ones dealing with disinformation issues. Disinformation had to go abroad, and this was already the patrimony of the diplomats. Litvinov feared, and, obviously, it is quite true that any information disseminated by this newly created bureau would immediately be refuted by the Soviet embassies and that such situations might affect the overall reputations of the Soviet embassies. Thus, the embassies should not be informed about the creation of such a disinformation bureau ["dezburo"].[27] Already in Litvinov's letter, according to Gorbunov, the foundations of the conflict—specifically the failure to develop a fruitful cooperation between counterintelligence and the Ministry of Foreign Affairs—were laid. Political disinformation, due to disagreements on several issues between the Commissariat of Foreign Affairs and the GPU, was not widely used. In such a situation the only capable organization which could conduct similar activities, and only in the military field, was military intelligence.[28]

In military intelligence, this new direction of activity was supervised by the Chief of Intelligence, Razvedupra Jan Berzin. Two years after the resolution on disinformation was adopted by the Politburo, the new chairman of the Revolutionary Military Council of the USSR and the chief of the General Staff of the Red Army, Mikhail Frunze, demanded from Berzin a report on the two-year work on disinformation. On January 21, 1925, report number 0226/ss was presented to Frunze. The detailed, 12-page typewritten document provided a fuller picture on the two-year work on disinformation.[29]

According to the report, the issue of creating a special body to develop false documents for disinformation purposes was developed within military intelligence back in 1921, but practical work on this issue began only after the Politburo decision was accepted. For practical work on the military, at the very first meeting of the disinformation bureau, it was decided to create a small three-person department within military intelligence, which in fact later became the working apparatus of this bureau. Gorbunov noted that the bureau's activities were so classified that even in the central apparatus of military intelligence they decided to limit the number of informed persons.[30] Disinformation materials on the political line were to be developed by the Counterintelligence Office of the Main Political Directorate (KPO OGPU) apparatus together with the People's Commissariat of Foreign Affairs.

The Department for Disinformation at military intelligence started work on December 22, 1922, and its tasks were to conduct a permanent record and study on information about their adversaries' awareness of the Red Army; to develop for KRO OGPU on its instructions, or on its own initiative, a number of false documents or messages to be transferred to the intelligence of the enemy. The general direction of such work was to be determined by the Revolutionary Military Council and controlled from a purely military point of view by the assistance of the chief of the general staff.[31]

Berzin noted that the general directive was given by then Revolutionary Military Council chairman, Lev Trotsky. On his instructions, military intelligence was instructed to list in its disinformation materials that the conditions and combat capability of the Red Army were 50%–60% higher than they were in reality. In the spring of 1924, this directive was confirmed, and its provisions upheld. By this time, the main opponents of the disinformation operations were also determined. They were the intelligence departments of the French, Polish, American, Italian, and Japanese military headquarters. "The Allies compiled a table of the number of weapons of the Red Army was based on our document of December 1923, plus the products of military factories," Berzin wrote in his report.[32]

However, the first experiences did not inspire the Soviet leadership, and Unshlikht's proposal to publish a new portion of fake articles on Poland and Romania was declared "untimely" by the party leaders. Officers of the OGPU prepared fake information on "Poland's preparations for attack on Germany" for publication in the newspapers "Pravda" and "Izvestia."[33] Most likely, the Central Committee quickly realized that when spreading false information, the reliability of the official Soviet media could be affected. After that, the Disinformburo started to use foreign newspapers.[34]

In 1923, a successful operation was carried out to discredit the Grand Duke Kirill Vladimirovich, who sought, through monarchical emigration, to recognize himself as the locum tenens of the throne. The exposé about him was done by the newspapers of Bavaria, where the grand duke lived. Along with the truth, for example, that Kirill supported the February Revolution, much false information was added to the publications. Reportedly, after that, not only did the Russian monarchists reject Kirill Vladimirovich but also the German bankers who financed him.[35]

Other successful operations of the Soviet intelligence organizations mainly based on disinformation were "Trest" and "Syndicate-2." Between 1921 and 1926, with the help of agents, Soviet intelligence "revealed" the existence of an underground monarchist organization on the territory of the USSR. The operations "Trest" and "Syndicate-2" allowed the OGPU to marginalize the anti-Soviet activities of the Russian emigration.[36] In the course of these events, another method for misinforming world public opinion was tested. Soviet intelligence allowed the well-known monarchist Vasily Shulgin, under an alien name and with the support of the fake conspirators, to visit his homeland and show him the USSR in the most favorable conditions possible. His book, "Three capitals" [*Tri stolitsy*], which predicted a final victory for the Bolsheviks, was the result of this voyage.[37]

In the 1930s, the methods of individual disinformation of prominent publicists were improved and simplified. For instance, the receptions of the French writer Henri Barbusse were allocated ever-increasing funds from the Soviet state treasury, which were fully paid off by his pro-Soviet publications.[38]

Prior to the German attack, the Soviets recognized deception as one of their primary tools for achieving surprise. According to the Regulations of the Red Army in 1939, deception involved concealment, simulation, misinformation, and demonstrations or feints. All these methods were described by the Soviets using the single Russian word "*maskirovka*." Maskirovka became integral to the formal planning process and part of the commander's decision. In 1943, the new Field Regulations emphasized the importance of maskirovka by making it a command responsibility.[39] During WWII, the Soviets conducted several deception operations, mainly using camouflage companies.

The American military expert Bruce R. Pirnie notes that, in accordance with Soviet military thought, there were three levels of maskirovka:

> At tactical level, units from battalion through division conducted deception, usually concentrating on concealment. At operational level, armies and fronts developed maskirovka plans to achieve operational surprise. Beginning in

the 1970's, the Soviets published extensive materials concerning operational maskirovka during the Second World War. Finally, at strategic level, the Supreme High Command and the General Staff developed maskirovka for strategic operations and campaigns.[40]

According to Pirnie, based on available sources, Soviet maskirovka was not sophisticated, but it was clever and effective. He emphasizes that Soviet deception operations distorted the German intelligence picture using their preferred collection means. During the later phases of the war, knowing German intelligence relied primarily upon radio intercepts, aerial photography, and agents in formerly occupied territory, the Soviets played to these three sources by systematically denying intelligence on forces as they concentrated on offensive operations while revealing other forces, both real and simulated. "As a result," writes Pirnie, "the Germans acquired intelligence that concealed Soviet operational intentions, or at least made these very uncertain."[41] Pirnie also stresses that the Soviets played well with the Germans mental attitude and used the optimism of their leadership regarding their own military and the weaknesses of the USSR.[42]

Aiming to outsmart their adversaries, the Soviet Union actively used various deception activities. One of them, which is known by its code name "Khorovod" ("dance circle"), was conducted in the 1950s. The Soviet security institutions decided to pursue a disinformation operation during their military parade. It should be noted that military parades, organized every year in the Soviet Union, were lovely events for foreign intelligence. Knowing this, the Soviet intelligence agency decided to make use of such an opportunity. During the aviation parade in August 1955, in the presence of foreign diplomats and military attaches, an armada of new-type heavy bombers flew over Red Square for 15 minutes at a low height. Those aircrafts were in larger numbers than expected by the foreign intelligence institutions. As a result, the guests had the impression that dozens and hundreds of bombers were steadily produced by the Soviet aircraft industry. In fact, the same squadron flew in a circle every three minutes, appearing over the heads of foreigners. The purpose of this maneuver was to create the appearance that the USSR intended to increase the power of its offensive forces and use its industrial potential to produce heavy bombers. The West was nudged to perceive that the USSR was prioritizing the use of strategic aviation in a possible war. While, in fact, the USSR was developing its intercontinental ballistic missile program.[43]

After the reformation of their main intelligence organization, the successor of the disinformation bureau was now in the service of the "active measures" of the First Main Directorate (Service A). It was established in 1962 on the basis of the "D" department, which in turn was established in 1959 on the basis of the KI [Komitet Informatsii] (Information Committee) disinformation service of the USSR Ministry of Foreign Affairs, which was established in 1949.

Projects realized by Service A were called "active measures." Active measures were large-scale campaigns meant to complement traditional diplomacy and weaken governments that were not already taking their directions from Moscow.

In the so-called "Intelligence Doctrine" approved in 1974, the task of the First Main Directorate [PGU KGB] regarding "active measures" was defined as:

> solving the foreign policy tasks of the Soviet Union; exposing and disrupting the ideological sabotage of the enemy against the USSR and the socialist community; consolidation of the international communist movement, strengthening of the national liberation and anti-imperialist struggle; the growth of the economic and scientific-technical strengths of the Soviet Union; exposing of the military preparations of states hostile to the USSR; to misinform enemy regarding the foreign policy, military, and intelligence activities being prepared or carried out by the USSR, and also about the real state of the country's military, economic, scientific, and technical potential; compromising the most dangerous anti-communist and anti-Soviet leaders, the worst enemies of the Soviet state.[44]

The document stressed the possibility of using not only the department's capabilities but also the tools of the KGB as a whole as well as other Soviet institutions, departments, organizations, and the armed forces in order to conduct active reconnaissance operations depending on the need.

Another interesting part of the "Intelligence Doctrine" involves the tasks of special operations, which included asymmetric approaches. According to the document, in the field of special operations, using particularly "acute methods of struggle" is required. Acute methods such as conducting special measures against the traitors to the Fatherland and the operation to put an end to the anti-Soviet activities of the most active enemies of the Soviet state; carrying out the seizure and secret delivery to the USSR of persons who are carriers of important state and other secrets of the enemy—weapons, equipment, secret documentation; creating prerequisites for the use in the interests of the USSR of certain hotbeds of the anti-imperialist movement and the partisan struggle in the territory of foreign countries; providing communications for special tasks and providing assistance to weapons, instructors, etc. to the leadership of fraternal communist parties, progressive groups, and organizations fighting in isolation from the outside world.[45]

Service A had grown into one of the most important units of the KGB. The service worked in close cooperation with the departments of the Central Committee of the CPSU: International, Propaganda, as well as with the Department of Socialist Countries. Foreigners resettled in the USSR advised Service A on the subtleties of a given language and details about life in their former countries. The service manufactured all sorts of fakes, falsifications, and materials. The work of the service was coordinated and monitored by the high-level institutions of the state. After the approval of the Politburo, the idea developed into plans, schedules were made, and then it was utilized. Realizations of so-called active measures were entrusted to the PR (political intelligence) in residencies, to foreign communist parties, and to all sorts of organizations that were in one way, or another, linked to the USSR. The Service coordinated a department of political publications of the APN, the Agency of Publishing "News" [*Agentstvo Pechati "Novosti"*] of the USSR.[46] This was the Soviet state media holding primarily tasked with promoting propaganda abroad. The agency also used as a cover for intelligence activities. The APN was a predecessor of the contemporary state media holding "Russia Today"—comprised of media such as Sputnik—and used by the state as a tool of information and influence operations. The successor of the APN also continues with practices strikingly similar to those of its predecessor.[47]

Disinformation articles were mainly published in lesser-known newspapers in the Third World and then reprinted in pro-Soviet and USSR-funded publications in Western Europe and the United States. Over the years of its existence, the staff of Service A allegedly found channels for the publication of disinformation in respectable Western publications. The former head of the First Main Directorate, Leonid Shebarshin, said that it was possible to find a journalist in any newspaper who agreed to publish the necessary text for reasonable money or just a drink. One of the veterans of the active measures told the Kommersant newspaper that they were unable to publish their materials in only one publication, the Washington Post.[48]

One particular active measure operation is helpful for understanding how these kinds of operations worked. In 1977 Nikolai Leonov, who was Fidel Castro's first KGB contact and had since risen to head of the First Main Directorate's Service No. 1 (analytical department), was involved in contacting the then president of Panama, General Omar Torrijos Herrera. Leonov, under diplomatic cover and with the approval of the KGB central office, arranged meetings with Torrijos every six to eight months, mainly with the aim of influencing the president's policy regarding the United States.[49] According to the Mitrokhin archives, a KGB officer operating under cover as a correspondent of TASS, the Soviet state news agency, was given responsibility for making the detailed arrangements for these meetings. In order to flatter Torrijos, another operations officer, also under TASS cover, was sent by the KGB to deliver Torrijos a personal letter from Leonid Brezhnev, the head of the Soviet Union. To reinforce Torrijos suspicion of the Carter administration, he was also given a bogus US State Department document forged by Service A, which discussed methods of dragging out the Panama Canal negotiations and removing Torrijos from power.[50]

In the last years of the USSR, Service A was used by KGB leaders trying to make a career under Mikhail Gorbachev. Former KGB chairman Viktor Chebrikov noted that, at the initiative of Vladimir Kryuchkov, the chief of foreign intelligence, Service A paid for the publication of articles, which glorified Gorbachev and perestroika in the Western media. This, in the eyes of the world public, seemed like genuine "Gorbachev mania."[51]

For disinformation operations in foreign countries and for propaganda campaigns among their own people, the Soviets used several possible narratives. One of them was "biological weapons against socialist states and populations." The Soviet Union's ideological and security institutions actively used biological weapons narratives in their information war against the West during the Cold War. For instance, in the 1960s, the Soviet propaganda machine spread fake news about how "the United States intentionally infected Eastern Europe with the Colorado potato beetles." According to Tamara Eidelman, one of the most complex fabrications regarding that narrative was a massive influx of Colorado potato beetles across the Baltic Sea. To strengthen their narrative, the Soviet propagandists "created" amphibian Colorado potato beetles.[52]

In 1950, the Soviet minister of agriculture addressed the "Report of the Minister of Agriculture of the USSR I. A. Benediktov to the Secretary of the Central Committee of the CPSU (b) M. A. Suslov on the danger of the spread of the Colorado potato beetle." In his report, the minister informed the Communist Party leadership about "the problems related to the Colorado potato beetles." Benediktov noted that between 1946 and 1949, the Soviet military administration carried out extensive measures to fight the Colorado beetles in the Soviet occupation zone of Germany and managed to reduce the number of pockets where the Colorado potato beetle could be found and almost completely eliminated it in the lands adjacent to Poland. But, he emphasized, "at the same time, the American, British, and French occupying authorities almost did not carry out any extermination measures against the Colorado potato beetle, thereby, creating extremely favorable conditions for the mass reproduction and spread of the beetle and the constant contamination of the areas of the German Democratic Republic adjacent to the western zones of occupation of Germany."[53] The Soviet minister concluded that "creating favorable conditions for the mass reproduction of the Colorado potato beetle, Americans simultaneously carry out atrocious acts of dropping a beetle in mass quantities from planes over several areas of the German Democratic Republic and in the Baltic Sea region in order to infect the Polish Republic with the beetle."[54] In the same report, measures for fighting the beetles were not about agricultural measures, but information or, in the Soviet parlance, ideological ones.[55]

Another similar case was utilized by the Soviets in North Korea and China. In the 1950s, the Soviet disinformation campaign claimed that "the United States used rodents and insects to infect North Korean people with several diseases." For this disinformation campaign, they used the groundless "conclusions" of an international commission of scientists, which had been established under Soviet control and whose conclusions were spread by the world's left-leaning press. The method applied at that time was the simplest and most effective. Soviet security organizations generously paid for the services of experts who turned a blind eye to the absence of facts and to publications, which were spreading fake information in North Korea and China.[56]

Besides the institutions that dealt with disinformation operations within the security institutions, the Soviet Communist Party also had its own propaganda structure. The Agitation and Propaganda Department (the Agitprop) of the Central Committee of the Russian Communist Party (b.) (the RCP (b.) was organized in the 1920s as part of the Secretariat of the Central Committee of the RCP (b.). It was the body through which the Central Committee united and directed all oral and printed agitation and propaganda materials of the Party. It should be noted that the department existed previously, under the subdivision of agitation and propaganda of the RCP (b).[57] The agitprop consisted of five subdivisions: (1) agitation; (2) propaganda; (3) consideration of local experience; (4) distribution of literature; and (5) national minorities.[58]

Agitprop, together with other institutions (Glavpolitprosveta, Moscow Party Committee, etc.), published a number of magazines covering issues of agitation and propaganda, such as Sputnik of agitator, Izba-Chitalnya, and Questions of patronage.[59] The department within the party existed under several names until the elimination of the Communist Party of the Soviet Union. It continued to work as the ideological department of the Central Committee of the CPSU between 1988 and 1991.[60]

*Red code breakers—the founding fathers of the Russian cyberwarfare army*

One of the methods actively used by Soviet intelligence was the code breaking of other states' cipher systems. The establishment of the organizational structures, which dealt with cryptography in the Soviet intelligence service and military, started in the first months of the Bolshevik government. The continued use of "Tsarist" and "underground" revolutionary period ciphers could not serve as a reliable means of protecting the secret information of the Soviet Republic involved in external and internal military conflicts. Bolshevik leaders understood that it was extremely important and necessary to create their own cryptographic secret services.

Already in December 1917, the "Encryption and Printing Division" was established in the structure of the People's Commissariat of Foreign Affairs and on April 29, 1918, it was reorganized into an independent cryptography department. After the reorganization of the People's Commissariat in August 1918, when the Office of the Commissariat of Foreign Affairs for the Western Affairs was renamed as the Department of the West, it also included the cryptographic division. At the beginning of May 1918, the responsibility for encrypting and decrypting telegrams in the military was assigned to the General Division of the Military Statistics Division of the Operational Directorate of the All-Russian General Staff of the Workers' and Peasants' Red Army.[61]

It should be noted that code breaking, or as it is officially called cryptography, was one of the most in-demand areas of the Soviet security organization activities. Cryptography had such importance for the Soviet state that there were several scientific institutions and departments in the service of the security organizations. The political and military leadership of the Soviet Union perceived the necessity of radio-communication intelligence, cryptography, and code breaking since WWII. From that point, and until the breakup of the USSR, several departments in the main intelligence and security organizations dealt with the issue.

From March 1953 to January 1954 (when the Ministry of State Security [MSS] and the Ministry of Internal Affairs [MIA] were merged), Department "S" (special communication) and the Eighth (cryptography) Directorate of the Ministry of Internal Affairs of the USSR were responsible for the security of communication of the state leadership and cryptography. When the Ministry of State Security became an independent institution again in January 1954, the Second Special Department dealt with cryptosecurity at the Ministry of Internal Affairs. The Eighth Directorate and Department "S" became part of the Ministry of State Security. In 1954, when the Ministry of State Security was reorganized as the Committee of the State Security (the KGB) under the Soviet government, two departments of the Eighth Main Directorate (government communications and cryptography) and the Sixteenth Directorate (radio-electronic warfare and cryptography) were primarily responsible for cryptographic activities. Moreover, the General Staff of the Red Army also had a department that dealt with radio-electronic warfare and cryptography.[62]

The greatest volume of Soviet intelligence on much of the Third World came from SIGINT rather than HUMINT. According to Andrew and Mitrokhin, by 1967, KGB code breakers were able to depict 152 cipher systems used by a total of 72 states. Every day, an inner circle within the Politburo—consisting (in 1980) of Brezhnev, Andropov, Gromyko, Kirilenko, Suslov, and Ustinov—was sent copies of the most important decrypts.[63] In many cases, especially in the Middle East, the tasks of KGB and GRU code breakers were greatly simplified thanks to the vulnerabilities of the weaker cipher systems used by the countries of the region.[64]

Soviet intelligence organizations benefited from their remarkable success in obtaining intelligence on cypher systems by penetrating the Moscow embassies of several countries. According to Ilya Dzhirkvelov, a Soviet defector, Soviet intelligence successfully realized breaking operations at the Egyptian, Syrian, Iranian, Turkish, and other Middle Eastern embassies in Moscow in the early 1950s. For the successful operations, Dzhirkvelov and his colleagues were rewarded with engraved watches and the title of "Honored Chekist."[65] According to the Mitrokhin archives, in the later stages of the Cold War, at least 34 KGB agents and confidential contacts took part in a highly successful operation to penetrate the Moscow Embassy of Syria, then the USSR's main ally in the Middle East.[66]

In the 1970s, Soviet cryptographers succeeded in intercepting a multitude of message exchanges between Washington and the airplanes on which the President of the United States, the Secretary of State, and other high-level members of the administration flew overseas. It was possible to penetrate Andrews Air Force Base's communications. Operational officers of the Soviet operational post "Pochin" were awarded orders of the Red Star for intercepting messages during the trip of US Secretary of State Henry Kissinger to London in July 1974 for talks with the British Foreign Secretary (and future Prime Minister) James Callaghan. Soon, "Pochin" managed to overhear the negotiations these two politicians had with the Minister of Foreign Affairs of Turkey, Turan Gunes. According to Russian sources, sometimes the KGB managed to intercept the private conversations of high-level Western politicians. For instance, one such case was Henry Kissinger's phone conversation with his fiancé, Nancy Maginnes, which took place shortly before their wedding in 1974. The KGB's psychological analysts extracted information from such private conversations. Analysis of private conversations of high-level and influential American politicians allowed the Soviet security institutions to better understand their character and prepare their psychological portraits.[67]

According to Vladimir Sever, who studied KGB history, the number of reports and transcripts of the interceptions of the Soviet Radio-Electron Warfare posts, which operated in several parts of the world, increased from 2,600 pages in 1975 to 7,000 in 1976. During these two years, eight hundred messages were prepared and sent to Moscow on the basis of intercepts by the Washington station. Among the intercepted messages sent to and from the Andrews airbase in 1976 were communications related to the visits of US Secretary of Defense Donald Rumsfeld to meetings of the NATO Nuclear Planning Group in January and June 1975 and to the headquarters of the US forces in Europe in February of the same year, as well as Henry Kissinger's meetings with the leaders of Great Britain, France, West Germany, and South Africa. In 1977, the volume of summaries and transcripts of the post-"Pochin" exceeded 10,500 pages, which covered the foreign visits of, among others, Vice President Walter Mondale and Secretary of State Cyrus Vance. However, the most valuable information given by the post-"Pochin" in the 1970s and early 1980s was military information. According to Sever, those intercepts provided top-secret information about American missiles and other military developments.[68]

The state put huge efforts into increasing the professional capacities of the staff of the security institutions in radio-electronic warfare, and cryptography. On October 19, 1949, the decision of the Politburo of the Central Committee of the CPSU (b) No. P71/426 adopted a number of important decisions for the development of Soviet cryptology. According to the decision, on the basis of the 6th Directorate of the MSS and the deciphering intelligence service of the General Staff of the Soviet Army, the Main Directorate of Special Services [*Glavnoe upravlenie spetsialnoi sluzhby*] (hereinafter—GUSS) was created under the Central Committee of the CPSU (b) (from October 13, 1952—the CPSU). Several measures were utilized to attract scientists both to perform the operational tasks of the cryptographic service and as teachers to train new highly qualified staff. Moreover, the Higher School of Cryptographers and the "closed" Department of the Faculty of Mechanics and Mathematics [*Mekhmat*] of Moscow State University were created.[69] In April 1953, by the decision of the country's leadership, the Special Service was reorganized. GUSS was abolished, and its functions were transferred to the Eighth Directorate of the USSR Ministry of Internal Affairs. With the formation of the State Security Committee (KGB) at the Council of Ministers of the USSR in 1954, the Eighth Main Directorate was recreated, to which the functions of the Special Service were transferred.[70] The state education projects continued until the breakup of the Soviet Union.[71] Although the names of the departments dealing with cryptography and code breaking were changed several times between 1917 and 1991, their tasks stayed the same until the collapse of the Soviet Union. The Soviet school of cryptography and services was the ancestor of cyber education and certain divisions of the security institutions in contemporary Russia. The initial knowledge regarding cybersecurity of several Russian experts and employees of the security services was formulated during the Soviet era.

*"Revolutionary wars"—the red insurgency*

The existence of nuclear weapons on both sides deterred the Soviet Union and the United States from becoming directly involved in military conflicts, that is, from using military force against each other, during the Cold War. However, both superpowers tested each other's battle capabilities not within their borders but in third countries. In this regard, Latin America, the Middle East, Southeast Asia, and Africa were the battlefields of the two superpowers. Both mainly supported their own proxies in several conflicts during the Cold War. Besides supporting friendly governments with military equipment and weapons, the main tools they utilized in the conflicts were insurgency, guerrilla warfare, and counterinsurgency. The final aims of which were the change of a regime or the propping up of a friendly government. These tools were the main forms of warfare in Latin America, especially where, in many cases, the Soviet Union supported insurgents and guerrillas while the United States supported the existing governments and counterinsurgency operations.

The interest of Moscow in challenging the United States in its own backyard was first aroused at the end of the 1950s by the emergence of a new generation of Latin American revolutionary leaders. Among them, Fidel Castro and Che Guevara, leaders of the Cuban Revolution, played key roles. Both were charismatic leaders through whom the Soviet leadership started to "export socialist revolutions" to the United States' backyard. Fidel Castro's eventual emergence, with some hesitation, as a reliable pro-Moscow loyalist was of immense importance for both Soviet foreign policy and intelligence institutions (mainly KGB and also GRU) operations.[72] It should be noted that from the very beginning, the KGB and GRU, rather than the foreign ministry, played the lead role in affairs with Latin America. As the (at that time) head of the Soviet Union, Nikita Khrushchev, was later informed, the first Soviet ambassador to Castro's Cuba "turned out to be unsuited for service in a country just emerging from a revolution" and had to be replaced by the KGB resident, who proved to be "an excellent choice."[73] A Lieutenant-General (retired) of the KGB Nikolai Leonov, who was one of the key KGB specialists on Latin America and who was in close relations with Cuban revolutionary leaders before they came to power, described how he had worked with several other political leaders in Latin America and how the Soviets helped them "to improve their knowledge on Marxism and Leninism."[74]

The contacts with Salvador Allende before his election as Chile's president in 1970 and with Juan and Isabel Peron before their return to Argentina in 1973 were also realized by KGB residents rather than Soviet diplomats. The KGB officers started contact with the Sandinistas almost two decades prior to their conquest of power in Nicaragua in 1979. According to Leonov, the initiative often came from the KGB's Latin American experts:

> We ourselves developed the program of our actions, guiding ourselves ... I might as well admit that sometimes we also wanted to attract attention to ourselves, to present our work as highly significant. This was to protect the Latin American direction in intelligence from withering away and dying out. On the whole we managed to convince the KGB leadership that Latin America represented a politically attractive springboard, where anti-American feeling was strong ....[75]

There are several cases—not only in Latin America—where the Soviet intelligence organizations supported, sometimes initiated, and even participated in regime changes or coup d'états during the Cold War. Moreover, sometimes the Soviets prepared such operations and realized several activities for final regime change operations years before they happened. In some cases, they were successful, but there were failures as well. In Nicaragua in the 1970s, the guerrillas, the Sandinistas, were trained and financed by the Soviet intelligence service.[76]

Support for radical groups, which used terrorist acts as one of the methods of their political struggle, was practiced by the Soviet security institutions too. In the early 1970s the KGB used organizations, which practiced terrorist methods as proxies in the Middle East and Europe. Andrew and Mitrokhin stress that while refusing to deal directly with either Carlos Jackal or Abu Nidal, the KGB leadership was content for other Socialist bloc intelligence agencies, such as the East German and Syrian secret services, to do so.[77]

## The Soviet Union's influence on contemporary Russia's security policy

Since the beginning formations of post-Soviet Russia's security policy in the 1990s, the Soviet Union's legacy has played a key role. It was especially emphasized during Putin's presidency. While simultaneously strengthening the positions of former Soviet security organization officers, the revitalization of Soviet practices in Russia's security policies also increased. There are a number of contemporary Russian security methods that are close, similar, or, in some cases, even the exact same as those previously utilized by the Soviets. For an explanation regarding how the Soviet Union's legacy has had such a huge influence on contemporary Russia's security policy, we are going to compare Russia's contemporary and the Soviet Union's approaches to realizing state security policies.

One of the more interesting cases which may be very useful in understanding the Soviet legacy in contemporary Russia's security institutions approaches is the case of medical scholars in 1947—one of Stalin's campaigns dubbed as the fight against "sycophancy" and cosmopolitanism. One of the most striking cases was against professors N. G. Klyueva and G. I. Roskin at the very beginning of the Cold War. Klyueva and Roskin created an effective, as they believed, medicine against cancer—"KR" (Krutsin). Experts from the United States were interested in the research, and they wanted to publish their book and offer a program of joint research. It should be noted that an agreement (with the permission of the Soviet authorities) was reached, and in November 1946, academician-secretary of the Academy of Medical Sciences V.V. Parin visited the United States. Instructed by the deputy minister of health, he took the manuscript of Klyueva and Roskin's book and an ampoule with the medicine to the American scientists. These caused Stalin's sharp discontent. Upon his return in early 1947, Parin was arrested and sentenced to 25 years for "treason against the Fatherland." Stalin personally pushed to launch the campaign against the "sycophancy" of the Soviet intelligentsia before the "bourgeois culture of the West" and the importance of "educating the Soviet intelligentsia in the spirit of Soviet patriotism." In 1947, the campaign covered the whole country. In the same year, the resolution on the establishment of "Courts of Honors" within USSR ministries and central departments was accepted by the

Political Bureau of the Central Committee of the All-Union Communist Party (Bolsheviks).[78]

According to a classified letter of the Central Committee of the CPSU (b) on the case of professors Klyueva and Roskin, "with the connivance of the former minister of health Miterev and with the active assistance of the American spy—the former secretary of the Academy of Medical Sciences Parin," Klyueva and Roskin passed to the United States information on the aforementioned medicine. The letter, which was mainly addressed to Stalin, stressed that the professors, "being doubtful citizens of the USSR, guided by considerations of personal fame and cheap popularity abroad, they could not resist the harassment of American intelligence officers and handed over to the Americans the scientific discovery, owned by the Soviet state, the Soviet people ... Neglecting the vital interests of the state and the people, forgetting about their duty to the Fatherland, which surrounded their work with care and attention, Klyueva and Roskin deprived Soviet science of priority (superiority) in this discovery and caused serious damage to the state interests of the Soviet Union," concluded the letter.[79]

The main reasons for Stalin's grievances and declaration of "the fight against cosmopolitanism" were sentiments and hopes within society for the liberalization of the regime following victory in the Second World War. Such thoughts were especially popular among the intelligentsia. In the struggle against the intelligentsia, Stalin resorted to sophisticated forms of ideological pressure. One of them was the campaign to organize the "honor courts" initiated by a resolution of the Central Committee of the CPSU (b) regarding the case of Klyueva and Rosskin and widespread in the next two years. Those who appeared before the "courts of honors" were accused of "sycophancy" before foreign countries and of anti-patriotism, which, according to official propaganda, directly led to "rootless cosmopolitanism."[80]

The campaign against cosmopolitanism meant the further self-isolation of the country. According to archival documents, the Communist Party leadership consistently led the country toward a drastic restriction in the exchange of mutual information, a limitation, and finally an almost complete rupture of the cultural and scientific ties between the USSR and the West.[81] V. V. Parin, N. G. Klyueva, G. I. Roskin, and the Minister of Health, G. A. Miterev, were victims of a political game by the Soviet leadership known as "the struggle against cosmopolitanism." The accusation made against them regarding the disclosure of state secrets (backdating all the work on cancer was classified) was arbitrarily qualified differently for each of the accused. V.V. Parin was subjected to crueler measures, including imprisonment and exile.[82]

Following the developments around the so-called "KR case," it is possible to better understand the decision-making mechanism in the Soviet leadership's security policies. The formation of the "case" by the apparatus of the Central Committee of the CPSU (b) reveals that at its essence, it was a means of influencing public consciousness and a tool for managing public opinion in the Soviet Union. Interestingly, similar cases can be found in contemporary Russia.

In recent years, Russian security organizations have declared a witch hunt against "spies of hostile states." This ranges from senior academics to members of anarchist youth organizations. Many of these sophisticated indictments and methods are not new. They are linked to the legacies of the Soviet era, with some additional new battlegrounds, such as social networks and the Internet in general.[83]

In 2018, the FSB arrested several individuals and searched a research facility controlled by the country's space agency, ROSCOSMOS, over the suspected leak of secrets about new hypersonic weapons to Western states.[84] As a result, 74-year-old scientist Viktor Kudryavtsev, an employee of the Central Scientific-Research Institute of Mechanical Engineering, was arrested. According to the FSB, Kudryavtsev passed classified technical information used in the design of hypersonic weapons (*Avangard* and *Kinzhal* missiles) through the von Karman Institute for Fluid Dynamics to NATO countries, including the United States.[85] It should be noted that several Russian and European scientific organizations conducted joint research within the framework of one of the European Union's FP7 projects, which was supported by an EU grant and confirmed by the Russian government, in 2011–2013.[86] The results of the research would be used in industry and aerospace missions. Viktor Kudryavtsev helped to coordinate this research.

In 2016, Vladimir Lapygin, a 76-year-old researcher who was Kudryavtsev's boss at the same institution, was jailed for seven years, also for treason. Kudryavtsev denied the accusations.[87] According to the prosecution, Kudryavtsev sent classified information to Belgian Institute researcher Patrick Rambo. According to the RBC, Rambo is a representative of the institute, which is the subject of the investigation and which, according to the FSB, is a "NATO structure." Kudryavtsev's lawyer, Ivan Pavlov, notes that the issue is not that intelligence agencies consider Rambo a spy but that the FSB considers the von Karman Institute an enemy espionage organization. A piece of evidence "proving" his guilt is an email found in the spam folder of Kudryavtsev's email account that allegedly approved an American residence permit (green card) for him. In fact, said Pavlov, this was a rather standard email scam.[88]

Another arrested academic is 64-year-old Andrey Temirev. According to his lawyer, the scientist from Novocherkassk was charged with passing data, together with a graduate student from Vietnam, about the equipment he created in the design office of IRIS (Intelligent Robust Integrated Systems). According to the intelligence services, Temirev sent secret information to Vietnam. "But this is all in the public domain, in books that are in every library," said the lawyer.[89] It should be noted that there may be more current cases that are hidden from the public. Moreover, the policies regarding the classification of information regarding such cases have been updated. Following the arrests in July 2018, Moscow court databases no longer display the names of those accused of treason and espionage in relation to the decision.[90]

One of the reasons for what is happening can be found in the amendments to Article 275 of the Criminal Code adopted in 2012. According to these, not only is the disclosure of state secrets considered treason but also the provision of "consulting services to other states." Judging by what little is known about the cases brought under Article 275, it is not necessary for a potential "criminal" to be a carrier of state secrets or to have secret information—simply communicating with foreigners is enough. There is one similar feature in most treason cases: the indicted or defendant cannot get access to full protection. Duty lawyers often work on these cases and are usually on the side of the investigation, persuading the defendants to plead guilty. The lawyers and former defendants in Article 275 cases interviewed by Medusa believe that the level of espionage increases in "troubled times" of economic crisis and local conflicts. The first surge in criminal cases of treason in Russia began in the late 1990s.[91]

According to the secretary of the committee for the protection of scientists, Ernest Cherny, the wave of persecution of "traitors" and "spies" is linked to tensions in relations between Russia and the West, specifically the United States. But security organizations have their own interests as well. "The motives of the FSB and the investigators are, as a rule, self-serving: for such cases they get new titles, awards … People try their best, understanding that no one from outside can monitor the case—all trials are classified."[92]

However, arrests of scholars on accusations of treason are continuing. Seventy-nine-year-old professor and president of the Arctic Academy, Valery Mitko was detained in 2020 while living under house arrest. According to investigators, he collected secret data on the instructions of the Chinese special services. Reportedly data related to developments in the field of hydroacoustics. His lawyer alleges that the case concerns a period of "lecturing to students at a university in China." Mitko was teaching at Dalian Maritime University between 2016 and 2020 as a visiting professor. He pointed out that Russia should pay special attention to the Arctic in order to keep up with the West. At the same time, he criticized the attitude of mining companies from different countries when it came to the Arctic environment when working with deposits where Russian Rosneft is also involved.[93] The 81-year-old professor faced 12–20 years in prison.[94] He died under house arrest in October 2022.

In 2021, several scholars involved in projects related to hypersonic technologies, including the general director and chief designer of the Scientific Research Enterprise of Hypersonic Systems, were arrested on charges of treason.[95] A tragic case occurred when well-known scholar Dmitry Kolker from Novosibirsk died in a Moscow pre-trial detention center. The 54-year-old physicist suffering from cancer was taken straight from the hospital on suspicion of treason by the FSB and departed for Moscow in June 2022.[96] Moreover, after Kolker, two more scholars in Novosibirsk were arrested, including the head of the Novosibirsk Institute of Theoretical and Applied Mechanics, Oleksandr Shiplyuk. All of them were arrested for allegedly transferring information about hypersonic weapons abroad.[97]

In addition to the increasing number of cases of state treason, in 2019, the Russian Ministry of Education and Science sent an official order to the universities and institutes with strict recommendations regarding contacts with foreigners. The document stated that at least two Russian scientists should be present at any meeting with foreigners. At the same time, such contacts outside of working hours are possible only with the permission of management, and following the meeting, the researchers must draw up a report with a brief description of the conversation, attaching scans of the participants' passports.[98] A year later, Russian President

Vladimir Putin signed the law "On amendments to Article 7 of the Federal Security Service." It prohibits the publication and dissemination of materials about the FSB without the permission of the leadership of the service.[99]

All of these are reminiscent of the developments in the Soviet Union of the 1950s, and since the invasion of Ukraine in 2022, the control that the security institutions exert over Russian society is only expected to increase. There are indeed already signs of this happening. However, it seems the Russian leadership did not learn well from the Soviet Union's experience. Despite tough measures focused on controlling society and it's witch hunt against foreign spies, the Soviet Union did not win the competition with the West.

## The legacy of the Soviet's asymmetric response

The Soviet influence on Russia's external security policy can also be found in its attitudes toward strategic deterrence issues. One of the more striking cases has been ongoing in recent years. Russia tried to respond to the United States' missile defense capabilities with asymmetric strategies. Such approaches can be readily found in Soviet history. This is mainly about Russia's new intercontinental and other hypersonic missile systems, which President Putin mentioned in his address to the Federal Assembly in 2018. Putin presented the newest types of Russian weapons, which "have no analogues" in the world during his address. These are the *Sarmat* intercontinental missile system, underwater UAVs, a cruise missile with a nuclear power plant, the *Kinzhal* (the Dagger) high-precision missile system, a laser, and hypersonic weapons. Putin stressed that the West did not really want to discuss with Russia its warnings about "the violation of strategic balance." According to Putin, at the time Moscow declared to NATO members that they would take the necessary measures "to neutralize the threats associated with the deployment of the US global missile defense system … Nobody listened to us. Listen now," Putin said.[100]

The system causing the most concern is a nuclear-powered and nuclear-armed cruise missile with intercontinental range, though the Status-6, a nuclear-powered and nuclear-armed long-range underwater vehicle, has also drawn some attention. One may ask why Russia, which has thousands of deployed strategic nuclear warheads already able to be delivered from existing ballistic and cruise missile systems, would invest in these new systems? According to Austin Long, the answer is deeply rooted in two of the defining events of modern Russian and Soviet history—the Great Patriotic War (or World War II) and the Cold War. "Far from being crazy, these 'new' Russian nuclear weapons have their origin in an abiding fear and respect for US nuclear and missile defense capabilities," emphasizes Long.[101] The lessons of the first years of the war with Germany revealed weaknesses of the Soviet Army, especially in air defense and during the Cold War the threat of nuclear strikes by a stronger adversary, the United States, pushed the Soviet political and military leadership to look for asymmetric responses for strategic defenses. In this regard, the Soviet Union started its nuclear arms program and created in 1950 a research and development organization focused on surface-to-air missiles that was essentially coequal with the atomic bomb and offensive missile projects. These missile programs were key to defending against high-flying nuclear bombers and, in the future, ballistic missiles.[102] The Soviets were well aware of the limits of both their offensive and defensive forces relative to the Americans. The United States in the mid-1960s had a vastly more capable offensive nuclear force and if it invested as extensively in missile defense as the Soviets had, it would likely have had a significant advantage in that area as well.[103] A 1966 CIA estimate on likely Soviet responses to various proposed US missile defense deployments, concluded:

> While we worry about their strengths and our vulnerabilities, they worry about our strengths and their vulnerabilities ... From their point of view either the [missile defense] Posture A or the Posture B program would threaten eventually to degrade the deterrent power of their strategic attack forces.[104]

Even in early 1980s, Soviet leadership was scared that the United States was developing the capability to neutralize the Soviet strategic deterrence with offensive strikes.[105] At that time, the head of the KGB—and shortly thereafter the head of the state—Yuri Andropov in a meeting with the leadership of the Stasi in 1981 stated that "the US is preparing for war but it is not willing to start a war":

> They are not building the factories and palaces in order to destroy them. They strive for military superiority in order to "check" us and then declare "checkmate" against us without starting a war. Maybe I am wrong. This is what they want, but we will not allow it.[106]

In 1983, US President Ronald Reagan announced the Strategic Defense Initiative (SDI), a missile defense program commonly known as the Star Wars Program. The SDI was one of the most controversial US projects of the Cold War. Initiated in 1983, it was a research program aimed at the development of a range of advanced missile defense technologies directed against the Soviet Union. It was intended to "counter the awesome Soviet missile threat" by giving the United States the capability "to intercept and destroy strategic ballistic missiles before they reached [US] soil."[107]

For the Soviets, being already concerned about US technical advantages in missile defense, the Strategic Defense Initiative was an obvious additional advantage of existing US capabilities to attack Soviet nuclear forces. According to some Soviet calculations, by the mid-1990s, when US nuclear modernization was complete, a highly effective missile defense might reduce the number of targets for a Soviet retaliatory strike by several factors.[108] The Strategic Defense Initiative was perceived by a significant part of the top Soviet leadership not only nervously, but almost hysterically. As academician Georgy Arbatov wrote in his memoirs, evaluating such a reaction from the Soviet leaders, US President Ronald Reagan believed that "there cannot be so bad a weapon against which the Russians are so fiercely protesting."[109]

*The Soviet legacy of Russia's security policy* 103

According to Austin Long, the Soviets began considering ways to neutralize the advantage of US missile defenses with mainly asymmetric approaches. One of these was attacking the space-based components of the system with anti-satellite weapons and building decoys for their existing missiles.[110] The CIA's professional journal notes that "General Secretary Yuri Andropov had considered such options as … developing and deploying underwater missiles that would not be affected by the space-based missile shield."[111] According to a US intelligence assessment in 1984, for countering US missile defenses, the Soviets might eventually pursue "nuclear powered intercontinental cruise missiles," which "would have a greater payload capability, range, and ability to deploy advanced defensive electronics than present small cruise missiles."[112]

Despite the fact that the majority of the military elite were adherents of symmetric responses to Reagan's initiative, the Soviet leadership supported an asymmetric strategy. Their "asymmetric response" to the US Strategic Defense Initiative program put forward by the US President in 1983 was one of the most interesting examples of an integrated strategy of their political-military plan. It included diplomatic and political-propaganda activities, and specific programs for the development of weapons systems and the scientific and technical base for them.

The components of the Soviet "asymmetric strategy" were developed in a number of research centers. It was developed in the Academy of Sciences of the USSR and in other institutions. For instance, among them were the Central Research Institute of Machine Building [*Tsentral'nyy nauchno-issledovatel'skiy institut mashinostroyeniya*TsNIImash] of the Ministry of General Engineering of the USSR and 4th Central Research Institute of the Ministry of Defense, and a number of other military research institutes. The main work on designing the strategy on an interdisciplinary basis was done by a group of scholars and specialists led by the vice president of the Academy of Sciences, academician Evgeny P. Velikhov. It was a unique interdisciplinary team. Velikhov's group included physicists, mathematicians, chemists, rocket engineers, spacecraft specialists, political scientists, economists, and professional military personnel.[113]

According to Andrei Kokoshin, one of the leaders of the strategy developers, the core of the "asymmetric response" was primarily based on the fact that the United States was deploying a multi-echelon missile defense (including with space capabilities) using various, "including the 'exotic' anti-ballistic missile defense systems, such as various types of directional energy transfer weapons- neutral particle accelerators, free electron lasers, excimer lasers, x-ray lasers, etc., electrodynamic mass accelerators, 'electromagnetic guns,' etc., providing for the possibility of 'unacceptable damage.'"[114] For this, diverse scenarios on the massive use of nuclear weapons by the Soviet Union were examined in order to pursue the most effective disarming and "decapitating strikes," which might disable the strategic nuclear weapons of the adversary and its control system. Computer modeling simultaneously played an important role.[115]

A special computer modeling laboratory, headed by a well-known Soviet specialist on artificial intelligence, V. M. Sergeev was also subordinated to Kokoshin. According to Kokoshin, the treatise of the ancient Chinese theorist and strategist

Sun Tzu played an important role in the formation of the "ideology of asymmetry" both in the military-technical and in the political psychological dimension. This treatise, stresses Kokoshin, is "imbued with a spirit of asymmetry." The ideas of asymmetry formed the basis for a series of scientific and technical reports prepared by the Velikhov group.[116]

It should be noted that there are similar ongoing weapon programs in contemporary Russia. Worries about the development of US space capabilities have led Russia to actively work on its anti-satellite capabilities in recent years.[117]

Considering the Soviet experience regarding strategic deterrence, Long concludes that the Soviet leadership, fearful of renewed missile defense competition and US nuclear modernization, began to mull exactly the sort of systems Putin revealed in March 2018:

> The Soviets doubted they could keep up in either competition—much less both—so asymmetric responses were their only hope. Within a few years the Cold War wound down peacefully, but historical experiences continued to underlie Soviet—now Russian—fears of missile defense.[118]

Contemporary Russia uses any available approach in its competition with their adversaries, as did the Soviets. In this regard, the Soviet leadership sometimes even evaded their official ideological obligations. During the Cold War, to achieve an advantage in their struggle with the United States in the Middle East, the Soviet political leadership avoided tough ideological attitudes toward the countries of the region. The dramatic loss of US confidence in dealing with the Muslim world after the fall of its ally, the Shah of Iran, and the rise of Ayatollah Khomeini was epitomized by the decision of the Carter administration not to send any congratulations to Muslim leaders to celebrate the 1,400th anniversary of Islam in 1979, for fear that it would somehow cause offense. The Soviet Union, by contrast, despite its official atheism, flooded Arab capitals with messages of congratulations.[119] Similar practices can be found in contemporary Russian foreign policy. Moscow poses itself as a defender of Christian values in the West, while at the same time it promotes itself as a defender of Muslim countries in the Middle East from US interventions and maintains a strategic partnership with Iran.

Russia's political and military leadership learned from their experiences in Afghanistan and the first war in Chechnya that, in fact, their military failures in both were attributable to the paradoxes of asymmetric conflict. According to Robert M. Cassidy, these paradoxes come into play whenever a great power faces a preindustrial and semifeudal enemy who is intrinsically compelled to mitigate the great power's numerous advantages with cunning and asymmetry.

"In other words, great powers often do poorly in small wars simply because they are great powers that must embrace a big-war paradigm by necessity."[120] As put by Cassidy, the goals in Chechnya, at the start of military operations in 1994, were almost the same as the goals sought in Afghanistan years earlier, to implant a pro-Russian government and to stabilize the Chechen Republic. Russian forces pulled out of Chechnya almost two years later after suffering close to 6,000 killed, having failed to meet their objectives just as Soviet forces had withdrawn in 1989 after suffering close to 14,000 killed, leaving behind a very precarious pro-Soviet government and an ongoing civil war in Afghanistan.[121]

The lesson as to how a superpower such as the Soviet Union could fail to win a small war in Afghanistan and also how Russia, a declining great power, failed to win the first war in Chechnya encouraged Russia's leadership to rely on asymmetric approaches in its security policy in light of its decreased economic and military capabilities of the 1990s. However, the performance of the Russian military during the invasion of Ukraine in 2022 showed that Russia did not or could not fully use its required strategic and tactical approaches against an asymmetric adversary.

## Summary

> The main method in the current struggle is political-ideological subversion. We were both absolutely right [in predicting this]. Yet the forms of political-ideological subversion keep changing. The Polish events are a case in point. They prove the effectiveness of US special services in the broadest sense. They want to differentiate among the socialist states and foment nationalism. They are backing away from individuals such as Sakharov, and are trying to infiltrate the working class. They are trying to fuel unrest and exploit weaknesses in our economy—where our economists are not flexible enough and have forgotten how to work with the people.
>
> Yuri Andropov, Chairman of the KGB, July 11, 1981, Moscow[122]

The use of asymmetric approaches in the security and foreign policies of the Soviet Union was based on the Soviet leadership's understanding of its weaknesses and fear of the economic and military capabilities of its stronger adversary. It was also initiated and justified by the official state ideology, Marxism-Leninism. Moreover, the economic weaknesses which accompanied the USSR from its establishment until its breakup also made asymmetric approaches in the security policy preferable for Moscow. They were preferable even during the Soviet Union's comparatively strong period between the 1960s and 1980s, when the existence of nuclear weapons on both sides deterred any direct war engagement, that is, conventional strategies, but such a situation encouraged both sides to use asymmetric methods. Moreover, Moscow and Washington accepted the fact that direct military conflict would result in tremendous military and civilian casualties and economic losses, if not outright Armageddon. Such possibilities pushed the two superpowers to fight each other indirectly, using asymmetric methods and strategies. In that competition, the battlefields were chosen in the territory of third countries, and even, at least officially, the warring sides also had to be made up of third-party fighters. In this regard, Moscow and Washington used proxy wars to weaken or diminish the influence of each other in several regions.

The goal of this chapter was to explain why, how, and what kind of asymmetric approaches were used by the Soviet Union and how their legacies influence contemporary Russia's security policy. Analyzing the main asymmetric methods used by Moscow during the USSR, the chapter emphasized information warfare, cryptography or code breaking, insurgency or guerrilla warfare, and the use of asymmetric strategies in conventional military deterrence. The chapter also analyzed other asymmetric warfare approaches of the Soviet Union's security policy. Similarities between Soviet and contemporary Russian security policies were also discussed.

The chapter argued that since the formation of post-Soviet Russia's security policy in the 1990s, the Soviet Union's legacy has played a key role. There is even a special emphasis on it during Putin's presidency. Since strengthening the positions of former Soviet security organization officers in the upper echelons of the political elite, the revitalization of Soviet practices in Russia's security policies has increased. There are a number of cases in contemporary Russian security approaches which are similar—and in some cases even the same—as the methods utilized by the Soviet Union. For explanations of this, examples of Russia's contemporary and the Soviet Union's security policies were compared.

## Notes

1 Chueh-Yuan, Wang (1976) *The Russians' Communists Strategies and Tactics for World Revolution*, World Anti-Communist League. China, Chapter: Asian Peoples' Anti-Communist League, Republic of China, Pamphlet XXII, no. 189, pp. 21–22.
2 Ibid., p 33.
3 Ibid., pp. 33–34.
4 Wang Chueh-Yuan (1976) *The Russians' Communists Strategies and Tactics for World Revolution* …, p. 20.
5 Kennan, George Frost (1961) *Russia and the West under Lenin and Stalin*. Boston; Toronto: Little, Brown and Company, p. 389.
6 Ibid.
7 Stalin, Joseph. V. (1925) "The Fourteenth Congress of the C.P. S.U. (B.): Political Report of the Central Committee", 1925, December 18–31. *Works*, Vol. 7, 1925, https://www.marxists.org/reference/archive/stalin/works/1925/12/18.htm.
8 Andrew, Christopher and Mitrokhin, Vasili (2005) *The world was going our way*. New York: Basic Books.
9 Kennan, George Frost (1961) *Russia and the West under Lenin and Stalin* …, p. 395.
10 Ibid.
11 Ibid.
12 Zimmerman, William (1969) *Soviet perspectives on international relations: 1956–1967*. Princeton: Princeton University Press, p. 161.
13 Federalnoe Sluzhba Bezopasnosti – FSB. "Istoria sozdania", http://www.fsb.ru/fsb/history.htm.
14 Sinitsin, Igor Yeliseevich (2015) *Andropov vblizi. Vospominania o vremenakh ottepeli I zastoia*. Electron book format, LitMir.ru, p. 80, https://www.litmir.me/br/?b=263687&p=80.
15 Ibid.
16 Amalrik, Andrei (1970) *Prosushchestvuet li Sovetskii Soyuz do 1984 goda?*. Amsterdam: Fond imeny Gertsena, p. 32.
17 Pipes, Richard (1974) *Russia under the old regime*. New York: Charles Scribner's Sons, pp. 109–110.
18 Damaskin, Igor (2004) *Stalin i razvedka*, Moskva: Veche, Glava 2. Nachalo, Biblioteka v elektronnoi formate fb2, e-book, http://litresp.ru/chitat/ru/%D0%94/damaskin-igorj-anatoljevich/stalin-i-razvedka.

## The Soviet legacy of Russia's security policy 107

19 Gorbunov, Yevgenii A. (2018) *Stalin i GRU*, Moskva: Rodina, e-book, https://history.wikireading.ru/186233.
20 Ibid.
21 Ibid.
22 Gorbunov, Yevgenii A. (2018) *Stalin i GRU ...*
23 Zhirnov, Yevgenii (2003) "Dezinformbyuro-80 let sovetskoy sluzhbe dezinformatsii", gazeta *"Kommersant"*, N 2, January 13, p. 7.
24 *Postanovleniye Politbyuro TSK RKP(b)* «O dezinformatsii» 1) 11.01.1923, PB № 43/82, APRF. F. 3. Op. 58. D. 2. L. 18, 129–130. Postanovleniye – podlinnik, predlozheniya – kopiya. Opubl.: Lubyanka. Stalin i VCHK–GPU–OGPU–NKVD. Yanvar' 1922 – dekabr' 1936. M., 2003. p. 73, online http://hrono.ru/dokum/192_dok/19230111ck.php.
25 Gorbunov, Yevgeniy (2006) "Faktor stabil'nosti – strategicheskaya dezinformatsiya", *"Nezavisomaya Gazeta"*, 12 May 2006, http://nvo.ng.ru/spforces/2006-05-12/7_spy.html.
26 Gorbunov, Yevgenii A. (2018) *Stalin i GRU ...*
27 Gorbunov, Yevgenii A. (2018) *Stalin i GRU ...*
28 Ibid.
29 *Doklad nachrazvedupra Shtaba RKKA YA.K. Berzina o rabote po dezinformatsii predsedatelyu Revvoyensoveta SSSR M.V. Frunze*, № 0226/st, Sovershenno sekretno, RGVA. F. 33987. Op.3. D. 99. L. 490–501. Podlinnik, 21.01.1925, available online at: http://www.hrono.info/dokum/192_dok/19250121berz.php.
30 Gorbunov, Yevgenii A. (2018) *Stalin i GRU ...*
31 *Doklad nachrazvedupra Shtaba RKKA YA.K. Berzina o rabote po dezinformatsii ...*
32 Ibid.
33 Yakovets E. N. (2013) "Osnovnyye napravleniya organizatsionnoy i pravovoy zashchity gosudarstvennoy tayny v Sovetskoy Rossii", *Istoriya gosudarstva i prava*, N 6, https://Centre-bereg.ru/h261.html.
34 Zhirnov, Yevgenii (2003) "Dezinformbyuro-80 let sovetskoy sluzhbe dezinformatsii", *Kommersant*, N 2, 13 January 2003, p. 7.
35 Ibid.
36 Sluzhba vneshney razvedki Rossiyskoi Federatsii (2019) "Operatsiya "Trest", Operatsiya 'Sindikat-2', Stanovlenie vneshnei razvedki (1921–1925), http://svr.gov.ru/history/stage02.htm; See also: Ioffe G. (1998) "Smertel'naya 'igra': operatsiya 'Trest'", *Nauka i Zhizn*, № 3, 1998, https://www.nkj.ru/archive/articles/10389/.
37 Zhirnov, Yevgenii (2003) "Dezinformbyuro-80 let sovetskoy sluzhbe dezinformatsii" ...
38 Ibid.
39 Pirnie, Bruce R. (Major) (1985) *Soviet Deception Operations during World War II*, Analysis Branch U.S. Army Centre of Military History, Washington, D.C., p. 1, online https://apps.dtic.mil/dtic/tr/fulltext/u2/a165980.pdf.
40 Ibid., p. 2.
41 Ibid.
42 Ibid.
43 Sever, Vladimir (2008) *Istoriya KGB*, Moskva: Algoritm Vega-Klub Veteranov Sluzhby Bezopasnosti, p. 22, online http://vegaclub.ru/files/istoriya_kgb.pdf.
44 Kolpakidi, Aleksandr and Prokhorov, Dmitrii (2001) *Vneshnyaya razvedka Rossii*, Saint Petersburg and Moscow: Olma-Press Neva, pp. 77–80.
45 Kolpakidi, Aleksandr and Prokhorov, Dmitrii (2001) *Vneshnyaya razvedka Rossii ...*, p. 80.
46 Shevyakin, Aleksandr (2013a) *Sistema bezopasnosti SSSR*, Chapter "Organy Gosudarstvennoy Bezopasnosti", Moscow: Algoritm, e-book, http://indbooks.in/mirror8.ru/?p=404710.
47 Borogan, Irina and Soldatov, Andrey (2007) "Kogda spetssluzhby snova stali pudrit' mozgi Zapadu", *"Ezhdnevnyi Zhurnal'"*, 16 January 2007, online https://web.archive.

org/web/20101207010427/http://www.agentura.ru/press/about/jointprojects/ej/pudritmozgi/.
48 Zhirnov, Yevgenii (2003) "Dezinformbyuro-80 let sovetskoy sluzhbe dezinformatsii" ...
49 Andrew, Christopher and Mitrokhin, Vasili (2005) *The world was going our way* ..., pp. 108–109.
50 Ibid., p. 110.
51 Shevyakin, Aleksandr (2013b) *KGB protiv SSSR. 17 mgnoveniy izmeny*, Moskva: EKSMO, online https://history.wikireading.ru/409740.
52 Eidelman, Tamara (2018) *Kak rabotaet propaganda*. Moskva: Individuum, pp. 80–84.
53 Ibid., pp. 81–82.
54 Ibid.
55 Eidelman, Tamara (2018) *Kak rabotayet propaganda* ..., p. 83.
56 Zhirnov, Yevgenii (2003) "Dezinformbyuro-80 let sovetskoy sluzhbe dezinformatsii" ....
57 *Agitatsionno-propagandistskii otdel TSK RKP(b) VKP(b)*, Spravochnik po istorii Kommunisticheskoi partii i Sovetskogo Soyuza 1898–1991, http://www.knowbysight.info/2_KPSS/00508.asp.
58 Shmidt, O.Yu. (ed.) (1926) *Bol'shaya sovetskaya entsiklopediya*, Tom pervyi, Moskva: A – Akolla, AO Sovetskaya entsiklopediya, Kolonka 423, online http://ponjatija.ru/node/14466.
59 Ibid.
60 Ideologicheskii otdel – Otdel propagandy i agitatsii – Ideologicheskii otdel TsK KPSS, *Spravochnik po istorii Kommunisticheskoi partii i Sovetskogo Soyuza 1898–1991*, http://www.knowbysight.info/2_KPSS/04284.asp.
61 Grebennikov, Vadim (2017) *Kriptologiya i sekretnaya svyaz'. Sdelano v SSSR*, Moskva: Algoritm, p. 144.
62 Sever, Vladimir (2008) *Istoriya KGB* ..., p. 108.
63 Andrew, Christopher and Mitrokhin, Vasili (2005) *The world was going our way* ..., p. 139; For more information on the Soviets code breakers activities see Andrew, Christopher and Mitrokhin, Vasili (1999) *The Sword and the Shield: The Mitrokhin Archive and the Secret History of the KGB* ..., ch. 21.
64 Andrew, Christopher and Mitrokhin, Vasili (1999) *The Sword and the Shield: The Mitrokhin Archive and the Secret History of the KGB,* New York: Basic Books; 1st edition, p. 337.
65 Dzhirkvelov, Ilya (1987) *Secret Servant: My life with KGB and the Soviet Elite*, London: Collins, pp. 211–214.
66 Andrew, Christopher and Mitrokhin, Vasili (2005) *The world was going our way* ..., p. 140.
67 Sever, Vladimir (2008) *Istoriya KGB* ..., pp. 107–108.
68 Sever, Vladimir (2008) *Istoriya KGB* ..., p. 108.
69 Grebennikov, Vadim (2017) *Kriptologiya i sekretnaya svyaz. Sdelano v SSSR*, Moskva: Algoritm, p. 228.
70 Ibid., p. 21.
71 Sever, Vladimir (2008) *Istoriya KGB* ..., p. 22.
72 Andrew, Christopher and Mitrokhin, Vasili (2005) *The world was going our way* ..., p. 29.
73 Talbott, Strobe (ed.) (1970) *Khrushchev Speaks, with introduction and commentary by Edward Crankshaw*, Boston: Little, Brown&Co., pp. 490–491; Andrew, Christopher and Mitrokhin, Vasili (2005) *The world was going our way* ..., p. 29.
74 Leonov, Nikolai (2019) Interview, "Ya opasayus' za sud'bu Kryma, Kaliningrada i Primor'ya", Interviewed by Sarkis Tsaturyan, *Eurasia Daily*, March 29, online https://eadaily.com/ru/news/2019/03/29/nikolay-leonov-ya-opasayus-za-sudbu-kryma-kaliningrada-i-primorya; See also: Andrew, Christopher and Mitrokhin, Vasili (2005) *The world was going our way*. New York: Basic Books, p. 29.
75 Leonov, Nikolai (1995) Likholet'e, *Mezhdunarodnye Otnosheniya*, p.112; Translated in Andrew, Christopher and Mitrokhin, Vasili (2005) *The world was going our way*. New York: Basic Books, p. 30.

76 Andrew, Christopher and Mitrokhin, Vasili (2005) The world was going our way …, p. 117.
77 Andrew, Christopher and Mitrokhin, Vasili (2005) The world was going our way …, p. 144. See also, Follain, John (1998) *Jackal: The Secret Wars of Carlos the Jackal*, London: Weidenfeld & Nicolson.
78 Esakov V. D. and Levina E. S. (1994a) "'Delo KR'. Iz istorii goneniy na sovetskuyu intelligentsiyu", *Kentavr*, № 2. pp. 65–69 and Esakov V. D. and Levina E. S. (1994b) "'Delo KR'. Iz istorii goneniy na sovetskuyu intelligentsiyu", *Kentavr*, № 3. pp. 96–114.; See also, Esakov V. D., Levina E. S.(1994c)"Delo «KR». (Iz istorii goneniy na sovetskuyu intelligentsiyu)", Iz arkhivnykh fondov, Institut Istorii Estestvoznaniya i Iekhniki im. S.I. Vavilova Rossiyskoy akademii nauk (IIET RAN), online available at: http://old.ihst.ru/projects/sohist/papers/kentavr/1994/kr.pdf.
79 Yakovlev A.N., Nadzhafov D.G. and Belousova Z.S. (ed) (2005) *Stalin i kosmopolitizm. 1945–1953. Dokumenty. Agitpropa*. TSK/S11, "Zakrytoye pis'mo TsK VKP(b) o dele professorov Klyuyevoy i Roskina", 16 July 1947, Sekretno, Zakrytoye pis'mo TsK VKP(b), Rossiya. XX vek, Moskva: MFD: Materik, pp. 123–128, online: https://www.alexanderyakovlev.org/fond/issues-doc/69339.
80 Ibid., p. 19.
81 Yakovlev A.N., Nadzhafov D.G. and Belousova Z.S. (ed) (2005) *Stalin i kosmopolitizm. 1945–1953. Dokumenty. Agitpropa* …, p. 20.
82 Levina E. S. (2000) "Krutsin" imeyet svoyu sud'bu …", *Voprosy Znaniya, Estestvennoznaniya i Tekhniki*, Vol. 1, 2000, online: http://vivovoco.astronet.ru/VV/JOURNAL/VIET/LEVINA.HTM.
83 Aliyev, Nurlan (2018) "Hunting "Spies" in Russia: Reasons and Implications for the Political Regime", *Diplomaatia*, International Centre for Defence and Security, No. 184, December 2018, available online at: https://icds.ee/hunting-spies-in-russia-reasons-and-implications-for-the-political-regime/.
84 Kommersant (2018) "FSB uslyshala utechku giperzvuka-Obyski po delu o gosizmene provodyatsya v Koroleve i Moskve", July 20, https://www.kommersant.ru/doc/3690575?tg.
85 Syun, Yurii and Sinergiyev, Ivan (2018) "Uchenyy izmenil s bel'giyskim institutom", August 3, https://www.kommersant.ru/doc/3702851.
86 *EU-Russia Cooperation for Strengthening Space Foundations (SICA)*, CORDIS (Community Research and Development Information Service), cordis.europa.eu/project/rcn/99134_en.html.
87 Alekhina, Margarita and Lymar, Yuliya (2018) "Grant stal gosizmenoy: kak uchenogo obvinili v peredache sekretov Bel'gii", August 3, https://www.rbc.ru/society/02/08/2018/5b62d1cc9a7947410d61e64b?from=newsfeed.
88 Alekhina, Margarita, Inna Sidorkova and Yevgenii Pudovkin (2018) "Pis'ma v NATO: kak FSB sochla institute v Bel'gii 'shpionskoy organizatsiei'", September 17, https://www.rbc.ru/society/17/09/2018/5b9fbe849a794720ccb0d597?utm_source=pushc.
89 Radio Ekho Moskvy (2018) "Stali izvestny novyye podrobnosti aresta 64-letnego uchenogo iz Novocherkasska Alekseya Temireva", July 30, https://echo.msk.ru/news/2249316-echo.html.
90 TASS (2018) "Baza sudov Moskvy perestanet otobrazhat' familii obvinyayemykh v gosizmene i shpionazhe", July 21, https://tass.ru/obschestvo/5392934.
91 Chelishcheva, Vera (2016) "Polezno dlya kar'yery Pochemu v Rossii vse chashche presleduyut za gosudarstvennuyu izmenu", February 4, https://meduza.io/feature/2016/02/04/polezno-dlya-kariery.
92 Chelishcheva, Vera (2018) "'Lyudi starayutsya izo vsekh sil'-V Rossii ocherednaya kampaniya po bor'be s izmennikami i shpionami", July 28, https://www.novayagazeta.ru/articles/2018/07/28/77321-lyudi-starayutsya-izo-vseh-sil.
93 Merzlikin, Pavel (2020) "FSB protiv gosudarstvennika Novoye delo o gosizmene", *Meduza*, June 15, https://meduza.io/feature/2020/06/15/fsb-protiv-gosudarstvennika.

110   *The Soviet legacy of Russia's security policy*

94  BFM.ru (2022) "Prezident Arkticheskoy akademii nauk ne priznal v sude vinu v gosizmene" August 10, https://www.bfm.ru/news/506325.

95  Petrova, Anastasia, Alexey Ramm and Anna Cherepanova (2021) "Novoye giperzvuchaniye: s chem svyazano ocherednoye ugolovnoye delo o gosizmene", *Izvestia*, August 12, https://iz.ru/1206477/anastasiia-petrova-aleksei-ramm-anna-cherepanova/novoe-giperzvuchanie-s-chem-sviazano-ocherednoe-ugolovnoe-delo-o-gosizmene.

96  BBC (2022) "Novosibirskiy fizik Kolker umer v SIZO. FSB uvezla yego iz bol'nitsy na IV stadii raka", *BBC Russian Service*, July 3, https://www.bbc.com/russian/news-62026909?utm.

97  Askerova, Ksenia and Vladislav Trifonov (2022) "Direktor Instituta teoreticheskoy i prikladnoy mekhaniki RAN Shiplyuk arestovan za gosizmenu", *Kommersant*, August 5, https://www.kommersant.ru/doc/5501207.

98  Merzlikin, Pavel (2019) "Minobrnauki pytayetsya ogranichit' kontakty uchenykh s inostrantsami. Uchenyye vspominayut sovetskiye vremena; chinovniki govoryat, chto eto 'prosto rekomendatsii'", *Meduza*, August 14, https://meduza.io/feature/2019/08/14/minobrnauki-pytaetsya-ogranichit-kontakty-uchenyh-s-inostrantsami-uchenye-vspominayut-sovetskie-vremena-chinovniki-govoryat-chto-eto-prosto-rekomendatsii.

99  Official Internet portal of legal information (2020) Federal'nyy zakon ot 31.07.2020 № 279-FZ "O vnesenii izmeneniy v stat'yu 7 Federal'nogo zakona "O federal'noy sluzhbe bezopasnosti", http://publication.pravo.gov.ru/Document/View/0001202007310049?index=1&rangeSize=1.

100  Putin, Vladimir (2018) "Poslaniye Prezidenta Federal'nomu Sobraniyu", March 1, http://kremlin.ru/events/president/news/56957.

101  Long, Austin (2018) "Red Glare: the origin and implications of Russia's 'new' nuclear weapons", March 26, *War on the Rocks*, online: https://warontherocks.com/2018/03/red-glare-the-origin-and-implications-of-russias-new-nuclear-weapons/.

102  Gruntman, Mike (2016) "Intercept 1961: from air defence Sa-1 to missile defence system A", *Proceedings of the IEEE*, Vol. 104, No. 4, April 2016, pp. 883–888, DOI: 10.1109/JPROC.2016.2537023; See also Holloway, David (1996) *Stalin and the Bomb – The Soviet Union and Atomic Energy, 1939–1956*, New Haven: Yale University Press.

103  Long, Austin (2018) "Red Glare: the origin and implications of Russia's 'new' nuclear weapons" …

104  Central Intelligence Agency, Office of National Estimates (1966) "Soviet Reactions to a US Decision to Deploy ABM Defences", 10 December 1966, online: https://www.cia.gov/library/readingroom/docs/CIA-RDP79R00967A001000070003-1.pdf.

105  Green, Brendan R. and Long, Austin (2017) "The MAD Who Wasn't There: Soviet Reactions to the Late Cold War Nuclear Balance", *Security Studies*, Volume 26, 2017, Issue 4, pp. 606–641, DOI:10.1080/09636412.2017.1331639.

106  The Wilson Centre Digital Archive, *Stasi note on meeting between minister Mielke and KGB chairman Andropov*, 11 July 1981, online: https://digitalarchive.wilsonCentre.org/document/115717.

107  Podvig, Pavel (2017) "Did Star Wars Help End the Cold War? Soviet Response to the SDI Program", *Science & Global Security*, Vol. 25, Issue 1, p. 3, DOI: 10.1080/08929882.2017.1273665.

108  Long, Austin (2018) "Red Glare: the origin and implications of Russia's 'new' nuclear weapons" …

109  Arbatov, Georgy. A. (2002) *Chelovek sistemy*. Moskva: Vagrius, p. 265.

110  Podvig, Pavel (2017) "Did Star Wars Help End the Cold War? Soviet Response to the SDI Program" …, p. 3.

111  Long, Austin (2018) "Red Glare: the origin and implications of Russia's 'new' nuclear weapons" …

112  The Central Intelligence Agency (1984) "Possible the Soviets Response to the US Strategic Defence Initiative", Interagency Intelligence Assessment, June 27, online https://www.cia.gov/library/readingroom/docs/CIA-RDP86B00420R000701360002-3.pdf.

113 Oznobishchev S.K., Potapov V.YA. and Skokov V.V. (2008) *Kak gotovilsya «asimmetrichnyy otvet» na 'Strategicheskuyu oboronnuyu initsiativu' R. Reygana: Velikhov, Kokoshin i drugiye*. Moskva: LENAND, online at: http://lawinrussia.ru/content/kak-gotovilsya-asimmetrichnyy-otvet-na-strategicheskuyu-oboronnuyu-iniciativu-r-reygana.
114 Kokoshin, Andrei (2007) "'Asimmetrichnyy otvet' vs. 'Strategicheskoy oboronnoy initsiativy'", *Mezhdunarodnaya zhizn'*, № 8, https://interaffairs.ru/jauthor/material/1650.
115 Ibid.
116 Oznobishchev S.K., Potapov V.YA. and Skokov V.V. (2008) *Kak gotovilsya «asimmetrichnyy otvet» na 'Strategicheskuyu oboronnuyu initsiativu' R. Reygana: Velikhov, Kokoshin i drugiye* …
117 It is largely discussed in the seventh chapter.
118 Long, Austin (2018) "Red Glare: the origin and implications of Russia's 'new' nuclear weapons" …
119 Rubinstein, Alvin Z. (1990) *Moscow's Third World Strategy*, Princeton, NJ: Princeton University Press, p. 237.
120 Cassidy, Robert M. (2003) *Russia in Afghanistan and Chechnya: military strategic culture and the paradoxes of asymmetric conflicts*. Carlisle Barracks: Strategic Studies Institute – U.S. Army War College, p. v.
121 Ibid., p. 1.
122 The Wilson Centre Digital Archive, *Stasi note on meeting between minister Mielke and KGB chairman Andropov*, 11 July 1981, https://digitalarchive.wilsonCentre.org/document/115717.

## Bibliography

*Agitatsionno-propagandistskii otdel TSK RKP(b) VKP(b)*, Spravochnik po istorii Kommunisticheskoi partii i Sovetskogo Soyuza 1898–1991, available at: http://www.knowbysight.info/2_KPSS/00508.asp, accessed 1 May 2019.

Alekhina, Margarita, and Yuliya Lymar' (2018) "Grant stal gosizmenoy: kak uchenogo obvinili v peredache sekretov Bel'gii", 3 August 2018, available at: https://www.rbc.ru/society/02/08/2018/5b62d1cc9a7947410d61e64b?from=newsfeed, accessed 23 May 2019.

Alekhina, Margarita, Inna Sidorkova, and Yevgenii Pudovkin (2018) "Pis'ma v NATO: kak FSB sochla institute v Bel'gii 'shpionskoy organizatsiei'", 17 September 2018, available at: https://www.rbc.ru/society/17/09/2018/5b9fbe849a794720ccb0d597?utm_source=pushc, accessed 23 May 2019.

Aliyev, Nurlan (2018) "Hunting "Spies" in Russia: Reasons and Implications for the Political Regime", *Diplomaatia*, International Centre for Defence and Security, No. 184, December 2018, available online at: https://icds.ee/hunting-spies-in-russia-reasons-and-implications-for-the-political-regime/, accessed 24 May 2019.

Amalrik, Andrei (1970) *Prosushchestvuet li Sovetskii Soyuz do 1984 goda?* Amsterdam: Fond imeny Gertsena.

Andrew, Christopher, and Vasili Mitrokhin (1999) *The Sword and the Shield: The Mitrokhin Archive and the Secret History of the KGB*, New York: Basic Books; 1st edition.

_____ (2005) *The world was going our way*, New York: Basic Books.

Arbatov, Georgy A. (2002) *Chelovek sistemy*, Moskva: Vagrius.

Askerova, Ksenia, and Vladislav Trifonov (2022) "Direktor Instituta teoreticheskoy i prikladnoy mekhaniki RAN Shiplyuk arestovan za gosizmenu", *Kommersant*, August 5, available at: https://www.kommersant.ru/doc/5501207, accessed 15 August 2022.

BBC (2022) "Novosibirskiy fizik Kolker umer v SIZO. FSB uvezla yego iz bol'nitsy na IV stadii raka", *BBC Russian Service*, July 3, available at: https://www.bbc.com/russian/news-62026909?utm, accessed 15 August 2022.

BFM.ru (2022) "Prezident Arkticheskoy akademii nauk ne priznal v sude vinu v gosizmene" August 10, available at: https://www.bfm.ru/news/506325, accessed 15 August 2022.

Borogan, Irina, and Andrey Soldatov (2007) "Kogda spetssluzhby snova stali pudrit' mozgi Zapadu", *"Ezhdnevnyi Zhurnal"*, 16 January 2007, online available at: https://web.archive.org/web/20101207010427/http://www.agentura.ru/press/about/jointprojects/ej/pudritmozgi/, accessed 30 April 2019.

Cassidy, Robert M. (2003) *Russia in Afghanistan and Chechnya: military strategic culture and the paradoxes of asymmetric conflicts*, Carlisle Barracks: Strategic Studies Institute—U.S. Army War College.

Central Intelligence Agency, Office of National Estimates (1966) "Soviet Reactions to a US Decision to Deploy ABM Defences", 10 December 1966, online available at: https://www.cia.gov/library/readingroom/docs/CIA-RDP79R00967A001000070003-1.pdf, accessed 25 May 2019.

Chelishcheva, Vera (2016) "Polezno dlya kar'yery Pochemu v Rossii vse chashche presleduyut za gosudarstvennuyu izmenu", 4 February 2016, available at: https://meduza.io/feature/2016/02/04/polezno-dlya-kariery, accessed 23 May 2019.

Chelishcheva, Vera (2018) "'Lyudi starayutsya izo vsekh sil'-V Rossii ocherednaya kampaniya po bor'be s izmennikami i shpionami", July 28, available at: https://www.novayagazeta.ru/articles/2018/07/28/77321-lyudi-starayutsya-izo-vseh-sil, accessed 23 May 2019.

Chueh-Yuan, Wang (1976) *The Russians' Communists Strategies and Tactics for World Revolution*, Asian Peoples' Anti-Communist League, Republic of China: World Anti-Communist League, China, Chapter, Pamphlet XXII, no. 189.

Damaskin, Igor' (2004) *Stalin i razvedka*, Moskva: Veche, Glava 2. Nachalo, Biblioteka v elektronnoi formate fb2, e-book, available at: http://litresp.ru/chitat/ru/%D0%94/damaskin-igorj-anatoljevich/stalin-i-razvedka, accessed 1 December 2018.

*Doklad nachrazvedupra Shtaba RKKA YA.K. Berzina o rabote po dezinformatsii predsedatelyu Revvoyensoveta SSSR M.V. Frunze*, № 0226/st, Sovershenno sekretno, RGVA. F. 33987. Op.3. D. 99. L. 490–501. Podlinnik, 21.01.1925, available online at: http://www.hrono.info/dokum/192_dok/19250121berz.php, accessed 13 April 2019.

Dzhirkvelov, Ilya (1987) *Secret Servant: My life with KGB and the Soviet Elite*, London: Collins.

Eidelman, Tamara (2018) *Kak rabotaet propaganda*, Moskva: Individuum.

Esakov, V. D., and E. S. Levina (1994a) "'Delo KR'. Iz istorii goneniy na sovetskuyu intelligentsiyu", *Kentavr*, Vol. 2, pp. 65–69.

_____ (1994b) "'Delo KR'. Iz istorii goneniy na sovetskuyu intelligentsiyu", *Kentavr*, Vol. 3, pp. 96–114.

_____ (1994c) "Delo «KR». (Iz istorii goneniy na sovetskuyu intelligentsiyu)", Iz arkhivnykh fondov, Institut Istorii Estestvoznaniya i Iekhniki im. S.I. Vavilova Rossiyskoy akademii nauk (IIET RAN), available online at: http://old.ihst.ru/projects/sohist/papers/kentavr/1994/kr.pdf, accessed 21 May 2018.

*EU-Russia Cooperation for Strengthening Space Foundations (SICA)*, CORDIS (Community Research and Development Information Service), available at: cordis.europa.eu/project/rcn/99134_en.html, accessed 23 May 2019.

Federalnoe Sluzhba Bezopasnosti – FSB. "Istoria sozdania", available at: http://www.fsb.ru/fsb/history.htm, accessed 5 March 2018.

Follain, John (1998) *Jackal: The Secret Wars of Carlos the Jackal*, London: Weidenfeld & Nicolson.

Grebennikov, Vadim (2017) *Kriptologiya i sekretnaya svyaz'. Sdelano v SSSR*, Moskva: Algorithm.

Green, Brendan R., and Austin Long (2017) "The MAD Who Wasn't There: Soviet Reactions to the Late Cold War Nuclear Balance", *Security Studies*, Vol. 26, No. 4, pp. 606–641. DOI: 10.1080/09636412.2017.1331639.

Gruntman, Mike (2016) "Intercept 1961: from air defence Sa-1 to missile defence system A", *Proceedings of the IEEE*, Vol. 104, No. 4, pp. 883–888. DOI: 10.1109/JPROC.2016.2537023.

Gorbunov, Yevgeniy (2006) "Faktor stabil'nosti – strategicheskaya dezinformatsiya", "*Nezavisomaya Gazeta*", 12 May 2006, http://nvo.ng.ru/spforces/2006-05-12/7_spy.html, accessed 1 April 2019.

Gorbunov, Yevgenii A. (2018) *Stalin i GRU*, Moskva: Rodina, e-book, available at: https://history.wikireading.ru/186233, accessed 15 January 2019.

Holloway, David (1996) *Stalin and the Bomb – The Soviet Union and Atomic Energy, 1939–1956*, New Haven: Yale University Press.

Ideologicheskii otdel – Otdel propagandy i agitatsii – Ideologicheskii otdel TsK KPSS, *Spravochnik po istorii Kommunisticheskoi partii i Sovetskogo Soyuza 1898–1991*, available at: http://www.knowbysight.info/2_KPSS/04284.asp, accessed 1 May 2019.

Ioffe, G. (1998) "Smertel'naya 'igra': operatsiya 'Trest'", *Nauka i Zhizn*, 3, 1998, available at: https://www.nkj.ru/archive/articles/10389/, accessed 14 April 2019.

Kennan, George Frost (1961) *Russia and the West under Lenin and Stalin*, Boston; Toronto: Little, Brown and Company.

Kokoshin, Andrei (2007) "'Asimmetrichnyy otvet' vs. 'Strategicheskoy oboronnoy initsiativy'", *Mezhdunarodnaya zhizn*, 8, 2007, available at: https://interaffairs.ru/jauthor/material/1650, accessed 1 November 2019.

Kolpakidi, Aleksandr, and Dmitrii Prokhorov (2001) *Vneshnyaya razvedka Rossii*, Saint Petersburg and Moscow: Olma-Press Neva.

Kommersant (2018) "FSB uslyshala utechku giperzvuka-Obyski po delu o gosizmene provodyatsya v Koroleve i Moskve", 20 July 2018, available at: https://www.kommersant.ru/doc/3690575?tg, accessed 23 May 2019.

Leonov, Nikolai (1995) Likholet'e, *Mezhdunarodnye Otnosheniya*.

_____ (2019) Interview, "Ya opasayus' za sud'bu Kryma, Kaliningrada i Primor'ya", Interviewed by Sarkis Tsaturyan, *Eurasia Daily*, 29 March 2019, online available at: https://eadaily.com/ru/news/2019/03/29/nikolay-leonov-ya-opasayus-za-sudbu-kryma-kaliningrada-i-primorya, accessed 9 May 2019.

Levina, E. S. (2000) "Krutsin" imeyet svoyu sud'bu …", *Voprosy Znaniya, Estestvennoznaniya i Tekhniki*, Vol. 1, 2000, online available at: http://vivovoco.astronet.ru/VV/JOURNAL/VIET/LEVINA.HTM, accessed 24 May 2019.

Long, Austin (2018) "Red Glare: the origin and implications of Russia's 'new' nuclear weapons", 26 March 2018, *War on the Rocks*, online available at: https://warontherocks.com/2018/03/red-glare-the-origin-and-implications-of-russias-new-nuclear-weapons/, accessed 25 May 2019.

Merzlikin, Pavel (2019) "Minobrnauki pytayetsya ogranichit' kontakty uchenykh s inostrantsami. Uchenyye vspominayut sovetskiye vremena; chinovniki govoryat, chto eto 'prosto rekomendatsii'", *Meduza*, August 14, available at: https://meduza.io/feature/2019/08/14/minobrnauki-pytaetsya-ogranichit-kontakty-uchenyh-s-inostrantsami-uchenye-vspominayut-sovetskie-vremena-chinovniki-govoryat-chto-eto-prosto-rekomendatsii, accessed 15 August 2022.

_____ (2020) "FSB protiv gosudarstvennika Novoye delo o gosizmene", *Meduza*, June 15, available at: https://meduza.io/feature/2020/06/15/fsb-protiv-gosudarstvennika, accessed 15 August 2022.

## 114  *The Soviet legacy of Russia's security policy*

Official Internet portal of legal information (2020) Federal'nyy zakon ot 31.07.2020 № 279-FZ "O vnesenii izmeneniy v stat'yu 7 Federal'nogo zakona "O federal'noy sluzhbe bezopasnosti", available at: http://publication.pravo.gov.ru/Document/View/0001202007310049?index=1&rangeSize=1, accessed 15 August 2022.

Oznobishchev, S.K., V.YA. Potapov, and V.V. Skokov (2008) *Kak gotovilsya «asimmetrichnyy otvet» na 'Strategicheskuyu oboronnuyu initsiativu' R. Reygana: Velikhov, Kokoshin i drugiye*. Moskva: LENAND, electronic version is available at: http://lawinrussia.ru/content/kak-gotovilsya-asimmetrichnyy-otvet-na-strategicheskuyu-oboronnuyu-iniciativu-r-reygana, accessed 1 November 2019.

Petrova, Anastasia, Alexey Ramm, and Anna Cherepanova (2021) "Novoye giperzvuchaniye: s chem svyazano ocherednoye ugolovnoye delo o gosizmene", *Izvestia*, August 12, available at: https://iz.ru/1206477/anastasiia-petrova-aleksei-ramm-anna-cherepanova/novoe-giperzvuchanie-s-chem-sviazano-ocherednoe-ugolovnoe-delo-o-gosizmene, accessed 15 August 2022.

Pipes, Richard (1974) *Russia under the old regime*, New York: Charles Scribner's Sons.

Pirnie, Bruce R. (Major) (1985) *Soviet Deception Operations during World War II*, Analysis Branch U.S. Army Centre of Military History, Washington, D.C., online available at: https://apps.dtic.mil/dtic/tr/fulltext/u2/a165980.pdf, accessed 19 April 2019.

Podvig, Pavel (2017) "Did Star Wars Help End the Cold War? Soviet Response to the SDI Program", *Science & Global Security*, Vol. 25, No. 1, DOI: 10.1080/08929882.2017.1273665.

*Postanovleniye Politbyuro TSK RKP(b)* «O dezinformatsii» 1) 11.01.1923, PB № 43/82, APRF. F. 3. Op. 58. D. 2. L. 18, 129–130. Postanovleniye – podlinnik, predlozheniya – kopiya. Opubl.: Lubyanka. Stalin i VCHK–GPU–OGPU–NKVD. Yanvar' 1922 – dekabr' 1936. M., 2003. p. 73, online available at: http://hrono.ru/dokum/192_dok/19230111ck.php, accessed 1 April 2019.

Putin, Vladimir (2018) "Poslaniye Prezidenta Federal'nomu Sobraniyu", *Kremlin*, 1 March 2018, available at: http://kremlin.ru/events/president/news/56957, accessed 24 May 2019.

Radio Ekho Moskvy (2018) "Stali izvestny novyye podrobnosti aresta 64-letnego uchenogo iz Novocherkasska Alekseya Temireva", 30 July 2018, available at: https://echo.msk.ru/news/2249316-echo.html, accessed 23 May 2019.

Rubinstein, Alvin Z. (1990) *Moscow's Third World Strategy*, Princeton, NJ: Princeton University Press.

Sever, Vladimir (2008) *Istoriya KGB*, Moskva: Algorithm Vega-Klub Veteranov Sluzhby Bezopasnosti, p. 22, online available at: http://vegaclub.ru/files/istoriya_kgb.pdf, accessed 30 April 2019.

Shevyakin, Aleksandr (2013a) *Sistema bezopasnosti SSSR*, Moscow: Algoritm, electron book, http://indbooks.in/mirror8.ru/?p=404710, accessed 30 April 2019.

_____ (2013b) *KGB protiv SSSR. 17 mgnoveniy izmeny*, Moskva: EKSMO, online available at: https://history.wikireading.ru/409740, accessed 1 May 2019.

Shmidt, O.Yu. (ed.) (1926) *Bol'shaya sovetskaya entsiklopediya*, Tom pervyi, Moskva: A – Akolla, AO Sovetskaya entsiklopediya, Kolonka 423, online available at: http://ponjatija.ru/node/14466, accessed 1 May 2019.

Sinitsin, Igor Yeliseevich (2015) *Andropov vblizi. Vospominaniya o vremenakh ottepeli I zastoia*. Electron book format, LitMir.ru, available at: https://www.litmir.me/br/?b=263637&p=80, accessed 14 December 2018.

Sluzhba vneshney razvedki Rossiyskoi Federatsii (2019) "Operatsiya "Trest", Operatsiya 'Sindikat-2', Stanovlenie vneshnei razvedki (1921–1925), http://svr.gov.ru/history/stages/stage02.htm, accessed 14 April 2019.

Stalin, Joseph. V. (1925) "The Fourteenth Congress of the C.P. S.U. (B.): Political Report of the Central Committee," 1925, December 18–31. *Works*, Vol. 7, 1925, available at: https://www.marxists.org/reference/archive/stalin/works/1925/12/18.htm, accessed 30 March 2018.

Syun, Yurii, and Ivan Sinergiyev (2018) "Uchenyy izmenil s bel'giyskim institutom", 3 August 2018, available at: https://www.kommersant.ru/doc/3702851, accessed 23 May 2019.

Talbott, Strobe (ed.) (1970) *Khrushchev Speaks, with introduction and commentary by Edward Crankshaw*, Boston: Little, Brown&Co.

TASS (2018) "Baza sudov Moskvy perestanet otobrazhat' familii obvinyayemykh v gosizmene i shpionazhe", 21 July 2018, available at: https://tass.ru/obschestvo/5392934, accessed 23 May 2019.

The Central Intelligence Agency (1984) "Possible The Soviets Response to the US Strategic Defence Initiative", Interagency Intelligence Assessment, 27 June 1984, online available at: https://www.cia.gov/library/readingroom/docs/CIA-RDP86B00420R000701360002-3.pdf, accessed 28 May 2019.

The Wilson Centre Digital Archive, *Stasi note on meeting between minister Mielke and KGB chairman Andropov*, 11 July 1981, online available at: https://digitalarchive.wilsonCentre.org/document/115717, accessed 28 May 2019.

Yakovets, E. N. (2013) "Osnovnyye napravleniya organizatsionnoy i pravovoy zashchity gosudarstvennoy tayny v Sovetskoy Rossii", *Istoriya gosudarstva i prava*, N 6, available at: https://Centre-bereg.ru/h261.html, accessed 14 April 2019.

Yakovlev, A.N., D.G. Nadzhafov, and Z.S. Belousova (ed) (2005) *Stalin i kosmopolitizm. 1945—1953. Dokumenty. Agitpropa. TSK/S11*, "Zakrytoye pis'mo TsK VKP(b) o dele professorov Klyuyevoy i Roskina", 16 July 1947, Sekretno, Zakrytoye pis'mo TsK VKP(b), Rossiya. XX vek, Moskva: MFD: Materik, pp. 123–128, online available at: https://www.alexanderyakovlev.org/fond/issues-doc/69339, accessed 22 May 2019.

Zhirnov, Yevgenii (2003) "Dezinformbyuro-80 let sovetskoy sluzhbe dezinformatsii", *Kommersant*, N 2, 13 January 2003.

Zimmerman, William (1969) *Soviet perspectives on international relations: 1956–1967*, Princeton: Princeton University Press.

# 4 Evolution of the Russian Federation's security concept

### Facets of Russia's security policy documents

Before analyzing Russia's security documents, it is essential to review which characteristics exert influence on the formation of the state's security policy and strategies since their development does not take place in a vacuum. They are products of several characteristics, political processes, internal and external situations, threat perceptions, the security thinking, and influences of ruling elites. In this regard, this chapter will discuss the main facets of Russia's security documents.

In comparing Russia's contemporary external security behavior with its traditional principles, Marcel de Haas correctly stresses the following four characteristics regarding the development of Russian security policy since the breakup of the USSR: a first is fear for the alien, "a feeling of being surrounded by enemies which finds its present side effect in an emphasis on external threats in security documents."[1] A second characteristic—an insatiable desire for security—expresses itself in expansion and buffer zones, such as those of occupations of Kazan, the Caucasus, and Central Asia between the 16th and 19th centuries or in the creation of the Warsaw Pact in the 20th century. Nowadays, this feature is reflected in the Russian-led military or economic cooperation organizations, such as the Collective Security Treaty Organization (CSTO), the Commonwealth of Independent States (CIS), and the Shanghai Cooperation Organization (SCO), and, to some extent, the separatist regions of several former Soviet republics, which present challenges to any integration into Euro-Atlantic projects. A third characteristic is a feeling of superiority, which is expressed in references to the unique status of Russia and its leading role in the world. This characteristic is linked to the "third Rome" idea, which is explained as being the global political, religious, and cultural center after Rome and Constantinople ended. This concept was established in the medieval ages, was subsequently strengthened until the 1917 revolutions, and continued under the Marxism-Leninism façade during the USSR. Under Putin and Medvedev, this idea was brought to the surface through frequent statements around Russia's great power status and how it no longer lets itself be ignored or humiliated by the West.[2] A fourth characteristic, writes Haas, is the return of centralized political power to the Kremlin and through an internal security policy that, under the pretext of terrorist threats, restrained democratic institutions during Putin's first presidency.[3]

DOI: 10.4324/9781003344391-5

Regarding strategies—although there are official documents on how to defend the country and wage the next wars—Russians might declare a particular intent but act/fight differently. This facet of security thinking of the military and political elites has been found since Russia's pre-revolutionary period. Historically, tactical and operational plans were more important for the military elites than any official or unclassified document, strategy, or doctrine. However, official documents are useful for understanding the trends in Russia's security policy.

The officially adopted Russian security and military doctrinal issues are mainly reflected in five groups: (1) the concept of national security; (2) the military doctrine, where only the fundamental, issues of organizing the defense of the country are reflected; (3) legislative, legal, and official documents such as "The Law on Security," "The Law on Defense," "The Law on Military Duty and Military Service," government decrees on matters of defense and military construction; (4) military regulations and manuals determining the activities of the armed forces and other troops in military operations; and (5) general military regulations and basic orders, manuals, and guidelines that govern the daily life and activities of the Russian armed forces and other troops.[4]

According to Mahmud Gareev, if the main essence of Russia's military doctrines would be summarized, they are fundamentally designed to address the following issues:

> the nature of modern threats to the security of Russia and the defense tasks arising from them; the kind of military organization needed in the Russian Federation (armed forces and other troops) to neutralize potential threats and accomplish defense tasks; possible uses of the armed forces and other troops; the types of wars and armed conflicts, presently and in the future, which could be imposed on Russia; the direction of military training and education of personnel; preparing for a defense of the country as a whole especially in economic, military-industrial, and moral-political terms.[5]

These issues put forth by Gareev in 2007 would be addressed in Russia's 2010 and 2011 military doctrines, which regarded developments in Russia's foreign and security policy alongside developments in the world.

In the early 2000s, Mahmud Gareev divided Russia's external threats into three groups: the first group of threats is the long-term policy of "certain international forces and powers" that sought to deprive Russia of its independence, by interfering in its internal politics and infringing upon the country's economic and national interests. The second group surrounds the possibility of nuclear weapons being used against Russia, the proliferation of nuclear weapons, and other types of weapons of mass destruction. Gareev emphasized that after the NATO "aggression against Yugoslavia, some countries come to the conclusion that nowadays without nuclear weapons it is impossible to defend the country's independence."[6] The third group is the ongoing race for the qualitative improvement of armaments, "the desire of the leading powers to make a breakthrough to the creation of dominant military-technical superiority."[7] Gareev also considered NATO enlargement a threat but did not refer to the alliance directly:

> Among the obvious external threats are the presence of powerful armed groups that disturb the balance of powers and hotbeds of conflicts near the borders of the Russian Federation and its allies, bringing them closer to Russia, creating hostile armed groups and terrorist groups in other countries, infiltrating them into Chechnya and other areas of Russian territory.[8]

As to the main internal threats, Gareev points to terrorism, as well as the separatist and extremist nationalist movements against the unity and territorial integrity of Russia. Moreover, he stressed that internal conflicts and terrorism are often fueled from outside.[9]

Based on a study of the nature of the threats, Gareev emphasized the importance in developing and controlling state policy regarding the use of non-military means in conflicts. He argued that it is not enough to recognize the significance and importance of non-military forms of struggle in upholding national interests. It is necessary to organize and coordinate their implementation at the state level. He regretfully noted in his 2003 article that until the theory and practice of conventional military defense of the state are developed and mastered, "the problems of using non-military means to defend Russia's national interests and countering new forms of struggle in the international stage remain poorly understood and undeveloped."[10] As to these shortcomings, he pointed to the lack of coordination of efforts by state bodies to prevent wars and conflicts through the use of non-military means of defense. These make it difficult to reasonably determine the scope of real defense tasks, the necessary composition of the armed forces and other troops, and the content and direction of military reform. Because the scale of military efforts and the defense budget largely depends on how fully and effectively the first part of the task of preventing threats and neutralizing them by political, diplomatic, and other non-military means is solved.[11]

For solving these problems, Gareev suggested holding a special meeting of the Security Council of the Russian Federation, where possible ways of upholding Russia's national interests and ensuring the country's defense with a wider and more active use of political-diplomatic, economic, informational, and other non-military means would be considered and the tasks and responsibilities of the government agencies in this area more clearly defined.[12]

The Russian Minister of Defense, between 2001 and 2007, Sergey Ivanov classifies three types of threats in his program article in 2004: external, domestic, and transnational. The Russian armed forces are assigned to neutralize these threats and they are not solely military. According to Ivanov, even traditional external threats are acquiring new aspects:

> These include interference in Russia's internal affairs by foreign states or organizations supported by them, instability in neighboring countries caused by the weakness of their governments, and several other aspects which are

relatively new for Russia's military planning. The Russian armed forces now play an increasingly significant role in countering the threat of weapons of mass destruction by individual states, coalitions of states, and political movements, as well as their access to the most dangerous types of weapons.[13]

He emphasizes the external threats that would require the Russian armed forces to perform various tasks around the world. He stresses that it is not possible to absolutely rule out the preventive use of force if this is required by Russia's interests or its alliance commitments.

As to the more important domestic threats the armed forces are assigned to neutralize, Ivanov highlights regime security-related problems specifically: attempts to change the constitutional system by force and the violation of Russia's territorial integrity; the formation, arming, training, and functioning of illegal armed groups; illegal arms, munitions, and explosives trafficking on the territory of the Russian Federation; large-scale activities of organized crime, threatening political stability on the scale of individual entities of the Russian Federation; the activities of separatist and radical religious or nationalist movements and terrorism.[14] That is why, according to Ivanov, the Russian Army should deal not only with external threats, but also with internal ones as well.

Ivanov's prognosis is that Russia's military planning will be determined by several uncertainty factors, that is, conflicts or processes, which may develop into factors that could essentially change the geopolitical situation in regions of priority for Russia's interests—CIS countries and adjacent regions—or create a direct threat to its security. He emphasizes the necessity to consider several types of armed conflicts. As a result, combat training, operational planning, and defense procurement must be as flexible as possible.[15]

Regarding the tasks for the Russian armed forces, Ivanov urges that they must take into consideration recent changes in the military-political situation in "the zones of Russia's interests" as well as possible trends in the principles of warfare.[16]

Russia's growing concerns about the West's role on the international stage and the "color revolutions" in former Soviet republics resulted in a sense of fear within official discourse regarding the possibility of similar events happening inside Russia. According to Aglaya Snetkov, in response, the regime widened its "*obraz vraga*" [the image of the enemy] to include any actor or group—domestic or foreign—that questioned the course and direction chosen for Russia by the Putin regime.[17]

Speaking on the structure and main content of the new Russian military doctrine (2010), Makhmut Gareev noted the need to develop a new version of the doctrine, following its approval in 2000 because "there were significant changes in the geopolitical and military-political situation, in the nature of threats to the state's defense security."[18] Moreover, some provisions of that doctrine were not viable. They did not meet the realities that had emerged in recent years and did not work for strengthening Russia's security. Gareev points to "the international situation," specifically the United States, as a justification for the changes in the military document. He believed that the political course pursued by the United States would inevitably lead to a confrontation with a significant part of the world and "objectively, there are conditions when Russia will have to act as a geopolitical arbiter." "At the same time, certain moderation is needed in defining and defending of national interests in order to firmly uphold only truly vital interests," he noted.[19] At the same time, he warned that the experience post-WWII proved that excessive "maximalism and unreality" of proclaimed national interests and goals, the desire to implement them rigidly and at any cost, gave rise to a confrontational foreign policy and military doctrine, which led to the destruction of the economy and the complete destruction of falsely understood national goals. According to Gareev, such an approach must not be allowed.[20]

Gareev noted two forms of threats and approaches that should be reflected in the doctrine. The first was adopted in the doctrine of 2000 which, according to Gareev, focused solely on military threats and ways to counter them by military means. Gareev emphasized that the second approach required proceeding from "the radical military-political changes" in the world and must consider a wide range of threats carried out by both military and non-military means. The threats were political, diplomatic, economic, and informational and were primarily non-military and asymmetric.

Gareev stressed that the "experience of the breakup of the USSR, Yugoslavia, the 'color revolutions' in Georgia, Ukraine, Kyrgyzstan, and other regions of the world convincingly shows that the main threats are carried out not only and not so much by military means, but mainly hidden" ones.[21] Therefore, military and non-military threats cannot be separated, they must be considered in "organic unity." He merges state security threats with the regime security as the main threats for Russia: "the policies and efforts of certain" international forces and states that encroach on Russia's sovereignty; infringe upon Russia's economic and "other" interests; political and informational pressure and subversive activities "as there were in the cases in Ukraine, Georgia, Kyrgyzstan;" territorial claims; and the threat to energy security. After defining the threats, Gareev notes that they require appropriate defense tasks specifically the prevention, localization, and neutralization of such threats by "politico-diplomatic, economic, informational, and other non-military means."[22]

At the same time, he stressed the necessity to reconsider conventional means in the military doctrine. Gareev believed that the use of nuclear weapons against Russia and the proliferation of weapons of mass destruction remained a threat.[23] However, Gareev also noted that nuclear weapons cannot be absolutized. The fact that "as long as there are nuclear weapons, the security of Russia is guaranteed" does not fully correspond to the new realities. He argued that nuclear weapons can no longer be universal; they cannot be used in such conflict situations as in Chechnya. It is not possible to neutralize economic, informational, and other subversive actions with the help of nuclear weapons. So, it is necessary to consider such threats and the relevant responses to them in the Russian military doctrine. He also suggested cooperation between the great powers for fighting against or preventing common threats, such as terrorism, and believed that transnational threats required the creation of transnational mechanisms to counter them. To do so, he proposed a division in the areas of responsibility between NATO and the CSTO in 2007.

Gareev suggested that it is necessary to consider—following the reduction of Russia's military capabilities after the collapse of the USSR—increasing and maintaining Russia's nuclear potential. At the same time, he argued that military doctrine should pay attention to the development of general-purpose forces (the Air Force, Navy, and ground forces). He emphasized that given the vast territory of Russia, the possibility of potential adversaries emerging in the east and south, and a reliance on military ground forces, Russia cannot do without sufficiently strong general-purpose forces.

The military doctrine of 2010 focused on the transformation of the armed forces, the creation of a unified system of aerospace defense, the use of contact and non-contact methods of warfare, conducting active preemptive strikes, and other issues of military construction, including the creation of mixed units and units consisting separately of professionals and conscripts. Nevertheless, the new military doctrine of Russia, according to General Gareev, would be actively defensive in nature.[24] Gareev's visions and suggestions regarding the development of military doctrine are important to consider when analyzing the military doctrine of 2014. Moreover, as noted above, General Gareev's public speeches and writings were considered and reflected upon by the Russian military and political elites in the process of developing the country's main military document. His thoughts can be found in the 2014 doctrine.

Since the breakup of the USSR, the changing external threat perceptions have been reflected in Russia's security documents. If we compare security documents between the 1990s and 2010s, it is possible to find how attitudes toward external threats changed.

In the first half of the 1990s, the development of Russia's national security policy demonstrated a realistic approach in that it saw mainly non-military, internal social-economic conditions as the main threat. Considering these problems, the Yeltsin government's foreign policy was oriented to the West. Consequently, Russian foreign policy was primarily directed at territorial cooperation, and the non-military means of Moscow's international policy received priority. In the second half of the 1990s, following the conflict in Yugoslavia and the enhanced role of NATO in international processes—especially in Europe—and the activation of its enlargement projects, along with increasing internal threats, specifically the military conflicts in Chechnya and the heavy criticism from the West regarding the high number of civilian casualties in those conflicts, Russian security policy and its documents changed drastically. These developments triggered a strengthening of thinking among Russia's political elite that Russia was facing internal and, once again, external threats.[25]

However, the main determinants of the security documents have not changed since the 1990s. At first glance, there seemed to be a watershed moment between Putin's presidential terms, which saw more resistance and a tougher position toward closer cooperation with the West. Marcel de Haas noted that Putin's constructive attitude toward the West in his first term was based solely on his statements and economic necessity: "the security documents had consistently contained anti-Western entries, e.g., considering NATO and the USA as threats."[26] Haas stressed that it was not a radical watershed in security policy but rather "a temporary and opportunistic change of course, anticipating return to the steadfast line when possible."[27]

Russian scholar Fyodor Lukyanov stressed that Putin's anti-Western position in 2012 was very different to the anti-Western position he took some five or six years before, when he delivered his famous Munich speech. If in 2007 it was an offensive position, in 2012, it was "very defensive." Lukyanov tries to justify Putin's stance toward the West.[28] Lukyanov notes that at the same time, Putin understood he could not close the country. That is why he was trying to achieve equilibrium—to isolate politically, but engage economically.[29] Such contradictions or zigzags between cooperative and assertive stances toward the West were reflected in the official security documents as well. In the documents accepted after 2013 (i.e., after the annexation of Crimea), the assertive attitude toward the West strengthened.

## The reflection of asymmetric methods in Russia's security policy documents

In analyzing how asymmetric methods are reflected in Russia's security documents, it is necessary to review Russian post-Soviet security concepts. Asymmetric approaches (both as threats and responses to them) are not mentioned separately; they are part of the same concept. The asymmetric methods and conventional approaches are merged into the same documents. The key aspect for understanding Russian strategy is that Russia's concepts are eclectic regarding methods and rely on a dialectic approach. As Janis Berzins notes, it is a methodological mistake to try to frame a theory developed independently by the Russian military as a theory developed in another country. He believes that Russia's case reflects another culture's way of thinking and strategic understanding about the way warfare should be conducted:

> Specifically, what the Russians call New Generation Warfare is a combination of Asymmetric warfare with Low-Intensity Conflict, Network-Centric Warfare and Sixth-Generation Warfare, combined with components of Reflexive Control. Its main aim is to achieve political objectives; therefore, the use of military power may not even be necessary. To fully comprehend the way Russia sees warfare, it is necessary to understand Russia's security ambitions—and therefore its tactical objectives—as well as its military doctrine.[30]

In post-Soviet Russia, three documents determine the official security policy. They are the National Security Strategy (the NSS), the Foreign Policy Concept (the FPC), and the military doctrine. The NSS focuses on the protection of national interests against internal and external threats. The FPC deals with actions in the international arena such as states and international institutions.[31] War, conflicts, crises and their prevention, deterrence and suppression of aggression, force generation and preparation of the armed forces, population and economy, securing vital interests of the state are reflected in the military doctrine.[32]

Although Russia's 2000 National Security Concept stressed that the internal social-economic and political weaknesses were the main problems for Russia's national security, factors such as the "strengthening of military-political blocs and alliances, above all NATO's eastward expansion," the "possible appearance of foreign military bases and large troop contingents in direct proximity to Russia's borders," and "a weakening of the integration processes in the Commonwealth of Independent States" were among the main external threats.[33]

In the official military document of the Ministry of Defense in 2003, the priority tasks of the development of the armed forces of the Russian Federation, three types of threats were emphasized: external, internal, and trans-border. The main external threats outlined in the document are the deployment of groups of forces and resources with the aim of launching a military attack against Russia or its allies; territorial claims to Russia; the threat of political or military seizure of parts of Russian territory; programs for creating weapons of mass destruction carried out by states, organizations and movements; interference in the internal affairs of Russia by foreign states or organizations supported by foreign states; demonstration of military power close to Russia's border; military exercises with provocative aims; seats of armed conflicts close to the borders of Russia or its allies which threaten their security; instability or weakness of state institutions in border countries; the build-up of groups of forces resulting in the disruption of the balance of forces close to the borders of Russia or its allies and adjacent seas; the expansion of military blocs and unions to the detriment of the military security of Russia or its allies; the operation of international radical groups and the strengthening of Islamic extremism close to Russia's borders; the deployment of foreign troops (without agreement of Russia or the UN Security Council) in the territory of adjacent and friendly countries; armed provocations, including attacks at Russian military facilities located in foreign states, as well as the facilities and structures on the state border of Russia or the borders of its allies; actions hindering the operation of the Russian systems of state and military management, of the strategic nuclear forces, early warning systems, ballistic missile defense, space control, and combat stability of troops; actions hindering Russia's access to strategic transport communications; discrimination against and infringement on the rights, freedoms, and legitimate interests of the citizens of Russia in foreign states; proliferation of equipment, technologies, and component parts used for the creation of nuclear and other weapons of mass destruction, as well as dual technologies that can be used for the creation of weapons of mass destruction and their delivery vehicles.[34]

The results of this threat assessment would be used subsequently in other official documents. The asymmetrical nature of a considerable part of the wars of the past decade was stressed in the document. And therefore the importance of preparation for such military conflicts was also noted.[35] Generally speaking, knowing that its ambitions are limited by both internal and external factors, Moscow actively encourages the use of asymmetric methods in its security policy. These asymmetric methods are also expressed in Russia's recent national security strategy.

If we compare Russia's recent security documents with the 2003 Ministry of Defense document, it would be possible to find a strengthening of the "fortress under siege" thinking. According to Ryszard Zięba, Russia's relations with the West have become even more exacerbated, as a result of among other things, NATO's expansion to include Croatia and Albania in April 2009, the announcement of the EU's Eastern Partnership—which Russia did not join—and the crisis in Ukraine beginning in the autumn of 2013. "This worsening of Russia's relations with the West," writes Zięba, "was reflected in the new security strategy adopted by President Putin on December 31, 2015."[36] According to Zięba, the shift in Russian doctrine toward the greater use of its armed forces for ensuring defense and security can be observed beginning in 2000, that is, after NATO's first post-Cold War round of expansion (to include Poland, the Czech Republic, and Hungary). "Then in 2009," he writes, "Moscow clearly formulated the postulate of shaping Russia into a world power."[37]

The military doctrine of 2014 and the 2015 National Security Strategy presented a Russia focused on influencing and strengthening its image as a global power.[38] In these documents, Russia is illustrated as a state accomplishing its aims while simultaneously feeling threatened by the United States and NATO "activities." Most of this could be found in previous documents, but there are also some facets that illustrated the changing security vision of Russia's political elite in recent years.

Both aforementioned documents list several levels of threats to Russia's national security. Some of the external threats are familiar from previous security and military strategies: global instability, proliferation of conventional weapons and weapons of mass destruction, terrorism, information warfare, the overthrow of legitimate regimes with Western support in Eurasia or "color revolutions," corruption, subversion, and a range of transnational threats. Russia also expresses concerns about the US missile defense systems stationed in Europe, global strike capabilities, high-precision weapons, and the militarization of space.

One of the significant changes in these documents is that the United States and its Western allies are openly described as adversaries that aim to contain Russia's increasing role in international relations. According to Olga Oliker, while past strategic documents implied a threat from the United States, 2014s military doctrine preferred to term US and NATO activities as dangers (in Russian military parlance, a danger is a concern, while a threat could spark conflict), although a number of specific capabilities (e.g., global strike) were classified as threats. "This strategy asserts that the US and its allies are seeking to contain Russia in order to maintain their dominance of world affairs, which Russia's independent foreign policy challenges," Oliker notes. "It describes NATO as a threat because the alliance is expanding its military infrastructure toward Russian borders (a phenomenon noted as a concern in the 2009 strategy)."[39] Moreover, in the last National Security Strategy, Western sanctions are described as a partial cause of Russia's economic woes, but are not tied to Ukraine, and, indeed, are given no particular background, leaving the casual reader to interpret them as simply one component of Western perfidy. Finally, the strategy depicts a United States which is leading its allies to undermine the global order and a Russia at risk because of its opposition to those policies.[40] "The strategy presents the world as dangerous for Russia," writes Oliker, "a world that the US and its allies are actively making more dangerous, in part to limit Russia's power. The broader dangers of terrorism, instability, and proliferation make cooperation with these countries necessary. However, they are also part of the problem, and cooperation is only possible if they accept Russia's leadership role."[41]

From the above analysis, we can see that one of the threats, in the official security documents, is the "color revolution," which relates to regime security, but is reflected as an external threat. Russia's ruling elite consider such revolutions as one of the main threats for the internal (regime security) and external security (Russia's sphere of influence). Even Russia's military leadership and scholars consider such revolutions as "non-military tools, threats in new generation warfare which are used by the West against Russia and its allies."[42]

One of the interesting facets of the 2015 National Security Strategy is that it emphasizes the importance of using asymmetric warfare methods in contemporary conflicts. According to Katri Pynnöniemi, the strategy reflects the idea that traditional military power, although important in intimidating Russia's weaker neighbors, is not sufficient for protecting Russia's strategic interests amid the changing security landscape.[43] "The new situation requires an 'asymmetric approach' whereby Russia's strengths (the weaponization of information, technology, and organizations) are coupled with its relative weakness in military-technological (force) development," Pynnöniemi notes.[44]

The main tools and aim of this approach are reflected in Article 36:

Interrelated political, military, military-technical, diplomatic, economic, informational, and other measures are being developed and implemented in order to ensure strategic deterrence and the prevention of armed conflicts. These measures are intended to prevent the use of armed force against Russia, and to protect its sovereignty and territorial integrity.[45]

Since the 2000s, the use of, and reflection on, non-military asymmetric approaches in Russia's security documents has only strengthened. Additionally, new facets such as energy resources and their security and color revolutions as threats have been emphasized in Russia's foreign security documents.

Marcel de Haas notes that energy had been gaining weight in Russian security thinking since Putin's second term in office. The critical importance of energy resources and security was also mentioned in the 2009 National Security Strategy. The strategy described energy as a power instrument to strengthen Moscow's influence in the international arena, and the need to use energy resources as strategic deterrence.[46] Haas notes that the latter was possibly "a hint to the applied policy of cutting off energy supplies for economic but also for political purposes, e.g., respectively to Belarus and Ukraine."[47] The importance of energy sources and their security is mentioned in the 2015 National Security Strategy several times.[48]

Moreover, in the 2015 NSS, color revolutions are considered one of the main threats to the state and public security of Russia. In the state and public security chapter of the strategy (Article number 43), it is stated that:

Activities of radical public associations and groups that use nationalist and extremist religious ideology, foreign and international non-governmental organizations, financial and economic structures, as well as private individuals, aimed at violating the unity and territorial integrity of the Russian Federation, destabilizing the internal political and social situation in the country, including inspiring "color revolutions," the destruction of traditional Russian spiritual and moral values.[49]

In fact, "color revolutions" are in line with threats such as nationalist and extremist religious ideologies and within the document are "contrasted with the countries traditional values." It should be noted that in the recent military doctrine of 2014, "color revolutions" are considered military threats. In the second chapter of the doctrine "Military risks and military threats to the Russian Federation," color revolution is noted as one of the main external military risks (Article number 12, subarticle-m) for the political regimes in the states adjacent to Russia specifically in those states which are preferable for Moscow. It states that, "the establishment of regimes in the states adjacent to the Russian Federation, including as a result of the overthrow of legitimate government bodies whose policies threaten the interests of the Russian Federation."[50]

Moreover, revolutions are considered one of the main internal military risks (Article 13, subarticle-a) since they have "activities aimed at forcibly changing the constitutional (political) system of the Russian Federation, destabilizing the internal political and social situation in the country, disrupting the functioning of government bodies, important state and military facilities and the information infrastructure of the Russian Federation."[51]

Revolutions or social-political protests are also referenced in Article 15 (Characteristics and specific features of modern military conflicts, subarticles—a, i, k) as a feature of modern military conflicts.[52] As reflected in the military doctrine, revolutions or political risks to the governing elite are considered asymmetric activities.

The 2021 National Security Strategy is not much different from its predecessors.[53] However, it is clear to see Russia's deteriorating relations with the West, which is mentioned in the text exclusively in negative terms, reflected. The idea that the West deliberately "erodes" Russian "traditional spiritual and moral values" is mentioned more than 20 times in the document.[54] As before, threats to regime security—specifically revolutions—are stressed. Cooperation possibilities with the "collective" West are narrowed in the document. The foreign policy section of the strategy has as such been reduced. A detailed review on Russia's relations with the United States and the European Union has disappeared entirely in the 2021 version. Moreover, the United States and some of its NATO allies are now officially mentioned as unfriendly states. In addition to US military deployments and NATO enlargement, the US "controlled" Internet, media, and the US dollar are considered instruments for containing Russia.[55] Consequently, Russia's relations with the two major Asian powers, China and India, are stressed. According to Russian scholar Igor Denisov, they are viewed more from pragmatic positions and designated as Russia's foreign policy priorities. At the same time, the strategy does not explicitly mention either China or India when talking about Russia's struggle with the West for moral leadership and competition in creating an attractive ideological basis for the future world order, stresses Denisov. Thus, according to Denisov, the Russia-India-China triangle is seen in the Kremlin through a regional rather than a global lens.[56] Looking back, the document can be seen as a strategy for a state preparing its country for war with the West. A war that would happen after February 24, 2022. However, as discussed above, Moscow's increasing grievances regarding relations with the West since the 2000s have also been reflected in the security documents.

Asymmetric approaches are reflected in other security documents as well. One of them, the 2015 Maritime Doctrine of the Russian Federation, reflects the asymmetric approaches in strategic interactions.[57] This doctrine is one of the most important doctrinal statements to emerge from Russia in recent years. It is Russia's most important recent official strategy of its maritime interests and goals, and therefore provides insight into how Moscow envisions Russia's global role.[58] The document itself provides extraordinary insight not only into current Russian maritime activities writ large but also into Russian ambitions for future maritime development. The Maritime Doctrine lists the roles and responsibilities of the resurgent Russian Federation Navy, both globally and regionally. The doctrine also provides insight into how Moscow might engage in a maritime conflict with the West including "mobilizing" its civilian fishing fleet, oceanographic vessels, and other ostensibly non-military vessels and installations to support a potential conflict. Michael B. Petersen stresses that the mobilization of civilian resources for use in conflict has a long history in Russia, and this doctrine provides a clear articulation of its practice in the maritime domain. "In any case, the doctrine envisions an active role for Moscow's improving military and its civilian resources," he concludes.[59] According to Richard Connolly, several broad points stand out regarding the doctrine and much of competition between states is likely to exist in either geographic areas of particular importance to Russia, including the Arctic, the Middle East, and on Russia's western borders, or in spheres of the global economy in which Russia is a key actor, especially natural resources.[60]

Connolly emphasizes that the threats defined in Russia's security documents, including the Maritime Doctrine, are as much "geoeconomic as they are geopolitical in nature." He notes that "Russia's existing domestic capabilities are seen as insufficient to deal with these myriad challenges ... As a result, strategic planning is viewed as a crucial step in mobilizing domestic resources to develop the capabilities—social, economic, and political—required to survive and even flourish in an increasingly competitive and multipolar world order."[61]

The 2022 Maritime Doctrine of the Russian Federation declares the strategic course of the United States and its allies on dominance in the oceans as a main challenge and a threat to Russia's national security in the world's oceans. The new doctrine also listed measures on how to mobilize Russian civilian vessels, installations, and ports to support the navy during a potential conflict.[62]

Comparing Russia's security documents with the strategies of other global powers, it is possible to find significant similarities and differences between them. One of the analyses on the issue gives important information and some interesting results for comparison. The Finland Institute on International Affairs (FIIA) report on analyses of the security documents of Russia, the United States, China, and European Union notes that all of the strategies reflect the complex nature and multiplicity of threats, and hence the need for a broad range of responses. In all of them, terrorism, economic security, and vulnerabilities in the spheres of cyber and energy are broadly shared concerns. Terrorism and mass destruction weapons are cited as threats in all the documents. One similarity in the documents of all the major global powers is the increasing emphasis on the role of military strength.

The report emphasizes that one of the distinguishing aspects of Russia's security documents is the complementing of military power with asymmetric approaches:

> At the same time, military power is complemented with various other instruments in sophisticated ways, notably in Russia's "asymmetric approach" whereby Russia's strengths such as the weaponization of information, technology and non-state organizations are used as a way to compensate for the relative weakness in the military-technological field. Correspondingly, the US stresses the need to be prepared to operate across multiple domains at once, in conflict scenarios possibly involving political, military, economic, and cyber spheres.[63]

The promotion of values is another key difference between the Western documents and Russian and Chinese ones. Values such as freedom, democracy, and human rights are still present in the strategies of both the EU and the United States, but are less central than in previous rhetoric. Meanwhile, China and Russia do emphasize their own values and the need to defend these against external influences.[64] In this respect, Ryszard Zięba notes that the Western states and institutions honor liberal ideology, which they consider to be the only proper one. According to Zięba, Russia, regardless of how it may describe itself as a democratic country, prefers so-called sovereign democracy and authoritarian methods of government. Consequently, the same phenomena and actions are viewed differently, "It can generally be stated that how the world is viewed and what security policy aims are formulated (with their ways and means) depends on the given state's ideology," Zięba notes.[65]

The FIIA report concludes that despite the differences, all four strategies tackle the rapid change of global structures and instruments of power and try to identify ways to shape these dynamics and adapt:

> A major common theme in the strategy documents is increased competition among major powers, which plays out in military, political, and economic fields as well as at the level of values. At the same time, the multiplicity of actors and diffusion of power is reflected in different ways in all four approaches.[66]

The head of the Russian General Staff, General Gerasimov, emphasized several times the asymmetric threats to Russia and the necessity of preparing responses for such threats in the annual conference of the Academy of Military Sciences in 2019. Gerasimov's speech represents a merging of the ideas discussed by the military elite over the past years, as well as a precursor to the new military doctrine. In the conference on the development of military strategy in modern condition, he notes that wars are expanding and their contents are significantly changing. The number of subjects involved in the armed struggle is increasing and along with the armed forces of states, various gangs, private military companies, and self-proclaimed "quasi-states" are fighting in wars:

> The means of economic, political, diplomatic, information, as well as demonstration of military power in the interests of enhancing the effectiveness of non-military measures are being actively used. Military force is used when it is not possible to achieve the goals set by non-military methods.[67]

But, on the other hand, Gerasimov notes that Russia's adversaries do not hide the fact that they are going to achieve political goals solely in local conflicts. According to Gerasimov, they are preparing to wage wars against a "high-tech adversary" using high-precision weapons from the air, sea, and space, with active information warfare. He stresses that under these conditions, the Russian armed forces must be ready to conduct new types of war and armed conflict, using classical and asymmetric methods of action. Therefore, the search for rational strategies for waging war with various adversaries is of paramount importance to the development of the theory and the practice of military strategy, believes Gerasimov.[68] He notes that in the course of its development, the military strategy has undergone several stages of evolution—from the "strategy of crushing" and the "strategy of attrition" to the strategies of global war, nuclear deterrence, and indirect actions.[69]

According to Gerasimov, the United States and its allies are developing offensive military actions, such as the Global Strike Program, multisphere battle, the technology of color revolutions, and soft power. Gerasimov explains the goals of such approaches as the elimination of "the statehood of undesirable countries, the undermining of sovereignty, and the change of lawfully elected bodies of state power." He notes that its goals were achieved in Iraq, in Libya, in Ukraine, and similar activities were observed in Venezuela. Here, in fact, Gerasimov mentions the threats to regime security, such as color revolutions and social protests, as this is rather standard thinking for Russia's political and military elite. He was presenting these threats as a wider part of the war strategy of Russia's adversaries.

Moreover, he claims that the Pentagon has begun to develop a new strategy of warfare, already dubbed the "Trojan Horse." The Pentagon means, according to Gerasimov, to use the protest potential of populations for destabilizing the situation in a targeted country while simultaneously striking high-precision weapons at important targets. According to Gerasimov, such a strategy actively uses asymmetric approaches, as it simultaneously uses military and non-military methods, which is why Russia must prepare for similar defensive and offensive operations. He also notes that Russia is ready to oppose any such strategies since, in recent years, military scholars—together with the General Staff—have developed conceptual approaches to neutralize "the aggressive actions of potential adversaries." The basis of Russia's response is the active defense strategy, which, given the defensive nature of the Russian military doctrine, provides for a set of measures to proactively neutralize threats to the security of the state, Gerasimov states.[70] Gerasimov stresses that this is one of the priority areas of state security and the development of responsive measures should be a priority for Russian military scholars, "We must be ahead of the enemy in the development of military strategy."[71] The active defense strategy is a combination of military and non-military tools, such as military force, including irregular and armed groups, information operations, cyberattacks, and diversion, as well as diplomatic, economic, and political measures. The term active defense has historical roots as it was used by the Red Army during the Great Patriotic War.[72]

It should be noted that "the United States' new war strategy" as Gerasimov mentioned is based on the speech made by Air Force Chief Staff General David Goldfein at the Brookings Institution in February 2019. In fact, General Goldfein talked about the necessity of using a multi-domain strategy in future military operations—using several approaches and forces in frame of the same operation. "This is about using our asymmetric advantage. All forms, conventional and non-conventional would be connected," said General Goldfein. He didn't mention the "Trojan horse" strategy or using the "protest potential of the fifth column" which Gerasimov stated.[73] David Goldfein's thoughts are similar to asymmetric approaches in their strategic interaction. Moreover, Goldfein conceded that it's a concept of operations not yet ready "to be doctrine," it refers to using:

> our asymmetric advantage as a joint team to be able to bring all of our capabilities to bear on an adversary, so that we can overwhelm them and cause so many simultaneous dilemmas for them that they either would choose not to take us on—i.e., we have effectively deterred, and if deterrence fails we are able to win because we can bring capabilities to bear that they can't counter.[74]

Gerasimov also emphasized this in his speech. "In modern conditions, the principle of warfare has evolved based on the coordinated use of military and non-military measures with the decisive role of the armed forces," he said.[75] Gerasimov notes that Russia will "have to" respond with mirror and asymmetric measures to military threats in space as well.

Gerasimov also mentioned a new Russian strategy of "limited actions" which, draw upon lessons from Russia's operations in Syria. The foundation for implementing such a strategy involves the creation of a self-sufficient grouping of troops based on force elements of one of the branches of the Russian armed forces possessing high mobility and the capability to make the greatest contribution to executing assigned missions. In Syria, that role was set aside for elements of the aerospace forces. According to Gerasimov, the most important conditions for the implementation of the strategy are winning and holding information superiority, the preemptive readiness of command-and-control and comprehensive support systems, as well as the covert deployment of the necessary grouping.[76]

While it may appear that the above-described strategy of limited actions is new, its essence reflects largely what the Russian military carried out in its operations in Syria. Such a strategy could also be considered asymmetric, that is, using small groups of forces rather than large military formations based primarily on economic calculations and it is mainly useful in small-scale operations. According to Roger McDermott, it does not represent a declaration to conduct "power projection" on a global scale, given the economic and military obstacles that would limit such ambitions, "Nonetheless, by using the term 'strategy of limited actions,' Gerasimov most likely sought to signal a conceptualization of the Syrian experience that may serve to guide future defense decision making," McDermott suggests.[77] However, Russia did not use such a strategy during the first phase of the invasion of Ukraine in 2022. Only since the beginning of the second phase of the war have the Russian Forces started to use such approaches.[78]

It should be noted that traditionally, the Academy of Military Sciences' annual conference is a platform for the exchange of views of military experts on the most topical and problematic issues facing Russian military science and the results of the conference essentially determine the future direction of Russian military strategy. Most likely, Gerasimov's speech, as well as others during the conference, will influence the design of Russia's next military doctrine ordered by President Vladimir Putin in December 2018. One can reasonably argue that the use of asymmetric approaches in the next Russian military strategy will only be strengthened. However, the 2022 invasion of Ukraine will surely result in corrections and changes in the development of the new doctrine.

## The contemporary role of security institutions in Russia and their influence on the formation of security policies

As mentioned in previous chapters, contemporary Russia's political elite inherited a rich tapestry of security thoughts from pre-revolutionary Russia and the Soviet Union. This security thinking was grounded mainly in Soviet, and partly in the Russian Empire, historical experiences and connected to the prism through which they both saw the world.

The weaknesses and fears emanating from them have always had a considerable influence on the Kremlin's security views. These characteristics caused—since approximately the medieval period—the Tsarist expansion over the Eurasian continent specifically enlarging the empire with regions such as Siberia, the Caucasus, and Central Asia. In 1991, an opposite development took place. With the annulment of the Warsaw Pact in July 1991, the USSR lost its security buffer zone in the West. And with the demise of the USSR on December 25, 1991, Russia inherited a framework state, having lost the South Caucasus, Central Asia, and Ukraine. Moreover, the collapse of the Soviet Union subsequently affected elite security thinking thereby influencing present-day Russian security policy.[79]

Since 1999, and under these conditions, the participation of security institution representatives in high-level political positions has increased. With them came security thinking and threat perception behaviors formulated during their service in the Soviet Union security organizations. Since then, such security thinking has been dominant among Russia's political elite.

According to Russian scholar Olga Kryshtanovskaya's data analysis, Vladimir Putin's Security Council of 2002 was more similar to the Soviet Politburo of the CPSU Central Committee, both in number and structure, than to Yeltsin's 1993 Security Council.[80] The major distinguishing features of Putin's elite

Kryshtanovskaya writes, "were decreasing of the share of 'intellectuals' who had scientific degrees; decreasing of the already extremely low level representation of women in the elite; 'regionalization' [*provintsializatsiya*] of the elite and a sharp increasing in the number of military personnel." By "military," she means officers "in uniforms of all types—officers of the army and navy, border guards, internal troops, security services and so on." Kryshtanovskaya explains that to denote this group of people in the 1990s in Russian political slang, the notion of "*siloviki*" was fixed, and the totality of the militarized departments of Russia began to be called "power structures."[81]

Notwithstanding its prominence, the validity of several core elements of Kryshtanovskaya's analysis—and other studies with similar conclusions on the role of siloviki in Putin's regime—has been criticized by several scholars.[82]

One of Kryshtanovskaya's most prominent critics, Bettina Renz questions the perception of the rising numbers of siloviki in Russian politics as a conscious strategy and the expression of a more authoritarian policy direction pursued by President Putin. Renz argues that personal links and loyalties characteristic of elite recruitment in Russia, and not an individual's institutional background in the force structures per se, have been the central rationale for political appointments under Putin, rather than a conscious policy to strengthen the political influence of the force structures.[83] Accordingly, she argues that within the context of the strongly personalized system fostered by Yeltsin, the emphasis on personal links and loyalty in the making of political appointments allowed Putin—even forced him to an extent—to build his team from trusted individuals he had previously worked with. From this point of view, the rising number of siloviki in recent years was determined by democratic deficits already inherent in the Russian political system when Putin came to power, rather than by a strategy of establishing a "well ordered police state."[84]

Renz also stresses that siloviki ought not to be treated as an analytical entity based on a taken-for-granted common "military mindset." Taking into account a microlevel study of a number of siloviki, with reference to general literature on Soviet elite transformation and military sociology, Renz concludes that the wide array of posts and opinions held by these figures precludes their analytical treatment as a homogenous entity, and that the potential "military mindsets" of such figures are likely to vary considerably.[85] However, Renz does not deny that there has been a rise in the numbers of siloviki under Putin's leadership, but she concludes that this cannot be explained merely as a particular project pursued by a single actor with the aim of implementing a more authoritarian policy direction.[86]

Scholars David W. Rivera and Sharon Werning Rivera question Kryshtanovskaya's dramatic data. They stress that, "both our analyses of Russia's societal elite and our re-analyses of Kryshtanovskaya's data on the political elite paint a rather different—and less alarming—picture of the depths to which siloviki have penetrated the corridors of power since 2000 than has been commonly depicted in both scholarship and the media."[87] In their work, Rivera and Rivera note that rather than the "almost half" figure for silovki that Kryshtanovskaya claims in her "The

Russian Elite in Transition," militarization under Putin actually peaked at one-fifth of Russian officialdom and just one-seventh of the elite.[88]

Despite claims of alarmism and exaggerations on the role and numbers of force structure representatives in politics, neither Renz nor the Riveras deny an increase of siloviki participation in Russia's political life under Putin's presidency.[89] Moreover, Russian expert Tatiana Stanovaya stresses that following the occupation of Crimea, the participation of the *siloviki* in high-level decision-making processes sharply increased, thus reducing the role of civil institutions.[90] In such a situation, the security institutions are the main providers of analytical information for top Russian leadership, as has happened in Russia's Ukraine policy.

In April 2022, there were reports that Colonel-General Sergei Beseda, head of the 5th Department of the FSB, was arrested in connection with the failure in Ukraine.[91] The 5th Department of the FSB (Service of Operational Information and International Relations) includes the Department of Operational Information, which, as Russian journalists Andrey Soldatov and Irina Borogan wrote, performs the functions of foreign intelligence and is also engaged in attempts to keep the post-Soviet countries in Russia's sphere of influence. According to Soldatov and Borogan, it was Beseda who was responsible for providing Russian President Vladimir Putin with information about political events in Ukraine on the eve of the invasion.[92]

However, the arrest was not confirmed and General Beseda, and his department, have reportedly been deemed untouchable. Additionally, there seem to be several services in the FSB, whose leaders occupy a similar position as Beseda.[93]

One operation reportedly conducted by the 5th Department is an interesting case to observe how they perform deceptive "measures." In June 2010, a website lubyanskayapravda.com (Lubyanskaya Pravda) published secret FSB documents, among which were various intelligence reports including 5th Department reports addressed directly to Putin. One of these discussed a document that was falsified to undermine relations between Ukraine and Turkmenistan. It was about a fake report of the Ukrainian special services on the financing of the Turkmen opposition. It was a classic FSB active measure: the 5th Department leaked a fake report to the Ukrainian media, but then something unexpected happened, Russian Foreign Intelligence (SVR) accepted this report as genuine and reported it to the Kremlin.[94]

The FSB Operational Information and International Relations Service (5th Service) is the third intelligence service in Russia, after the GRU and the SVR, working beyond Russia's borders. According to Andrey Soldatov, the 5th Department is "promoting the Kremlin's agenda, using all available means, in the post-Soviet countries" and "not only in them."[95]

The reason that the security institutions are the main, and perhaps only, reliable sources of information for the Russian President and the ever-increasing influence of the security institutions in the hierarchy of the Russian political decision-making, is Putin himself—specifically his past professional experiences in the KGB and, after 1991, the FSB. Moreover, Putin's isolation during the COVID-19 pandemic reportedly contributed to the increased role of the security institutions as the main sources of information regarding developments internally and abroad, including in Ukraine. Accordingly, the isolation has made it almost impossible for Putin, already distinguished by excessive suspicion, to convey an alternative point of view that did not already coincide with the opinion of the security services. As a result, Putin, when deciding to invade Ukraine, relied mainly on the reports of his former colleagues, including the 5th Service of the FSB.[96]

One characteristic of the Russian ruling elite is that they mostly apply thinking for the worst-case scenario. Fiona Hill and Clifford Gaddy note that, such thinking has governed Putin's policies as Russia's preeminent leader since 2000, and he "applies his worst-case scenario thinking to the state level." Hill and Gaddy also stress surviving in explaining President Putin's behavior. "Surviving in a hostile and competitive world means thinking about the worst thing or things that could happen, and having something to rely upon to ensure yourself, and the state, when the external shocks come along," they write.[97] Such thinking, on the one hand, is based on the mindset of Russian society. On the other hand, the political elite are effectively a societal role model and exert influence on public perception through the state-controlled media.

According to data from the Levada Analytical Center (Levada-Center), the percent of persons who believed that external military threats existed for Russia went from 13% in 1990 to 57% in 2017.[98] It is important to note that during this period and in subsequent years, elite security thinking exerted influence on the public's threat perception. Throughout history, elites strongly influenced the security thoughts of the masses and formerly played a determining role in it. With contemporary Russia's more sophisticated mass media possibilities, elites can exert even more influence on public security thinking and even guide it. For instance, after the meeting between Presidents Putin and Trump in July 2018, Russian attitudes toward the United States changed positively. According to the Levada-Center survey, for the first time in years, a positive attitude about the United States began to prevail over negative ones. In May 2018, 69% of the respondents had a "bad" assessment (20% were "positive"), while in July positive assessments rose to 42% as negative ones fell to 40%.[99] Russian scholar Georgiy Satarov states that such changes in attitude are caused by the influence of political elites. According to Satarov, as in every country, at least 60% of Russia's society has a very flexible and conformist world view while their "unstable positions are influenced by propaganda" and "leaders become the models of thinking,"

> In the last years of the USSR, when the leaders of unofficial public opinion were people like Dmitry Sergeevich Likhachev or Andrei Dmitrievich Sakharov, it was a completely different society. Then they were gone, and no one could replace them. However, there were numerous television provocateurs, and another society was born. And television provocateurs appeared, because they are the most important, special tools in the hands of the authorities. This is all called circumstance. And under these circumstances, the large, conformist part of society and public opinion is adapting. But the most important thing is that the position of this majority does not define anything, except for the headlines of newspapers.[100]

According to the director of the Levada-Center, Lev Gudkov, public opinion does not exert any special influence on decision-making in the Kremlin. He emphasized that the overwhelming majority of the population (80%–85%) believe that they are in no way capable of influencing the policy of the country's leadership:

> Here you can talk about less or more approval of certain actions of the authorities, on the worries and fears that they cause. But resistance, especially with regard to foreign policy, is very small. The annexation of the Crimea actually consolidated the entire Russian population, split the middle class, and split those who went to anti-Putin rallies in 2011–2012. The share of those who condemned the annexation of the Crimea and the unleashed war in the Donbass was 7–12%.[101]

The start of the Russian invasion of Ukraine in 2022 led to an increase in Putin's support among the mass public.

As the Levada-Center's survey shows, in March, the approval of the main state institutions increased significantly: 83% approved of the president's activities, 71% the prime minister, 70% the government, and 59% the State Duma.[102] The proportion of those that believed the country was moving in the right direction sharply increased and United Russia was rated positively by 54%.[103] These numbers did not change significantly in August. According to the survey conducted by the Levada-Center, in August, the proportion of those that believed things in the country were going in the right direction amounted to 67% and Putin's support was at 83%.[104]

According to the Levada-Center's survey, the majority of respondents in the first months of the invasion supported the actions of the Russian armed forces in Ukraine (53% "definitely support", 28% "rather support") and 14%, did not support, another 6% found it difficult to respond.[105] The Levada-Center explains that support was highest among those who approved of President Putin's actions, and with older respondents. There was slightly less support in Moscow and other major cities. The lowest support was found among those that disapproved of Vladimir Putin's actions as president and with the youngest Russians.[106] After several months, in July, there were no significant changes in the attitudes of Russians to the "special operation." The level of public support for the actions of the Russian armed forces in Ukraine changed slightly: 76% of respondents supported the "special operation" (48% definitely support it, 28% rather support), 18% do not support it (8% definitely, 10% rather).[107] In August, there were no significant changes in support (46% "definitely support" the actions of the Russian armed forces in Ukraine with another 30% saying they "rather support" while 17% of respondents did not support (definitely and rather) the actions.[108] Although the public's tendency not to share their true attitudes most certainly influences the results of such surveys, the support for the invasion was still high.[109] Although anti-Ukrainian sentiment was fueled by the Russian state-run media from the mid-2000s, these efforts had little effect until, in the 2010s, the propaganda turned on the theme of "Ukrainian nationalism" and "fascism," destroying the sense of unity with Ukrainians, writes Lev Gudkov.[110] According to Gudkov, in general, up until August 2022, the reaction of society to the war went through three stages: insufficiently consolidated support, the greatest consolidation, and the period of routinization:

> Insufficiently consolidated support for the war against the backdrop of fear and shock at first gave way to a period of the greatest consolidation and mobilization of its supporters. March and April became the months of maximum declarative support for the war. However, since May, as the war took on a protracted character, a period of routinization began. It is characterized, on the one hand, by a drop in interest in news from Ukraine, most noticeable among young people and opponents of the war, who, realizing the impossibility of changing the course of things, began to fence themselves off from the problem. On the other hand, there is a certain increase in anxiety about the victims and destruction of the war, its protracted nature, and the uncertainty of the future. And although the proportion of those who feel responsible for the deaths involved and the continuation of hostilities has somewhat increased, the dominant mechanism for compensating for this anxiety remains the "transfer of responsibility" for what is happening to "external forces."[111]

Based on survey data, Lev Gudkov explains that a majority didn't want war prior to February 24, and that they were afraid. They weren't afraid necessarily for moral reasons but rather feared for their own well-being, feared that the war would quickly spread to Russian territory and capture the layman himself. Gudkov notes, "this fear was very significant, and I thought that it would be an occasion for rationalizing the policy pursued, the consequences of the war, and my own existence."[112] But it turned out that this was not the case. Gudkov explains this by firstly noting the fact that the authorities prepared for this and dampened the negative consequences by promising payments. Secondly, they reassured the people that this would not spread to the territory of Russia, and that the Russian Army will be able to protect them from NATO expansion (this being one of the main threats according to public attitudes). Through this "special operation"—which is local in time or territory—the people were placated. But the head of the Levada-Center believes that this is not exactly support but rather a lack of moral human sympathy and resistance to war.[113]

There were hopes that the increasing Russian losses and the effects of sanctions would influence the public's mood and a change in their attitudes regarding the invasion would be visible. Since September 2022, the support for the actions of the Russian armed forces in Ukraine has decreased slightly. In December 2022, while support remained high, there was a slight decrease: 41% "definitely support" the actions of the Russian armed forces in Ukraine (November—42%), with another 30% saying they "rather support" (November—32%) while 21% of respondents declared that they did not support the actions.[114]

Despite the mobilization and losses in the war, most probably it is the influence of Russia's state media propaganda, which plays a huge role in the attitudes of the respondents. The Levada-Center reported that the highest support for the actions of the Russian armed forces comes from those groups that cite Russian state TV channels as their main source of news (86%) and approve of the president's activities (82%), as well as those respondents aged 55 and older.[115]

This is already having a clear impact. Arrests in different regions are becoming more common. The public and journalists often find out about new "traitors and spies" by chance. It is not possible to argue that President Putin does not understand the challenges of strengthening the role of the security institutions in the state and society. Indeed, he maintains his role as an arbitrator in conflicts among state institutions including the security organizations. The fact is that the role of the security services in Russia's daily life and in the regime's security (partly thanks to Putin himself) is so huge that it is almost impossible to diminish. If the political regime would decide to do so, they would be practically shooting themselves in the foot. On the other hand, even sophisticated security services could not save the political regime in an emergency if most of the population resisted. The recent history of Russia, the August 1991 putsch, is proof of this claim. According to Nikolay Leonov, a retired KGB lieutenant general who was in charge of the organization's analytical department, KGB officers did not defend the Soviet Union during the August 1991 putsch because they knew that the people were against the regime. Despite the fact that the KGB had the capacity to act, it chose not to. There were 60,000 armed KGB personnel in Moscow alone, but they did not leave their barracks or offices on August 21.[116]

**Summary**

In reviewing Russia's security documents following the breakup of the Soviet Union, this chapter mainly focused on the strategies prepared after 2000. The main reason being that this is when the asymmetric approaches began to show more distinctly in these documents. The chapter explored asymmetric approaches in Russia's security documents and explained the asymmetric methods found within them.

This chapter also aimed to analyze how the threat perceptions of Russia's political elite, which are influenced by the Soviet past, processes in international relations, and Russian domestic politics, are depicted in these security documents. In conjunction with a historically established threat perception, Soviet experiences exert influence on the security thinking of Russia's political elites and this thinking is reflected in Russia's security documents.

Using the existing data of social surveys and qualitative analyses, the chapter explained that since 1999, the participation of security institution representatives in high-level political positions has increased. It stressed that they brought their security thinking and threat perception behaviors from their time in the Soviet Union's security organizations. Such security thinking has dominated Russia's political elite and directly influences the formation of the security policy documents of the state.

The results of several surveys, which date between 1990 and 2023, on the Russian elite and the public's security thinking, are used in the chapter. The chapter reviewed the official security documents of the post-Soviet period and analyzed how threat perceptions and developments in international relations are reflected in them. It analyzed how and why asymmetric approaches have appeared in the documents since the 2000s. The chapter explored the influences of the political elite's security thinking on public threat perception. It argued that the political elite are effectively a societal role model and exert significant influence on the public's threat perceptions. The chapter clarified what differentiates Russia's security documents from three other world powers (the United States, China, and the European Union) and analyzed those differences.

We can conclude that the reflection of asymmetric approaches is one of the main distinguishing aspects of Russia's security documents. Understanding its weaknesses in the face of a stronger adversary, that is, the West, Russia has, since the 2000s, been strengthening the use of asymmetric methods in its official documents. Moreover, this chapter analyzed the thinking of Russia's military elites regarding the next military doctrine and, based on this, explained that we can expect an increased role for asymmetric approaches in any future security document.

## Notes

1 Odom, W.E. (1998) *The collapse of the Soviet Military*, New Haven, CT: Yale University Press, cited in Haas, Marcel de (2010) *Russia's foreign security policy in the 21st century: Putin, Medvedev and beyond*, Abingdon; New York: Routledge, p. 3.
2 Bezemer, J.W. (1988) Een geschiedenis van Rusland, Amsterdam: Van Oorschot. pp. 26, 33–34, cited in Haas, Marcel de (2010) *Russia's foreign security policy in the 21st century: Putin, Medvedev and beyond*, Abingdon; New York: Routledge, p. 3; see also: Surkov, Vladislav (2018) "Odinochestvo polukrovki", April 9, https://www.global affairs.ru/global-processes/Odinochestvo-polukrovki-14-19477.
3 Haas, Marcel de (2010) *Russia's foreign security policy in the 21st century: Putin, Medvedev and beyond*, Abingdon; New York: Routledge, p. 3.
4 Gareev, Makhmut (2007) "Struktura i osnovnoye soderzhaniye novoy voyennoy doktriny", doklad prezidenta Akademii Voyennykh Nauk generala armii Makhmuta Gareeva na voyenno-nauchnoy konferentsii (Makhmudov's speech), AVN, gazeta *Voenno-Promyshlennyi Kur'er*, № 3 (169), January 24, https://vpk-news.ru/articles/4824.
5 Ibid.
6 Gareev, Makhmud (2003) "O kharaktere i oblike vooruzhennoi bor'by budushchego", "*Armeiskii sbornik*", Vol. 4, http://www.soldiering.ru/war/war.php.
7 Ibid.
8 Gareev, Makhmud (2003b) "O kharaktere i oblike vooruzhennoi bor'by budushchego" …
9 Ibid.
10 Gareev, Makhmud (2003b) "O kharaktere i oblike vooruzhennoi bor'by budushchego" …
11 Ibid.
12 Gareev, Makhmud (2003b) "O kharaktere i oblike vooruzhennoi bor'by budushchego" …
13 Ivanov, Sergei (2004) "Russia's Geopolitical Priorities and Armed Forces", *Russia in Global Affairs*, №1, 2004, February 17, https://eng.globalaffairs.ru/number/n_2571.
14 Ivanov, Sergei (2004) "Russia's Geopolitical Priorities and Armed Forces" …
15 Ivanov, Sergei (2004) "Russia's Geopolitical Priorities and Armed Forces" …
16 Ibid.
17 Snetkov, Aglaya (2015) *Russia's security policy under Putin: a critical perspective*, London; New York: Routledge, p. 106.
18 Litovkin, Viktor (2007) "General Gareev: Rossiya menyaet svoiu voennuiu doktrinu", interview with General Makhmud Gareev, January 16, https://ria.ru/20070116/59124252. html.

19 Ibid.
20 Ibid.
21 Litovkin, Viktor (2007) "General Gareev: Rossiya menyaet svoiu voennuiu doktrinu" …
22 Ibid.
23 Ibid.
24 Litovkin, Viktor (2007) "General Gareev: Rossiya menyaet svoiu voennuiu doktrinu" …
25 Haas, Marcel de (2010) Russia's foreign security policy in the 21st century: Putin, Medvedev and beyond, Abingdon; New York: Routledge, p. 7.
26 Haas, Marcel de (2010) Russia's foreign security policy in the 21st century: Putin, Medvedev and beyond …, p. 158.
27 Ibid.
28 Lukyanov, Fyodor (2012) "Talking point: the logic of Russian foreign policy. Marie Mendras and Fyodor Lukyanov join oDRussia editor Oliver Carroll for a debate in Paris", the speech, *Russia in Global Affairs*, December 13, https://eng.globalaffairs.ru/event/Talking-point-the-logic-of-Russian-foreign-policy-Marie-Mendras-and-Fyodor-Lukyanov-join-oDRussia-ed.
29 Ibid.
30 Bērziņš, Jānis (2019) "Not 'Hybrid' but New Generation Warfare", *Russia's military strategy and doctrine*, (ed.) Glen E. Howard and Matthew Czekaj, The Jamestown Foundation, p. 158.
31 Manilov, V.L. (2000) *Voyennaya Bezopasnost Rossii*, Moskva: Probel, pp. 165, 231–232; Translated in Haas, Marcel de (2010) *Russia's foreign security policy in the 21st century: Putin, Medvedev and beyond* …, p. 5.
32 Zabolotin, V.D. (2000) *Slovar Voyennykh Terminov*, Moskva: OOO NIT's Kosmo, p. 16; Translated in Haas, Marcel de (2010) *Russia's foreign security policy in the 21st century: Putin, Medvedev and beyond* …, p. 5.
33 *National Security Concept of the Russian Federation* (2000) January 10, http://www.mid.ru/en/foreign_policy/official_documents/-/asset_publisher/CptICkB6BZ29/content/id/589768.
34 MOD – The Ministry of Defence of the Russian Federation (2003) *The priority tasks of the development of the armed forces of the Russian Federation*. October, 2003, pp. 45–46, http://red-stars.org/doctrine.pdf.
35 Ibid., p. 51.
36 Zięba, Ryszard (2018) *The Euro-Atlantic security system in the 21st century: from cooperation to crisis*. Springer, p. 103.
37 Ibid., pp. 124–125.
38 *Voennaia Doktrina Rossiyskoi Federatsii (2014) Rossiyskoya Gazeta*, December 30, https://rg.ru/2014/12/30/doktrina-dok.html; *Strategiya natsionalnoi bezopasnosty Rossiiskoi Federatsii* (2015) Kremlin.ru, December 31, http://static.kremlin.ru/media/events/files/ru/l8iXkR8XLAtxeilX7JK3XXy6Y0AsHD5v.pdf.
39 Oliker, Olga (2016) "Unpacking Russia's New National Security Strategy", 7 January 2016, the Center for Strategic and International Studies (CSIS), https://www.csis.org/analysis/unpacking-russias-new-national-security-strategy.
40 Ibid.
41 Oliker, Olga (2016) "Unpacking Russia's New National Security Strategy" …
42 Gerasimov, Valerii (2013) "Tsennost nauki v predvidenii", February 26, Voenno-Promishlenniy Kurer, https://www.vpk-news.ru/articles/14632; Nagornikh, Irina (2016) "'Tsvetnim revoliutsiyam' otvetiat po zakonam gibridnikh voin", March 1, Kommersant.ru, https://www.kommersant.ru/doc/2927168,.
43 Pynnöniemi, Katri (2018) "The National Security Strategy of Russia". *The security strategies of the US, China, Russia and the EU: Living in different worlds*, Report 56. Finnish Institute of International Affairs – FIIA. June, p. 46, https://www.fiia.fi/en/publication/the-security-strategies-of-the-us-china-russia-and-the-eu.
44 Ibid., p. 47.

45 *Strategiya natsionalnoi bezopasnosty Rossiiskoi Federatsii* (2015) Kremlin.ru, December 31, http://static.kremlin.ru/media/events/files/ru/l8iXkR8XLAtxeilX7JK3XXy6Y0 AsHD5v.pdf; Pynnöniemi, Katri (2018) "The National Security Strategy of Russia". *The security strategies of the US, China* ..., p. 47.
46 Haas, Marcel de (2010) *Russia's foreign security policy in the 21st century: Putin, Medvedev and beyond* ..., p. 87.
47 Ibid.
48 *Strategiya natsionalnoi bezopasnosty Rossiiskoi Federatsii (2015)* ...
49 *Strategiya natsionalnoi bezopasnosty Rossiiskoi Federatsii* (2015) ...
50 *Voennaia Doktrina Rossiyskoi Federatsii* (2014) ...
51 Ibid.
52 Ibid.
53 *Strategiya natsionalnoi bezopasnosty Rossiiskoi Federatsii* (2021) *Ofitsial'nyy internet-portal pravovoy informatsii*, July 3, http://publication.pravo.gov.ru/Document/View/0001202107030001.
54 Gol'ts, Aleksandr (2021) "Starcheskiye strakhi kremlya", *Ezhednevnyi Zhurnal*, July 5, https://www.ej2020.ru/?a=note&id=36282&utm.
55 *Strategiya natsionalnoi bezopasnosty Rossiiskoi Federatsii* (2021) ...
56 Denisov, Igor (2021) "What Russia's National Security Strategy Has to Say About Asia", *The Diplomat*, July 14, https://thediplomat.com/2021/07/what-russias-national-security-strategy-has-to-say-about-asia.
57 *Morskaya doktrina Rossiyskoy Federatsii* (2015) utv. Prezidentom RF, July 26, http://static.kremlin.ru/media/events/files/ru/uAFi5nvux2twaqjftS5yrIZUVTJan77L.pdf.
58 Maritime Doctrine of the Russian Federation (2015) Translated by Anna Davis, Russia Maritime Studies Institute of the United States, Naval War College, p. 2.
59 Ibid.
60 Connolly, Richard (2019a) "Fundamentals of the state policy of the Russian Federation in the field of naval activities for the period until 2030", *Russian Studies Series 02/2019*, NATO Defence College, January 22, http://www.ndc.nato.int/research/research.php?icode=574#_edn1.
61 Ibid.
62 Morskaya doktrina Rossiyskoy Federatsii (2022) "Utverzhdena Morskaya doktrina Rossiyskoy Federatsii", *Kremlin.ru*, July 31, pp. 49–50, http://kremlin.ru/acts/news/69084.
63 Raik Kristi, Aaltola Mika, Kallio Jyrki and Pynnöniemi Katri (2018) "The security strategies of the US, China, Russia and the EU- living in different worlds", *FIIA report*, Finish Institute of international Affairs, June 2018/56, p. 64.
64 Ibid.
65 Zięba, Ryszard (2018) *The Euro-Atlantic security system in the 21st century: from cooperation to crisis*. Springer, p. 120.
66 Raik Kristi, Aaltola Mika, Kallio Jyrki and Pynnöniemi Katri (2018) "The security strategies of the US, China, Russia and the EU- living in different worlds", *FIIA report*, Finish Institute of international Affairs, June 2018/56, p. 64.
67 Gerasimov, Valerii (2019) "Vektory razvitiya voyennoy strategii", speech, Anastasiya Sviridova, "*Krasnaya Zvezda*", March 4, http://redstar.ru/vektory-razvitiya-voennoj-strategii/.
68 Ibid.
69 Gerasimov, Valerii (2019) "Vektory razvitiya voyennoy strategii" ...
70 Ibid.
71 Gerasimov, Valerii (2019) "Vektory razvitiya voyennoy strategii" ...
72 Westerlund, Fredrik and Oxenstierna Susanne (eds) (2019) "Russian Military Capability in a Ten-Year Perspective – 2019", *FOI report*, December 3, p. 88, https://www.foi.se/rapportsammanfattning?reportNo=FOI-R–4758–SE.
73 *Air Force Chief Staff General David Goldfein Speaks at Brookings Institution*, February 19, minutes 15–21, https://www.youtube.com/watch?v=3HsHbsGDyfc.

74 Twardowskii, Adam (2019) "General David Goldfein on building the Air Force of the future", February 22, https://www.brookings.edu/blog/order-from-chaos/2019/02/22/general-david-goldfein-on-building-the-air-force-of-the-future/.
75 Gerasimov, Valerii (2019) "Vektory razvitiya voyennoy strategii" …
76 Interfax (2019) "V RF razrabotana strategiya ogranichennykh deystvii po zashchite ee interesov za predelami natsional'noi territorii – Gerasimov", March 2, http://militarynews.ru/story.asp?rid=1&nid=503181&lang=RU.
77 McDermott, Roger (2019) "Gerasimov Unveils Russia's 'Strategy of Limited Actions'", *Eurasia Daily Monitor*, Vol. 16, Issue 31, March 6, https://jamestown.org/program/gerasimov-unveils-russias-strategy-of-limited-actions/.
78 It is largely discussed in the seventh chapter.
79 Haas, Marcel de (2010) *Russia's foreign security policy in the 21st century: Putin, Medvedev and beyond* …, p. 3.
80 Kryshtanovskaya, Olga (2005) *Anatomia rossiiskoi elity*, Moscow: Zakarov, p. 150, online https://vrn-politstudies.nethouse.ru/static/doc/0000/0000/0134/134217.swusdllkvr.pdf.
81 Kryshtanovskaya, Olga (2005) *Anatomia rossiiskoi elity* …, p. 157.
82 Aliyev, Nurlan (2020) "Determinants of Russia's Political Elite Security Thought: Similarities and Differences between the Soviet Union and Contemporary Russia", *Problems of Post-Communism*, Vol. 67, No. 6, pp. 467–477, p. 471. DOI: 10.1080/10758216.2019.168982.
83 Renz, Bettina (2006) "Putin's Militocracy? An Alternative Interpretation of Siloviki in Contemporary Russian Politics." *Europe-Asia Studies*, Vol. 58, No. 6, pp. 907–911, pp. 903–924. DOI: 10.1080/09668130600831134.
84 Ibid, p. 922.
85 Renz, Bettina (2006) "Putin's Militocracy? An Alternative Interpretation of Siloviki in Contemporary Russian Politics" …, p. 912.
86 Ibid., p. 905.
87 Rivera, David W., and Sharon Werning Rivera (2014) "Is Russia a Militocracy? Conceptual Issues and Extant Findings regarding Elite Militarization", *Post-Soviet Affairs*, Vol. 30, No. 1, pp. 27–50, pp. 42–43, DOI: 10.1080/1060586X.2013.819681.
88 Rivera, David W., and Sharon Werning Rivera (2018) "The Militarization of the Russian Elite under Putin." *Problems of Post-Communism*, Vol. 65, No. 4, pp. 221–232. p. 229. DOI: 10.1080/10758216.2017.1295812. For the Kryshtanovskaya's mentioned work see: Kryshtanovskaya, Olga (2008) "The Russian Elite in Transition", *Journal of Communist Studies and Transition Politics*, Vol. 24, No. 4, pp. 585–603, p. 596. DOI: 10.1080/13523270802510602.
89 Aliyev, Nurlan (2020) "Determinants of Russia's Political Elite Security Thought: Similarities and Differences between the Soviet Union and Contemporary Russia", *Problems of Post-Communism*, Vol. 67, No. 6, pp. 467–477, p. 471. DOI: 10.1080/10758216.2019.168982.
90 Stanovaya, Tatiana (2018) "Minimaya stabilnost. Pochemu rezhim Putina kak nikogda gotov k peremenam", June 28, Carnegie Moscow Center, https://carnegie.ru/commentary/76700.
91 Meduza (2022) "Zhurnalist Andrey Soldatov: rukovoditel' vneshney razvedki FSB Sergey Beseda pereveden v SIZO 'Lefortovo'", April 8, https://meduza.io/news/2022/04/08/zhurnalist-andrey-soldatov-rukovoditel-vneshney-razvedki-fsb-sergey-beseda-pereveden-v-sizo-lefortovo.
92 Soldatov, Andrey and Borogan, Irina (2022) "Putin nachal repressii protiv 5-y sluzhby FSB", March 11, https://meduza.io/feature/2022/03/11/putin-nachal-repressii-protiv-5-y-sluzhby-fsb-imenno-ona-nakanune-voyny-obespechivala-prezidenta-rossii-dannymi-o-politicheskoy-situatsii-v-ukraine.
93 Anin, Roman (2022) "Kak Putin prinyal resheniye o voyne", *Vazhnye Istorii*, May 16, https://istories.media/opinions/2022/05/16/kak-putin-prinyal-reshenie-o-voine/?fbclid=IwAR08xSTjo_TynjkrgEYz9e8bHQIcaXTaW3_VZ43vnnlq3W21sydDMI9iLtw.

94 Soldatov, Andrey i Irina Borogan (2022) "Putin nachal repressii protiv 5-y sluzhby FSB", March 11, https://meduza.io/feature/2022/03/11/putin-nachal-repressii-protiv-5-y-sluzhby-fsb-imenno-ona-nakanune-voyny-obespechivala-prezidenta-rossii-dannymi-o-politicheskoy-situatsii-v-ukraine.
95 Soldatov, Andrey (2022) "Neizvestnaya razvedka", January 17, https://agentura.ru/investigations/neizvestnaja-razvedka/.
96 Anin, Roman (2022) "Kak Putin prinyal resheniye o voyne" …
97 Hill, Fiona and Gaddy, Clifford G. (2013) *Mr. Putin: operative in the Kremlin*. Washington: Brookings Institution Press, p. 84.
98 Levada Analytical Center (Levada-Center) (2017) "Rossiiskaia Armiia", Opros, February 20, https://www.levada.ru/2017/02/20/rossijskaya-armiya-2/.
99 Levada Analytical Center (2018) "Rossia i Zapad – Opros", August 2, https://www.levada.ru/2018/08/02/rossiya-i-zapad-3/.
100 Gostev, Aleksandr (2018) "'Drama starikh suprugov'. Rossiyane ochutili legkiy vsplesk lubvi k SShA", August 4, *Radio Svoboda*, https://www.svoboda.org/a/29412642.html.
101 Drakokhrust, Yurii (2018) "Direktor 'Levada-Sentra': Putin viydavil Lukashenko iz massovogo soznaniia rossiian", August 23, https://news.tut.by/economics/605475.html?crnd=18256.
102 Levada Analytical Center (2022a) "Odobreniye institutov, reytingi partiy i politikov", March 30, https://www.levada.ru/2022/03/30/odobrenie-institutov-rejtingi-partij-i-politikov/.
103 Ibid.
104 Levada Analytical Center (2022d) "Odobreniye institutov, reytingi partiy i politikov", August 31, https://www.levada.ru/2022/08/31/odobrenie-institutov-rejtingi-politikov/.
105 Levada Analytical Center (2022b) "Konflikt s Ukrainoy", March 31, https://www.levada.ru/2022/03/31/konflikt-s-ukrainoj/.
106 Ibid.
107 Levada Analytical Center (2022c) "Konflikt s ukrainoy: iyul' 2022 goda", August 1, https://www.levada.ru/2022/08/01/konflikt-s-ukrainoj-iyul-2022-goda/.
108 Levada Analytical Center (2022e) "Konflikt s ukrainoy – avgust 2022 goda", September 1, https://www.levada.ru/2022/09/01/konflikt-s-ukrainoj-avgust-2022-goda/.
109 Levinson, Alexey (2022) "Why continue polling in Russia?", June 21, https://ridl.io/why-continue-polling-in-russia/.
110 Gudkov, Lev (2022) "Tri fazy adaptatsii", *RE:Russia*, July 5, https://re-russia.net/expertise/009/.
111 Gudkov, Lev (2022) "Tri fazy adaptatsii" …
112 Medvedev, Sergey (2022) "'Obizhennyy, zlobnyy i mstitel'nyy'- Portret 'cheloveka putinskogo'", *Golos Svobody*, August 14, https://www.svoboda.org/a/chelovek-obizhennyy-zlobnyy-mstiteljnyy-lev-gudkov-o-homo-putinus-/31983907.html.
113 Ibid.
114 Levada Analytical Center (2022f) "Konflikt s ukrainoy: otsenki dekabrya 2022 goda", December 23, https://www.levada.ru/2022/12/23/konflikt-s-ukrainoj-otsenki-dekabrya-2022-goda/.
115 Ibid.
116 Leonov, Nikolay (2018) "Pochemu KGB ne spas SSSR", interviewed by Igor' Latunskii, https://versia.ru/v-avguste-91-go-po-moskve-xodili-60-tysyach-vooruzhyonnyx-chekistov.

## Bibliography

*Air Force Chief Staff General David Goldfein Speaks at Brookings Institution*, February 19, minutes 15–21, available at: https://www.youtube.com/watch?v=3HsHbsGDyfc, accessed 1 March 2019.

## Evolution of the Russian Federation's security concept 143

Aliyev, Nurlan (2020) "Determinants of Russia's Political Elite Security Thought: Similarities and Differences between the Soviet Union and Contemporary Russia", *Problems of Post-Communism*, Vol. 67, No. 6, DOI:10.1080/10758216.2019.1689827, available at: https://www.tandfonline.com/doi/full/10.1080/10758216.2019.1689827.

Anin, Roman (2022) "Kak Putin prinyal resheniye o voyne", *Vazhnye Istorii*, May 16, available at: https://istories.media/opinions/2022/05/16/kak-putin-prinyal-reshenie-o-voine/?fbclid=IwAR08xSTjo_TynjkrgEYz9e8bHQIcaXTaW3_VZ43vnnlq3W21sydDMI9iLtw, accessed 19 May 2022.

Bērziņš, Jānis (2019) "Not 'Hybrid' but New Generation Warfare", *Russia's military strategy and doctrine*, Glen E. Howard and Matthew Czekaj (ed.). Washington: The Jamestown Foundation.

Bezemer, J.W. (1988) *Een geschiedenis van Rusland*, Amsterdam: Van Oorschot.

Connolly, Richard (2019a) "Fundamentals of the state policy of the Russian Federation in the field of naval activities for the period until 2030", Russian Studies Series 02/2019, NATO Defence College, January 22, available at: http://www.ndc.nato.int/research/research.php?icode=574#_edn1, accessed 30 January 2019.

Denisov, Igor (2021) "What Russia's National Security Strategy Has to Say About Asia", *The Diplomat*, July 14, available at: https://thediplomat.com/2021/07/what-russias-national-security-strategy-has-to-say-about-asia, accessed 17 August 2022.

Drakokhrust, Yurii (2018) "Direktor 'Levada-Sentra': Putin viydavil Lukashenko iz massovogo soznaniia rossiian", August 23, available at: https://news.tut.by/economics/605475.html?crnd=18256, accessed 31 August 2018.

Gareev, Makhmud (2003) "O kharaktere i oblike vooruzhennoi bor'by budushchego", "*Armeiskii sbornik*", Vol. 4, available at: http://www.soldiering.ru/war/war.php, accessed 28 November 2018.

_____ (2007) "Struktura i osnovnoye soderzhaniye novoy voyennoy doktriny", doklad prezidenta Akademii Voyennykh Nauk generala armii Makhmuta Gareeva na voyenno-nauchnoy konferentsii (Makhmudov's speech), AVN, gazeta *Voenno-Promyshlennyi Kur'er*, 3 (169), January 24, available at: https://vpk-news.ru/articles/4824, accessed 27 November 2018.

Gerasimov, Valerii (2013) "Tsennost nauki v predvidenii", 26 February 2013, Voenno-Promishlenniy Kurer, available at: https://www.vpk-news.ru/articles/14632, accessed 10 June 2018.

_____ (2019) "Vektory razvitiya voyennoy strategii", speech, Anastasiya Sviridova, "*Krasnaya Zvezda*", 4 March 2019, available at: http://redstar.ru/vektory-razvitiya-voennoj-strategii/, accessed 8 March 2019.

Gol'ts, Aleksandr (2021) "Starcheskiye strakhi kremlya", *Ezhednevnyi Zhurnal*, July 5, available at: https://www.ej2020.ru/?a=note&id=36282&utm, accessed 17 August 2022.

Gostev, Aleksandr (2018) "'Drama starikh suprugov'. Rossiyane ochutili legkiy vsplesk lubvi k SShA", August 4, *Radio Svoboda*, available at: https://www.svoboda.org/a/29412642.html, accessed 6 August 2018.

Gudkov, Lev (2022) "Tri fazy adaptatsii", *RE:Russia*, July 5, available at: https://re-russia.net/expertise/009/, accessed 19 August 2022.

Haas, Marcel de (2010) *Russia's foreign security policy in the 21st century: Putin, Medvedev and beyond*, Abingdon; New York: Routledge.

Hill, Fiona, and Clifford G. Gaddy (2013) *Mr. Putin: operative in the Kremlin*, Washington: Brookings Institution Press.

Interfax (2019) "V RF razrabotana strategiya ogranichennykh deystvii po zashchite ee interesov za predelami natsional'noi territorii – Gerasimov", March 2, available at: http://militarynews.ru/story.asp?rid=1&nid=503181&lang=RU, accessed 8 March 2019.

Ivanov, Sergei (2004) "Russia's Geopolitical Priorities and Armed Forces", *Russia in Global Affairs*, 1, 2004, February 17, available at: https://eng.globalaffairs.ru/number/n_2571, accessed 28 November 2018.

Kryshtanovskaya, Olga (2005) *Anatomia rossiiskoi elity*, Moscow: Zakarov. Online available at: https://vrn-politstudies.nethouse.ru/static/doc/0000/0000/0134/134217.swusdllkvr.pdf, accessed 1 April 2018;

_____ (2008) "The Russian Elite in Transition", *Journal of Communist Studies and Transition Politics*, Vol. 24, No. 4, DOI: 10.1080/13523270802510602.

Leonov, Nikolay (2018) "Pochemu KGB ne spas SSSR", interviewed by Igor' Latunskii, available at: https://versia.ru/v-avguste-91-go-po-moskve-xodili-60-tysyach-vooruzhyonnyx-chekistov, accessed 19 May 2019.

Levada Analytical Centre (Levada-Centre) (2017) "Rossiiskaia Armiia", Opros, February 20, available at: https://www.levada.ru/2017/02/20/rossijskaya-armiya-2/, accessed 1 June 2018.

_____ (2018) "Rossia i Zapad – Opros", August 2, available at: https://www.levada.ru/2018/08/02/rossiya-i-zapad-3/, accessed 8 August 2018.

_____ (2022a) "Odobreniye institutov, reytingi partiy i politikov", March 30, available at: https://www.levada.ru/2022/03/30/odobrenie-institutov-rejtingi-partij-i-politikov/, accessed 19 May 2022.

_____ (2022b) "Konflikt s Ukrainoy", March 31, available at: https://www.levada.ru/2022/03/31/konflikt-s-ukrainoj/, accessed 19 May 2022.

_____ (2022c) "Konflikt s ukrainoy: iyul' 2022 goda", August 1, available at: https://www.levada.ru/2022/08/01/konflikt-s-ukrainoj-iyul-2022-goda/, accessed 19 August 2022.

_____ (2022d) "Odobreniye institutov, reytingi partiy i politikov", August 31, available at: https://www.levada.ru/2022/08/31/odobrenie-institutov-rejtingi-politikov/, accessed 1 September 2022.

_____ (2022e) "Konflikt s ukrainoy – avgust 2022 goda", September 1, available at: https://www.levada.ru/2022/09/01/konflikt-s-ukrainoj-avgust-2022-goda/, accessed 17 September 2022.

_____ (2022f) "Konflikt s ukrainoy: otsenki dekabrya 2022 goda", December 23, available at: https://www.levada.ru/2022/12/23/konflikt-s-ukrainoj-otsenki-dekabrya-2022-goda/, accessed 23 January 2023.

Levinson, Alexey (2022) "Why continue polling in Russia?", June 21, available at: https://ridl.io/why-continue-polling-in-russia/, accessed 19 August 2022.

Litovkin, Viktor (2007) "General Gareev: Rossiya menyaet svoiu voennuiu doktrinu", interview with General Makhmud Gareev, 16 January 2007, available at: https://ria.ru/20070116/59124252.html, accessed 5 January 2019.

Lukyanov, Fyodor (2012) "Talking point: the logic of Russian foreign policy. Marie Mendras and Fyodor Lukyanov join oDRussia editor Oliver Carroll for a debate in Paris", the speech, *Russia in Global Affairs*, December 13, available at: https://eng.globalaffairs.ru/event/Talking-point-the-logic-of-Russian-foreign-policy-Marie-Mendras-and-Fyodor-Lukyanov-join-oDRussia-ed, accessed 23 February 2019.

Manilov, V.L. (2000) *Voyennaya Bezopasnost Rossii*, Moskva: Probel.

Davis, Anna(Ed.) (2015) *Maritime Doctrine of the Russian Federation*, Russia Maritime Studies Institute of the United States: Naval War College.

McDermott, Roger (2019) "Gerasimov Unveils Russia's 'Strategy of Limited Actions'", *Eurasia Daily Monitor*, Vol. 16, No. 31, March 6, available at: https://jamestown.org/program/gerasimov-unveils-russias-strategy-of-limited-actions/, accessed 8 March 2019.

Meduza (2022) "Zhurnalist Andrey Soldatov: rukovoditel' vneshney razvedki FSB Sergey Beseda pereveden v SIZO 'Lefortovo'", April 8, available at: https://meduza.io/news/2022/04/08/zhurnalist-andrey-soldatov-rukovoditel-vneshney-razvedki-fsb-sergey-beseda-pereveden-v-sizo-lefortovo, accessed 3 May 2022.

Medvedev, Sergey (2022) "'Obizhennyy, zlobnyy i mstitel'nyy' – Portret 'cheloveka putinskogo'", *Golos Svobody*, August 14, available at: https://www.svoboda.org/a/chelovek-obizhennyy-zlobnyy-mstiteljnyy-lev-gudkov-o-homo-putinus-/31983907.html, accessed 19 August 2022.

MOD – The Ministry of Defence of the Russian Federation (2003) *The priority tasks of the development of the armed forces of the Russian Federation*. October, 2003, pp. 45–46, available at: http://red-stars.org/doctrine.pdf, accessed 13 May 2018.

*Morskaya doktrina Rossiyskoy Federatsii* (2015) utv. Prezidentom RF, 26 July 2015, available at: http://static.kremlin.ru/media/events/files/ru/uAFi5nvux2twaqjftS5yrIZUVTJan77L.pdf, accessed 7 February 2019.

*Morskaya doktrina Rossiyskoy Federatsii* (2022) "Utverzhdena Morskaya doktrina Rossiyskoy Federatsii", *Kremlin.ru*, July 31, pp. 49–50, available at: http://kremlin.ru/acts/news/69084, accessed 17 August 2012.

Nagornikh, Irina (2016) "'Tsvetnim revoliutsiyam' otvetiat po zakonam gibridnikh voin", 1 March 2016, Kommersant.ru, available at: https://www.kommersant.ru/doc/2927168, accessed 10 June 2018.

*National Security Concept of the Russian Federation* (2000) 10 January 2000, available at: http://www.mid.ru/en/foreign_policy/official_documents/-/asset_publisher/CptICkB6BZ29/content/id/589768, accessed 3 May 2018.

Odom, W.E. (1998) *The collapse of the Soviet Military*, New Haven, CT: Yale University Press.

Oliker, Olga (2016) "Unpacking Russia's New National Security Strategy", 7 January 2016, the Centre for Strategic and International Studies (CSIS), available at: https://www.csis.org/analysis/unpacking-russias-new-national-security-strategy, accessed 5 May 2018.

Pynnöniemi, Katri (2018) "The National Security Strategy of Russia". *The security strategies of the US, China, Russia and the EU: Living in different worlds*, Report 56. Finnish Institute of International Affairs –FIIA. June 2018, p. 46, available at: https://www.fiia.fi/en/publication/the-security-strategies-of-the-us-china-russia-and-the-eu, accessed 15 January 2019.

Kristi, Raik, Aaltola Mika, Kallio Jyrki, and Pynnöniemi Katri (2018) "The security strategies of the US, China, Russia and the EU-living in different worlds", *FIIA report*, Finish Institute of international Affairs, June 2018/56.

Renz, Bettina (2006) "Putin's Militocracy? An Alternative Interpretation of Siloviki in Contemporary Russian Politics", *Europe-Asia Studies*, Vol. 58, No. 6, pp. 903–924. DOI: 10.1080/09668130600831134.

Rivera, David W., and Sharon Werning Rivera (2014) "Is Russia a Militocracy? Conceptual Issues and Extant Findings regarding Elite Militarization", *Post-Soviet Affairs*, Vol. 30, No. 1, pp. 27–50, DOI: 10.1080/1060586X.2013.819681.

―――― (2018) "The Militarization of the Russian Elite under Putin", *Problems of Post-Communism*, Vol. 65, No. 4, pp. 221–232, DOI: 10.1080/10758216.2017.1295812.

Snetkov, Aglaya (2015) *Russia's security policy under Putin: a critical perspective*, London; New York: Routledge.

Soldatov, Andrey (2022) "Neizvestnaya razvedka", January 17, available at: https://agentura.ru/investigations/neizvestnaja-razvedka/, accessed 19 May 2022.

Soldatov, Andrey, and Irina Borogan (2022) "Putin nachal repressii protiv 5-y sluzhby FSB", March 11, available at: https://meduza.io/feature/2022/03/11/putin-nachal-repressii-protiv-5-y-sluzhby-fsb-imenno-ona-nakanune-voyny-obespechivala-prezidenta-rossii-dannymi-o-politicheskoy-situatsii-v-ukraine, accessed 3 May 2022.

Stanovaya, Tatiana (2018) "Minimaya stabilnost. Pochemu rezhim Putina kak nikogda gotov k peremenam", June 28, Carnegie Moscow Centre, available at: https://carnegie.ru/commentary/76700, accessed 29 March 2019.

*Strategiya natsionalnoi bezopasnosty Rossiiskoi Federatsii* (2015) Kremlin.ru, 31 December 2015, available at: http://static.kremlin.ru/media/events/files/ru/l8iXkR8XLAtxeilX7JK3XXy6Y0AsHD5v.pdf, accessed 4 May 2018.

*Strategiya natsionalnoi bezopasnosty Rossiiskoi Federatsii* (2021) *Ofitsial'nyy internet-portal pravovoy informatsii*, July 3, available at: http://publication.pravo.gov.ru/Document/View/0001202107030001, accessed 17 August 2022.

Surkov, Vladislav (2018) "Odinochestvo polukrovki", April 9, available at: https://www.globalaffairs.ru/global-processes/Odinochestvo-polukrovki-14-19477, accessed 27 June 2018.

Twardowskii, Adam (2019) "General David Goldfein on building the Air Force of the future", February 22, available at: https://www.brookings.edu/blog/order-from-chaos/2019/02/22/general-david-goldfein-on-building-the-air-force-of-the-future/, accessed 1 March 2019.

*Voennaia Doktrina Rossiyskoi Federatsii* (2014) *Rossiyskoya Gazeta*, 30 December 2014, https://rg.ru/2014/12/30/doktrina-dok.html, accessed 3 May 2018.

Westerlund, Fredrik, and Oxenstierna Susanne (eds.) (2019) "Russian Military Capability in a Ten-Year Perspective – 2019", FOI report, December 3, p. 88, available at: https://www.foi.se/rapportsammanfattning?reportNo=FOI-R–4758–SE, accessed 4 December 2019.

Zabolotin, V.D. (2000) *Slovar Voyennykh Terminov*, Moskva: OOO NIT's Kosmo.

Zięba, Ryszard (2018) *The Euro-Atlantic security system in the 21st century: from cooperation to crisis*, Springer.

# 5 Functions of Russia's foreign security policy

New approaches

**Russia's external security approaches: hybrid or not?**

Since Russia's intervention in Ukraine in 2014, its activities and tactics have been considered from several angles by scholars and decision-makers. There is no common approach for defining what kind of strategy/warfare methods are used by Russia among these scholars. However, since its "unlabeled" military operations in Crimea and in eastern Ukraine, Russia's contemporary warfare approaches have been one of the subjects of concern in international security.

There are continuing discussions among experts regarding the name of Russia's warfare approaches. Labeled as "hybrid war" immediately after Russia's intervention in Ukraine in 2014, the terminology was useful to highlight how Russia's approach in Crimea differed from previous wars in Chechnya and Georgia. Russian military approaches that resulted in swift victory were termed differently. As one of the key experts that developed the concept of "hybrid war," Frank Hoffman stressed, in his 2007 article, that the world was entering a time when multiple forms of warfare would be used simultaneously by flexible and sophisticated adversaries who understand that successful conflicts must take on a variety of forms designed to fit one's needs/goals at that particular time.[1] Although there are several similarities in Russia's approaches and original hybrid warfare theory, this concept mainly regards the use of conventional and non-conventional methods simultaneously in framing a given military operation. Analyzing Russia's activities and Russian military scholars' thinking, Janis Berjins described it as new-generation warfare.[2] Several experts compared Russia's approaches to Messner's non-linear warfare terminology, which was also used by Surkov in his writing. Michael Kofman explained Russia's behavior in Ukraine and Syria as 20th-century raiding operations.[3] Mark Galeotti proposed the idea of Russian political war, which was ultimately based on George Kennan's concept from the 1940s.[4]

In the aftermath of the Crimea annexation in March 2014, the "hybrid warfare" concept quickly gained popularity because it appeared particularly relevant to a situation where non-military tools and the use of information played a central role. According to Bettina Renz, few of the analysts applying the concept to Russia, however, have explicitly based their conclusions on Frank Hoffmann's specific understanding of the term and instead have tended to refer loosely to the general

DOI: 10.4324/9781003344391-6

idea of "hybridity" as a mix of military and non-military tools. "This has resulted in widely varying understandings and definitions of what exactly 'hybrid warfare' entails and enabled the extreme stretching of the concept ultimately to frame Russian foreign policy in general."[5]

Analyzing Gerasimov's famous article, which was published about a year before the operations in Ukraine and mistakenly called "Gerasimov's Doctrine" in the West, Charles K. Bartles stressed that probably the most misunderstood aspect of Gerasimov's article is the idea of "indirect and asymmetric methods," which has been interpreted by the West as hybrid war:

> Of note, there is a general consensus in Russian military circles that hybrid war is a completely Western concept as no Russian military officer or strategist has discussed it, except to mention the West's use of the term, or to mention the West's use of hybrid warfare against Russia. The Russian military has been adamant that they do not practice a hybrid-war strategy. Moreover, there have been many Russian commentaries that state this concept is nothing new, that the aspects of hybrid war mentioned by Western analysts have been practiced since warfare began.[6]

Russia's Defense Minister Sergei Shoigu explains his visions on the hybrid war "waged by the West" stating that "patterns and algorithms for overthrowing any legal authority" have long been created in any country that is inconvenient for "them." He claims that all of this is done under the banner of promoting democracy.[7] Furthermore, he highlights that "Western colleagues" like to accuse Russia of waging "hybrid wars" but the West itself is waging the "real hybrid wars."[8]

Generally, proponents of the "Russian hybrid war" concept argue that with "hybrid warfare" as demonstrated in Ukraine, Russia, had found new methods of warfare which its adversaries are unable to stand against. Skeptical authors on the concept, in contrast, explain that "hybrid warfare" is not new because indirect approaches and unconventional tactics, such as the use of proxy forces, information warfare, psychological operations, or sabotage, have long been tools in the arsenal of most states' military.[9] Bettina Renz argues that the problems pertaining to the "hybrid warfare" concept go beyond the fact that the tactics used by Russia in Crimea are nothing new. Discussing the concept in the context of other presumed war-winning approaches in the history of strategic thought, she rightfully points out that the effectiveness of Russia's operation in Crimea was not the result of applying a new war-winning formula. Instead, the swift achievement of objectives in this case was the result of extremely favorable circumstances—such as a Russian or Russian-speaking majority, an already stationed Russian military base, and a severely weakened Ukrainian political and military leadership unable or unwilling to put up any measure of resistance—which are unlikely to work in a different scenario.[10] As Russian security analyst Vladimir Mukhin asserted, the relative success of a "hybrid war" in Crimea was due to ethnic factors, "Obviously, a Russian 'hybrid war' would not have succeeded in Crimea if the majority of the population there had been Crimean

Tatars."[11] Additionally, agreements on transit of troops in Ukraine between Moscow and Kyiv enabled deployments and methods that would not otherwise have been possible.

Renz stresses that the focus on Russian "hybrid warfare" capabilities does not adequately reflect the direction of ongoing Russian military modernization:

> Contrary to the claims made by some observers, the perfection of "hybrid warfare" capabilities, where the use of actual military force will play at best a secondary role, is not a Russian ambition. As such, an exaggeration of the centrality of "hybrid warfare" thinking in Russian military policy can lead to a one-sided understanding of Russian military capabilities.[12]

This thought would be confirmed during Russia's invasion of Ukraine in 2022.

According to Michael Kofman and Matthew Rojansky, non-linear or non-traditional warfare, as it is understood in Moscow, is simply Russia's attempt to catch up conceptually to the realities of modern war. The realities of which the United States have been grappling with for over a decade in Iraq, Afghanistan, and elsewhere. "By labeling Russia's response to these broad realities as a new and special kind of 'hybrid war,' the West has incorrectly elevated Russia's particular operations in Ukraine to the level of a coherent or preconceived doctrine."[13]

All of the aforementioned explanations can be justified by Russia's external security approaches. Many of these claims can also be recognized as appropriate when considering Russia's contemporary military approaches. But only if all of the aforementioned warfare approaches are considered together, not separately, even possibly in frame of the same operational strategy. Such a thought could be explained by the changing, dialectical characteristics of Russia's methods. The use of any method that is both possible and affordable in its confrontation with a stronger adversary or adversaries might be the best formula to understand Russia's contemporary approaches. Given Russia's foreign and security policy goals, from the confirmation of its "legitimate zone of interests" regarding most parts of the former Soviet Union to acceptance of its status as a global power, Russia faces several adversaries simultaneously. In the global power competition Russia has stronger competitors, such as the West or possibly China in the future, while in stark contrast, in approaches toward the former Soviet republics, which are not members of NATO, Russia has weaker targets. All these influence the formation of Russia's security policy. But the main problems in realizing the goals of these plans are Russia's economic and other internal problems. In such a situation where a state has ambitious international goals but does not have the required economic possibilities, it is inclined to behave as a small actor in an asymmetric war. In other words, Russia with its goals, threat perception, and possibilities has to use asymmetric strategies and instruments rather than symmetric ones.

As the regime's primary internal concern is regime security, Russian elites publicly state that the pattern of forced "US-sponsored" regime change has largely been supplanted by a new method. According to Charles K. Bartles, from a Russian military perspective, this new Western way of war has many implications that can be easily identified in Gerasimov's 2013 article[14] and Russia's current military doctrine:

> If in the past, the primary threat of foreign-forced regime change has come from an army storming across the border, in contrast, today, the threat is coming increasingly from more indirect and asymmetric methods. This change in the nature of the threat to Russia's sovereignty is causing Russian military development to increasingly focus on obtaining improved capabilities to counter those asymmetric and indirect threats. The means required to implement these capabilities will be as diverse and asymmetric as the threats they are intended to counter and could come in the form of undeclared conventional forces, peacekeepers, special operators, Cossacks, private military companies, foreign legionnaires, biker gangs, Russian-sponsored NGOs, and cyber/propaganda warriors.[15]

According to Bartles, one of the most interesting aspects of Gerasimov's article is his view on the relationship between non-military and military measures in war. Bartles notes that leveraging all the means of national power in an effort to achieve the state's ends is nothing new for Russia, but now the Russian military is seeing war as something more than a simple military conflict:

> These non-military measures include economic sanctions, disruption of diplomatic ties, and political and diplomatic pressure. The important point is that while the West considers these non-military measures as ways of avoiding war, Russia considers these measures as war.[16]

Bartles emphasized that although some analysts in the West, having read Gerasimov's article and viewed Russian operations in Crimea and eastern Ukraine, have created models for a new Russian way of warfare, but these are unrealistic visions. "In Gerasimov's own words, 'each war represents an isolated case, requiring an understanding of its own particular logic, its own unique character,'" he writes.[17] Bartles notes that although Russia may respond similarly to two different situations, this is not an indicator of a specific formula for action; rather, "it just means the similarity of the situations required similar responses."[18] According to him, at the tactical level, models and formulas are essential for determining the correlation of forces needed for victory, "but at the operational and strategic levels, a much different approach is required."[19]

## Instruments of security policy

The instruments used by Russia cannot be identified as simply military or non-military. It is also difficult to determine the lines between the conventional and nonconventional methods utilized. But, if Russia's activities were to be analyzed in an asymmetric warfare frame, it is possible to find that in many cases Russia's instrument choices depend on the strategic relationship of asymmetric approaches. As explained above, the main issue for succeeding in asymmetric war is the asymmetry of a chosen strategy. For instance, if Russia were to face a stronger adversary, that is, the United States or NATO, Moscow would try to avoid directly involving themselves in conflict or if that's impossible they'd try to focus on using indirect methods (mainly information and cyber warfare tools) or strategy (e.g., for a response to threats such as strikes from cosmic forces, it may target adversaries military satellites and develop its electron warfare capabilities) against a certain enemy. On the other hand, if the adversary is weaker, Russia may prefer to use both conventional—for a quick victory (as Moscow tried to conduct at the beginning of the 2022 invasion of Ukraine)—and also non-conventional in order to destabilize the targeted society and influence the adversary's decision-makers and public in the hopes of achieving an inexpensive victory. To achieve these aims faster, Russia would consider the most affordable methods or instruments rather than more expensive approaches.

In short, Russia tries to find affordable methods for its defensive and offensive approaches. This is not something new in Russia's security policy. Since the establishment of the Soviet Union, such approaches in security policy have been quite familiar. The Russian version of the idea "all's fair in love and war" [v bor'be s vragom vse metody khoroshi] is popular among Russia's political and military elites. To realize these "fair" approaches, it needs to focus on the vulnerabilities in a targeted state. Stalin's 1936 explanation of this aspect of Soviet security thinking is appropriate when considering the current security thinking of the Russian elite. According to Stalin, "history shows that when any state intends to make war against another state, even not adjacent, it begins to seek for frontiers across which it can reach the frontiers of the state it wants to attack, usually, the aggressive state finds such frontiers."[20]

According to Christopher S. Chivvis, a quarter century after the end of the Cold War, the Kremlin has clearly returned to its Cold War practices and is engaging in a far-reaching political warfare effort against US interests in Europe and elsewhere. Chivvis notes that Russia's current political warfare efforts are similar to those of the Soviet Union in the 1980s, but they go further and take advantage of new tools and opportunities. Although Russia used information operations in the Cold War, the volume and ambition of Moscow's information campaigns today are far greater "and they are facilitated by the internet, cable news, and especially social media."[21] The existence of new tools, such as cyber, has dramatically changed the picture, giving Russia new means of exerting both direct and indirect influences over the Western political scene:

> Because Russia and the world are much more closely linked than during the Cold War, it is easier for Russia to penetrate Western societies. Russia's use of political warfare tactics also appears to be less ideological than during the Cold War, when the Kremlin held a hidebound Marxist worldview. Russia's outlook today is less bound to any ideology, and Moscow may be shrewder as a result.[22]

Any possible and affordable instrument can be used for such activities. Russia uses any available possibility against a stronger adversary, which can make them stronger in a particular niche. These niches can be the information sphere, the Internet, cyber tools, social media, etc. Using non-kinetic warfare instruments, Russia does not eschew conventional military force. However, in conventional military confrontations—or potential arms races—Russia prefers asymmetric strategies. In non-kinetic methods, Russia is focused on influencing the populations of targeted countries. Though it is hard to measure the effects of Russian non-conventional operations, they have likely had some influence on elections in the West and elsewhere. It should be noted that the factors that make a given state vulnerable to Russia's asymmetric non-conventional approaches can be geographical proximity to Russia, cultural or historical affinities with Russia, high levels of corruption, political, ethnic, religious, and other conflict situations in the particular state.

It is difficult to exactly classify which institutions are responsible for non-conventional asymmetric approaches in Russia. In some cases, it might be a public institution or a common operation of various security institutions; in other cases, it might be government-affiliated businesses or NGOs. According to Mark Galeotti, there is no single Russian "doctrine" on non-conventional operations. He notes that Russia's campaign is dangerous precisely because it has no single organizing principle, let alone a controlling agency:

> There is a broad political objective—to distract, divide, and demoralize—but otherwise it is largely opportunistic, fragmented, even sometimes contradictory. Some major operations are coordinated, largely through the presidential administration, but most are not. Rather, operations are conceived and generally carried out by a bewildering array of 'political entrepreneurs' hoping that their success will win them the Kremlin's favor: diplomats and spies, criminals and think-tankers, oligarchs, and journalists.[23]

One of the main lessons from Ukraine in 2014 that could prove useful in analyzing developments in Russia's external security instruments is the coordination, management, and involvement of not only state and non-state actors but also government-affiliated institutions in the operation. Samuel Charap notes that Moscow coordinated the arms of national power effectively to achieve its objectives. He highlighted that in previous post-Soviet military operations, Russia was not able to do so. Conversely, the operation in Ukraine included the successful use of subversion, cyber, proxies, conventional military interventions, and military exercises to deter and coerce, all conducted under the cover of the nuclear umbrella, which Russian officials regularly brought to the world's attention. One of the outcomes of the Ukraine intervention in 2014 was the creation of a new body to deal with such issues, the National Center for the Management of Defense of the Russian Federation, a 24/7 interagency nerve center that came online in early 2014.[24]

According to Lawrence Freedman, one of the possible successes of Russia's approach in Ukraine in 2014 was its projection of a more menacing image than Russia's actual strength warranted, which served to deter the West from escalating the conflict.[25] As highlighted by Michael Kofman and Matthew Rojansky from the Russian perspective, an approach to war that combines different types of power projection is not itself reflective of any newly devised strategy. Rather, it is an illustration or acknowledgment by Russia of a growing trend in how wars are fought, whoever may be fighting them. According to Kofman and Rojansky, modern wars, simply put, are waged through a combination of many elements of national power stating that, "in Washington, this conventional wisdom has long been characterized by the beltway catchphrase of 'using all the tools in the toolkit,' or the more recent mantra of using 'smart power.'"[26]

The tools and methods used by Russia, such as information operations, propaganda, cyberoperations, coercive diplomacy, use of political groups, NGOs or public individuals, economic pressing, etc., are not new nor are they used solely by Russia. Such methods were used, and are currently used, by several states and in international relations in one way or another. However, their dimension and role in the state security policy are distinguished in Russia's case. Another of contemporary Russia's distinctive characteristics in international security is its new take on the Soviet's entire country war concept, that is, using the state's external security policy not only in regards to government institutions but also to engage (either voluntarily or with the state's encouragement or coercion) businessmen, criminal groups, and others as necessary. Now, we are going to examine the main tools Russia has used in recent years.

**The role of information warfare in Russia's security approaches**

In contemporary Russia, information plays a huge role in statecraft, including external security. The role of propaganda in military operations is so great that Russian Nobel Prize-winning journalist Dmitry Muratov explained the obedience of an essential part of Russian society with the invasion of Ukraine in 2022 as "propaganda is the new religion, Putin is the new God."[27]

As with any form of warfare, information attacks are used by adversaries in all forms of war, including asymmetric warfare. But, according to the asymmetric nature of this type of aggression, communication is used as one of the main tools of warfare. Both state and non-state actors actively use communication interventions in the form of propaganda or information operations to achieve their political goals. In this respect, the role of communication in the military, especially in asymmetric warfare has increased. In these circumstances, the information environment becomes a key element of the operational environment assessment for military leaders. Nowadays, information influences as well as communication tools and skills are as important in the military as in public life. The complex nature of conflict today is represented by the convergence of different types of war throughout various domains in an unclear environment, which challenges policymakers and military strategists alike.[28] Such information operations use disinformation, fake news, and psychological warfare as its primary tools. Information operations are employed together with cyberoperations.

According to Russian sociologist Denis Volkov, there are three phases of the Putin administration's information campaign: in the first stage, from the moment Vladimir Putin came to power in 2000, state control over TV broadcasters was extended, such as Ren TV or Channel 1; in the second phase, which gathered momentum after the post-election protests in 2011, the government shut down independent print and online publications, such as Lenta; the third phase—war propaganda—began with Georgia in 2008 and resumed with Ukraine in February 2014.[29] It should be noted that during the Russian-Georgian war and the intervention in Ukraine, Russian government controlled news channels began broadcasting strikingly similar, if not identical, messages. These positions coincided with the Kremlin's vision regarding the military operations in Georgia and Ukraine.

Russia's successful information operations were observed during the invasion of Ukraine in 2014. Russia's information warfare in Crimea and the Donbas in 2014 can be divided into the following phases:

1 The creation of loyalty through cultural, linguistic, and ideological ties of Russian minority and Russian-speaking communities of these regions toward Russia.
2 Spreading fear among the population regarding the governments' crackdowns against them. In this phase, the role of the Soviet Army in liberating them from the occupation of Nazi Germany during WWII was emphasized.
3 The defense of these regions by the Russian military/civilian forces and the humanitarian intervention to promote them joining Russia.[30]

Russian information operations in Crimea and Donbas dates back to the "First Maidan" in 2004. Since the majority of the population in these areas are Russian speakers and have close historical, cultural, and economic ties with Russia, Moscow could successfully carry out information operations there.

In addition to media institutions, Russia also used educational and cultural institutions for propaganda in Crimea. For instance, the local branch of the Moscow State University (MSU-*MGU*) played an important role in the propaganda campaign among the local youth. The MSU's branch, which acted independently in its early years, was known as the educational institution that brought international experts for lectures and organized high-quality educational programs. However, the branch's directory was changed later and the institution became a vehicle for "brainwashing." Then MSU invited only Russian experts, notably the propagandists of "Russian World" (*Russkiy Mir)* to deliver lectures. Local businessmen with close ties to Russia started to organize charity events, such as the creation and repair of museums, galleries, and exhibitions dedicated to the Great Patriotic War. These businessmen played an important role in the promotion of "George's ribbons." Local experts who witnessed these events pointed to five reasons for the success of Russia's information operations in Crimea:

1 Ethnic factor—presentation of the Crimean Tatars and their non-Slavic roots as a threat;
2 The failure of Ukraine's policy (working with the media, counterpropaganda, social-cultural, and poor awareness) aimed at the Russian-speaking population;
3 The failure of Ukrainian nationalist ideas in Crimea where a large number of the Russian-speaking population lives;

4 The presence of a strong, local self-identification; and
5 The promotion of the idea, immediately before the invasion of Crimea, that Ukraine would collapse as the Soviet Union did (this envisaged "legalization" of the idea of secession of Crimea from Ukraine among the local population).[31]

Russia created an alternative reality in the information space using historical factors (the "Russification" of these regions during the Russian Empire and the USSR) that were formed in Donetsk and Luhansk many years ago. These factors created historical weaknesses with the identification of Donbas' population toward Ukraine. Both during the Soviet period and until 2014, the negligent attitude of Kyiv toward its eastern regions played a role in the creation of these conditions. In addition to other factors, the lack of sufficient Ukrainian content in these Russian-speaking regions (as in Crimea) and the activities of "Russian World" played an important role in the formation of an alternative reality. When the active phase of the conflict started, Kyiv's confusion regarding its information policy and a lack of timely measures were serious factors. In this phase, civil society was the main actor taking measures against Russia's information war. The information operations carried out by Russia used narratives popular during the Soviet period and postindependence, declaring that the eastern regions "supply the main products of the entire country." On the other hand, Yanukovych fleeing had a huge psychological impact on the population of the country's eastern regions. During the presidency of Yanukovych, who was originally from eastern Ukraine, these regions regarded themselves as necessary and important provinces. Yanukovych's resignation gave rise, in the eastern regions, to the so-called "complex of abandoned" syndrome. The regional factor, an approach created by the Ukrainian political elites and widely used during the years of independence to their benefit, was now used by Russia against Ukraine on the eve of the conflict in 2014.[32]

Another narrative used for psychological effect in the information operation was the inconceivable "fact" of "Nazi attacks against the civilian population." The "Nazi" terminology in Russian propaganda is used to reflect nationalist organizations (especially the "Right Sector") and generally western Ukraine. Ukrainian journalists and civil society activists captured by the separatist military forces were tortured and forced to make "confessions" (for the purpose of generating hatred and using them as anti-heroes) and was widely used by Russia in the information warfare operations.[33]

Understanding why a majority of audiences believe this type of false information can be explained by several factors:

1 This type of information/propaganda is meant to be confusing and it is non-stop. In such a situation, it is not possible for an unprepared person to understand and analyze the information received;[34]
2 Quantitative factors—the amount of interconnected information was incredibly high such that the majority of people are inclined to believe subconsciously that the information is connected and of the same type;

3 Trust in broadcasting—this feature is applicable to most of the population groups in the former Soviet Union (especially middle and older generations). The approach of "if the TV says so, then it is true;"
4 Limited or non-existent access to alternative sources of information;
5 Lower formal education level of the population (as the less educated tend to more readily believe false information for propaganda purposes).[35]

The last two factors play an important role for countermeasure efforts in the information war. The domination in the information space, the reflection of different views to make the population believe the media, and the education level of the population is of great importance in the information war. For instance, Latvia encouraged the opening of local Russian language media for the protection of their Russian-speaking community from the influence of Russian propaganda-style media. Even though some local Russian-language websites have sharply criticized the Latvian government, such approaches and measures envisage the prevention of an "explosion" of "negative energies" of the Russian-speaking people and aims to minimize the chances that Russia could benefit from possible social clashes.

An active civil society can play an important role in deterring information war operations. In the first period of the 2014 invasion of Ukraine, Ukraine's civil society actively fought the information attacks of Russia. To combat the fake news and propaganda disseminated by the Russian information TV channels, various Internet portals, groups, and journalistic accounts of public activists in social media have done important work in this area.[36]

Despite Russia's successful information operations during the previous Ukraine invasion, Moscow could not achieve similar effects in the invasion of 2022. Primarily because it was impossible to hide Russia's invasion and how obsolete the Russian propaganda narratives such as "to liberate Ukrainians from fascists" or "together we will be happy" were. In any event, Russia did not perform influential information operations during its 2022 invasion of Ukraine and has been using approaches based on the same narratives as in 2014. The other reason for the failure of Russian information operations, most probably, was the work among the Ukrainian public and civil institutions since 2014, which seems to have inoculated the majority of Ukrainian society from Russia's information attacks.

*"Biological warfare laboratories" within Russia's borders: an information campaign*

Another interesting case for analyzing Russia's information operations is the claim that the United Sates has biological weapon laboratories on Russia's borders. Using biological weapons as narratives for information attacks is nothing new for Russia's security institutions. During the Cold War, Soviet security organizations also used "biological weapon" narratives in information operations against the West. But in the age of the Internet and hi-tech instruments Russia realizes more sophisticated information operations based on Soviet experiences.

Since the establishment of a partnership between the United States and several post-Soviet republics in biological studies at the end of the 1990s, Moscow has considered such cooperation a threat. The main targets for Russian officials and experts' accusations are the laboratories in Georgia, Azerbaijan, Ukraine, and more recently Kazakhstan, and Uzbekistan. Projects such as the so-called "Lugar's laboratories" were part of the Nunn-Lugar Biological Threat Reduction program. The program sought to dismantle the Soviet Union's massive biological weapons of mass destruction (WMD) research, development, and production infrastructure. Moreover, it operates to prevent the proliferation of expertise, materials, equipment, and technologies that could contribute to the development of biological weapons. Under the program, the Defense Threat Reduction Agency has carried out the implementation of bio threat reduction projects in Russia, Kazakhstan, Uzbekistan, Georgia, Azerbaijan, and Ukraine.[37] The cooperation, almost since its inception, has been accompanied by accusations from Russia. Some of the Russian media, politicians, and experts periodically accused the United States and the aforementioned republics of "suspected biological activities" in areas close to Russia's borders.

Moscow's concerns regarding the laboratories and cooperation can be classified mainly in three approaches: (a) the United States projects the conduct of researches in cooperation with local scientists who could potentially be involved in the production of bacteriological weapons; (b) the transfer of information and samples of pathogens to the United States can mean the disclosure of military and biological secrets not only of the USSR, but of Russia, which is its legal successor; (c) With the disclosure of Soviet secrets to Washington, such activities of the leadership of Georgia, Azerbaijan, and other countries threaten Russia's interests.[38] These laboratories, according to Moscow, are conducting research that could potentially be used for the production of bacteriological weapons while the transfer of information and samples of pathogens to the United States could disclose not only Soviet but also Russian military and biological secrets. These "military-biological" labs near Russia are described as external threats in Russia's latest National Security Strategy.[39]

Although such accusations are refuted by officials and experts of Georgia, Azerbaijan, Ukraine, and Kazakhstan, the spread of negative information about the laboratories has intensified in recent years.[40]

Such accusations are stated by experts and officials. High-level officials of Russia's MFA accused the United States of being in violation of the Biological and Toxin Weapons Convention requirements.[41] A former head of the Federal Service for the Protection of Consumers Rights and the country's Chief Sanitary Physician Gennady Onishchenko alleged that these laboratories are an important part of the US biological weapons program and even stated that the US military microbiologists in Georgia can purposely infect mosquitoes with the Zika virus.[42] During a briefing in Moscow on October 4, 2018, General-Major Igor Kirillov, commander of Russia's radiological, chemical, and biological defense troops, stated that following experiments of certain medicines on people—medicines produced by a company of former US Secretary of Defense Donald Rumsfeld—73 Georgian citizens died.[43] Kirillov stated that the United States financed biological laboratories in Ukraine, Azerbaijan, and in Uzbekistan are continuing their work and that most likely the United States, "under the guise of peaceful research, is building up its military-biological potential."[44] He also pointed to a so-called "Lugar Laboratory" in Georgia. According to him, "the Lugar Center is only a small element of the extensive US military-biological program and vigorous activity has been launched in the territory of states adjacent to Russia, where laboratories under the control of the Pentagon also operate ... there is data that the United States is developing the tools of delivery for the use of biological weapons, which is contrary to the agreements to ban it."[45] He mainly referred to the former Minister of Georgian State Security Igor Georgadze's accusations. Georgadze was in the KGB service between the 1970s and 1990s and holds the title of "Honorary Officer of the KGB of the USSR." About a month before Kirillov's press conference, Igor Georgadze launched a campaign against the Public Health Research Center in Tbilisi in the Russian media. He argued that he had obtained thousands of pages of documents from "Georgian friends" and that they contained very "strange facts." Georgadze's "facts" enjoyed widespread pro-government media coverage.[46] Moreover, the accusations came on October 4, 2018 at the same time as the United Kingdom and the Netherlands were accusing Russian spies of being behind an attempted attack on the OPCW in the Hague.[47]

In 2016, media in Armenia blamed the Richard Lugar Public Health Research Center in Georgia for the death of more than 10 people from swine flu (H1N1). The absurdity of such scandalous publications was recognized even in the Russian media.[48] Negative information about the aforementioned laboratories appeared in Azerbaijan and Kazakhstan's media as well.[49] Moreover, Dagestanian journalists—led by Mukhtar Amirov—alleged that a Georgian laboratory assisted in the use of biological weapons in Dagestan and Chechnya. He also created a petition addressed to Vladimir Putin, to initiate "an investigation into the activities of Lugar's laboratory in connection with the threat to biological safety of Russian citizens," as well as the imposition of sanctions against individuals and legal entities related to this laboratory.[50] Such accusations are regularly made by high Russian officials as well. Russia used similar accusations during its invasion of Ukraine in 2022.

Since the beginning of Russia's invasion of Ukraine in 2022, Moscow has accused the United States and Kyiv of operating "biological weapons laboratories" in Ukraine to create weapons for use against Russians. Similar accusations have been leveled by the Russian political and military leadership and in war briefings of the Defense Ministry. Besides progovernment media and propagandist journalists, Putin himself stated that the "military biological activities of the United States in Ukraine poses a huge danger both for Russia and for the whole of Europe."[51] Secretary of the Russian Security Council Nikolai Patrushev claimed that "Washington is in every possible way afraid of the publicity of its research on the development of biological weapons in the territory of the post-Soviet states, and the investigation should shed light on the true intentions and consequences of the work that took place in bio-laboratories in Ukraine with the participation of the United States."[52] Defense Minister Shoigu also joined this campaign saying that "under the guidance of US specialists, components of biological weapons were developed in Ukraine."[53]

Moreover, the Russian Defense Minister published "documents" on the activities of the biological laboratories of the United States in Ukraine which mainly focused on the Science and Technology Center in Ukraine (STCU).[54] STCU aims to advance global peace and prosperity through cooperative chemical, biological, radiological, and nuclear (CBRN) risk mitigation by supporting civilian science and technology partnerships and collaboration that address global security threats and advance non-proliferation. STCU provides scientists from Azerbaijan, Georgia, Moldova, Ukraine, and Uzbekistan the ability to conduct research with full grant support.[55] The "investigation" of the Russian Defense Minister seems to have used information from the STCU website and interpreted it as required for the propaganda campaign.

Using these types of accusations, Moscow pressed CIS countries to allow Russia access to their health-related cooperation and especially to work of those institutions created by the financial and technical support of the United States and joint programs with the West. For instance, in 2021 Russia signed memorandums on "ensuring biological safety" with Armenia and Turkmenistan.[56] Russia and Kazakhstan are in the final stage of preparing a similar memorandum.[57] Moreover, Russia is supported by China in this. In 2021, foreign ministers of the two states issued a joint statement on strengthening "the Convention on the Prohibition of the Development, Production and Stockpiling of Bacteriological (Biological) and Toxin Weapons and on Their Destruction." The statement emphasizes that "the foreign military biological activities of the United States and its allies (more than 200 American biological laboratories, whose activities are secret and non-transparent and are located outside the national territory of the United States) raise serious concerns and questions from the international community regarding compliance with the BTWC." The parties further state their opinion that such activities pose a serious threat to the national security of Russia and China and damage the security of the respective regions.[58]

Russia had not previously been in favor of a verification protocol to the Biological and Toxin Weapons Convention (BTWC) during the Ad Hoc Group negotiations. But recently Russia proposed a return to negotiations to develop a verification mechanism. Roger Roffey and Anna-Karin Tunemalm ask why they change of heart:

> At this time, many states within the EU are advocating a need for measures for compliance monitoring. Russia is well aware that the United States is not in favor of verification or in resuming negotiations, as they believe that the BTWC and compliance with it cannot be verified. So, the question arises if this new Russian interest in negotiations and verification is genuine or more directed at trying to present a picture of the United States stopping the previous negotiations at a critical stage and how it will now be perceived as preventing any progress in the BTWC.[59]

They conclude that this could then well fit in with "the anti-American propaganda insinuating that the United States is trying to hide a biological weapons program. Another aim can be to try to cause a wider gap in the positions of the EU and the United States on how to proceed in the BTWC arena at a time when the BTWC really needs to be strengthened."[60]

It is very difficult to explain exactly what Russia intends in using these biological weapons narratives mainly because they have several potential aims. They may be geopolitical (i.e., increasing confrontation with the West); preventing any increase in the security cooperation between the West and the former Soviet republics; spreading mistrust among the population against the West and local governments; security concerns regarding declassification of the Soviet biological weapons program secrets; or even realizing information attacks on a targeted country to cause panic among the population. Using the Soviet legacy, biological weapon threat perceptions have not completely disappeared from the public consciousness in the former Soviet republics. Russia may also be trying to pose as a defender or is intending to create such an image of itself. Moscow uses such narratives to accuse the United States and its allies of using the "populations of the former Soviet republics for laboratory tests and purposefully harming their health" on the one hand, while on the other, "preparing biological weapons against Russia's population on their borders."

According to a RAND Corporation report, using information cartography (information maps with artificial intelligence technologies), it is possible to map key Russian sources as part of Russian information operations against a target state.[61] These sources might include: Russian and target country think tanks; foundations; authorities; television stations; pseudo-news agencies and multimedia services; cross-border social and religious groups; social media and Internet trolls; Russian regime-controlled companies and organizations; Russian regime-funded political parties and other organizations in a target country; Russian propaganda directly targeting journalists, politicians, and individuals in the target countries in particular and the EU in general.

Rand Waltzman writes that the mapping of target state receivers as part of Russian information operations against a target state might include: national government organizations; military; intelligence community; industry; media; independent think tanks; academia and citizen-organized groups.[62]

It should be noted that although various methods are used in Russia's information operations, the use of psychological methods and cyber tools in frame of the same operation are basic facets. The specific methods are adapted to the demands of a given state, as well as the psychological, religious, ethnic, and cultural characteristics of its society. Common-sensitive problems prevailing among a segment of the targeted country can be identified and, if necessary, manipulated for a given purpose. Russia's organizations conduct surveys, roundtables with experts in countries that are of interest (especially in the former Soviet republics and in former socialist-bloc countries) through their own or third-party organizations.

In the former Soviet republics where democratic institutions are developed, Russian institutions or cooperating local organizations act in a more open way, while in countries where authoritarian rulers are strong, they try to use more careful means.

For example, the marginalization of opposition political parties and independent businessmen by Lukashenko's government led Russia to use an indirect form of influence in Belarus for organizational activities and propaganda purposes. It should be noted that this form is relevant not only for Belarus but also for other similar former Soviet republics. Such forms are utilized in countries where the activities of political life are under the full control of governments. They aim to obtain analytical information about the socio-political and economic situation in the targeted country, and to use these forces in future scenarios to promote Russia's interests. It is possible that one of the main purposes of the "Political Culture in Belarus and Comparative Analysis of Moldova, Azerbaijan, Kyrgyzstan, and Belarus" research, which started in 2016 by a Russian foundation, was to find vulnerable points for in-depth analysis into the country's political situation. Funding for this research was provided by the Russian State National Charitable Fund and was implemented by the Eurasian Dialogue organization. It should be noted that the Eurasia Dialogue and the "Since" public union conducted similar projects in Moldova, Azerbaijan, and Kyrgyzstan in 2015–2016. Questions such as the sensitive problems for populations, what major issues are likely to cause public unrest, the public's attitude about political regimes, and the identification of local and foreign media with a wide range of influence were studied in these projects. Respondents who were involved in in-depth interviews and focus group discussions were local experts and business representatives.[63]

As a result of such research, information about a targeted country's public consciousness, general trends in society, and sensitive aspects could be collected for various reasons, including for psychological information purposes. Such characteristics of the public mood are also known as "cognitive vulnerability." According to Rand Waltzman, for the specialists that prepare information attacks, *cognitive vulnerability* is a premise that the audience is already predisposed to accept because it appeals to their already existing fears or anxieties.[64]

However, as Russia's invasion of Ukraine in 2022 showed, such surveys are not always effective, or their results are not properly perceived by top Russian decision-makers. According to *The Washington Post* report, pre-war polls by an organization (Research & Branding) linked to Russia's security service, FSB, found that 48% of Ukrainians were prepared to fight to defend the country, and that only 2% would regard the "appearance" of Russian forces as a "liberation."[65] While the number had to be interpreted as a sign of resolve, showing that millions of citizens were ready to take up arms against Russia, the FSB, however, might have drawn a different conclusion from the same data, believing that only a minority of Ukrainians were committed to defending their country, explains the report. Moreover, the results of the second survey conducted in January, just several weeks before the war, showed that 84% of respondents across Ukraine perceived "appearances of the Russian military forces in Ukraine" as an occupation. However, it is unclear whether the results of these surveys were accurately relayed to the Kremlin or if they were, whether they were correctly perceived by them.[66]

**The cyber tools of Russia's warfare approaches**

In recent years, Russia has been conducting a wide range of cyber espionage and sabotage operations. The first publicly known attacks were by Moonlight Maze. Intrusions began as early as 1996. The early targets: a vast number of US military and government networks, including Wright Patterson and Kelly Air Force Bases, the Army Research Lab, the Naval Sea Systems Command in Indian Head, Maryland, NASA, and the Department of Energy labs. By mid-1998, the FBI and Department of Defense investigators had forensic evidence pointing to Russian Internet service providers (ISPs).[67]

Another known case is the Pentagon breach in 2008. The "malware" strike, thought to be orchestrated from inside Russia, hit combat zone computers and the US Central Command overseeing Iraq and Afghanistan.[68] Another operation blacked out Kyiv in 2016. At midnight, a week before Christmas, hackers struck an electric transmission station north of Kyiv, blacking out a portion of the Ukrainian capital equivalent to a fifth of its total power capacity. According to cyber researchers, it was the first real-world malware attack on physical infrastructure since Stuxnet.[69]

According to the Joint Statement from the Department Of Homeland Security and Office of the Director of National Intelligence on Election Security, the US Intelligence Community (USIC) is confident that the Russian government directed the compromise of emails from US persons and institutions, including US political organizations during the presidential election campaign in 2016.[70] "The recent disclosures of alleged hacked emails on sites like DCLeaks.com and WikiLeaks and by the Guccifer 2.0 online persona are consistent with the methods and motivations of Russian-directed efforts," said the statement. "These thefts and disclosures are intended to interfere with the US election process."[71]

One of the largest and most devasting cyberattacks in history was NotPetya. It targeted an entire nation, crippled ports, paralyzed corporations, and froze government agencies. The NotPetya attack was likely more explosive than even its creators intended:

> Within hours of its first appearance, the worm raced beyond Ukraine and out to countless machines around the world, from hospitals in Pennsylvania to a chocolate factory in Tasmania. It crippled multinational companies including Maersk, pharmaceutical giant Merck, FedEx's European subsidiary TNT Express, French construction company Saint-Gobain, food producer Mondelēz, and manufacturer Reckitt Benckiser. In each case, it inflicted nine-figure costs. It even spread back to Russia, striking the state oil company Rosneft. The result was more than $10 billion in total damages.[72]

US intelligence agencies also confirmed that Russia's military—the prime suspect in any cyber war attack targeting Ukraine—was responsible for launching the malicious code.[73]

As it is largely described in Chapter 3, technological espionage has been a familiar tool for Russia's intelligence agencies since the Soviet Union. The KGB had high-level technical capabilities for spying on signals intelligence. In contemporary Russia, following the dissolution of the Soviet Union, KGB signals intelligence functions were divided between three Russian special services: the Federal Security Service (FSB), the Foreign Intelligence Service (SVR) and the Federal

Protective Service (FSO). In addition, the Russian Military Intelligence Service (GRU) has considerable powers to carry out cyber and signals intelligence.[74]

Currently, Russia's institutional tools for cyberoperations can be identified in two ways: military and civilian institutions. However, in some cases, this characteristic is relative. Because, the information and cyber groups under the control of the Defense Ministry are often engaged in operations targeting public and political spheres, while the private security companies controlled by the Federal Security Service (FSB) or government-affiliated organizations with civilian and political goals might also have military targets. Russia's security organizations use cyber tools for information operations and for intelligence gathering (Cyber Intelligence-CYBINT).

In February 2017, Russian Defense Minister Sergei Shoigu announced the creation of Information Operations Troops [*Voyska informatsionnykh operatsiy*; VIO] under the Ministry of Defense.[75] In fact, it is possible that such a group was operating before the invasion of Ukraine in 2014. The Information Operations Troops, first publicly mentioned in 2014, seek to integrate and synthesize these activities, judging from numerous Russian officials' statements.[76] According to the US sanctions imposed against Russian malign influence actors in April 2021, the VIO oversees Unit 54777 and is responsible for "cyber espionage, influence, and offensive cyberoperations."[77]

The military exercises in 2017 also included information operations. Under the Ministry of Defense, a group engaged in cyberoperations under the Main Directorate (GRU) has operated for years. There are reports about hacker groups known as APT 28, or Fancy Bear (which, according to some experts, operate under the same name) managed by the GRU.[78] The names of these groups were mentioned in a number of hacking operations including the Ukrainian cyberattacks, the United States in 2016, and during the 2017 presidential elections in France. The Main Directorate of the General Staff (GRU) had multiple units, including Units 26165 and 74455, engaged in cyberoperations involving the staged releases of documents stolen through computer intrusions. These units conducted large-scale cyberoperations to interfere with the 2016 US presidential election. Before the 2016 presidential election, American officials stated that Units 26165 and 74455 hacked into the servers of the Democratic National Committee and the Clinton campaign, and then published embarrassing internal communications.[79] Special counsel Robert Mueller's indictment of 12 Russian intelligence officers for their hacking and attack on the 2016 presidential election emphasized the activities of these groups. The hackers got their public Fancy Bear moniker from the security firm CrowdStrike, which spotted the phrase "Sofacy" in some of the unit's malware, reminding analysts of Iggy Azalea's song "Fancy."[80] Russia's Foreign Intelligence Service (SVR) controls Advanced Persistent Threat (APT) 29, a shadowy group of skilled hackers who seemingly focus on illicitly obtaining information through espionage while avoiding disruptive operations.[81]

In addition to its official cybersecurity unit, the FSB reportedly controls the hacker groups Cozy Bear and The Dukes (which, according to some experts, is a single group). FSB employees and representatives of private cyber companies were suspected of having links with the Shaltay Baltay hacking group, which led to the arrests, in late 2016 and early 2017, of several FSB officers as a result of a criminal investigation into this group.[82] Russia's Federal Security Service (FSB) almost certainly has several components dedicated to offensive cyberoperations, including Centers 16 and 18. Center 16 is a direct descendant of the Soviet-era KGB's 16th Directorate.[83]

Besides the already mentioned organizations, several other state and non-state institutions are involved in Russia's cyber warfare operations. The private company widely known to be involved in Russia's information operations is the Internet Research Agency, also known as the "Troll Factory." The owner of the company, based in St. Petersburg, is Sergei Prigozhin (nicknamed "chef") is known for his close ties to the Kremlin. It is worth noting that Prigozhin's name was among the 13 Russian citizens mentioned in the first indictment on Russia's secret influences in the 2016 US presidential election initiated by Robert Muller and his team.[84] In addition to the troll factory, Prigozhin owns a media group known as a "media factory" with several online outlets. Prigozhin is also an owner of the private military company Wagner, which engaged in military operations in Ukraine, Syria, and other countries.

In addition to the troll factory, Russia has a powerful "bots army," which has a significant stake in the botnet network. Peter Levashov, the owner of one of those "armies" and the operator of the Kelihos Botnet Software, was arrested in April 2017 in Barcelona at the request of the United States. Levashov, known as the "spam king" in the botnet and nicknamed Peter Severa, has been accused of various cybercrimes (including thousands of computer bots, phishing-emails or personal data stealing operations, banking Trojans, etc.) between 2010 and 2016. According to reports, Levashov's bot army also participated in Russian information campaigns in the 2016 US elections. Interestingly, although US law enforcement did not give full information on the issue, Levashov's active defense in the Russian state-owned media reinforces the suspicion that there was a relationship between the bot army and the official Russian authorities.[85] Despite Russia's efforts, Levashov was extradited to the United States in February 2018.[86]

According to the key findings of the research conducted by Omri Ben-Bassat from Intezer and Itay Cohen from Check Point Research, every actor or organization under the Russian Advanced Persistent Threat (APT) umbrella has its own dedicated malware development teams, working for years in parallel on similar malware toolkits and frameworks. Findings of the report suggest that Russia is investing a lot of effort into its operational security. By avoiding different organizations reusing the same tools on a wide range of targets, they overcome the risk that one compromised operation will expose other active operations, the report notes.[87]

The researchers verified previously reported connections between different groups, supporting these connections with code similarity analysis as evidence. Moreover, by analyzing thousands of samples in order to map connections between different cyberespionage organizations in Russia, they concluded that Russian-attributed actors are part of a larger picture in which Russia is one of the strongest powers in cyberwarfare today stating, "their advanced tools, unique approaches, and solid infrastructures suggest enormous and complicated operations that involve different military and government entities inside Russia."[88]

Besides using the cybersphere as a tool in its external security approaches, the Russian government also tries to keep tough controls over its domestic cybersecurity. There is a popular thought among the current political and military elites that the Internet is controlled by the United States. The Russian leadership, and particularly the most influential part of it—*siloviki*—look upon the West and especially the United States suspiciously and believe that Washington fully controls the web because it was a CIA project. Andrei Soldatov and Irina Borogan highlight the fact that Putin's regime wants to end that supremacy. "Just as he (Vladimir Putin) attempted to change the rules inside Russia, so too did he attempt to change them for the world," they wrote.[89] Since the end of the 2000s, Russia has been trying to make other countries—especially the United States—accept Russia's right to control the Internet within its borders.[90]

Triggered by the thought that the Internet, particularly social media, could be used by any opposition free from government control during possible political protests—as happened during the revolutions in Arab countries and in some former Soviet republics—the Kremlin tries to neutralize such threats. One method is by reusing the Soviet period SORM device (an acronym in Russian for Systema Operativno-Rozysknykh Meropriatii-the System of Operative Search System), invented by the KGB, which allows the state security institutions to not only, as it was once, intercept phone calls but to now monitor emails, Internet usage, Skype, cell phone calls, text messages, and social networks.[91] The government is trying to realize a so-called "sovereign internet" project. In 2019, the State Duma adopted the law on "Ensuring the safe and stable functioning" of the Internet in Russia.[92] Separate provisions—on cryptographic protection of information and on the national domain name system—came into effect on January 1, 2021.[93]

After analyzing the previous information, it is possible to conclude that cybertools are used by the Russian state intelligence and security organizations for external security approaches and in internal politics for the regime's security.

### *Cyberoperations during the invasion of Ukraine in 2022*

In its invasion of Ukraine in 2022, Russia conducted cyberwar operations as well. Although the invasion of Ukraine increased the intensity of Russian cyberoperations compared to 2014–2021, at least until March 2023, it had not inflicted significant damage on Ukrainian infrastructure. Reports published after February 2022 offer two competing explanations for the failure of Russia's cyberattacks. According to findings of Tetyana Malyarenko and Borys Kormych, the first assumes that Russia's cyberwar against Ukraine had already reached its highest possible level of complexity, so there is either too little room for qualitative growth on the Russian side or sufficient resilience on the Ukrainian side. The second explanation is based on published reports from government agencies and private companies, such as Microsoft, which show that Russian cyberattacks have improved and increased since January 2022, but attention and intervention by the United States and other international cyberspecialists helped Ukraine neutralize the attacks and successfully counterattack.[94] Of course, there are no easy answers to whether Russian CW operations were just not that sophisticated, or if Ukrainian cyber defenses were formidable; perhaps it is some combination of the two.[95]

However, since the beginning of the war there have been several known cyberoperations conducted by Russia. In the beginning of the invasion the main goal of Russian cyberattacks was to paralyze Ukraine's information systems, which would make it easier to achieve military goals in other domains of war. Russia's invasion was preceded by a massive cyberattack on the Ukrainian government's websites in January 2022.[96] Reportedly Russian cybergroups hacked the state-run Diya app's known vulnerabilities to gain access to the data of 2.6 million individuals, businesses, law firms, and government agencies.[97]

Microsoft reported that since the beginning of its Ukraine invasion, Russian cyberthreat groups have been performing actions supporting the military's strategic and tactical objectives. As Microsoft observed a timeline of military strikes and cyberintrusions, it found several examples of computer network operations and military operations seeming to work in tandem against a shared target set, though it is unclear if this was in actuality coordination, centralized tasking, or merely a common set of understood priorities driving the correlation.[98] The report found that Russia's cyberoperations since the beginning of the war have been consistent with actions designed to degrade, disrupt, or discredit the Ukrainian government, military, and economic functions, secure footholds in critical infrastructure, and to reduce the Ukrainian public's access to information.[99] Moreover, cyber and kinetic military operations appeared to be directed toward similar military objectives, according to Microsoft's report.[100] The State Service for Special Communications and Information Protection of Ukraine also stated that Russian hackers are acting in sync with the Russian military.[101] From February 23 to April 8, nearly 40 discrete destructive attacks permanently destroyed files across hundreds of systems in dozens of organizations in Ukraine. Up to the end of April 2022, more than 40% of all destructive attacks were aimed at organizations in critical infrastructure sectors that could have negative second-order effects on the government, military, economy, and people. Another 32% affected Ukrainian government organizations at the national, regional, and city levels.[102] Microsoft also notes that the Russian threat actors are slightly modifying the malware to evade detection with each wave of deployment.[103]

Through the end of June 2022, Microsoft's Threat Intelligence Centre (MSTIC) detected Russian network intrusion efforts on 128 targets in 42 countries outside Ukraine. According to MSTIC, a range of strategic espionage targets were targeted which were likely involved in direct or indirect support of Ukraine's defense, 49% of these being government agencies. Another 12% were NGOs, typically think tanks advising on foreign policy or humanitarian groups involved in providing aid to Ukraine's civilian population or refugees.[104] As the report shows while these targets are spread around the globe, 63% of the observed activity has involved NATO members and that Russian cyberespionage operations focused on targets in the United States more than any other country (12% of the global total outside Ukraine).[105]

One such case was Russia's cyberattack on the US satellite communications provider Viasat at the start of the invasion, an incident that triggered satellite service outages across Central and Eastern Europe.[106] Although the primary target of the attack is believed to have been the Ukrainian military, which relies on satellite communications, the February 24 attack also impacted Internet service for thousands of Viasat customers in Ukraine and tens of thousands of customers across Europe.[107] The attack also affected the operations of some 5,800 wind turbines across Germany as they relied on Viasat routers for remote monitoring and control.[108] In addition to those named here, there have been several other Russia's cyberoperations conducted during the invasion of Ukraine in 2022.[109]

**Asymmetric approaches in the military**

As discussed in Chapter 1, the importance of using asymmetric approaches in contemporary wars has been emphasized since the 1990s by Russian military scholars in addition to military and political leadership. Despite claims that Russian military experts and leaders mainly consider using non-military methods in contemporary conflicts when they refer to asymmetric methods, they also use asymmetric strategy or methods as terminology to describe the use of non-symmetric strategies in conventional military operations. It should be noted that in Russia's military thinking, strategies, and tactics, the use of conventional military approaches specifically military force is dominant.

There are debates among Russian experts about the effectiveness of asymmetric warfare approaches and whether asymmetry becomes the preferable military strategy of the weaker side when it faces a stronger adversary. For instance, one of the interesting works on this was written by officers of the Russian General Staff Academy, Sergey G. Chekinov and Sergey A. Bogdanov, in 2010. They emphasized that in the current circumstances, asymmetric actions are characterized by a qualitative difference in the use of new (non-traditional) weapons, forms, and methods of warfare from both (weak and strong) warring parties, as well as completely opposite declared ultimate goals of military campaigns. Chekinov and Bogdanov noted that even though the power of countries at a lower level of economic, technological, and military development are several times lower than that of developed states, the former nevertheless retain the ability to exert a comparable effect and consequences on the latter for the first time in history.[110]

Chekinov and Bogdanov drew parallels between asymmetric approaches and Liddell Hart's classic work on indirect approaches. It should be noted that in fact, there are many similar and common approaches between asymmetric warfare and Liddell Hart's indirect approaches. He analyzed historical cases of indirect methods from Greek wars to World War II.[111]

Chekinov and Bogdanov stressed that the wars of the 20th century brought a lot to the development of indirect methods and that these methods acquired an enormous spatial scope, which was the result of the strategy's globalization. This is expressed in the spread of armed struggle to all continents, seas, oceans, and airspace, as well as in the creation of a unified system of command and control of the armed forces. According to them, "indirect actions" ["*Nepryamye deistvie*"] have been manifested in improving methods of maneuvering by large strategic-operational cells; increasing the importance of surprise and the time factor in achieving military goals; using new varieties of split and flanking attacks; increasing the role of mobile groups with high mobility and great striking power; the capability of rapidly developing tactical success at the operational level; increasing the depth of simultaneous fire impact on the enemy, and conducting operations to pursue and defeat its major groups:

> The indirect actions strategy which in the past mainly acted as a "second star," since the "power strategy" was the dominant one which consisted of achieving defeat of the enemy by creating numerical superiority in forces and weapons, is being highlighted in modern conditions, and the ability to use it is becoming a sign of a high-level of leadership skill.[112]

Chekinov and Bogdanov stressed that an analysis of the major military operations of the past decade of the 20th century, the features of wars and armed conflicts of the beginning of the 21st century, as well as trends in the development of weapons of war, suggests that the United States and NATO widely use the so-called "indirect actions" concept. Russia, in response, prefers "asymmetric approaches and measures" during hostilities. This means "striking targets in areas of national security where opponents are most vulnerable." For such strikes to be effective, Chekinov and Bogdanov emphasize the role of the latest highly effective weapons systems and indirect, non-contact forms of troop usage and methods in operations:

> Unacceptable consequences for the aggressor may be the result of both defensive (direct) actions and the result of asymmetric measures, the main content of which is to cause unacceptable damage to the enemy in other areas of national security, which will compensate or minimize its superiority in power. The combination of defensive actions in order to repel aggression and asymmetric, based on the effectiveness of modern high-precision strategic weapons systems in conventional equipment, as well as on the use of sabotage and reconnaissance groups, creates important prerequisites for forcing the enemy to cease hostilities on conditions favorable to Russia.[113]

Put succinctly, Chekinov and Bogdanov suggested using the combination of high-precision weapons strikes and classic asymmetric warfare techniques in the frame of one operation. Similar operations would be implemented by Russia years later in Ukraine (during both invasions but especially in 2022) and Syria where the combination of the "defensive and asymmetric actions" was utilized in the frame of the same operations.

Chekinov and Bogdanov even suggest possible targets within the European Union. They are strategically important facilities, including systems of higher state and military administration; large enterprises of industry and the energy sector of the economy (steel-making, machine-building, oil refineries, enterprises of the military-industrial complex, power plants and substations, points of production, reception and storage of oil and gas, life support facilities for the population, etc.); critical communications facilities throughout enemy territory (railway junctions, bridges, strategically important ports, airfields, tunnels, etc.); potentially hazardous objects (dams of hydroelectric power plants and hydroelectric power plants, reactors of nuclear power plants, technological plants of chemical plants, nuclear industry enterprises, warehouses of potent toxic substances, etc.).[114] These type of targets have been the focus of strikes in Ukraine since February 2022.

According to them, each will have a different impact on the stabilization or termination of any military conflict. Chekinov and Bogdanov conclude that a clear understanding by a potential adversary that the outcome of the outbreak of hostilities may not be victory and achievement of its goals, but an environmental and socio-political disaster, will be an effective deterrent. Thus, direct military measures to protect Russia's national interests, to prevent and repel possible aggression should combine both "direct (symmetrical) actions involving the preparation and conduct of operations with decisive goals to defeat the invading enemy troops, and asymmetric measures, the main content of which may consist in inflicting unacceptable damage on adversary in other (non-military) areas of security."[115]

Other Russian authors propose to confront the United States and its allies' network-centric warfare strategies through the use of asymmetric approaches. Recognizing that it would be difficult to reach the West's achievement in network-centric warfare, the authors emphasized the necessity of using asymmetric methods. For reducing the effectiveness of the adversary's network technologies of warfare, they point to "a more realistic direction" to develop different tactics and "qualitatively different weapons, military, special and other equipment." In the case of network-centric warfare, they propose the creation of models designed for the complete and long-term destruction of the network-centric systems, with short-term effects focusing on the destruction of the adversary's means for a certain period of time and, finally, they suggest "a sharp refusal to copy network-centric systems of the enemy" and the transition to "manual" control at all tactical levels, up to the battalion.[116] As seen in the war in Ukraine, the Russian military suffered greatly from their tough hierarchical command and control system and in this respect, almost nothing has changed since the Soviet days.[117]

According to Michael Kofman, the Russian General Staff sees the world in terms of theaters of operations, strategic directions, correlations, and asymmetries. Kofman argues that the overarching Russian concept is driven by an assumption that the initial period of war will be decisive because deflection, attrition, and disorganization will stop the US military from executing its preferred way of war, and a US failure to attain quick victory will decisively affect American political resolve. He emphasizes that although the Russian General Staff would love to impose a cost to theater access and maneuver, they expect a US aerospace blitzkrieg, which cannot be blocked at the outset. "Their answer is to deflect, degrade, suppress, or preempt in order to functionally destroy the adversary's ability to fight, and ultimately win the attrition exchange," Kofman writes.[118]

Analyzing Russia's anti-access and area denial (A2/Ad) capabilities, Kofman notes that investments in air defense reflect Russia's desire to create a defensive mass rather than a bubble and force the US military to attain superiority through attrition. He believes that this is why Russian defenses are echeloned and oriented to provide coverage for critical objects, as opposed to providing area defense around Russian forces. "It is a theory of victory based on resilience, mass, and cost imposition, tethered to the perception that an asymmetry of interests will favor Russia in terms of political resolve," explains Kofman.[119]

Asymmetric approaches in military can also be found in Russia's most strategic issues such as cooperation with China in order to challenge the United States. On October 3, 2019, President Vladimir Putin stated that Russia and China would continue to work together in outer space exploration and cooperate in the military-technical sphere. According to Putin, Russia helped China create a missile attack warning system.[120] It should be noted that military cooperation between Russia and China has increased in recent years. They conducted joint exercises, held regular and extensive talks, and conducted education projects for each other's officers. Besides imports of Russian produced armaments and military technologies, Chinese officers have trainings at Russian military academies.[121] According to the Russian Defense Minister, up to the end of 2016, more than 3,600 Chinese officers were trained in Russian military academies and training centers.[122] However, Putin's statement signaled a new level of developments in regards to security relations.

Early-warning missile attack systems rely on long-range ground-based radars and space-based technologies to detect missile launches and predict their trajectory. Hong Kong-based military analyst Song Zhongping said the system would help Beijing and Moscow set up a joint early ballistic missile network to counter "American global hegemony." "If the US wants to attack China [with its ICBMs], their missiles are likely to be launched from the Arctic, and that will be covered by Russia's early warning system, and that means Moscow will have the capability to alert Beijing," said Song while also adding that China could provide reciprocal help to Russia.[123]

According to Beijing-based military expert Zhou Chenming, Putin's remarks served as a veiled warning to US President Donald Trump who had taken the unilateral step of withdrawing from the Intermediate Range Nuclear Forces Treaty, signed between the United States and Russia in 1987. Chenming also emphasized the asymmetric facet of the cooperation on the early-warning missile attack systems. According to him, cooperation will help both Russia and China to save costs "because early warning ballistic missile systems are very expensive."[124]

Besides economic benefits and similarities of the political regimes, Moscow also uses its military cooperation with China as a response to the development and deployment of missile defense by the US close to Russia. Moreover, Moscow was concerned about the fate of the new START Treaty between the United States and Russia. After the United States' withdrawal from the 1987 Intermediate-Range Nuclear Forces (INF) in 2019, Moscow had growing suspicions that the new START Treaty also would not be prolonged or replaced after it expired in 2021. Most probably, to prepare for such a scenario Moscow tried to develop military cooperation with China with the aim of sharing the cost of any potential arms race in the coming years or even just to threaten Washington with such a possibility.

However, the main driver of their close relations in the international arena is the rivalry with a common adversary: the United States. Most probably, until the United States is not perceived by both as the main adversary and main source of a common threat, or in the event of some black swan scenarios such as a change of the political regime in Russia (involving not only Putin leaving the presidency), military cooperation between Moscow and Beijing will probably increase in the coming years.[125] According to Dmitry Gorenburg, bilateral cooperation is unlikely to advance to the level of a full alliance because of differences in geopolitical interests and asymmetries of power, with Russia remaining reluctant to fully acknowledge China's geopolitical rise. "But US actions to pressure both Russia and China have the effect of pushing the two countries closer together," Gorenburg writes.[126]

Most probably, at least for the immediate future, military and security cooperation between Russia and China will increase but both sides will keep an eye on the other with the aim of not repeating past mistakes.[127] However, despite the fact that the New START Treaty was prolonged in 2021 and the sides agreed to extend the treaty through February 4, 2026, Russia's cooperation with China on the strategic issues is continuing and most probably—amid the invasion of Ukraine and growing confrontation with the West—it may increase further.

**Guerrilla warfare, insurgency, and PMCs or semi-official military groups**

> In the culture of any state, there must be such phenomena as Wagner. I have spoken more than once about Robin Hood, Three Bogatyrs and 300 Spartans. Now Wagner.
>
> (Yevgeny Prigozhin[128])

Guerrilla warfare was used by Russia in several historical military conflicts. Guerrilla warfare was actively used by the Russians during the French invasion, known in Russia as the Patriotic War of 1812.[129] Moreover, Bolsheviks used guerrilla warfare methods from the civilian war in 1917 until the breakup of the Soviet Union in conflicts around the world. The main characteristic of the Bolshevik's military strategy in the civilian war was the coordination of military operations of the Red Army with guerrilla groups behind adversary lines.[130] In December 1919, the number of insurgents reached 50,000.[131] The Soviet Union's guerrilla war was a nightmare for the Nazi Army during WWII.[132] Moreover, during the Cold War, the Soviet Union supported several insurgent movements in Asia, Africa, and South America.[133]

Marlene Laruelle explains the growing role of militia in contemporary Russia's security policy in recent years as multilayered. They can be increasingly used as an outsourced tool for repressing the opposition and performing "hybrid" duties abroad, as well as a coercive force serving the power ministries against civilian authorities in case of conflicting interests.[134] The more highly trained groups sometimes become paramilitary forces within private military companies that can be recruited by the state to perform military duties in parallel with official military troops, such as Wagner.[135]

Already in 2012, Vladimir Putin, Prime Minister at the time, supported the idea of creating in Russia a system of private military companies (PMCs) that could provide security services for facilities and train foreign military abroad without the participation of government institutions.[136] PMCs are banned in Russia, the Criminal Code provides for punishment for mercenaryism: Art. 359, part 3 of the Criminal Code of the Russian Federation provides for from three to seven years in prison for the participation of a mercenary in an armed conflict or hostilities.[137] However, amid the war in Ukraine, a draft law on PMCs has been submitted to the State Duma and according to it, their activities are allowed outside the Russian Federation.[138]

Russia has actively used non-official or semi-official military establishments in military operations abroad in recent years. These can be private military companies (PMCs) or private military and security companies (PMSCs) in which the owners are usually linked to official institutions. Russian PMCs appeared in Syria, Iraq, Ukraine, and in several countries of Africa; the so-called insurgents (in eastern Ukraine) were unofficially coordinated by the militaries of Russia or Russian-backed separatist military groups (South Ossetian, Abkhazian military). Those military groups used guerrilla warfare tactics as well. The Russian PMC's performance in Syria and Ukraine showed that such semi-official military companies were beginning to play a special role in Russia's contemporary military operations abroad. If Syria became the "birthplace" of contemporary Russian PMCs in the 2010s, Ukraine should be viewed as a "testing ground" that helped to overcome the initial deficiencies of the early Syrian period.[139] Sergey Sukhankin stressed that in Syria (2013–2018), Russian "quasi-PMCs" were allocated a crucial role in ground military hostilities from the very inception of their mission, acting as shockwave troops and bearing the greatest amount of hardships in frontal attacks against anti-Assad forces.[140]

Russian PMCs can, at the same time, be involved in insurgency and counterinsurgency operations. For instance, one of the famous Russian PMC's Wagner supported insurgence groups in Ukraine in 2014 and was involved in counterinsurgent operations in Syria and Iraq. Recently, the group began to operate in several African countries as well. They've performed security tasks, such as diamond-mining policing, cross-border security, and strategic objects protection, among others.[141] Despite Moscow officially rejecting the Kremlin's cooperation with PMCs, there are several reports regarding their relations with state institutions and their involvement in several military conflicts around the world. According to several journalist investigations and reports, the Wagner Group is owned by Russian businessmen Yevgenii Prigozhin, known as "the Chef." Prigozhin is related to several high-level officials and his companies officially provide catering services for Kremlin organized events.[142] Prigozhin admitted to founding Wagner only in September 2022.[143]

In Africa, which is beset by jihadist insurgencies and ethnic conflicts, Moscow explores possibilities for strengthening multidimensional cooperation through its security institutions and its extractive industry companies. In recent years, Russian

PMCs expanded geographic theaters. Their geographical expansions are accompanied by increasing Russian involvement in Africa. In many cases, Moscow explains the presence of its PMCs in Africa as technical supports for the Russian military to assist its training and capacity building of local military forces. The presence of Russian private military contractors has been officially confirmed in several African countries including the Central African Republic (CAR), Sudan, and Libya (in 2012). Unofficially, they operated in Burundi, Gabon, the Democratic Republic of Congo (DRC), Yemen, and Mozambique.[144] The Central African Republic has a close relationship with Russia. According to the Financial Times, Russian mercenaries and PMCs—reportedly supplied by a company with connections to the Kremlin—guard President Faustin-Archange Touadéra, who also appointed a former Russian spy as his top security adviser. Furthermore, Russian companies have received diamond mining concessions from the CAR government. According to Isaac Fokuo, a lot of relationships have been based around military areas, but are now beginning to open up to deals in other sectors. "All sides want to reengage from a business standpoint," he said adding that "the sweet spots are technology, energy, power; areas where Russia is traditionally strong and African countries have particular needs."[145]

Having past experiences of security and economic cooperation during the Soviet Union, Moscow has intensified its pursuit of opportunities on the African continent. Russia is competing in Africa against the likes of China, the United States, and France so its use of PMCs is meant to increase the economic benefits in cooperation. In such circumstances the use of PMCs can be explain as an asymmetric approach, as they attempt to cement their own security presence with fewer costs.

Marlène Laruelle believes that, at a minimum, a militia fosters social consensus around the political regime and its values, but also secures access to thousands of patriotic-minded and trained citizens potentially ready to be recruited.[146] An estimated 12–15,000 Russian civilians, mostly representatives of far-right nationalist groups, volunteered in the war in Donbass in 2014–2015.[147] During the invasion of Ukraine in 2022, the Wagner group seemingly went from a PMC to an almost state military organization, and in several cases the group's owner and commanders played the role of semi-official recruiters who also had access to the prisons. Before that, there were several reports that since Wagner's establishment in the 2010s it has been coordinated by the Russian Defense Ministry.[148] On the other hand, in a country such as Russia where security institution controls are high and legally it was impossible to have PMCs, and where the participation in such an organization was classified as "mercenary" and punishable by the Russian Criminal Code, the involvements of the government institutions are obvious. Bellingcat's investigation even suggested that the Wagner mercenaries are integrated into the overall chain of command under central Kremlin control within its military intelligence, the Main Directorate of the General Staff (GU/GRU) apparatus.[149]

Meduza reported that although the Wagner Group remains completely dependent on the Defense Ministry's infrastructure and equipment, it has established an independent network of recruiters. Ahead of the invasion of Ukraine, as part of its wider effort to manage mercenary groups more directly, the Defense Ministry seized control of the online network that Wagner used to advertise vacancies.[150]

Around March 2022, Wagner once again made international headlines with the arrival of around 1,000 of its fighters onto the battlefields in Ukraine.[151] However, Russian media reported that in the first weeks of the invasion, most of the Russian mercenaries fighting in Ukraine were from a private military company called "Redoubt" and that the company sits under the Russian Defense Ministry's complete control.[152] However, since the summer of 2022, the Russian military began to use Wagner's combatants as one of its main strike forces in Ukraine, "renting out" the mercenaries to forward army units and as a result, the PMC's troops suffered heavy losses.[153] But in return an owner of the Wagner, Prigozhin received a Gold Star medal and the Hero of Russia honorary title for getting the group's combatants to Ukraine's frontlines and he was permitted to recruit fighters from the Russian prisons. Referring to messages on the Gulagu.net project hotline for the protection of the rights of prisoners, it was reported in July that prisoners were being recruited to participate in the war from prisons in different regions.[154] Moreover, Russian media reported about the visits of Yevgeny Prigozhin to various prisons and how he offered prisoners a chance to take part in the war in Ukraine in exchange for money and a pardon.[155] The Russian Behind Bars foundation reported that the Wagner PMC has recruited more than 1,000 prisoners from 17 Russian colonies and that those who refuse are sent to punishment cells.[156] By the end of 2022, their numbers had increased several times and in early 2023, the US Department of the Treasury designated the Russian PMC, Wagner Group as a transnational criminal organization.[157]

Amid Russia's manpower problems, which have been strikingly revealed in the second phase of the war in Ukraine—especially until the announcement of the partial mobilization in September—Moscow tried to solve the problem by heavily using PMCs. Besides Wagner, other Russian PMCs and paramilitary groups reportedly participated in the invasion of Ukraine, such as the "Borey" group and "Don" the Cossack group.[158] Anyway, they did not solve Russia's manpower problems. However, since the summer of 2022, the Wagner group has been equipped with its own artillery and aviation and has been one of Russia's main military forces in Ukraine. According to the United Kingdom Defense Intelligence update on the situation in Ukraine for January 2023, Wagner almost certainly commanded up to 50,000 fighters and had become a key component of the Ukraine campaign.[159]

**Summary**

According to the above analysis, since Russia's intervention in Ukraine in 2014, its activities and strategy have been considered from several angles by scholars and decision-makers. There is no commonly accepted definition of what kind of strategy or warfare methods are used by Russia. There are also ongoing discussions among experts on the name of Russia's warfare approaches. All of the claims can be justified by Russia's external security approaches.

Based on the findings, it is argued that many of these claims can be recognized as appropriate in the case of Russia's contemporary security and military approaches. But only if all of those warfare approaches would be considered together, not separately, even possibly in the frame of one operational strategy. Such a thought could be explained by the changing, dialectical characteristics of Russia's methods. However, the use of any possible, but also affordable, method in its confrontations with a stronger adversary or adversaries might be the best formula for understanding Russia's contemporary approaches. In such a situation in which the state has several ambitious international goals but does not have the required economic and technological possibilities, it is inclined to behave as a small actor in an asymmetric war. In other words, Russia with its goals, threat perception, and possibilities, has to use mostly asymmetric strategies and instruments rather than symmetric ones, especially with adversaries such as the United States or NATO.

The instruments for such attacks can be anything possible and affordable. The main tools used by Russia in its asymmetric approaches were analyzed: Tools in information operations, in cyberoperations, asymmetric approaches in military and the use of guerrilla warfare strategies in contemporary wars, such as involvement of the Russian military semi-private companies in insurgency and counterinsurgency operations. The latter tool of Russia's security approaches is considered one of the main forces used by Russian military operations abroad.

As Mark Galeotti put it, the Russians understanding that the role of non-military methods for achieving political and strategic goals in contemporary wars has increased and are supplemented by military means such as using special forces for peacekeeping or humanitarian operations in a concealed manner push them to use similar methods as countermeasures.[160] Moreover, Russia's political and military leadership considers possible operations against Russia as having been very similar to the Kosovo or Libya operations. In the Russian view, the United States and its allies can use in the frame of the same operation, military conventional, and non-military-unconventional methods with the aim of forcing regime change with help from internal opposition groups, NGOs, and media.[161] According to Kofman and Rojansky, the 2014 iteration added commentary on the "participation of irregular armed force elements and private military companies in military operations," and, "use of indirect and asymmetric methods of operations."[162]

The preferred tools for Russia's military and security institutions depend, and will depend, on the affordability and suitability of those tools in a given circumstance and as the operation demands. As Algirdas Revaitis rightly put it, all these types of warfare and the practical recommendations to the Russian armed forces formulated on their basis lead to the assumption that contemporary armed conflict in the future will continue to transform into a hi-tech war with intensive planning for and execution of high-precision military, electromagnetic, and information strikes against the enemy's key object.[163]

It can be emphasized here that Russia tries to use any possibility against a stronger adversary which may make it stronger in a given niche. These can be the information sphere, the Internet, cyber tools, and social media. Using these non-kinetic warfare instruments, however, Russia does not largely eschew conventional military force. However, in conventional military confrontations or arms races Russia prefers asymmetric strategies.

**Notes**

1 Hoffman, Frank (2007) *Conflict in the 21st century: The rise of hybrid wars*. Arlington, VA: Potomac Institute for Policy Studies.
2 Berzinš, Janis (2014a) "Russia's New Generation Warfare in Ukraine: Implications for Latvian Defence Policy". Policy Paper no 02, National Defence Academy of Latvia Centre for Security and Strategic Research; See also: Berzinš (2014b) "The new generation of Russian warfare". *Aspen Review*, 3, pp. 63–67.
3 Kofman, Michael (2018) "Raiding and International Brigandry: Russia's Strategy for Great Power Competition", *War on the Rocks*, June 14, https://warontherocks.com/2018/06/raiding-and-international-brigandry-russias-strategy-for-great-power-competition/.
4 Galeotti, Mark (2019. *Russian political war: moving beyond the hybrid*, London; New York: Routledge; See also Kennan, George (1948) "Policy Planning Staff Memorandum". National Archives and Records Administration, RG 273, Records of the National Security Council, NSC 10/2. Washington, 4 May 1948, http://academic.brooklyn.cuny.edu/history/johnson/65ciafounding3.htm.
5 Renz, Bettina (2016) "Russia and 'hybrid warfare'", *Contemporary Politics*, Vol. 22, No. 3, p. 285, DOI: 10.1080/13569775.2016.1201316, accessed 1 October 2019.
6 Bartles, Charles K. (2016) "Getting Gerasimov Right", January-February 2016 *Military Review*, Combined Arms Centre, Fort Leavenworth, Kansas, p. 34.
7 Shoygu, Sergey (2019) "Sergey Shoygu rasskazal, kak spasali rossiyskuyu armiyu", interviewed by Mikhail Rostovskiy, September 22, https://www.mk.ru/politics/2019/09/22/sergey-shoygu-rasskazal-kak-spasali-rossiyskuyu-armiyu.html.
8 Ibid.
9 Renz, Bettina (2016) "Russia and 'hybrid warfare'" …, p. 284.
10 Ibid., p. 288.
11 Mukhin, Vladimir (2013) "Krym vziali v ramkakh gibridnoi voiny". *Nezavisimaia gazeta*, 13 February 2015, http://www.ng.ru/armies/2015-02-13/3_kartblansh.html. Translated in Renz, Bettina (2016) "Russia and 'hybrid warfare'" …, p. 288.
12 Renz, Bettina (2016) "Russia and 'hybrid warfare'" …, p. 284.
13 Kofman, Michael and Rojansky, Matthew (2015) "A closer look at Russia's 'hybrid war'". Kennan Kable, 7, https://www.wilsonCentre.org/sites/default/files/7-KENNAN%20CABLE-ROJANSKY%20KOFMAN.pdf.
14 Gerasimov, Valerii (2013) "Tsennost nauki v predvidenii", February 26, *Voenno-Promishlenniy Kurer*, https://www.vpk-news.ru/articles/14632.
15 Bartles, Charles K. (2016) "Getting Gerasimov Right", January-February 2016 *Military Review*, Combined Arms Centre, Fort Leavenworth, Kansas, p. 33.
16 Ibid., p. 34.
17 Bartles, Charles K. (2016) "Getting Gerasimov Right" …, pp. 34–35.
18 Ibid., p. 35.
19 Ibid.
20 Stalin, Joseph (1936) "Comrade Stalin granted an interview to Roy Howard, President of Scripps-Howard Newspapers". 1 March 1936, *Works*, Vol. 14, Red Star Press Ltd., London, 1978, Transcription/HTML Markup: Salil Sen for MIA, 2008, Marxists Internet Archive (2008), https://www.marxists.org/reference/archive/stalin/works/1936/03/01.htm.
21 Chivvis, Christopher S. (2017) "Hybrid war: Russian contemporary political warfare", *Bulletin of the Atomic Scientists*, Vol. 73, No. 5 (How dangerous is hybrid war?), pp. 316–317, DOI: 10.1080/00963402.2017.1362903.

22 Ibid.
23 Galeotti, Mark (2018) "I'm Sorry for Creating the 'Gerasimov Doctrine'", March 5, https://foreignpolicy.com/2018/03/05/im-sorry-for-creating-the-gerasimov-doctrine/.
24 Charap, Samuel (2015) "The ghost of hybrid war". *Survival*, Vol. 57, p. 53, DOI: 10.1080/00396338.2015.1116147.
25 Freedman, Lawrence (2017) *The future of war: a history*. Bristol: Allen Lane, p. 225.
26 Kofman, Michael and Rojansky, Matthew (2015) "A closer look at Russia's 'hybrid war'" …
27 Solodnikov (2022) "Dmitriy Muratov: 'Russkiye pozvonochniki'", interview, *YouTube*, September 29, https://www.youtube.com/watch?v=mMBpbo8Wkwo.
28 Perry, Bret (2015) "Non-Linear Warfare in Ukraine: The Critical Role of Information Operations and Special Operations", August 14, http://smallwarsjournal.com/jrnl/art/non-linear-warfare-in-ukraine-the-critical-role-of-information-operations-and-special-opera.
29 Rettman, Andrew (2015) "EU to strike back at Russian propaganda", March 19, https://euobserver.com/foreign/128071.
30 Thornton, Rod (2015) "The Changing Nature of Modern Warfare-Responding to Russian Information Warfare", *The RUSI Journal*, Vol. 160, No. 4, 2015, pp. 40–48, DOI: 10.1080/03071847.2015.1079047.
31 Author's interviews and discussions with local experts, media representatives and activists in Ukraine (including originally from Donbas and Crimea), July–August, 2016.
32 Aliyev, Nurlan (2017) "Information Operations in the Hybrid/Non-Linear Warfare", *Grasping the virtual: (geo)politics, economics and privacy in a digital era*, WEASA, College of Europe Natolin Campus, Warsaw, pp. 38–39, https://www.weasa.org/wp-content/uploads/2018/02/WEASA_2017_publication_final.pdf.
33 Tsentr globalistiki "Strategiya KHKHÍ" (2016) "Gibressiya Putina. Nevoyennyye aspekty voyn novogo pokoleniya", March 23, 2016, http://geostrategy.org.ua/images/Hybression_finversion.pdf.
34 Pocheptsov, Georgii (2015) "Rol' informatsii v gibridnykh voynakh", *Prportal.com.ua*, September 19, http://prportal.com.ua/Peredovitsa/rol-informacii-v-gibridnyh-voynah.
35 Aliyev, Nurlan (2017) "Information Operations in the Hybrid/Non-Linear Warfare" …, p. 39.
36 Aliyev, Nurlan (2017) "Information Operations in the Hybrid/Non-Linear Warfare" …, p. 40.
37 Defence Threat Reduction Agency (2018) "Cooperative Biological Engagement Program", http://www.dtra.mil/Missions/Partnering/CTR-Biological-Threat-Reduction/.
38 Kartveli, Georgii (2017) "Biolaboratornyy «frontir» SSHA v Gruzii i Azerbaydzhane", April 2, http://vpoanalytics.com/2017/04/02/biolaboratornyj-frontir-ssha-v-gruzii-i-azerbajdzhane/.
39 *Strategiya Natsional'noi Bezopasnosti Rossiiskoi Federatsii* (2015) Kremlin.ru, December 31, http://static.kremlin.ru/media/events/files/ru/l8iXkR8XLAtxeilX7JK3XXy6Y0AsHD5v.pdf.
40 Aliyev, Nurlan (2018b) "Russa's 'Biological' Information Operation Against the US and Georgia", *The Central Asia-Caucasus Analyst,* November 27, https://www.cacianalyst.org/publications/analytical-articles/item/13545-russas-biological-information-operation-against-the-us-and-georgia.html.
41 RIA Novosti (2016) "Ryabkov: SSHA podryvayut konventsiyu o zapreshchenii biologicheskogo oruzhiya", May 27, https://ria.ru/20160527/1439959087.html; Golobokov, Nikita (2016) "Rabota amerikanskikh biolaboratoriy vyglyadit podozritel'no", September 1, https://vz.ru/politics/2016/9/1/830073.print.html.
42 Goodenough, Patrick (2013) "Russian Official Accuses US of Using Lab in Caucasus for Bio-Warfare", October 15, https://www.cnsnews.com/news/article/patrick-goodenough/russian-official-accuses-us-using-lab-caucasus-bio-warfare; see also: Gamov, Aleksandr (2016) "Gennadiy Onishchenko: Voyennyye mikrobiologi SSHA v Gruzii mogut namerenno zarazhat' komarov virusom Zika", https://www.kp.ru/daily/26493/3362692/.

## 178  Functions of Russia's foreign security policy

43 RIA Novosti (2018a) "Minoborony: v Gruzii 73 cheloveka pogibli iz-za eksperimentov tsentra Lugara", October 4, https://ria.ru/20181004/1529985745.html?inj=1.
44 RIA Novosti (2018b) "V Minoborony soobshchili o rekonstruktsii laboratoriy SSHA v trekh stranakh SNG", October 4, https://ria.ru/20181004/1529983608.html.
45 Departament informatsii i massovykh kommunikatsii Ministerstva oborony Rossiyskoi Federatsii (2018) "V Minoborony Rossii proshel brifing, posvyashchennyy analizu voyenno-biologicheskoy deyatel'nosti SSHA na territorii Gruzii", October 4, https://function.mil.ru/news_page/country/more.htm?id=12198232@egNews.
46 Aliyev, Nurlan (2018a) "Russia Claims Threat of US 'Biological Weapons Program' in Several Former Soviet Republics", *Eurasia Daily Monitor*, Vol. 15, No. 148, October 18, https://jamestown.org/program/russia-claims-threat-of-us-biological-weapons-program-in-several-former-soviet-republics/.
47 Aliyev, Nurlan (2018b) "Russa's 'Biological' Information Operation Against the US and Georgia", The Central Asia-Caucasus Analyst, November 27, https://www.cacianalyst.org/publications/analytical-articles/item/13545-russas-biological-information-operation-against-the-us-and-georgia.html.
48 Roks, Yurii (2016) "Bakteriologicheskaya laboratoriya Gruzii vnov' okazalas' v tsentre skandala", http://www.ng.ru/cis/2016-01-20/7_gruzia.html.
49 Aliyev, Nurlan (2018b) "Russa's 'Biological' Information Operation Against the US and Georgia", *The Central Asia-Caucasus Analyst*, November 27, https://www.cacianalyst.org/publications/analytical-articles/item/13545-russas-biological-information-operation-against-the-us-and-georgia.html.
50 Ibid.
51 Interfax-AVN (2022a) "Putin v khode razgovora s prem'yerom Lyuksemburga zaostril vnimaniye na neprekrashchayushchikhsya raketnykh udarakh ukrainskikh silovikov po Donbassu – Kreml'", March 19, https://www.militarynews.ru/story.asp?rid=1&nid=570725&lang=RU.
52 RIA Novosoti (2022) "Rassledovaniye pokazhet tsel' rabot v laboratoriyakh na Ukraine, zayavil Patrushev", March 15, https://ria.ru/20220315/laboratorii-1778285956.html.
53 Interfax-AVN (2022b) "Na Ukraine pod rukovodstvom spetsialistov SSHA razrabatyvalis' komponenty biologicheskogo oruzhiya – Shoygu", August 24, https://www.militarynews.ru/story.asp?lang=RU.
54 Arkadiev, Andrey and Alexandrov, Sergey (2022) "V MO RF raskryli imena zapadnykh kuratorov, zadeystvovannykh v realizatsii voyenno-biologicheskikh programm na Ukraine", April 14, https://tvzvezda.ru/news/20224141612-yTCt8.html.
55 Science and Technology Centre in Ukraine, Vision Statements, http://www.stcu.int/weare/index.php.
56 ArmenianReport (2021) "Armeniya i Rossiya podpisali memorandum o biologicheskoy bezopasnosti" May 6, https://armenianreport.com/print/280607/, And, Turkmen-Portlal (2021) "Glavy MID Turkmenistana i Rossii podpisali Memorandum", April 1, https://turkmenportal.com/blog/35608/glavy-mid-turkmenistana-i-rossii-podpisali-memorandum.
57 Informburo.kz (2022) "V MID otvetili, budet li Kazakhstan sotrudnichat' s Rossiyey v voyenno-biologicheskoy sfere", April 4, https://informburo.kz/novosti/v-mid-otvetili-budet-li-kazahstan-sotrudnichat-s-rossiej-v-voenno-biologicheskoj-sfere.
58 SIN'KHUA Novosti (2021) "Sovmestnoye zayavleniye ministrov inostrannykh del Rossiyskoy Federatsii i Kitayskoy Narodnoy Respubliki ob ukreplenii Konventsii o zapreshchenii razrabotki, proizvodstva i nakopleniya zapasov bakteriologicheskogo (biologicheskogo) i toksinnogo oruzhiya i ob ix unichtozhenii", October 8, http://russian.news.cn/2021-10/08/c_1310232124.htm.
59 Roffey, Roger and Tunemalm, Anna-Karin (2017) 'Biological Weapons Allegations: A Russian Propaganda Tool to Negatively Implicate the United States", *The Journal of Slavic Military Studies*, Vol. 30, No. 4, p. 540, DOI: 10.1080/13518046.2017.1377010.

60 Ibid.
61 Waltzman, Rand (2017) "The Weaponization of Information – The Need for Cognitive Security", The RAND Corporation CT-473, 2017, CT-473, Testimony presented before the Senate Armed Services Committee, Subcommittee on Cybersecurity 27 April, p. 5, https://www.rand.org/pubs/testimonies/CT473.html.
62 Waltzman, Rand (2017) "The Weaponization of Information – The Need for Cognitive Security" ..., p. 5.
63 Fond "Evraziiskii dialog" (2015) "Fond 'Evraziiskii dialog' poluchil prezidentskiy grant", Grant 2015 goda, http://evrazia-d.ru/news/68-novost-2.
64 Waltzman, Rand (2017) "The Weaponization of Information – The Need for Cognitive Security" ..., p. 3.
65 Miller, Greg and Belton, Catherine (2022) "Russia's spies misread Ukraine and misled Kremlin as war loomed", *The Washington Post*, August 19, https://www.washingtonpost.com/world/interactive/2022/russia-fsb-intelligence-ukraine-war/.
66 Ibid.
67 Guerrero-Saade, Juan Andres; Raiu, Costin; Moore, Daniel and Rid, Thomas (2017) "Penquin's Moonlit Maze – The Dawn of Nation-State Digital Espionage", King's College London, April 3, https://media.kasperskycontenthub.com/wp-content/uploads/sites/43/2018/03/07180251/Penquins_Moonlit_Maze_PDF_eng.pdf.
68 Barnes, Julian E. (2008) "Cyber-attack on Defence Department computers raises concerns". *The Los Angeles Times*, November 28, https://web.archive.org/web/20090221124901/http://articles.latimes.com/2008/nov/28/nation/na-cyberattack28.
69 Greenberg, Andy (2017) "'Crash Override': The Malware That Took Down a Power Grid", December 6, *WIRED*, https://www.wired.com/story/crash-override-malware/.
70 DHS Press Office (2016) "Joint Statement from the Department Of Homeland Security and Office of the Director of National Intelligence on Election Security", October 7, https://www.dhs.gov/news/2016/10/07/joint-statement-department-homeland-security-and-office-director-national.
71 Ibid.
72 Greenberg, Andy (2018) "The Untold Story of NotPetya, the Most Devastating Cyberattack in History", *WIRED*, August 22, https://www.wired.com/story/notpetya-cyberattack-ukraine-russia-code-crashed-the-world/.
73 Ibid.
74 The Estonian Foreign Intelligence Service (2018) "International Security and Estonia-2018, Report, p. 54, https://www.valisluureamet.ee/pdf/raport-2018-ENG-web.pdf.
75 RIA Novosti (2017) "V Rossii sozdany voiska informatsionnykh operatsii", February 22, https://ria.ru/defence_safety/20170222/1488596879.html.
76 Cheravitch, Joe (2021) "The Role of Russia's Military in Information Confrontation", *CNA Report, p. 10*, https://www.cna.org/reports/2021/06/role-of-russian-military-in-information-confrontation.
77 US Department of the Treasury (2021) "Treasury Escalates Sanctions Against the Russian Government's Attempts to Influence US Elections", April 15, https://home.treasury.gov/news/press-releases/jy0126.
78 Kramer, Andrew E. (2016) "How Russia Recruited Elite Hackers for Its Cyberwar", *The New York Times*, December 29, https://www.nytimes.com/2016/12/29/world/europe/how-russia-recruited-elite-hackers-for-its-cyberwar.html?hp&action=click&pgtype=Homepage&clickSource=story-heading&module=a-lede-package-region&region=top-news&WT.nav=top-news&_r=1.
79 The Department of Justice of the United Staes (2018) *Conspiracy to Commit an Offense Against the United States*, the United States District Court for the District of Columbia, https://www.justice.gov/file/1080281/download.
80 Graff, Garrett M. (2018) "PM Indicting 12 Russian Hackers Could Be Mueller's Biggest Move Yet", July 13, https://www.wired.com/story/mueller-indictment-dnc-hack-russia-fancy-bear/.

81 Cheravitch, Joe (2021) "The Role of Russia's Military in Information Confrontation", *CNA Report*, p. 9, https://www.cna.org/reports/2021/06/role-of-russian-military-in-information-confrontation.
82 Yuditskaya, Anastasiya and Rozhdestvenskii, Il'ya (2017) "SMI uznali yeshche ob odnom areste v FSB po delu o gosizmene", January 26, https://www.rbc.ru/politics/26/01/2017/588a0bda9a7947c9635cd8d2.
83 Cheravitch, Joe (2021) "The Role of Russia's Military in Information Confrontation", *CNA Report*, p. 9, https://www.cna.org/reports/2021/06/role-of-russian-military-in-information-confrontation.
84 Vice.com (2018) "13 Russian nationals indicted for meddling in US election", February 16, https://news.vice.com/en_us/article/vbp3kx/breaking-13-russian-nationals-indicted-for-meddling-in-us-election.
85 Krebsonsecurity.com (2017) "Alleged Spam King Pyotr Levashov Arrested", 10 April, https://krebsonsecurity.com/2017/04/alleged-spam-king-pyotr-levashov-arrested/.
86 Krebsonsecurity.com (2018) "Alleged Spam Kingpin 'Severa' Extradited to US", 5 February 2018, https://krebsonsecurity.com/2018/02/alleged-spam-kingpin-severa-extradited-to-us/.
87 Ben Bassat, Omri and Cohen, Itay (2019) "Mapping the Connections Inside Russia's APT Ecosystem", the Report, *Intezer*, September 24, https://www.intezer.com/blog-russian-apt-ecosystem/.
88 Ibid.
89 Soldatov, Andrei and Borogan, Irina (2015) *The red web: the struggle between Russia's digital dictators and the new online revolutionaries*, New York: Public Affairs, p. 223.
90 Ibid., pp. 223–238.
91 Ibid., pp. 65–84.
92 Duma.gov.ru (2019) *O vnesenii izmeneniy v Federal'nyy zakon 'O svyazi' i Federal'nyy zakon "Ob informatsii, informatsionnykh tekhnologiyakh i o zashchite informatsii"*, https://sozd.duma.gov.ru/bill/608767-7.
93 Meduza.io (2019) "Gosduma prinyala zakon ob izolyatsii Runeta", April 16, https://meduza.io/news/2019/04/16/gosduma-prinyala-zakon-ob-izolyatsii-runeta; See also: Prokopenko, Aleksandra (2019) "Zakon o suverennom runete. Kak on voznik i k chemu privedet". April 18, https://carnegie.ru/commentary/78928.
94 Malyarenko, Tetyana and Kormych, Borys (2022) "Russia's Cyberwar Against Ukraine: A De-Modernized Regime Against a Networked Society", *Ponars Eurasia*, Policy Memo, July 22, https://www.ponarseurasia.org/russias-cyberwar-against-ukraine-a-de-modernized-regime-against-a-networked-society/.
95 Aliyev, Nurlan (2022) "Cyber Operations During Russia's Invasion of Ukraine in 2022", *Riddle*, November 24, https://ridl.io/cyber-operations-during-russia-s-invasion-of-ukraine-in-2022/.
96 Malyarenko, Tetyana and Kormych, Borys (2022) "Russia's Cyberwar Against Ukraine …
97 Bykvu.com (2022) "'Diya' personal data leak: Ukraine's Digital Transformation Ministry called out over social media manipulation and use of bots", January 23, https://bykvu.com/eng/bukvy/diya-personal-data-leak-ukraine-s-digital-transformation-ministry-called-out-over-social-media-manipulation-and-use-of-bots/.
98 Microsoft (2022a) "Special Report: Ukraine – An overview of Russia's cyberattack activity in Ukraine", Digital Security Unit, *Microsoft Corporation*, April 27, p. 08 of 21, https://query.prod.cms.rt.microsoft.com/cms/api/am/binary/RE4Vwwd.
99 Microsoft (2022a) "Special Report: Ukraine …", p. 10 of 21.
100 Ibid.
101 Orlova, Violetta (2022) "Ataki rossiyskikh khakerov sovpadayut s obstrelami ukrainskikh gorodov – Gosspetszvyazi", May 7, https://www.unian.net/war/rossiyskoe-vtorzhenie-ataki-vrazheskih-hakerov-sovpadayut-s-obstrelami-ukrainskih-gorodov-novosti-vtorzheniya-rossii-na-ukrainu-11817174.html.

102 Microsoft (2022a) "Special Report: Ukraine …", pp. 03–04 of 21.
103 Ibid., p. 04 of 21.
104 Microsoft (2022b) "Defending Ukraine: Early Lessons from the Cyber War", *Microsoft Corporation,* June 22, 2022, p. 10, https://query.prod.cms.rt.microsoft.com/cms/api/am/binary/RE50KOK.
105 Ibid., p. 11.
106 Page, Carly (2022a) "Viasat cyberattack blamed on Russian wiper malware", *TechCrunch+*, March 31, https://techcrunch.com/2022/03/31/viasat-cyberattack-russian-wiper/.
107 Page, Carly (2022b) "US, UK and EU blame Russia for 'unacceptable' Viasat cyberattack" *TechCrunch+*, May 10, https://techcrunch.com/2022/05/10/russia-viasat-cyberattack/.
108 Sheahan, Maria; Christoph Steitz and Andreas Rinke (2022) "Satellite outage knocks out thousands of Enercon's wind turbines", *Reuters*, February 28, https://www.reuters.com/business/energy/satellite-outage-knocks-out-control-enercon-wind-turbines-2022-02-28/.
109 Hurska, Alla (2022) "Ukraine's Other Front: The Battle in the Cyber Domain", April 19, https://jamestown.org/program/ukraines-other-front-the-battle-in-the-cyber-domain/.
110 Chekinov S. G. and Bogdanov S.A. (2010) "Asimmetrichnye deystviya po obespecheniyu voyennoy bezopasnosti Rossii", *Voennaya mysl'*, № 3/2010, pp. 13–22, http://militaryarticle.ru/voennaya-mysl/2010-vm/10291-asimmetrichnye-dejstvija-po-obespecheniju-voennoj.
111 Liddell Hart, Sir Basil Henry (1954) *Strategy: the indirect approach*, London: Faber and Faber.
112 Chekinov S. G. and Bogdanov S. A. (2010) "Asimmetrichnye deystviya po obespecheniyu voyennoy bezopasnosti Rossii" …
113 Chekinov S. G. and Bogdanov S. A. (2010) "Asimmetrichnye deystviya po obespecheniyu voyennoy bezopasnosti Rossii" …
114 Chekinov S. G. and Bogdanov S. A. (2010) "Asimmetrichnye deystviya po obespecheniyu voyennoy bezopasnosti Rossii" …
115 Ibid.
116 Dul'nev P.A., Kovalev V.G., Il'in L.N. (2011) "Asimmetrichnoe protivodeystvie v setetsentricheskoi voine", *Voyennaya Mysl'*, № 10/2011, pp. 3–8, http://militaryarticle.ru/voennaya-mysl/2011-vm/10357-asimmetrichnoe-protivodejstvie-v-setetricheskoj.
117 These and other problems of the Russian military performed during the invasion of Ukraine in 2022 are largely discussed in Chapter 7.
118 Kofman, Michael (2019) "It's Time to Talk about A2/Ad: Rethinking the Russian Military Challenge, "War on the Rocks", September 5, https://warontherocks.com/2019/09/its-time-to-talk-about-a2-ad-rethinking-the-russian-military-challenge/.
119 Ibid.
120 Kremlin.ru (2019) "Valdai Discussion Club session, Vladimir Putin spoke at the final plenary session of the 16th meeting of the Valdai International Discussion Club", October 3, http://en.kremlin.ru/events/president/news/61719.
121 Kashin, Vasily (2018) "Russian-Chinese Security Cooperation and Military-to-Military Relations", December 21, https://www.ispionline.it/en/pubblicazione/russian-chinese-security-cooperation-and-military-military-relations-21828.
122 Tvzvezda.ru (2017) "Rossiya postavit v Kitay S-400, protivokorabel'nyye rakety i istrebiteli Su-35", February 21, https://tvzvezda.ru/news/opk/content/201702211445-41k8.htm.
123 Ibid.
124 Ibid.
125 Aliyev Nurlan (2020) "Military Cooperation Between Russia and China: The Military Alliance Without an Agreement?", Dilomaatia, June, N200, https://icds.ee/military-cooperation-between-russia-and-china-the-military-alliance-without-an-agreement/.

## 182  Functions of Russia's foreign security policy

126 Gorenburg, Dmitry (2020) "An Emerging Strategic Partnership: Trends in Russia-China Military Cooperation", Security Insights No. 54, The George C. Marshall European Center for Security Studies, April 29, https://www.marshallcenter.org/sites/default/files/files/2020-04/SecurityInsights_54.pdf.
127 Aliyev Nurlan (2020) Military Cooperation Between Russia and China …
128 Rukobratskiy, Valeriy and Gorbachov, Sergey (2022) "Iskusstvo voyny. Eksklyuzivnoye interv'yu Yevgeniya Prigozhina dlya aif.ru", September 30, https://aif.ru/society/safety/iskusstvo_voyny_eksklyuzivnoe_intervyu_evgeniya_prigozhina_dlya_aif_ru.
129 See Andreev P. (1940) *Narodnaya voina v Smolenskoi Gubernii v 1812 godu.* Smolensk: Smolenskoe Oblastnoe Gosudarstvennoe Izdatelstvo, http://militera.lib.ru/research/0/pdf/andreev_pg01.pdf.
130 Sokolovskiy, Vasili Danilovich (ed.) (1962) *Voennaya strategia.* The second edition. Moscow: Voenizdat, p. 142.
131 Ibid., p. 143.
132 Mil.ru. *Rukovodstvo bor'boy naroda v tylu vraga,* Guidelines, https://encyclopedia.mil.ru/files/morf/VoV_Vol11_Rukovodstvo_borboi_naroda.pdf?utm_.
133 See Andrew, Christopher and Mitrokhin, Vasili (2005) *The world was going our way.* New York: Basic Books.
134 Laruelle, Marlène (2019) "Russia's Militia Groups and their Use at Home and Abroad", Russie.Nei.Visions, No. 113, *Ifri*, April, p. 31, https://www.ifri.org/en/publications/notes-de-lifri/russieneivisions/russias-militia-groups-and-their-use-home-and-abroad.
135 Ibid., p. 5.
136 RIA Novosty (2012) "Putin podderzhal ideyu sozdaniya v Rossii chastnykh voyennykh kompaniy", April 11, https://ria.ru/20120411/623227984.html.
137 RBK(2018) "CHVK v zakone: zachem Sergey Lavrov predlagayet legalizovat' 'soldat udachi'", January 15, https://www.rbc.ru/politics/15/01/2018/5a5ca1219a7947afc1b76bfd.
138 Zamakhina, Tatyana (2022) "V Gosdumu vnesen proyekt o chastnykh voyennykh kompaniyakh", March 31, https://rg.ru/2022/03/31/v-gosdumu-vnesen-proekt-o-chastnyh-voennyh-kompaniiah.html.
139 Sukhankin, Sergey (2019) "'A black cat in the dark room': Russian Quasi-Private Military and Security Companies (PMSCs) – 'Non-existent,' but Deadly and Useful", *Canadian Military Journal (CMJ),* http://www.journal.forces.gc.ca/vol19/no4/page43-eng.asp.
140 Ibid.
141 Kamakin, Andrei (2018) "Safari dlya Vagnera", 12 June 2019, https://www.novayagazeta.ru/articles/2018/06/13/76787-safari-dlya-vagnera?utm_source=novaya&utm_medium=fb&utm_campaign=regular; See also: Svoboda.org (2019) "SBU opublikovala dannyye rossiyskikh grazhdan, nazvav ikh nayomnikami iz 'CHVK Vagnera'", January 28, https://www.svoboda.org/a/29736520.html.
142 Malkova, Irina and Bayev, Anton (2019) "Chastnaya armiya dlya prezidenta: istoriya samogo delikatnogo porucheniya Yevgeniya Prigozhina", Journalist investigation, January 29, https://thebell.io/41889-2/.
143 RBK (2022) "Prigozhin rasskazal ob istokakh gruppy Vagnera", September 26, https://www.rbc.ru/politics/26/09/2022/63314cef9a7947bf65368f6c.
144 Sukhankin, Sergey (2019) "'A black cat in the dark room': Russian Quasi-Private Military and Security Companies (PMSCs) – 'Non-existent,' but Deadly and Useful" …
145 Foy, Henry and Munshi, Neil (2019) "Putin seeks friends and influence at first Russia-Africa summit", October 22, https://www.ft.com/content/f20dbcc2-f17b-11e9-ad1e-4367d8281195.
146 Laruelle, Marlène (2019) "Russia's Militia Groups and their Use at Home and Abroad", Russie.Nei.Visions, No. 113, *Ifri*, April, p. 5. IFRI, p. 31.
147 Laruelle, Marlène (2019) "Russia's Militia Groups and their Use at Home and Abroad", Russie.Nei.Visions, No. 113, *Ifri*, April, p. 5. IFRI, p. 26.

148 Yapparova, Lilia, Andrey Pertsev and Alexey Slavin (2022) "A mercenaries' war How Russia's invasion of Ukraine led to a 'secret mobilization' that allowed oligarch Evgeny Prigozhin to win back Putin's favor", July 14, https://meduza.io/en/feature/2022/07/14/a-mercenaries-war.
149 Bellingcat Investigation Team (2020) "Putin Chef's Kisses of Death: Russia's Shadow Army's State-Run Structure Exposed", August 14, https://www.bellingcat.com/news/uk-and-europe/2020/08/14/pmc-structure-exposed/.
150 Yapparova, Lilia, Andrey Pertsev and Alexey Slavin (2022) "A mercenaries' war How Russia's invasion of Ukraine led to a 'secret mobilization' that allowed oligarch Evgeny Prigozhin to win back Putin's favor", July 14, https://meduza.io/en/feature/2022/07/14/a-mercenaries-war.
151 The UK Defense Intelligence update on the situation in Ukraine – 28 March 2022, *Twitter*, https://twitter.com/DefenceHQ/status/1508543191565406208?s=20&t=aGJ1Z-Ep352F_ThSQq2NPw.
152 Yapparova, Lilia, Andrey Pertsev and Alexey Slavin (2022) "A mercenaries' war …
153 Ibid.
154 Gulagu.net (2022) "Soobshcheniya s goryachey linii Gulagu.net", on *Telegram*, July 8, https://t.me/NetGulagu/2927, accessed 29 September 2022.
155 Pavlova, Anna and Elizabeth Nesterova (2022) "V pervuyu ochered' interesuyut ubiytsy i razboyniki — vam u nas ponravitsya", August 6, https://zona.media/article/2022/08/06/prigozhin.
156 The Insider (2022) "Wagner PMC has recruited more than 1,000 prisoners in 17 Russian colonies" August 8, https://theins.ru/en/news/253921.
157 US Department of the Treasury (2023) "Treasury Sanctions Russian Proxy Wagner Group as a Transnational Criminal Organization", January 26, https://home.treasury.gov/new/press-releases/jy1220.
158 Sheldon, Michael (2022) "Meet the Irregular Troops Backing up Russia's Army in the Kharkiv Region", June 17, https://www.bellingcat.com/news/2022/06/17/meet-the-irregular-troops-backing-up-russias-army-in-the-donbas/.
159 Ministry of Defence of the United Kingdom (2023) "Latest Defence Intelligence update on the situation in Ukraine – 20 January 2023", Twitter, https://twitter.com/DefenceHQ/status/1616323761392812033?s=20&t=Ep1-yuQimoaoFqJzRLUOPA.
160 Galeotti, Mark (2019) *Russian political war: moving beyond the hybrid*. London; New York: Routledge, p. 27. This issue is also discussed in Chapter 7.
161 It is largely discussed in the subchapter, "Colour revolutions" and "regime change" as main threats, of the second chapter – "Determinants of Russia's security policy".
162 Kofman, Michael and Rojansky, Matthew (2015) A closer look at Russia's 'hybrid war'. Kennan Kable 7, April, https://www.wilsoncenter.org/sites/default/files/media/documents/publication/7-KENNAN%20CABLE-ROJANSKY%20KOFMAN.pdf.
163 Revaitis, Algirdas (2018) "Contemporary Warfare Discourse in Russia's Military Thought", *Lithuanian Annual Strategic Review 2017–2018*, Vol. 16, p. 293.

## Bibliography

Aliyev, Nurlan (2017) "Information Operations in the Hybrid/Non-Linear Warfare", *Grasping the virtual: (geo)politics, economics and privacy in a digital era*, WEASA, College of Europe Natolin Campus, Warsaw, pp. 38–39, available at: https://www.weasa.org/wp-content/uploads/2018/02/WEASA_2017_publication_final.pdf, accessed 18 October 2019.

―――― (2018a) "Russia Claims Threat of US 'Biological Weapons Program' in Several Former Soviet Republics", *Eurasia Daily Monitor*, Vol. 15, No. 148, October 18, available at: https://jamestown.org/program/russia-claims-threat-of-us-biological-weapons-program-in-several-former-soviet-republics/, accessed 20 September 2022.

_____ (2018b) "Russa's 'Biological' Information Operation Against the US and Georgia", *The Central Asia-Caucasus Analyst,* November 27, available at: https://www.cacianalyst.org/publications/analytical-articles/item/13545-russas-biological-information-operation-against-the-us-and-georgia.html, accessed 20 September 2022.

_____ (2020) "Military Cooperation Between Russia and China: The Military Alliance Without an Agreement?", Dilomaatia, June, N200, available at: https://icds.ee/military-cooperation-between-russia-and-china-the-military-alliance-without-an-agreement/, accessed 27 September 2022.

_____ (2022) "Cyber Operations During Russia's Invasion of Ukraine in 2022", *Riddle*, November 24, available at: https://ridl.io/cyber-operations-during-russia-s-invasion-of-ukraine-in-2022/, accessed 19 February 2023.

Andreev, P. (1940) *Narodnaya voina v Smolenskoi Gubernii v 1812 godu.* Smolensk: Smolenskoe Oblastnoe Gosudarstvennoe Izdatelstvo, available at: http://militera.lib.ru/research/0/pdf/andreev_pg01.pdf, accessed 11 November 2019.

Andrew, Christopher, and Vasili Mitrokhin (2005) *The world was going our way*, New York: Basic Books.

Arkadiev, Andrey, and Sergey Alexandrov (2022) "V MO RF raskryli imena zapadnykh kuratorov, zadeystvovannykh v realizatsii voyenno-biologicheskikh programm na Ukraine", April 14, available at: https://tvzvezda.ru/news/20224141612-yTCt8.html, accessed 15 September 2022.

ArmenianReport (2021) "Armeniya i Rossiya podpisali memorandum o biologicheskoy bezopasnosti" May 6, available at: https://armenianreport.com/print/280607/, accessed 15 September 2022.

Barnes, Julian E. (2008) "Cyber-attack on Defence Department computers raises concerns". *The Los Angeles Times*. November 28, available at: https://web.archive.org/web/20090221124901/http://articles.latimes.com/2008/nov/28/nation/na-cyberattack28, accessed 26 September 2019.

Bartles, Charles K. (2016) "Getting Gerasimov Right", January–February 2016 *Military Review*, Combined Arms Centre, Fort Leavenworth, Kansas.

Bellingcat Investigation Team (2020) "Putin Chef's Kisses of Death: Russia's Shadow Army's State-Run Structure Exposed", August 14, available at: https://www.bellingcat.com/news/uk-and-europe/2020/08/14/pmc-structure-exposed/, accessed 29 September 2022.

Ben Bassat, Omri, and Itay Cohen (2019) "Mapping the Connections Inside Russia's APT Ecosystem", the Report, Intezer, September 24, available at: https://www.intezer.com/blog-russian-apt-ecosystem/, accessed 28 September 2022.

Berzinš, Janis (2014a) "Russia's New Generation Warfare in Ukraine: Implications for Latvian Defence Policy". Policy Paper no 02, National Defence Academy of Latvia Centre for Security and Strategic.

_____ (2014b) "The new generation of Russian warfare". *Aspen Review*, 3.

Bykvu.com (2022) "'Diya' personal data leak: Ukraine's Digital Transformation Ministry called out over social media manipulation and use of bots", January 23, available at: https://bykvu.com/eng/bukvy/diya-personal-data-leak-ukraine-s-digital-transformation-ministry-called-out-over-social-media-manipulation-and-use-of-bots/, accessed 26 September 2022.

Charap, Samuel (2015) "The ghost of hybrid war". *Survival*, 57, p. 53, DOI: 10.1080/00396338.2015.1116147.

Chekinov, Sergey G., and Sergey A. Bogdanov (2010) "Asimmetrichnye deystviya po obespecheniyu voyennoy bezopasnosti Rossii", *Voennaya mysl*, 3/2010, pp. 13–22, available at: http://militaryarticle.ru/voennaya-mysl/2010-vm/10291-asimmetrichnye-dejstvija-po-obespecheniju-voennoj, accessed 11 October 2022.

Cheravitch, Joe (2021) "The Role of Russia's Military in Information Confrontation", *CNA Report*, p. 10, available at: https://www.cna.org/reports/2021/06/role-of-russian-military-in-information-confrontation, accessed 23 September 2022.

Chivvis, Christopher S. (2017) "Hybrid war: Russian contemporary political warfare", *Bulletin of the Atomic Scientists'*, Vol. 73, No. 5 (How dangerous is hybrid war?), pp. 316– 317, DOI: 10.1080/00963402.2017.1362903.

Defence Threat Reduction Agency (2018) "Cooperative Biological Engagement Program", available at: http://www.dtra.mil/Missions/Partnering/CTR-Biological-Threat-Reduction/ accessed 1 November 2019.

Departament informatsii i massovykh kommunikatsii Ministerstva oborony Rossiyskoi Federatsii (2018) "V Minoborony Rossii proshel brifing, posvyashchennyy analizu voyenno-biologicheskoy deyatel'nosti SSHA na territorii Gruzii", 4 October 2018, available at: https://function.mil.ru/news_page/country/more.htm?id=12198232@egNews, accessed 15 November 2019.

DHS Press Office (2016) "Joint Statement from the Department Of Homeland Security and Office of the Director of National Intelligence on Election Security", October 7, available at: https://www.dhs.gov/news/2016/10/07/joint-statement-department-homeland-security-and-office-director-national, accessed 29 September 2019.

Dul'nev, P.A., V.G. Kovalev, and L.N. Il'in (2011) "Asimmetrichnoe protivodeystvie v setetsentricheskoi voine", *Voyennaya Mysl*, 10/2011, pp. 3–8, available at: http://militaryarticle.ru/voennaya-mysl/2011-vm/10357-asimmetrichnoe-protivodejstvie-v-setecentricheskoj, accessed 15 October 2019.

Duma.gov.ru (2019) *O vnesenii izmeneniy v Federal'nyy zakon 'O svyazi' i Federal'nyy zakon "Ob informatsii, informatsionnykh tekhnologiyakh i o zashchite informatsii"*, available at: https://sozd.duma.gov.ru/bill/608767-7, accessed 27 September 2019.

Fond "Evraziiskii dialog" (2015) "Fond 'Evraziiskii dialog' poluchil prezidentskiy grant", Grant 2015 goda, available at: http://evrazia-d.ru/news/68-novost-2, accessed 13 February 2018.

Foy, Henry, and Neil Munshi (2019) "Putin seeks friends and influence at first Russia-Africa summit", October 22, available at: https://www.ft.com/content/f20dbcc2-f17b-11e9-ad1e-4367d8281195, accessed 23 October 2019.

Freedman, Lawrence (2017) *The future of war: a history*, Bristol: Allen Lane.

Galeotti, Mark (2018) "I'm Sorry for Creating the 'Gerasimov Doctrine'", 5 March 2018, available at: https://foreignpolicy.com/2018/03/05/im-sorry-for-creating-the-gerasimov-doctrine/, accessed 5 September 2019.

―――― (2019) *Russian political war: moving beyond the hybrid*, London; New York: Routledge.

Gamov, Aleksandr (2016) "Gennadiy Onishchenko: Voyennyye mikrobiologi SSHA v Gruzii mogut namerenno zarazhat' komarov virusom Zika", available at: https://www.kp.ru/daily/26493/3362692/, accessed 15 November 2019.

Gerasimov, Valerii (2013) "Tsennost nauki v predvidenii", 26 February 2013, *Voenno-Promishlenniy Kurer*, available at: https://www.vpk-news.ru/articles/14632, accessed 10 June 2018.

Golobokov, Nikita (2016) "Rabota amerikanskikh biolaboratoriy vyglyadit podozritel'no", 1 September 2016, available at: https://vz.ru/politics/2016/9/1/830073.print.html, accessed 15 November 2019.

Goodenough, Patrick (2013) "Russian Official Accuses U.S. of Using Lab in Caucasus for Bio-Warfare", 15 October 2013, available at: https://www.cnsnews.com/news/article/patrick-goodenough/russian-official-accuses-us-using-lab-caucasus-bio-warfare, accessed 15 November 2019.

Gorenburg, Dmitry (2020) "An Emerging Strategic Partnership: Trends in Russia-China Military Cooperation", Security Insights No. 54, *The George C. Marshall European Center for Security Studies*, April 29, available at: https://www.marshallcenter.org/sites/default/files/files/2020-04/SecurityInsights_54.pdf, accessed 27 September 2022.

Graff, Garrett M. (2018) "PM Indicting 12 Russian Hackers Could Be Mueller's Biggest Move Yet", July 13, available at: https://www.wired.com/story/mueller-indictment-dnc-hack-russia-fancy-bear/, accessed 1 October 2019.

Greenberg, Andy (2017) "'Crash Override': The Malware That Took Down a Power Grid", December 6, *WIRED*, available at: https://www.wired.com/story/crash-override-malware/, accessed 29 September 2019.

_____ (2018) "The Untold Story of NotPetya, the Most Devastating Cyberattack in History", *WIRED*, August 22, available at: https://www.wired.com/story/notpetya-cyberattack-ukraine-russia-code-crashed-the-world/, accessed 30 September 2019.

Guerrero-Saade, Juan Andres, Costin Raiu, Daniel Moore, and Thomas Rid (2017) *Penquin's Moonlit Maze – The dawn of nation-state digital espionage*, King's College London, April 3, available at: https://media.kasperskycontenthub.com/wp-content/uploads/sites/43/2018/03/07180251/Penquins_Moonlit_Maze_PDF_eng.pdf, accessed 26 September 2019.

Gulagu.net (2022) "Soobshcheniya s goryachey linii Gulagu.net", on *Telegram*, July 8, available at: https://t.me/NetGulagu/2927, accessed 29 September 2022.

Hoffman, Frank (2007) *Conflict in the 21st century: The rise of hybrid wars*, Arlington, VA: Potomac Institute for Policy Studies.

Hurska, Alla (2022) "Ukraine's Other Front: The Battle in the Cyber Domain", April 19, available at: https://jamestown.org/program/ukraines-other-front-the-battle-in-the-cyber-domain/, accessed 26 September 2022.

Informburo.kz (2022) "V MID otvetili, budet li Kazakhstan sotrudnichat' s Rossiyey v voyenno-biologicheskoy sfere", April 4, available at: https://informburo.kz/novosti/v-mid-otvetili-budet-li-kazakhstan-sotrudnichat-s-rossiej-v-voenno-biologicheskoj-sfere, accessed 15 September 2022.

Interfax-AVN (2022a) "Putin v khode razgovora s prem'yerom Lyuksemburga zaostril vnimaniye na neprekrashchayushchikhsya raketnykh udarakh ukrainskikh silovikov po Donbassu – Kreml'", March 19, available at: https://www.militarynews.ru/story.asp?rid=1&nid=570725&lang=RU, accessed 15 September 2022.

_____ (2022b) "Na Ukraine pod rukovodstvom spetsialistov SSHA razrabatyvalis' komponenty biologicheskogo oruzhiya – Shoygu", August 24, available at: https://www.militarynews.ru/story.asp?lang=RU, accessed 15 September 2022.

Kamakin, Andrei (2018) "Safari dlya Vagnera", 12 June 2019, available at: https://www.novayagazeta.ru/articles/2018/06/13/76787-safari-dlya-vagnera?utm_source=novaya&utm_medium=fb&utm_campaign=regular, accessed November 13.

Kartveli, Georgii (2017) "Biolaboratornyy «frontir» SSHA v Gruzii i Azerbaydzhane", 2 April 2017, available at: http://vpoanalytics.com/2017/04/02/biolaboratornyj-frontir-ssha-v-gruzii-i-azerbajdzhane/, accessed 15 November 2019.

Kashin, Vasily (2018) "Russian-Chinese Security Cooperation and Military-to-Military Relations", December 21, available at: https://www.ispionline.it/en/pubblicazione/russian-chinese-security-cooperation-and-military-military-relations-21828, accessed 10 October 2022.

Kennan, George (1948) "Policy Planning Staff Memorandum". National Archives and Records Administration, RG 273, Records of the National Security Council, NSC 10/2. Washington, 4 May 1948, available at http://academic.brooklyn.cuny.edu/history/johnson/65ciafounding3.htm, accessed 4 September 2019.

Kofman, Michael, and Matthew Rojansky (2015) "A closer look at Russia's 'hybrid war'". Kennan Kable, 7, available at: https://www.wilsonCentre.org/sites/default/files/7-KENNAN%20CABLE-ROJANSKY%20KOFMAN.pdf, accessed 18 September 2019.

Kofman, Michael (2018) "Raiding and International Brigandry: Russia's Strategy for Great Power Competition". War on the Rocks, 14 June 2018, available at: https://warontherocks.com/2018/06/raiding-and-international-brigandry-russias-strategy-for-great-power-competition/, accessed 31 August 2019.

⸺ (2019) "It's Time to Talk about A2/Ad: Rethinking the Russian Military Challenge, "War on the Rocks", 5 September 2019, available at: https://warontherocks.com/2019/09/its-time-to-talk-about-a2-ad-rethinking-the-russian-military-challenge/, accessed 18 October 2019.

Kramer, Andrew E. (2016) "How Russia Recruited Elite Hackers for Its Cyberwar", *The New York Times*, December 29, available at: https://www.nytimes.com/2016/12/29/world/europe/how-russia-recruited-elite-hackers-for-its-cyberwar.html?hp&action=click&pgtype=Homepage&clickSource=story-heading&module=a-lede-package-region&region=top-news&WT.nav=top-news&_r=1, accessed 29 September 2019.

Krebsonsecurity.com (2017) "Alleged Spam King Pyotr Levashov Arrested", 10 April, available at: https://krebsonsecurity.com/2017/04/alleged-spam-king-pyotr-levashov-arrested/, accessed 26 September 2019.

⸺ (2018) "Alleged Spam Kingpin 'Severa' Extradited to US", 5 February 2018, available at: https://krebsonsecurity.com/2018/02/alleged-spam-kingpin-severa-extradited-to-us/, accessed 26 September 2019.

Kremlin.ru (2019) "Valdai Discussion Club session, Vladimir Putin spoke at the final plenary session of the 16th meeting of the Valdai International Discussion Club", October 3, available at: http://en.kremlin.ru/events/president/news/61719, accessed 10 October 2019.

Laruelle, Marlène (2019) "Russia's Militia Groups and their Use at Home and Abroad", Russie.Nei.Visions, No. 113, *Ifri*, April, p. 31, available at: https://www.ifri.org/en/publications/notes-de-lifri/russieneivisions/russias-militia-groups-and-their-use-home-and-abroad, accessed 29 September 2022.

Hart, Liddell, and Sir Basil Henry (1954) *Strategy: the indirect approach*, London: Faber and Faber.

Malkova, Irina, and Anton Bayev (2019) "Chastnaya armiya dlya prezidenta: istoriya samogo delikatnogo porucheniya Yevgeniya Prigozhina", Journalist investigation, January 29, available at: https://thebell.io/41889-2/, accessed 13 November 2019.

Malyarenko, Tetyana, and Borys Kormych (2022) "Russia's Cyberwar Against Ukraine: A De-Modernized Regime Against a Networked Society", *Ponars Eurasia*, Policy Memo, July 22, available at: https://www.ponarseurasia.org/russias-cyberwar-against-ukraine-a-de-modernized-regime-against-a-networked-society/, accessed 26 September 2022.

Meduza.io (2019) "Gosduma prinyala zakon ob izolyatsii Runeta", April 16, available at: https://meduza.io/news/2019/04/16/gosduma-prinyala-zakon-ob-izolyatsii-runeta, accessed 27 September 2022.

Microsoft (2022a) "Special Report: Ukraine – An overview of Russia's cyberattack activity in Ukraine", Digital Security Unit, *Microsoft Corporation*, April 27, p. 08 of 21, available at: https://query.prod.cms.rt.microsoft.com/cms/api/am/binary/RE4Vwwd, accessed 26 September 2022.

⸺ (2022b) "Defending Ukraine: Early Lessons from the Cyber War", *Microsoft Corporation*, June 22, p. 10, available at: https://query.prod.cms.rt.microsoft.com/cms/api/am/binary/RE50KOK, accessed 26 September 2022.

Mil.ru. *Rukovodstvo bor'boy naroda v tylu vraga*, Guidelines, available at: https://encyclopedia.mil.ru/files/morf/VoV_Vol11_Rukovodstvo_borboi_naroda.pdf?utm_, accessed 29 September 2022.

Miller, Greg, and Catherine Belton (2022) "Russia's spies misread Ukraine and misled Kremlin as war loomed", *The Washington Post*, August 19, available at: https://www.washingtonpost.com/world/interactive/2022/russia-fsb-intelligence-ukraine-war/, accessed 21 September 2022.

Ministry of Defence of the United Kingdom (2023) "Latest Defence Intelligence update on the situation in Ukraine – 20 January 2023", Twitter, available at: https://twitter.com/DefenceHQ/status/1616323761392812033?s=20&t=Ep1-yuQimoaoFqJzRLUOPA, accessed 20 January 2023.

Mukhin, Vladimir (2013) "Krym vziali v ramkakh gibridnoi voiny". *Nezavisimaia gazeta*, 13 February 2015, available at: http://www.ng.ru/armies/2015-02-13/3_kartblansh.html, accessed 1 September 2019.

Orlova, Violetta (2022) "Ataki rossiyskikh khakerov sovpadayut s obstrelami ukrainskikh gorodov – Gosspetszvyazi", May 7, available at: https://www.unian.net/war/rossiyskoe-vtorzhenie-ataki-vrazheskih-hakerov-sovpadayut-s-obstrelami-ukrainskih-gorodov-novosti-vtorzheniya-rossii-na-ukrainu-11817174.html, accessed 26 September 2022.

Page, Carly (2022a) "Viasat cyberattack blamed on Russian wiper malware", *TechCrunch+*, March 31, available at: https://techcrunch.com/2022/03/31/viasat-cyberattack-russian-wiper/, accessed 26 September 2022.

_____ (2022b) "US, UK and EU blame Russia for 'unacceptable' Viasat cyberattack" *TechCrunch+*, May 10, available at: https://techcrunch.com/2022/05/10/russia-viasat-cyberattack/, accessed 26 September 2022.

Pavlova, Anna, and Elizabeth Nesterova (2022) "V pervuyu ochered' interesuyut ubiytsy i razboyniki — vam u nas ponravitsya", August 6, available at: https://zona.media/article/2022/08/06/prigozhin, accessed 29 September 2022.

Perry, Bret (2015) "Non-Linear Warfare in Ukraine: The Critical Role of Information Operations and Special Operations", 14 August 2015, available at: http://smallwarsjournal.com/jrnl/art/non-linear-warfare-in-ukraine-the-critical-role-of-information-operations-and-special-opera, accessed 1 September 2019, accessed 30 September 2022.

Pocheptsov, Georgii (2015) "Rol' informatsii v gibridnykh voynakh", *Prportal.com.ua*, September 19, available at: http://prportal.com.ua/Peredovitsa/rol-informacii-v-gibridnyh-voynah, accessed 20 September 2022.

Prokopenko, Aleksandra (2019) "Zakon o suverennom runete. Kak on voznik i k chemu privedet", 18 April 2019, available at: https://carnegie.ru/commentary/78928, accessed 27 September 2019.

RBK (2018) "CHVK v zakone: zachem Sergey Lavrov predlagayet legalizovat' 'soldat udachi'", January 15, available at: https://www.rbc.ru/politics/15/01/2018/5a5ca1219a7947afc1b76bfd, accessed 2 October 2022.

_____ (2022) "Prigozhin rasskazal ob istokakh gruppy Vagnera", September 26, available at: https://www.rbc.ru/politics/26/09/2022/63314cef9a7947bf65368f6c, accessed 2 October 2022.

Renz, Bettina (2016) "Russia and 'hybrid warfare'", *Contemporary Politics*, Vol. 22, No. 3, pp. 283–300. DOI: 10.1080/13569775.2016.1201316.

Rettman, Andrew (2015) "EU to strike back at Russian propaganda", March 19, available at: https://euobserver.com/foreign/128071, accessed 18 September 2019.

Revaitis, Algirdas (2018) "Contemporary Warfare Discourse in Russia's Military Thought", *Lithuanian Annual Strategic Review 2017–2018*, Vol. 16, pp. 269–301, DOI: 10.2478/lasr-2018-0010.

RIA Novosty (2012) "Putin podderzhal ideyu sozdaniya v Rossii chastnykh voyennykh kompaniy", April 11, available at: https://ria.ru/20120411/623227984.html, accessed 2 October 2022.

―――― (2016) "Ryabkov: SSHA podryvayut konventsiyu o zapreshchenii biologicheskogo oruzhiya", 27 May 2016, available at: https://ria.ru/20160527/1439959087.html, accessed 15 November 2019.

―――― (2017) "V Rossii sozdany voiska informatsionnykh operatsii", February 22, available at: https://ria.ru/defence_safety/20170222/1488596879.html, accessed 29 September 2019.

―――― (2018a) "Minoborony: v Gruzii 73 cheloveka pogibli iz-za eksperimentov tsentra Lugara", 4 October 2018, available at: https://ria.ru/20181004/1529985745.html?inj=1, accessed 15 November 2019.

―――― (2018b) "V Minoborony soobshchili o rekonstruktsii laboratoriy SSHA v trekh stranakh SNG", 4 October 2018, available at: https://ria.ru/20181004/1529983608.html, accessed 15 November 2019.

Roffey, Roger, and Anna-Karin Tunemalm (2017) "Biological Weapons Allegations: A Russian Propaganda Tool to Negatively Implicate the United States", *The Journal of Slavic Military Studies*, Vol. 30, No. 4, p. 540, DOI: 10.1080/13518046.2017.1377010.

Roks, Yurii (2016) "Bakteriologicheskaya laboratoriya Gruzii vnov' okazalas' v tsentre skandala", available at: http://www.ng.ru/cis/2016-01-20/7_gruzia.html, accessed 15 November 2019.

―――― (2022) "Rassledovaniye pokazhet tsel' rabot v laboratoriyakh na Ukraine, zayavil Patrushev", March 15, available at: https://ria.ru/20220315/laboratorii-1778285956.html, accessed 15 September 2022.

Rukobratskiy, Valeriy, and Sergey Gorbachov (2022) "Iskusstvo voyny. Eksklyuzivnoye interv'yu Yevgeniya Prigozhina dlya aif.ru", September 30, available at: https://aif.ru/society/safety/iskusstvo_voyny_eksklyuzivnoe_intervyu_evgeniya_prigozhina_dlya_aif_ru, accessed 2 October 2022.

Sheahan, Maria, Christoph Steitz, and Andreas Rinke (2022) "Satellite outage knocks out thousands of Enercon's wind turbines", *Reuters*, February 28, available at: https://www.reuters.com/business/energy/satellite-outage-knocks-out-control-enercon-wind-turbines-2022-02-28/, accessed 26 September 2022.

Sheldon, Michael (2022) "Meet the Irregular Troops Backing up Russia's Army in the Kharkiv Region", June 17, available at: https://www.bellingcat.com/news/2022/06/17/meet-the-irregular-troops-backing-up-russias-army-in-the-donbas/, accessed 3 October 2022.

Shoygu, Sergey (2019) "Sergey Shoygu rasskazal, kak spasali rossiyskuyu armiyu", interviewed by Mikhail Rostovskiy, 22 September 2019, available at: https://www.mk.ru/politics/2019/09/22/sergey-shoygu-rasskazal-kak-spasali-rossiyskuyu-armiyu.html, accessed 23 September 2019.

SIN'KHUA Novosti (2021) "Sovmestnoye zayavleniye ministrov inostrannykh del Rossiyskoy Federatsii i Kitayskoy Narodnoy Respubliki ob ukreplenii Konventsii o zapreshchenii razrabotki, proizvodstva i nakopleniya zapasov bakteriologicheskogo (biologicheskogo) i toksinnogo oruzhiya i ob ix unichtozhenii", October 8, available at: http://russian.news.cn/2021-10/08/c_1310232124.htm, accessed 15 September 2022.

Science and Technology Centre in Ukraine, Vision Statements, available at: http://www.stcu.int/weare/index.php, accessed 15 September 2022.

Sokolovskiy, Vasili Danilovich (ed.) (1962) *Voennaya strategia*. The second edition. Moscow: Voenizdat.

Soldatov, Andrei, and Irina Borogan (2015) *The red web: the struggle between Russia's digital dictators and the new online revolutionaries*, New York: Public Affairs.

Solodnikov (2022) "Dmitriy Muratov: 'Russkiye pozvonochniki'", interview, *YouTube*, September 29, available at: https://www.youtube.com/watch?v=mMBpbo8Wkwo, accessed 30 September 2022.

Stalin, Joseph (1936) "Comrade Stalin granted an interview to Roy Howard, President of Scripps-Howard Newspapers". 1 March 1936, *Works*, Vol. 14, Red Star Press Ltd., London, 1978, Transcription/HTML Markup: Salil Sen for MIA, 2008, Marxists Internet Archive (2008), available at: https://www.marxists.org/reference/archive/stalin/works/1936/03/01.htm, accessed 11 September 2019.

*Strategiya Natsional'noi Bezopasnosti Rossiiskoi Federatsii* (2015) Kremlin.ru, 31 December 2015, available at: http://static.kremlin.ru/media/events/files/ru/l8iXkR8XLAtxeilX7JK3XXy6Y0AsHD5v.pdf, accessed 15 November 2019.

Sukhankin, Sergey (2019) "'A black cat in the dark room': Russian Quasi-Private Military and Security Companies (PMSCs) – 'Non-existent,' but Deadly and Useful", *Canadian Military Journal (CMJ)*, available at: http://www.journal.forces.gc.ca/vol19/no4/page43-eng.asp, accessed 12 November 2019.

Svoboda.org (2019) "SBU opublikovala dannyye rossiyskikh grazhdan, nazvav ikh nayomnikami iz 'CHVK Vagnera'", January 28, available at: https://www.svoboda.org/a/29736520.html, accessed 13 November 2019.

The Department of Justice of the United Staes (2018) *Conspiracy to Commit an Offense Against the United States*, the United States District Court for the District of Columbia, available at: https://www.justice.gov/file/1080281/download, accessed 1 October 2019.

The Estonian Foreign Intelligence Service (2018) "International Security and Estonia-2018, Report, p. 54, available at: https://www.valisluureamet.ee/doc/raport/2018-en.pdf., accessed 26 September 2019.

The Insider (2022) "Wagner PMC has recruited more than 1,000 prisoners in 17 Russian colonies" August 8, available at: https://theins.ru/en/news/253921, accessed 29 September 2022.

Thornton, Rod (2015) "The Changing Nature of Modern Warfare-Responding to Russian Information Warfare", *The RUSI Journal*, 2015, Vol. 160, No. 4, pp. 40–48. DOI: 10.1080/03071847.2015.1079047.

Tsentr globalistiki "Strategiya KHKHÍ" (2016) "Gibressiya Putina. Nevoyennyye aspekty voyn novogo pokoleniya", March 23, 2016, available at: http://geostrategy.org.ua/images/Hybression_finversion.pdf, accessed 13 October 2019.

TurkmenPortlal (2021) "Glavy MID Turkmenistana i Rossii podpisali Memorandum", April 1, available at: https://turkmenportal.com/blog/35608/glavy-mid-turkmenistana-i-rossii-podpisali-memorandum, accessed 15 September 2022.

Tvzvezda.ru (2017) "Rossiya postavit v Kitay S-400, protivokorabel'nyye rakety i istrebiteli Su-35", February 21, available at: https://tvzvezda.ru/news/opk/content/201702211445-41k8.htm, accessed 10 October 2019.

U.S. Department of the Treasury (2021) "Treasury Escalates Sanctions Against the Russian Government's Attempts to Influence U.S. Elections", April 15, available at: https://home.treasury.gov/news/press-releases/jy0126, accessed 23 September 2022.

_____ (2023) "Treasury Sanctions Russian Proxy Wagner Group as a Transnational Criminal Organization", January 26, available at: https://home.treasury.gov/news/press-releases/jy1220, accessed 26 January 2026.

Vice.com (2018) "13 Russian nationals indicted for meddling in U.S. election", February 16, https://news.vice.com/en_us/article/vbp3kx/breaking-13-russian-nationals-indicted-for-meddling-in-us-election, accessed 26 September 2019.

Waltzman, Rand (2017) "The Weaponization of Information – The Need for Cognitive Security", The RAND Corporation CT-473, 2017, CT-473, Testimony presented before the Senate Armed Services Committee, Subcommittee on Cybersecurity 27 April, p. 5, https://www.rand.org/pubs/testimonies/CT473.html, accessed 19 September 2019.

Yapparova, Lilia, Andrey Pertsev, and Alexey Slavin (2022) "A mercenaries' war How Russia's invasion of Ukraine led to a 'secret mobilization' that allowed oligarch Evgeny Prigozhin to win back Putin's favor", July 14, available at: https://meduza.io/en/feature/2022/07/14/a-mercenaries-war, accessed 29 September 2022.

Yuditskaya, Anastasiya, and Il'ya Rozhdestvenskii (2017) "SMI uznali yeshche ob odnom areste v FSB po delu o gosizmene", January 26, available at: https://www.rbc.ru/politics/26/01/2017/588a0bda9a7947c9635cd8d2, accessed 26 September 2019.

Zamakhina, Tatyana (2022) "V Gosdumu vnesen proyekt o chastnykh voyennykh kompaniyakh", March 31, available at: https://rg.ru/2022/03/31/v-gosdumu-vnesen-proekt-o-chastnyh-voennyh-kompaniiah.html, accessed 2 October 2022.

# 6 The implementation of Russia's foreign policy and the role of its security policy

### A second Cold War or an asymmetric competition between Russia and the West over the world order?

Since the 2000s, developments in Russia's foreign policy have reflected the country's struggle to preserve its status as a "great power" and to regain its "sphere of influence." Russia's ambitions and the accompanying security policy activities are the primary reasons for the increasing confrontation with the West. However, the chief drivers of Russia's foreign policy are the same as during the Soviet Union, if not earlier. Main among these drivers are Russia's desire for strategic depth and secure buffer zones against external threats due to its geography and an absence of natural protective barriers between it and neighboring powers, its ambition for recognition as a great power, and its complicated relationship with the West, which combines a fierce rivalry with the need for cooperation.[1]

The main cracks in its relations with the West stem from Russia's grievances around NATO enlargement, the West's democracy promotion in the post-Soviet area, and Moscow's unwillingness to accept the United States' role as hegemon in the international system.[2] In other words, Moscow's dissatisfaction with the unipolar system turned it into a firm supporter of multipolarity. The Russian scholar Fyodor Lukyanov notes that the West views Russia as a revisionist power, which challenges the post-Cold War order in Europe and the world. But, meanwhile Moscow believes that "there was no real order properly established at the end of the 20th century, but just an attempt (largely unsuccessful) to impose US hegemony."[3] According to Lukyanov, the Kremlin believes that a revisionist policy was carried out by a West "confident of its own right (as a moral and political victor) to change the world as it saw fit."[4] Lukyanov emphasizes that no "new world order" has been built, Western dominance in the world is seriously challenged, and that this strongly encourages Russia to prove that the collapse of the old one in 1991 was not legitimate. He argues that "the deep crisis in the EU and problems caused by the US' global dominance prompt Russia to revise the declared results of the Cold War."[5] It should be noted that Lukyanov's thoughts also mirror the narratives from Russia's political elite regarding the international system.

In its support for the multipolar system, Moscow advocates for self-determination and sovereignty in international relations. In this realm, Moscow

DOI: 10.4324/9781003344391-7

uses a nationalistic discourse. As John Mearsheimer stated, the diversity of opinion about what constitutes the best governing system makes the process of spreading liberal democracy around the world extremely difficult, especially in competition with nationalism. As Mearsheimer put it, "nationalism, after all, is a remarkably powerful political force that places great emphasis on self-determination and sovereignty."[6]

Mearsheimer notes that even the dominant state would be strongly inclined to wage war on minor powers to promote liberal democracy, it rarely ever attacks major powers for that purpose, especially if they possess nuclear weapons. It is because the costs would be too great, and the chance of success especially low. Therefore, US policymakers in the post-Cold War period have never seriously considered invading China or Russia. "Nevertheless, the United States has been committed to turning China and Russia into liberal democracies and absorbing them into the US-dominated liberal world order," Mearsheimer notes.[7] Mearsheimer emphasizes that "China and Russia have also resisted the spread of the liberal order for realist reasons, because it would allow the United States to dominate the international system economically, militarily, and politically."[8]

Russian political elites and experts supported the current foreign policy which emphasized international processes. They expect Russia's current and future position in the international system, along with the world order, to be defined by:

> the crisis of the European Union; the actual collapse of the old alignment of forces; the shift of international geopolitical and economic activity towards Asia and increasing role of China; increased international focus on Eurasia; "the beginning of a new rearrangement of the global economic regulation system through the formation of mega-blocs;" and "the United States starting to revise their strategic approaches."[9]

These are considered by Moscow the key factors for the realization of its foreign policy goals. These considerations and the current state of relations between Russia and the West raise an important question. Can the current situation be called a second or new Cold War? Despite several approaches on the question, we are going to try to understand the differences between the Cold War and the current confrontation between Russia and the West. In his 2018 analysis of this problem, Stephen Walt noted that the current situation is bad but to call it a "new Cold War" is misleading more than it is enlightening. Walt believes that if one compares the two situations more carefully, what is happening today is a mere shadow of that earlier rivalry:

> Viewing today's troubles as a new Cold War downplays the role that human agency and bad policy decisions have played in bringing the United States and Russia to the current impasse, distracts us from more important challenges, and discourages us from thinking creatively about how to move beyond the present level of rancor.[10]

After reviewing characteristics of the Cold War—such as the bipolar competition, parity of the two superpowers, and competition between the two rival political ideologies: liberal capitalism and Marxism-Leninism—Walt noted that the world today is not bipolar. It is either still unipolar or drifting toward some sort of multipolar system, with the United States still ahead and the other major powers catching up. If bipolarity eventually would return, it will be China, not Russia, as the other pole. Second, there was a certain rough parity during the Cold War, whereas today the United States is vastly stronger than Russia in nearly every category that matters. Third, there is no serious ideological rivalry. Fourth, "the real Cold War" "was a global competition, whereas the geopolitical issues that divide the United States and Russia today are confined to areas close to Russia's borders, like Ukraine, or to a small part of the Middle East."[11]

Emphasizing the main difference between the Soviets and Russia's foreign policy approaches, Dmitri Trenin points to the ideological cause. According to him, the Soviet Union used to march around the world spending huge resources on a lost ideological cause and an outsized geopolitical ambition while contemporary Russia has learned from this:

> When it travels abroad, it goes for security buffers as in Ukraine, status as in Syria and mostly money elsewhere. There is no grand design, but a lot of opportunity-seeking, based on the merits of each potential engagement. Russia imposes no models on others and in its present state, hardly serves as a model for anyone.[12]

According to Michael Kofman, today's competition is not the result of a balance of power, or universalist ideology *per se*, but instead "conscious decisions made by leaders, the strategies they pursued, and a series of definable disagreements in international politics." Kofman stresses that Russian leaders are desperate to avoid any further reduction in Russia's influence or territory, which is why they see the need to maintain buffer states and impose their will on neighbors in order to secure their own borders.[13] He believes that Russia is not a declining regional power, but rather that after a period of internal balancing, military reforms, and modernization, Russia is more than capable of holding its ground in its historic backyard, projecting power to other adjacent regions, and able to exact punishment on distant adversaries via non-military means. Russia is a potent military power in its near-abroad, has the proven ability to conduct political and cyber warfare, and readily contests the information domain, thus making contemporary Russia a weak, great power.[14] In this respect, answering SPIEGEL's question whether Putin acts out of weakness or out of strength, Henry Kissinger stated, "I think out of strategic weakness masked as tactical strength."[15] Kissinger's comment is the best explanation for developments in Russia's foreign and security policy in recent years.

There are some who believe a confrontation with Russia distracts the United States from the far more serious challenges it faces from a rising China.[16] However, Moscow considers the increasing competition between the United States and China as a possibility and tries to use it to promote its own interests. According to

Russian Foreign Minister Sergey Lavrov, the United States is "stubbornly" striving to mobilize all of its external partners to deter Russia and China, while at the same time, "they do not hide the desire to make trouble between Moscow and Beijing, to upset and undermine multilateral associations and regional integration structures developing outside of American control in Eurasia and the Asia-Pacific region."[17] Dmitry Trenin notes that Moscow and Beijing will continue to have their differences, and they are not entirely free from reciprocal phobias, but the chances of a China-Russia collision over those differences are minimized by the US policy of dual containment. "This policy, ironically, also relieves both countries' elites of lingering suspicions that the United States might build a bond with either China or Russia at the expense of the other."[18]

However, Russia's invasion of Ukraine in 2022 has further increased its confrontation with the West and deepened Russia's asymmetry in relations with China. Beijing, however, tries to keep its distance and does not support, at least not openly, the invasion.

Considering the above, it is possible to state that the current confrontation between Russia and the United States is not a new or second Cold War. Even as we consider the invasion of Ukraine in 2022 where Russia, in fact, waged war against a partner of the West and even after mutual sanctions and an energy war, which further deepened the confrontation, we cannot define this as a new Cold War. Based on the asymmetry between the adversaries' power capabilities, it can best be explained as an asymmetric confrontation happening between a declining or weak great power, Russia and an almost superpower, the West.

**Primakov's "doctrine"**

One of the main characteristics of Russia's contemporary foreign policy is the huge influence of the Soviet Union. Julia Gurganus and Eugene Rumer explain this well. They do not agree with Western perceptions that post-Soviet Russia has been heavily affected by the country's economic and political implosion and the foreign policy retreat of the 1990s, or that the ambition and dynamism of Russian foreign policy since Putin's 2012 return to the presidency is a relatively new phenomenon. They believe that Moscow's post-2012 foreign policy fits comfortably in the longstanding historical and intellectual tradition of the Soviet and even pre-Soviet Russian foreign policy.[19]

In this respect, even the very phrase "a new world order," a lovely phrase of the foreign policy elite, was introduced by Mikhail Gorbachev at the very beginning of his *perestroika* policy in 1986 to describe what the world should be like after the end of the Cold War.[20] Fyodor Lukyanov notes that all reform-minded members of the Soviet government were looking for ways to break the Cold War gridlock, and imagined some sort of "joint venture" between the two opponents as a solution. "In other words, they saw 'a new world order' as some agreement on mutually acceptable rules of global governance, as a compromise worked out through equal rapprochement."[21]

The legacy of the Soviet Union is also strengthened by the fact that the majority of Russia's foreign policy elites worked or studied during the reign of USSR.

In this respect, the legacy of Yevgeni Primakov, who was in key political positions in the Soviet Union and contemporary Russia, including foreign minister from 1996 to 1998, is greatly respected among the elites. Primakov's thoughts on international relations and the role of Russia in it merge the Soviet experience with Russia's interests and needs in the international system. Primakov's thoughts are so respected the among political elites and scholars in Russia that his foreign policy concepts are referred to as "Primakov's doctrine." "I think that in the near future, historians will formulate such a concept as 'Primakov's doctrine,'" Russian Foreign Minister Sergey Lavrov said in 2014.[22] He notes that since Primakov took office in the Russian Foreign Ministry, a foreign policy breakthrough occurred, "it went out of the rut that our Western partners tried to drive it into after the breakup of the USSR, and embarked on independent rails."[23] Lavrov recalled that Yevgeny Primakov was the first to put forward the idea of strengthening cooperation in the format of the Russia-India-China (RIC), which gave rise to BRICS.[24]

Since the second half of the 1990s, the trends of Russian foreign policy have been set by pragmatic realists. Generally, their foreign policy views can be called the "Primakov Doctrine." Ivan Safranchuk believes that the "Primakov Doctrine" proceeded from the assumption that the USSR actively participated in the formation of international law and, to a large extent, was its beneficiary. Safranchuk stresses that for Russia, which inherited all the positions of the Soviet Union in this area, international law was generally beneficial, especially given the country's weakness and its unpreparedness for "extra-legal disassembly." Russia was not strong enough to openly pursue its national interests and was, perhaps, not even able to articulate them clearly. "That is why Moscow should have waited for better times under the cover of international law," writes Safranchuk.[25]

It should be noted that this doctrine has never been formulated in writing. Moreover, it was not even clearly verbalized, but it was precisely this logic that has been visible in Russian foreign policy since 1996, when Yevgeny Primakov was appointed the foreign minister. Significant diplomatic efforts were then aimed precisely at deterring the United States and NATO within the framework of international law. Despite the declarative statements that they were a priority of Russian foreign policy, Primakov's approach implied the allocation of limited efforts to foreign policy in relation to the countries of the post-Soviet space.[26]

Primakov urged the necessity of pursuing a multi-vector, balanced foreign policy to counterbalance the West. Such a policy is vital because it creates the best conditions for Russia's internal development as it is not relying on one center of power, but several. He urged that without a doubt the number of poles will not remained fixed and that new ones will be formed. He pointed to the rapid economic growth of Brazil and South Africa. Integration processes will be developed in Latin America, Asia, Africa, and the Middle East and there are new "group" centers of the world economy and politics forming. Moreover, with the uneven development of world centers, the multipolar system itself is reliably stable. The multipolar characteristic of the present world is being built on the foundation of a particular phase of globalization, which not only enhances the interdependence of various centers but also makes their existence impossible under economic, scientific, and technological isolation.[27] Primakov highlighted that the dialectic between the emerging multipolarity and the interdependence of the emerging centers of the international system creates a real picture of today's world.[28]

Primakov noted that the supporters of rapprochement at all costs with the West assumed that an alternative to this would be an inexorable slide into confrontation but stated that this is not true. He stressed that Russia can and should seek equal partnerships with all and should find fields of shared interests. And where interests do not align, Russia should strive to find solutions that, on the one hand, ensure the vital interests for Russia and, on the other hand, do not lead to confrontation. "Obviously, this is the dialectic of the foreign policy of the Russian Federation in the period after the Cold War. If fields of shared interests are ignored, this is, at best, the Cold War again."[29]

He questioned whether Russia had enough capabilities to realize a multivector foreign policy. Primakov recognized that it would be difficult to use Russia's generally limited possibilities in all directions. Nevertheless, he believed that if taking into account the objectively accumulated political influence, the special geopolitical position, the existence of nuclear weapons, their status as a permanent member of the UN Security Council, the potential economic opportunities, as well as the advanced military, intellectual, and scientific-technical potential, then Russia would have the necessary basis of a multi-vector foreign policy. He emphasized that another incentive to its implementation is the indisputable reluctance of the predominant number of states to accept a world order determined by a single power.[30]

Can such a policy be considered a reorientation of Russia's foreign policy toward the East/China? Primakov's answer is negative:

> Russia would like to normalize relations with the United States and Europe, but it would be unreasonable to ignore the rapidly growing importance of China and other countries that are part of the Asia-Pacific economic cooperation. We are often intimidated by the fact that we are threatened to become a raw materials appendix of China. By the very nature of its capabilities, Russia cannot be and never will be any raw materials appendage.[31]

Neither ideological issues or values should be decisive in determination of partners or alliances, only Russia's interests. "There are no permanent opponents, but there are permanent national interests," realistically believed Primakov. He wrote that during the Soviet period, Russia often deviated from this vital truth, and as a result, in some cases, "the national interests of our state were sacrificed in the struggle against 'permanent opponents' or support of 'permanent allies.'"[32]

As shown above, Primakov offered flexible and maneuverable multivector foreign policy approaches which could allow Russia to balance between several vectors in the international system. It should be noted that he was not a promoter of strikingly anti-Western thoughts. As Secretary Madeleine Albright put it, "Yevgeny Primakov was always a staunch protector of Russian national interests … He loved his country. Yet he was pragmatic. He believed in the importance of solving difficult issues in US-Russian relations."[33]

Primakov cautiously stressed the need to not demonize the United States.[34] In one of his last speeches, he noted that Russia should cooperate with the United States and its NATO allies against real threats to humanity—terrorism, drug trafficking, conflict situations, and so on:

> Without this, not to mention the interest of Russians in eliminating dangerous international phenomena, we will lose our country as a great power. In such a case, Russia will not be able to occupy a main place for those states that are ready to accept support.[35]

**Russia as a "Liberal Empire"**

Until the 2000s, most of Russia's foreign policy efforts were focused on relations with the United States, NATO, the G7, and other issues related to the West. In the early 2000s, when the Russian economy began strengthening, Russia's political elite started to seriously consider the development of relations with the post-Soviet countries. In 2003, the concept of "Liberal Empire" was announced by Anatoly Chubais, who was one of the authors and implementers of the Russian economic reforms in the 1990s and considered among the political elite until the start of the invasion of Ukraine in 2022. According to this concept, the main task of the Russian Federation over a 35-year perspective was to build a liberal empire by expanding Russia's economic and political influences in the post-Soviet area. But it did not mean that Russia should be a hegemon; on the contrary, it should be a source of progress and a guarantor of human rights.[36] According to Chubais, Russia should not join either the EU or NATO. He considered one of the goals to be an economic space between Russia, Ukraine, Belarus, and Kazakhstan.[37] Chubais stated that the strategy of the "Liberal Empire" regarding Ukraine should be manifested in the expansion of Russian business in the Crimea.[38]

Chubais himself explained the "Liberal Empire" as a mission to carry freedom, human rights, private property, enterprise, and responsibility while also declaring that "this approach is already being implemented. First of all, by the penetration of our business abroad."[39]

Business should play a primary role in the "Liberal Empire." According to Chubais, compared to other post-Soviet countries, Russia was already ahead in terms of GDP per capita, in the quality of life, and in many other key indicators. Chubais highlighted that Russian business was confidently crossing borders. Since starting from the same position, Russia had outstripped all of the CIS countries. Therefore, this fact must not only be recognized but also be declared by Russia's leadership as the state's long-term goal:

> After all, there are things in politics that cannot be calculated in percentage terms—spirit, atmosphere, energy. A country like Russia should set itself not small, but big goals. The Liberal Empire is an ambitious goal.[40]

However, the "Liberal Empire" similar to Primakov's doctrine was not formulated. It was proposed by Chubais before the parliamentary election in 2003 and according to several Russian experts, simply a part of the election campaign. However, it did face huge criticism. Russian political expert Dmitry Orlov noted that an empire in the Russian version cannot exist only in an economic format and that influences of *siloviki* still matter:

> Inevitably, a situation will arise in which power arguments and special services take over the control and will coordinate the implementation of imperial ideas. And I am not at all convinced that Chubais, putting forward this theory now, will be able to keep the security institutions from its very peculiar interpretation at that time.[41]

Despite the liberal characteristics of Chubais' proposal, it could not avoid Russia's great power temptation and stressed Russia's spheres of interests, although in "liberal" terms. As Richard Sakwa put it, liberals define Russia's national interests in terms of "international economic integration and adaptation to the prevalent norms, although even they are not immune to great power temptations."[42] Generally, it was a liberal conception and supported by the so-called liberal members of Putin's first presidency. However, the "Liberal Empire" concept and its supporters were beaten by "Primakov's doctrine" and its promoters in the 2010s.

### Does Russian foreign policy favor "Primakov's doctrine," Chubais' "Liberal Empire," or something else?

Contemporary Russian foreign policy favors Primakov's thoughts rather than Chubais' ideas. Russian Foreign Minister Sergei Lavrov highlights that Primakov is the author of key provisions of Russia's current foreign policy doctrine:

> The principles he formulated, including our independence in world affairs, have stood the test of time and proved effective in practice. He fully realized that the country was capable of overcoming the difficulties it was facing and that Russia could not become a peripheral, second-rate state by virtue of its centuries-long history, unique geostrategic position and substantial military-political, economic, cultural, and, most important, human potential.[43]

It should be noted that Russia's recent Foreign Policy Concept named the strengthening of its economic presence in Asia-Pacific and the creation of security architecture there as a priority, as had been proposed by Primakov. In the presidential address to the Federal Assembly in 2013, President Putin highlighted Russia's reorientation toward the Pacific and the dynamic development in the eastern territories, declaring that these would not only open up new economic opportunities and new horizons but also provide additional instruments for an active foreign policy.[44] Alexander Korolev's thoughts reflect almost exactly the political leadership's view on Russia's pivot to the East. Korolev explains that for Russia, reorientation to the East means the transformation of its role in the world from "a 'zealous student' of the West, as it was during the 1990s, into a country that interacts with the West only when it deems it profitable and necessary." He continues by stating that "at the same time, by turning to Asia, Russia is gaining access to more instruments for promoting its agenda of balancing the United States and enhancing multipolarity."[45]

However, despite the Russian foreign policy elite's admiration for Primakov's ideas, in reality "Primakov's doctrine" is not fully realized or adhered to by Moscow. This is especially true in regards to his insistence on avoiding military conflict, which would lead to a heightened confrontation with the West as shown by Russia's invasion of Ukraine in 2022. Russian foreign policy elites now emphasize perspectives of long-term confrontation with the West. A new version of the Russian Foreign Policy Concept will likely be more assertive regarding relations with the West—who may even be transferred from "partners" to "adversaries." Director of the Foreign Policy Planning Department of the Russian Foreign Ministry, Alexey Drobinin—who is directly involved in development of the concept—wrote that regardless of the duration and outcome of the war in Ukraine, it can already be said that the 30-year era of generally constructive, albeit problematic, cooperation with the West has irrevocably ended, and that there will be no return to the situation as it stood prior to February 24 in regards to Russia's relations with "the North American and European countries."[46]

**Russia's great power temptations—hopes and realities of multipolarity**

Since the breakup of the Soviet, the idea of restoring Russia's great power status has been a popular concept among the Russian political elite and society at large. Resurrecting its great power status following its "humiliating defeat" by the West is the same as restoring Russia's dignity for a majority of the current ruling elite. But in reality, as Angela Stent put it, the USSR was not defeated in war; it perished from self-inflicted damages. It is difficult for many Russians to accept how such a nuclear superpower, which, despite its precarious economic situation, still possessed enormous natural resource wealth, could just disintegrate, literally petering out. Stent explains that therefore, Russia's domestic and foreign policy adjustments to its reduced status has been more complicated—albeit less violent—than that of the other former empires. "Its continuing role as a nuclear superpower—despite its economic weakness—made that transition away from empire more complex," Stent stresses.[47] According to Richard Sakwa, Russia's resistance was not to the global governance mechanisms promoted by international society, but "to the monist international relations practiced at the inter-state level." Sakwa stresses that the external dimension intersected with Russia's attempt to resist its diminished regional power status: "The post-imperial syndrome is particularly complex when the empire in question is not across the water but contiguous to a truncated state amidst a divided nations."[48]

The Russian elite, on the other hand, proposes that no stable international order has been created following the end of the Cold War. Fyodor Lukyanov highlights that "the idea about a Western-centric unipolar world has failed, and a multipolar system is yet to emerge, though it's hard to comment on how it may function properly."[49] He stresses that due to its size, geopolitical location, resource potential, tradition of being a great power, and aspiration to restore its might and prestige, Russia finds itself in the middle of the most important trends, which will shape the future world order.[50]

Despite Russia's vision that a multipolar world would be appropriate for resurrecting its status as one pole in such an international system, there are rising suspicions among Russian experts about whether the country would be able to. According to Dmitry Trenin, of course Russia should welcome the idea of a world of geopolitical and geoeconomic equilibrium as it corresponds to the interests of the country." "At the same time," writes Trenin, "Putin's obsession with the idea of changing the existing global order, i.e., making active efforts to eliminate the global hegemony of the US, is harmful."[51] He explains this with the idea that supporting parties solely because they oppose the global hegemony of Washington does not reinforce Russia's own position, "it creates additional problems. What is important for Russia is not the global order in itself, but Russia's place in this global order."[52] As Fyodor Lukyanov recognized, it is not the multipolar order that was expected by Russia:

The multipolar world, to which we really aspired, turned out to be in reality, well, let's say, not quite as pleasant as we thought. It is rather a chaotic development of events. These are nonlinear processes. And this is one of the illusions of world leaders, I mean—large countries of the world, which a lot depends on them. Rather, how? Much depends on them, but now much less depends on them than before. Therefore, we are not yet ready for a multipolar world.[53]

Suspicions regarding the supposed good conditions for Russia in the coming multipolar world can also be found in the statements of the ruling elites. For instance, Putin's former adviser Vladislav Surkov wrote that Russia for four centuries went to the East and for another four centuries went to the West but that neither of them "had taken root." Now the ideologies of the third path, "the third type of civilization, the third world, the third Rome, will be in demand," Surkov proposes.[54] But he concludes that, Russia must choose to be something between the West and the East, "Russia is a West-Eastern half-breed country. With its two-headed statehood, a hybrid mentality, intercontinental territory, bipolar history, it is charismatic, talented, beautiful, and lonely."[55]

According to Andrei Tsygankov, the Kremlin is seeking to adjust its policies to the global transition of power and international rules and during this process, Russia aims to preserve its international interests and great power status using the foreign policy tools available. However, Russia remains dependent on the West and is not likely to engage in actions that fundamentally disrupt the existing international order, believes Tsygankov.[56] He emphasizes that despite Russia's internal institutional differences from Western nations, Russia sees itself as an indispensable part of the West and will continue to reach out to Western leaders in order to demonstrate its relevance as a great power, "this part of Russia's historic identity is well established and will keep the country open to the West on international matters even when the latter refuses to recognize its potential contribution."[57] Explaining Russia's resistance to the liberal order, Richard Sakwa claims that this is tempered by Moscow's "aspirations to become part of a transformed power system, and by the weakness, both material and ideational, of the foundations of its opposition."[58]

Dmitry Trenin writes that even though the Russian elite and public traditionally perceived the country as a great power, this status needs a reinterpretation. He assesses the main characteristics[59] of great power status and notes the diminishing of those characteristics in modern Russia as compared to the Soviet Union.[60]

Trenin emphasizes that in quantitative terms, Russia has a much smaller impact in the international arena now than in the 20th or even the 19th century. Therefore, it should proceed from reality, not from memory. He highlights that great power status is not so much a whim of Russian rulers but rather a necessity for a traditionally lonely country and one of the most important conditions for its survival. However, in modern conditions, according to Trenin, Russia can claim the status of a great power in a different sense than before. Russia is no longer a hegemon and not a leader, but, nevertheless, it is one of the few countries that does not recognize the hegemony, dominance, or leadership of other states.[61]

This raises the question about what conditions Moscow wants to achieve or, more specifically, what is Russia's approach to the world order and its status in the international system? Andrey Baykov's thoughts on these questions provide a good explanation. What Russia mainly wants is "to be an autonomous player, to uphold its identity of a great power which is strategically independent."[62] From Moscow's point of view, Russia's strategy in the international system must be to gain opportunities from chaos. As Sarah Topol put it, "Russia did not break the back of the international world order, as much as it recognized the opportunities created by American withdrawal and the new era of global *bardak [chaos]*."[63] Yet at the same time, Russia pursues hegemonic ambitions in its relations with the post-Soviet republics. Russia considers those states, excluding the Baltic republics, as its "legitimate sphere of influence." This is an important part of Russia's approach to retaining its global power status. And as the Russian invasion of Ukraine in 2022 showed, Russia can conduct aggression against those states even in situations that result in possible negative consequences for itself.

**Russia's vision for the world order and how to maintain its role as a great power**

Russia's main problems with the liberal world order are from its place in it, its ability to maintain the regime's longevity, and Moscow's control over the former Soviet republics and its "legitimate sphere of interest." To have large maneuvering possibilities in a multipolar world is considered essential by Moscow. Especially because in such an international system the demands for democracy or regime change through elections and democratic reforms would be secondary and possibly lose all credibility and relevance, at least, according to the Russian political elite's thinking.

It is possible to find similar ideas in the statements and writing of Russian officials and experts. According to Russia's Foreign Minister Sergey Lavrov, what

Russia offers first of all is a recognition that the process of forming a polycentric architecture of the world order is irreversible. Lavrov stresses that most countries do not want to be at the mercy of "other's geopolitical calculations,"

> They are determined to pursue a nationally oriented domestic and foreign policy. It is in the common interest to ensure that multipolarity does not rely on a purely balance of powers, as it was at previous historical stages (for example, in the 19th and first half of the 20th centuries), but was fair, democratic, unifying in nature, taking into account the approaches and concerns of all participants, without exemption, may contribute to a stable and secure future."[64]

If one were to read between the lines, Lavrov's statement declares Moscow's vision on the contemporary and future world orders. But what is Russia's view on international relations? Are there any new approaches being applied by Russia? What are Russia's expectations from the international system? It is possible to find answers to these questions in what is said and written by scholars and Russian politicians.

According to Fyodor Lukyanov, Russia's view on international relations, with the exception of the early Soviet period, has always been based on the realist school of thought—states act in the international arena by certain laws, regardless of their own political system. But in the post-Cold War period, the West advocated for a liberal approach which "established a close interconnection between the internal system of government in a state and its foreign policy." Therefore, notes Lukyanov, the idea of advancing democracy as a guarantor of peace, stability, and security for the West. "If the West sees Russia as a country trying to revise the international order," writes Fyodorov, "Russia is afraid of Western zeal to revise those who don't stick to Western imposed standards."[65]

In recent years, Russia has demonstrated its will to maintain its great power status. After several years of calm and a relatively stable fluctuation of its acceptance and non-acceptance of its role as a regional power, Russia, in recent years and often aggressively, demonstrates the new approaches of its foreign policy and its role as a global power. Despite the shortcomings in achieving its diplomatic goals in Ukraine, its dynamic foreign policy approaches were demonstrated in the Middle East, following the commencement of military operations in Syria in 2015. Moscow kept a unique position as a player and peace broker between antagonistic regional actors. It can maintain high diplomatic contacts with all the main actors in the region. Russia succeeded in keeping its role as peace broker between such states as Iran, Israel, Turkey, Saudi Arabia, and Qatar, all of which have very complicated relations with each other and antagonistic goals regarding the resolution of the military conflict in Syria.

Dmitry Trenin explains that Russia achieved its direct aims in Syria by deploying its armed forces in relatively modest volumes, at a relatively low cost, and with limited losses. Trenin notes that for the first time since the breakup of the Soviet Union, Moscow has been accepted in the region as a serious player and the successful outcome stems from the fact that Russia's activities were clearly focused on its interests, not on ideology, "in its refusal to impose some geopolitical model on other countries; in a good knowledge of the region and the capability and readiness to pursue a policy based on local realities."[66] Trenin emphasizes that Syria, and in general the Middle East, were a signal that Russia was returning to the global arena and once again becoming a global player, "but a rather different player from the USSR. Instead of expending enormous efforts on trying to export its model to the rest of the world, Moscow is now trying to find niches that it can exploit to its own benefit."[67] But Trenin's enthusiasm would not last long. Since the start of the Ukraine invasion, Russia has been behaving as a weak and declining power, whose allies try to keep their distance or will not support the occupation of Ukrainian territories, at least publicly. Moreover, Russia's poor military performance and Western sanctions signal the further decline of Russia as a great power in the international system. Finally, it seems we will have a state that feels and wants to behave as a great power, but with a weaker economy and conventional military, an authoritarian political regime with a large territory, rich natural resources, and nuclear weapons. This is what Russia may look like without regime change or any tangible political reforms implemented by a new leader from the current authoritarian regime, as in the case of the Soviet Union in the 1980s.

Given the current situation where Moscow has had some success in the Middle East and in Eastern and South-Eastern Asia, while at the same time, has seen a significant increase in its confrontation with the West after the start of the Ukraine invasion, what does Russian foreign policy see as its priorities and threats?

According to Russia's latest Foreign Policy Concept (2016), the state prioritizes issues such as "creating a stable and sustainable system of international relations based on the generally accepted norms of international law and principles of equal rights, mutual respect, and non-interference in domestic affairs of States, so as to ensure solid and equal security for each and every member of the global community;" "to maintain the UN coordinator role and ensuring the Security Council's decisions authorities in important issues in international relations;" "ensuring the rule of law in international relations;" "strengthening international security;" "international economic and environmental cooperation;" even "international humanitarian cooperation and human rights;" and "information support for foreign policy activities" of the Russian Federation.[68]

Moreover, the Concept emphasizes "regional foreign policy priorities" covering issues such as "developing bilateral and multilateral cooperation with member States of the Commonwealth of Independent States (CIS) and further strengthening integration structures within the CIS involving Russia;" "expanding strategic cooperation with the Republic of Belarus within the Union State with a view to promoting integration in all areas;" "strengthening and expanding integration within the Eurasian Economic Union (EAEU);" and "the Collective Security Treaty Organization (CSTO) as one of the key elements of the current security framework in the post-Soviet space."[69] Although the Concept declares that Russia "strongly advocates a political and diplomatic settlement of conflicts in the post-Soviet space," it states that "assisting the establishment of the Republic of Abkhazia and the Republic of

South Ossetia as modern democratic States, strengthening their international positions, and ensuring reliable security and socioeconomic recovery remains a priority for Russia."[70] The Concept additionally emphasizes issues such as NATO and EU enlargement. The goal is to either have Moscow lead or be involved in integration and cooperation platforms as a counterbalance to any Euro-Atlantic project.

In recent years, Russian foreign policy elites have promoted the creation of the Greater Eurasian Partnership—a broad integration path with the participation of members of the EAEU, the Shanghai Cooperation Organization, ASEAN and all other states of the continent, including EU countries.[71] Sergey Lavrov writes that "consistent movement in this general creative direction will not only ensure the dynamic development of the national economies of the participating countries, it removes the barriers to goods, capital, labor and services, but also creates a solid foundation for security and stability in vast areas from Lisbon to Jakarta."[72] This idea is actually a continuation of Mikhail Gorbachev's Common European Home from the 1980s and Dmitry Medvedev's European Security Treaty at the end of 2009 as well as Vladimir Putin's concept of a Greater Europe from Lisbon to Vladivostok in 2010.[73] These concepts promote Russia as a member of a greater European security architecture but without, or with limited, NATO involvement and a strong recognition of Russia's interests. The main problem is that Moscow would prefer to gain something like a veto rather than a voice in the European security architecture.

The key priorities for Russian foreign policy in the coming years are to maintain the status of Russia as a great power outside the post-Soviet space, to deter the further expansion of NATO in Eastern Europe, and lessen the country's political isolation. "Moscow's strategy is to build a situation in which former partners, and now rivals and mainly the US will be forced to recognize Russia's security interests as they are defined by the Kremlin, not by Washington, and Russia's significance as a great power to be reckoned with on the world stage," Dmitry Trenin explained Russia's goals.[74] Such a strategy emphasizes the activities that can potentially change international reality in various regions and in functional areas favorable to Russia. Trenin stresses that this is a strategy of struggle "not so much for a new world order as for Russia's high place in any world order that will exist."[75] Negotiations, and the search for diplomatic solutions, are considered an important tool of foreign policy, but more as instruments for recording the results of the struggle. The United States and the West were considered unreliable partners in recent years, and following the start of the Ukraine invasion even adversaries, and the expectation is that they are not inclined to compromise with the Kremlin.

Obviously, Russia's foreign policy, and its role in international relations, was tremendously affected by the invasion of Ukraine in 2022. After the invasion, a Russian MFA official explained Russia's main foreign policy goal as a "missionary mission" in transferring the international system to the multipolar world.[76] Vladimir Putin himself explained the formation of a multipolar world order as "transitioning from a liberal globalist US egocentrism to a truly multipolar world based on genuine sovereignty of nations and civilizations."[77]

The current war in Ukraine will also influence the upcoming updated Foreign Policy Concept. Russian MFA official Alexey Drobinin, who is directly involved in the development of the concept, writes that injecting more sovereignty across the board, including "in the world of ideas, politics, culture, research, economics, finance, and other spheres while remaining open to broad mutually enriching equitable international cooperation" can place Russia well on the path to steady development and secure the place it deserves in the multipolar world order.[78] Drobinin praises the civilizational approach in the multipolar world. He explains that global-level players will include politically consolidated civilizational communities headed by a leading state "such as Russia and the Eurasian community, China and the East Asian community, the United States and the Anglo-Saxon sphere, as well as the Indian, Arab-Muslim, continental European and other civilizations."[79] Such an approach is supported by Russians because they understand that they will not be one of the poles in the bipolar world system. Another novelty in the new concept may be a statement regarding not only the threat of NATO enlargement, but of the EU as well.[80]

After reviewing Russia's foreign policy priorities and how Moscow considers the existing and the expected world orders as well as their own place in them, let's consider whether the Kremlin uses new or different approaches as it does in its external security. It should be noted that the use of several terms for the explanation of Russia's foreign policy approaches may overstate or conceal what they really are.

The thinking that Russia is waging asymmetric war or hybrid war against the West with its foreign policy dumbs down Russian foreign policy and explains nothing about the possible intentions and aims behind such alleged methods. According to Bettina Renz, such an approach is also counterproductive inasmuch as it unnecessarily militarizes the West's language regarding its relations with Russia in an already tense situation and it does not adequately reflect the Kremlin foreign policy complexity, "finally, the implied notion of Western weakness in the face of superior Russian 'hybrid warfare' capabilities plays directly into Putin's hands."[81]

Observing how Russia's foreign policy functions and discussing the challenges caused by its use of various tools are different things entirely. Russia uses several tools to conduct its interests and depends on specific goals and targeted states. The explanation of almost every Russian activity as part of a well-organized campaign, or even strategy against the West, exaggerates Russia's strategic power capabilities. As Renz put it, claiming almost every Russian foreign policy activity as a part of a wider "hybrid warfare" campaign is not useful:

> Referring to Russian actions ranging from the use of social media to military provocations as 'hybrid threats' not only exaggerates the notion of newness where there is in fact a high level of consistency. It also implies a coherence of effort and level of strategic foresight that is simply unrealistic and risks making Russia and its leadership look stronger than it actually is.[82]

Russia's recent achievements in the Middle East, specifically the development of its relations with the Gulf States, its flexible semi-alliances with Turkey and Iran while at the same time maintaining a close relationship with Israel, its recently revived military ties with Egypt, its involvements in Libya and generally in Africa, can be evaluated as successes of Moscow's foreign policy. These are supported by its external security approaches. When closely analyzing all of these, it is possible to find that the main characteristics of these developments relate to Russia's security policy approaches, including its asymmetric methods. Moreover, Russia promotes an active foreign policy in other parts of the world, such as its involvement in a political settlement in Afghanistan and fostering closer relations with several South American states specifically Venezuela and Cuba. Additionally, besides Latin America's leftist regimes, Moscow has close relations with Brazil, Mexico, and Argentina. All of these would seem to be proof of Russia's global power status and the strength of its place in the international system. Moscow will pursue its economic and security interests through its involvement in several regions if the economy, facing heavy sanctions after the invasion of Ukraine in 2022, will allow.

Besides realistic approaches and without any ideological component, Moscow needs to use effective methods and strategies that due not inflict huge costs on its weakened economy. To this end, asymmetric approaches are, and will remain, preferable for Russia. In recent years, what Russia has done in its military operations abroad are mainly based on asymmetric approaches. As Michelle Dunne notes regarding Russia's activities in Syria, "Putin has played a clever hand on the cheap, without really investing that much in it."[83] According to Dmitry Trenin's estimation, the cost at roughly $4 million per day, which is "reasonably affordable" for the state budget. By contrast, the United States' mission in Syria as part of Operation Inherent Resolve, cost $54 billion from 2014 to 2019, or $25 million per day.[84]

In most cases, Russia's success is the result of America's withdrawal from the Middle East. In this respect, Nicole Ng and Eugene Rumer highlight that Russia's activities in several countries, such as Venezuela, the Central African Republic, and Libya, say more about Russia's knack for seizing opportunities than about a new sense of adventurism. According to them, the risks for Russia in these regions so far appear modest and calculated, though the benefits have yet to be realized. "Rather than panicking about Russian footprints across the globe, Western analysts should strive for a clear assessment of Moscow's ambitions, capabilities, and propensity for risk," suggest Nicole Ng and Eugene Rumer.[85]

Despite the mentioned successes in recent years, Russia's foreign policy has many shortcomings. Dmitry Trenin claims that although Russian leadership is often blamed for the lack of a foreign policy strategy, this is not entirely true. The problem is rather a lack of realism of the stated goals or a lack of opportunities to solve the tasks.[86] It should not be forgotten that Russia's foreign policy is determined by various geopolitical concerns, as well as internal and external policy factors. For instance, what Russia wants to achieve vis-à-vis the United States or NATO differs from what it wants from its relationship with China, the European Union, and the former Soviet republics. Moscow even differentiates its approaches toward individual CIS, EAUE, or CSTO member states. To realize its foreign policy goals when facing stronger competitors, Russia primarily resorts to intimidation and attrition approaches adjusted based on the situation or resolution sought. For instance, in the case of Ukraine, the West generally supported the position of Ukraine and pushed Russia for resolution of the conflict, so this desire for negotiation was noted.[87] Believing that Western politics inclined toward the "business as usual" approach and that they did not seem ready to defend Ukraine—or any other post-Soviet country—militarily, Moscow persistently demanded solutions align with its foreign policy goals. But Russia's beliefs were shattered during the 2022 invasion when the West provided essential political, military, financial, information, and humanitarian support to Ukraine.

The decision to wage war in Ukraine has been changing Russia's foreign policy approach as well. The world and Moscow, of course, now see the limits of Russia's real power capabilities. As Fyodor Lukyanov put it, Russia is in a period where many of the achievements of the previous 20 years, "as it was fashionable to promote two years ago, are being reset—that is, those methods of conducting foreign policy and those practices that brought success step by step are now disappearing or simply becoming unnecessary."[88] In such a situation, Russia is more inclined to use asymmetric approaches to achieve its foreign and security policy goals. Stressing that the challenge Russia is facing is unparalleled in its history—following the Ukraine invasion—and confirming that Russia has no allies, or even potential partners in the West, Dmitry Trenin suggests they explore the possibilities and limits of situational cooperation with various political and social groups in the West, as well as with other temporary potential allies outside the West, whose interests in certain issues coincide with Russia's. "The task is not to inflict damage on the enemy anywhere," writes Trenin, "but to use various irritants to divert his attention and resources from the Russian direction, as well as to influence the domestic political situation in the United States and Europe in a direction favorable to the Russian Federation."[89] The head of the Carnegie Moscow Centre— until the Russian government banned its activities—stressed that the most important goal in this regard is to develop a strategy for the emerging confrontation between the United States and China.[90] What Trenin suggests, in fact, is the use of asymmetric methods to achieve Russia's foreign policy goals.

## The impact of Russia's security institutions on its foreign policy implementation

Based on an analysis of Russia's goals and activities above, it is possible to note that there are no asymmetric or hybrid strategies in Russia's foreign policy. However, the methods of Russia's external security policy, in many cases, can be assessed as asymmetric approaches, and they directly exert influence on the implementation of the state's foreign policy. Moreover, the participation of security institutions and their representatives in the implementation and decision-making process of the state also exerts influence over foreign policy.

Andrey Kortunov writes that the role of the military in formulating and implementing foreign policy is growing throughout the world and in the case of Russia, it appears that the balance between military officers and diplomats has been increasingly drifting in favor of the former.[91] He explains that generally the fact that the position of the security organizations is strengthening is not necessarily a cause for concern, and that military commanders are mostly known for their cautious and pragmatic behavior—they know practically the dangers of crossing the line between peace and war. However, believes Kortunov, the flip side of this process is exactly what is happening now, the degradation of the art of diplomacy.[92]

According to Andrei Tsygankov, those more critical of Dmitry Medvedev's foreign policy in 2008–2012 were those with strong ties to the defense and security establishment and whose foreign policy priorities differed from those with commercial and political relations with the West.[93] "By highlighting Russia's obligations to preserve global strategic balance and influence in Europe, Eurasia, and other regions," Tsygankov writes, "these groups defended a more muscular and assertive foreign policy."[94] Tsygankov highlights that this group's modernization priorities also differed from Medevedev's, "Those supported by Deputy Prime Minister Igor Sechin prioritized the development of the energy and military sectors, as opposed to the diversification highlighted by Medvedev."[95] Tsygankov emphasizes that Putin mostly was sympathetic to the Sechin's ideas.[96]

Russian foreign-policy decision-making remains reliably hidden from the outside world as it was before and during the Soviet era. As stated by Edwards Keenan, it closely mirrors the Soviet political elite's decision-making process:

> … one of the characteristic operative features of this system is, whether one is dealing with the sixteenth century or with the twentieth, the rule ""*Iz izby soru ne vynesi*" "(literally, "Do not carry rubbish out of the hut") remains in operation: i.e., one does not reveal to non-participants authentic information concerning politics, political groupings, or points of discord. Like several other rules of this culture, this rule of conspiratorial and mutually protective silence (modern official parlance "*neglasnost*") is quite normally adhered to even during the bitterest of political conflicts.[97]

The Security Council of the Russian Federation is the main body where important issues for the state and the political regime are discussed before a final decision is made by the president. The scope of responsibilities of the Russian Security Council is noticeably wider than purely national security issues, as is found in Western countries.

Dmitry Trenin assumes that a group of senior advisers—"namely advisers, and not colleagues or comrades"—who are members of the Security Council, help Putin in shaping foreign policy.[98] The televised Russian Security Council where recognition of the "independence" of the eastern Ukrainian territories of Donetsk and Luhansk was discussed, confirmed this.[99] Trenin also claims that Putin's foreign policy decisions are mainly based on the information he receives from the intelligence services:

> Now that a serious political and economic confrontation has arisen between Russia and the West, as well as an information war, the Russian intelligence services functioned as the general headquarters of the army in wartime. The leadership of these structures acts as military commanders: they plan campaigns, get Putin's approval, and carry out his orders, often remaining outside the range of vision of public.[100]

Trenin highlights that—for them—international relations are the endless struggle of several powerful countries for dominance and influence.[101]

In recent years, there has been an increasing trend of political statements by high-level representatives of the security agencies or military on developments in international relations. Pavel Felgenhauer characterizes their political statements on international developments as "the world is changing, a new world order is emerging, the West's influence and power is diminishing, but the US rejects the new reality and is determined to maintain its historically doomed 'global leadership' at all costs, 'including military means.'"[102] It is noticeable that their statements do not differ from those of high-level diplomats or the political leadership's declarations on the issue. One similar statement was issued by Sergei Naryshkin, the director of Russia's Foreign Intelligence Service [*Sluzhba Vneshney Razvedki*—SVR] in 2018. Speaking at the seventh annual Moscow International Security Conference (MCIS-2018), organized by the defense ministry, he stated that the West and the US are unable "to face the truth and reconcile themselves with their inevitable downgrading." Naryshkin claimed that the West and the United States are resisting the new emerging world order and looking to revitalize the "colonialist and imperialist" practices of domination "while masquerading their dictate and blackmail with a show of Euro-Atlantic and international solidarity."[103] Russia is considered by the West as "the main locomotive of change in the world" and is being singled out for attack by "retrograde and reactionary forces." Naryshkin stated that the US obsession with the "non-existent Russian threat" has produced a new cold war."[104] An almost identical speech was given by Naryshkin a year later at MCIS-2019.[105] In recent years, this type of thinking is generally visible in the speeches of other high-level representatives of Russia's security institutions.

One of the distinguishing characteristics of Russia's contemporary foreign policy implementation is that in several cases high-level representatives of *siloviki*, not the departments of the Ministry of Foreign Affairs or its officials, coordinate foreign policy issues. For instance, according to reports, the Secretary of the Security Council, Nikolai Patrushev, has had a significant role in Russia's Balkans policy in recent years. Mark Galeotti writes that the Kremlin had thought its policy toward the Balkans had suffered from not having a single, powerful "curator" and as a result, in either late 2015 or, more likely, the first half of 2016, Putin appears to have made Patrushev the Kremlin's point man for the Balkans.[106]

Patrushev, who is a former KGB officer and previously a head of the FSB and also famous for his anti-Western statements, together with Balkans expert Leonid Reshetnikov (a former senior figure within the KGB and SVR, who from 2009 to 2017 was head of the Russian Institute of Strategic Studies[RISI]) dealt with the region until 2017. One of the results of this cooperation was the attempted coup d'état in Montenegro, which aimed to deter the country's NATO membership in 2016. Russia's controversial billionaire Konstantin Malofeev—who was also involved in Russia's security activities in Ukraine—actively participated in developments in the Balkans, including in Montenegro. He organized propagandist events across several countries. For instance, he was an organizer of the controversial visit by the Russian Cossacks to Banja Luka, capital of *Republika Srpska*, in a show of force in support of nationalist leader Milorad Dodik.[107] However, despite Russia's efforts the coup attempt failed. "Montenegro joined NATO, Patrushev was forced to go to Belgrade and apologize, and Reshetnikov lost his position as head of RISI."[108]

Russia's foreign policy implementation is closely intertwined with its external security conduct. Yes, it is true that in every state those two policies are implemented in close relation. But in some cases, including Russia's, the security policy conduct is emphasized to such a degree that it seems as though foreign policy is simply complementing the former. And in such a situation, the reputation of activities of the foreign ministry can be affected by the activities of the security institutions of a given state.

There are several reports on how Russia uses shadowy approaches abroad to achieve its foreign policy goals. For instance, the Wall Street Journal reported how a shadowy figure, Maxim Shugaley working for Kremlin ally Yevgeniy Prigozhin, came to the Afghan capital with the goal of finding areas where the Taliban could work with the political and security network led by Mr. Prigozhin. He was among the first Russians to arrive in Kabul after the Taliban takeover in August. And this is despite the fact that Russia did not close its embassy in Kabul after the Taliban takeover in August 2021. The unusual career path of Shugaley as a political operator and sociologist, from Libya to Madagascar and now Afghanistan, provides an insight into how Moscow seeks to make friends and influence governments in places where America's sway is fading.[109]

Russian security organizations engaging in assassination attempts abroad is another case. According to a UK investigation, the attempted assassination of Sergei V. Skripal in 2018 was conducted by members of Unit 29155, a division within Russia's military intelligence agency, known as the GRU, that specializes in sabotage and assassination, and a European court blamed Russia for Alexander V. Litvinenko's murder in 2006. The European Court of Human Rights concluded that Litvinenko's assassins in 2006 were acting as "agents of the Russian state."[110]

An investigation by Bellingcat and its partners—The Insider and Der Spiegel— has uncovered that the assassination of Zelimkhan Khangoshvili, a former Chechen fighter opposed to Russian military operations in Chechnya, in Berlin in August 2019 was planned and organized by Russia's FSB security agency. That same investigation also revealed that the FSB has a department which deals specifically with these types of operations abroad. The investigation also revealed that FSB Department V nonofficially engages in extraterritorial assassinations.[111]

Moreover, the investigation revealed that one of the key members of the same GRU group that poisoned businessman Emilian Gebrev in Bulgaria, previously worked under diplomatic cover in the Russian representation at the WTO in Geneva. Reportedly that member worked as a diplomat with a rank of third secretary, and also participated in special operations along with those that participated in poisoning Skripal.[112] There are several similar cases where Russian security institutions have provided diplomatic immunity for their agents for several operations.

Recently the United States warned that Russia would step up its covert political influence to undermine sanctions over the war in Ukraine and that Russia would increasingly turn to covert political financing in the coming months. A review by the US intelligence community of Russia's efforts to influence other countries' politics found that Russia had transferred more than $300 million to foreign political parties, officials, and politicians in more than two dozen countries since 2014.[113]

All such activities of the Russian security institutions abroad affect the reputation of Russian foreign policy and their diplomats on the international stage.

The invasion of Ukraine in 2022, however, hugely affected Russia's ability to spy in Europe. Richard Moore, the head of MI6, Britain's foreign intelligence service, stated that Russia is losing steam in its invasion of Ukraine, and has lost its ability to spy in Europe "by half" following the expulsion of more than 400 Russian intelligence officers from cities across Europe and the arrest of several deep-cover spies posing as civilians.[114] In this respect, it is quite possible that new examples of Russian security institutions operations abroad will be revealed in which representatives of the country's foreign ministry are involved. As such, Putin's recent reminder to intelligence officers regarding the importance of industrial espionage amid the sanctions over the invasion of Ukraine, should be noted. Putin considers one of the main tasks of the Foreign Intelligence Service (SVR) "to promote the development of industrial potential." In his opinion, this is especially important in the context of Western sanctions.[115]

In the realization of its foreign policy goals, Moscow does not only use official diplomatic and security institutions or individuals. Moscow can use any affordable channels or tools. According to Julia Gurganus and Eugene Rumer, Russian "agents did not cause long-term conflicts or cleavages inside Western societies, but they have used them to advance their goals, which vary depending on the circumstances."[116] Concerning toolkits, they note that in many cases Moscow "has relied on a diverse toolkit that creates the appearance of operating one step removed from the Russian government through a range of actors including state-owned corporations such as Rosatom and Rosneft, private security companies such as the Wagner Group, organized crime syndicates, hackers, and information operation organizations such as the Internet Research Agency."[117] In this respect—not only in the West but elsewhere in the world—conflicts, such as those in the Middle East, Afghanistan, and Africa, or the post-conflict situation in the Balkans or frozen conflicts in post-Soviet states, have presented Russia with opportunities to involve themselves and use the conflicts to their own ends and attempt to create new realities on the ground. Such approaches work especially well when Russia does not face significant pushback, but rather a hesitant adversary, such as the United States.

### Implications of Russia's foreign policy for its position in the international system

After analyzing facets of Russia's foreign policy and how its external security policy approaches exert influence on it, let us explore the implications of Moscow achieving its goals.

Syria can be considered the main success story of Russian foreign policy in recent years but it is also a result of military operations there. Syria was the first time that Russia's military was deployed and extensively used in real combat conditions beyond the boundaries of the former Soviet Union following the breakup of the USSR.[118]

Vision, prejudices, the historically formulated state of foreign policy approaches along with beliefs and conduct in Russia affect Moscow's approaches toward its relations with Western countries. Andrey Kortunov notes that in the Russian political tradition, hierarchy plays an important role; this also fully applies to Russian foreign policy as well. Therefore, having faced such a complex, ambiguous, and controversial structure as the European Union, decision-makers in Moscow tried to identify the most accessible entry points using their previous experience and their understanding of European hierarchy.[119] From Moscow's point of view, it was only realistic to focus on "key players" specifically partners of Russia from the "old Europe" such as Germany, France, and Italy. The premise was that the mentioned countries should be Russia's lobbyists within the EU, using their powers to influence other member states including those very critical of Russia. However, the expectations that "old Europe"—Germany in particular—would solve all of Russia's problems with the European Union gave Moscow a plausible pretext not to seriously engage in managing the negative Soviet legacy in Russia's relations with the Central European and Baltic states.[120]

Kortunov emphasizes that unlike Germany after WWII, Russia after the Cold War did not consider the possibility of creating a belt of friendly partners out of its smaller neighboring countries to be a top foreign policy goal. If German leaders had a sense of guilt for the crimes of the Nazi regime regarding neighboring nations, Russia had a different belief, "Russian leaders, on the contrary, believed that they had dismantled the Communist system of their own free will and therefore deserved appreciation and gratitude from the part of Central European and Baltic states."[121]

Such beliefs are applied toward its relations with the post-Soviet republics as well.

In analyzing Russia's foreign policy, in recent years, Dmitry Trenin highlights that the absence of a long-term strategy and the gusto for cunning opportunism and tactical maneuvering condemns its foreign policy to substantial risks.[122] According to Kortunov, the fundamental problem of Russian foreign policy is not about how to cope with the external reality, but rather how to define it. Kortunov stresses the influences of the Soviet legacy among the foreign policy cadres. He explains that most of the Russian public officials and bureaucrats, who ran the policy toward the European Union since the early 1990s, had received a standard Soviet university education. "In other words, they were explicit or implicit Marxists/Neo-Marxists with a profound belief in the primacy of economic factors in international relations," Kortunov notes.[123]

Nicu Popescu notes that Russia's foreign power has been not so much "expanding as mutating and shifting ... Not every noisy Russian diplomatic step made out on Twitter to be a great success has actually gained Russia influence." Rather, as Popescu explains, in the global market of geopolitics, Russia has been behaving like a company finding itself squeezed out of traditional markets and desperately trying to find new places to offer its services and products:

> But, in all, this the company's overall "influence turnover" has not changed much. It has just shifted to less lucrative, more competitive, and harder-to-sustain markets.[124]

Russia's foreign policy behavior toward the former Soviet republics in recent years, including claims such as "legitimate sphere of influence," suggest that Russia considers a *bandwagoning* rather than alliance with them. This is especially reliable for the former republics, which do not have membership in NATO or the EU. According to Stephen Walt, the familiar phenomenon of a "sphere of influence" is created when a threat from a proximate great power leads to *bandwagoning*, "Small states bordering a great power may be so vulnerable that they choose to bandwagon rather than balance, especially if their powerful neighbor has demonstrated disability to compel obedience."[125]

Walt notes that states with large offensive capabilities are more likely to provoke an alliance than those who are either militarily weak or capable only of defending. But he highlights that the effects of this vary. On the one hand, the immediate threat that capabilities such as strong military power pose may lead small states to balance by allying with others.[126] Thanks to Moscow's foreign policy behavior this is what almost all the former Soviet republics have tried to do, "balance by allying with others." It was on their agendas since the breakup of the Soviet Union, but it has been an especially striking problem after Russia's invasions of Georgia and Ukraine in recent years.

Some former Soviet republics (Georgia, Ukraine, Uzbekistan, Azerbaijan, and Moldova) tried to develop an alliance in frame of GUUAM or GUAM in the 1990s and early 2000s but they could not succeed. However, Walt writes that when offensive power can succeed to reach rapid conquest, weaker states "may see little hope in resisting:"

> Balancing may seem unwise because one's allies may not be able to provide assistance quickly enough. This is another reason why "spheres of influence" may form: states bordering those with large offensive capabilities (and who are far from potential allies) may be forced to bandwagon because balancing alliances are simply not viable.[127]

This thought can appropriately explain the behavior of some post-Soviet countries after the United States involvement in the former Soviet Union space decreased. Although many CIS member states are inclined toward an alliance with Russia, Moscow's approaches to bandwagon them, and its aggressive behavior toward Georgia and Ukraine, pushed them to look for other powers for balancing. Russia's offensive behavior in fact scared the CIS member states, which were inclined toward an alliance with Russia. However, the lack of significant power and will among them to establish a balancing alliance against Russia, and the proximity problems regarding the United States, create appropriate conditions for China, especially with regard to the Central Asian republics. Moreover, in recent years, former Soviet republics such as Belarus, Ukraine, and South Caucasian states also have developed deeper relations with China. It should be noted that Russia's aggressive policies toward Georgia and Ukraine, historical experiences, and Russia's economic and technological unattractiveness, incline the CIS countries to avoid bandwagoning or forming a close alliance with

Moscow. Moreover, some of them, especially the Turkic states, also developed relations with Turkey. As Stephen Walt put it, "if an aggressor's intentions are impossible to change, then balancing with others is the best way to avoid becoming a victim."[128]

It should be noted that historical experiences, and their negative assessments, hugely affect Russia's foreign policy. As Fyodor Lukyanov notes, one of Russia's main problems, both for internal and especially for external behavior, "is obsession with past grievances, an enduring desire to prove that the collapse of status and potential almost 30 years ago was an accident and, first of all, foreign (Western) guilt."[129] Even if we are right about everything, this discussion is no longer interesting to external interlocutors, notes Lukyanov. "Previous shocks, of course, are very important, because Russia lives in their legacy of effects, but not their lessons will determine the future," he notes.[130]

The invasion of Ukraine in 2022 has further affected Russia's relations with the West, its neighboring states, and even Moscow's allies.

Now, Russia is facing a mobilized, and as Russian experts call it, collective West. Since the beginning of the invasion of Ukraine, the unity of the United States, Europe, and their allies in Asia has been almost unprecedented. Great Britain, Poland, and the Baltic states as well as Germany, France, Italy, and Spain took a strikingly strong stand against Russia's invasion. Russian expert Trenin recognized that for the first time in Russian history, Russia in the West does not have allies, or even "interlocutors" capable of playing the role of intermediaries.[131] The traditional neutrality of a number of European countries does not apply to Russia's invasion. Finland and Sweden decided to join NATO. Relations with one of the key economic partners of Moscow in the EU—Germany—have been deteriorating ever since February 24.

The expectation that Western countries, acting in their own economic interests, would mitigate the consequences of the invasion did not happen. A particularly painful disappointment for Moscow was the collapse of energy ties with Europe. Many in Moscow counted on the fact that the Russian energy weapon—natural gas—would keep the European Union from breaking with Russia. This was the Kremlin's miscalculation as well. The EU's decision to renounce the import of Russian oil and coal, along with the introduction of restrictions on gas imports, broke the most important material bond between Russia and Europe.[132]

Apart from Belarus, none of Russia's allies in the CSTO or EAEU officially supported the invasion of Ukraine. One of Russia's main allies among the former Soviet republics, Kazakhstan and its leader Kassym-Jomart Tokayev announced the non-recognition of the "quasi-states" of "the Donetsk People Republic" and "the Luhansk People Republic."[133] Moreover, he refused to accept the order for cooperation with Russia in the summer of 2022.[134] The symbolic case of Moscow's further declining reputation among its allies and strategic partners was vividly illustrated at the summit Council of Heads of State of the Shanghai Cooperation Organization (SCO) in Uzbekistan in September 2022. Putin, who is known to be late in official meetings, had to wait for leaders of Turkey, India, Azerbaijan, and Kyrgyzstan while in front of the cameras.[135]

216  *Implementation of Russia's foreign policy*

However, the war, and the Kremlin's shrinking opportunities to choose its foreign partners, has forced Moscow to put a higher value on its ties to the Central Asian countries. Russia's trade turnover with all five nations was growing in 2022.[136] Although this growth is largely linked to new trade patterns caused by sanctions, as well as to the mass exodus of Russians who fled to Central Asia following the war and the start of mobilization, Moscow is now paying noticeably more attention to the region. In 2022, Putin visited all five Central Asian countries. It was not just to use such visits to show that Moscow has allies, as reportedly some of the Central Asian countries have been used by Moscow during the war. Tajikistan, for example, reportedly provided Russia with Iranian attack drones that have been used in Ukraine, though Dushanbe denies it.[137] Reportedly, the Russian private military company Wagner is also recruiting convicts from the prisons in Turkmenistan to send to Ukraine.[138] Deliveries of telescopic sights from Kyrgyzstan to Russia increased sevenfold in 2022.[139] Bloomberg reported that the growth in imports of home appliances from the EU to Kazakhstan is reportedly due to the microchips from those goods being used in the Russian military complex.[140] There are also other developments since the beginning of the war in Ukraine, which show that Russian influence in Central Asia remains in several areas, and is not threatened with collapse in the near future, but that over the long term it is expected to decrease.[141] The same can be said regarding Russia's influence in other CIS countries, such as Armenia and Azerbaijan.

Global powers such as China and India increasingly state their concerns over the invasion of Ukraine. At the same summit of SCO in Samarkand, Indian Prime Minister Narendra Modi stated during his meeting with the Russian President that now was not the time for war, directly assailing Putin in public over the war in Ukraine.[142] For the Russian president, this was not the only awkward moment at the summit, Putin had to acknowledge China's concerns over Russia's invasion during a meeting with Chinese leader Xi Jinping.[143] However, India and China are both happy to buy cheapening Russian oil and other natural resources amid the Western sanctions.

As we can see, the invasion of Ukraine in 2022 has affected Russia's position in the international system and in the multipolar world that Moscow eagerly awaits.

**Summary**

In analyzing Russia's attitudes toward international relations, it can be emphasized that the drivers of Russia's vision of the world order are based on such factors as historical legacy, self-determination and sovereignty in international relations, and the survival of its political leadership. This chapter has attempted to explain Russia's preferences for a multipolar world order. Despite confrontations between the West and Russia, the current situation cannot be called a second or new Cold War. There are significant differences between the Cold War and the current state of relations as explained in this chapter. The two main approaches, "Primakov's doctrine" and Chubais' "liberal Empire" concept, are reflected in the formation of contemporary Russian foreign policy.

Facets of Russia's foreign policy, and how asymmetric approaches of external security policy exert influence on them, were analyzed. The implications of the methods used for achieving Moscow's goals were also explored. After analyzing these, it noted that there are both positive and adverse effects regarding the implications of the foreign policy for Russia. These were analyzed by looking at Russia's recent foreign policy successes, especially in the Middle East, and it highlighted that this was a result of Moscow's non-ideological and purely interest-driven approaches and, quite possibly, US reluctance to involve itself in particular regions. The reality and potential of Russia's foreign policy following the invasion of Ukraine were also discussed.

Russia's foreign policy approaches toward the former Soviet republics in recent years and its goals such as keeping a "legitimate sphere of influence" can suggest that Russia considers bandwagoning rather than an alliance with them.

Based on the analysis of Russia's goals and activities, it can be emphasized that there are no asymmetric or hybrid strategies in Russia's foreign policy but that the methods of Russia's external security policy, in many instances, use asymmetric strategies and that these exert influence on the implementation of Moscow's foreign policy.

**Notes**

1 Gurganus, Julia and Rumer, Eugene (2019) "Russia's Global Ambitions in Perspective", *Carnegie Endowment*, February 20, https://carnegieendowment.org/2019/02/20/russia-s-global-ambitions-in-perspective-pub-78067.
2 Zięba, Ryszard (2018) *The Euro-Atlantic Security System in the 21st Century: From Co-operation to Crisis*, Cham: Springer International Publishing, pp. 153–182; Bandeira, Moniz and Alberto, Luiz (2017) *The Second Cold War: Geopolitics and Strategic Dimension of the USA*, Berlin; Heidelberg: Springer, passim.
3 Lukyanov, Fyodor (2016) "A Failed New World Order and Beyond: Russian View", *Strategic Analysis*, Vol. 40, No. 6 (Russia in Global Affairs), p. 482.
4 Ibid.
5 Lukyanov, Fyodor (2016) "A Failed New World Order and Beyond …", p. 482.
6 Mearsheimer, John J. (2019) "Bound to Fail: The Rise and Fall of the Liberal International Order", *International Security*, Spring 2019, Vol. 43, No. 4, p. 32.
7 Ibid., p. 34.
8 Ibid.
9 Lukyanov, Fyodor (2016) "A Failed New World Order and Beyond: Russian View" …, p. 475.
10 Walt, Stephen (2018) "I Knew the Cold War. This Is No Cold War", *Foreign Policy*, March 12, http://foreignpolicy.com/2018/03/12/i-knew-the-cold-war-this-is-no-cold-war/.
11 Walt, Stephen (2018) "I Knew the Cold War. This Is No Cold War" …
12 Trenin, Dmitry (2019c) "Russia's Comeback Isn't Stopping With Syria", November 12, https://www.nytimes.com/2019/11/12/opinion/russias-comeback-isnt-stopping-with-syria.html.
13 Marcus, Jonathan (2018) "Russia v the West: Is this a new Cold War?", April 1, http://www.bbc.com/news/world-europe-43581449#.
14 Marcus, Jonathan (2018) "Russia v the West: Is this a new Cold War?" …
15 Kissinger, Henry (2014) "Do We Achieve World Order Through Chaos or Insight?", Interview conducted by Juliane von Mittelstaedt and Erich Follath, *Spiegel*, November 13, http://www.spiegel.de/international/world/interview-with-henry-kissinger-on-state-of-global-politics-a-1002073.html.

16. Walt, Stephen (2018) "I Knew the Cold War. This Is No Cold War" …
17. Lavrov, Sergey (2019) "Mir na pereput'ye i sistema mezhdunarodnykh otnosheniy budushchego", *Rossiya v global'noy politike*, September 20, http://www.mid.ru/ru/foreign_policy/news/-/asset_publisher/cKNonkJE02Bw/content/id/3792556.
18. Trenin, Dmitry (2019b) "China, Russia and the United States contest a new world order" …
19. Gurganus, Julia and Rumer, Eugene (2019) "Russia's Global Ambitions in Perspective", *Carnegie Endowment*, February 20, https://carnegieendowment.org/2019/02/20/russia-s-global-ambitions-in-perspective-pub-78067.
20. Gorbachev, Mikhail Sergeevich (1987) *Perestroika: New Thinking for Our Country and the World*, New York: Harper & Row.
21. Lukyanov, Fyodor (2016) "A Failed New World Order and Beyond: Russian View" …, pp. 480–481.
22. Lavrov, Sergey (2014) "V nedalekom budushchem istoriki sformuliruyut takoye ponyatiye, kak 'doktrina Primakova'", October 28, https://tass.ru/politika/1537769.
23. Ibid.
24. Ibid.
25. Safranchuk, Ivan (2014) "Rossiyskaya politika v Tsentral'noy Azii". *Strategicheskiy kontekst*. Zapiska Analiticheskogo tsentra Observo, CCI France Russie, No. 8, November, p. 4.
26. Safranchuk, Ivan (2014) "Rossiyskaya politika v Tsentral'noy Azii" …
27. Primakov, Yevgeny M. (2009) *Mir bez Rossii? K chemu vedet politicheskaya blizorukost'*. Moscow: IIK "Rossiyskaya gazeta", electron version, p. 11. http://yanko.lib.ru/books/politologiya/primakov.mir_bez_rossii.2-l.pdf.
28. Ibid., p. 12.
29. Primakov, Yevgeny M. (2015a) *Vstrechi na perekrestkakh*. Moskva, "Tsentrpoligraf" (Nash XX vek), https://history.wikireading.ru/82808.
30. Ibid.
31. Primakov, Yevgeny (2015c) "Ne prosto rabotat', a znat' vo imya chego" *Rossiyskaya gazeta*, Stolichnyy vypusk, 3(6574), January 13, https://rg.ru/2015/01/13/primakov-site.html.
32. Primakov, Yevgeny M. (2015a) *Vstrechi na perekrestkakh* …
33. Albright, Madeleine (2015) "Remembering Yevgeny Primakov", *Foreign Policy*, June 29, https://foreignpolicy.com/2015/06/29/remembering-yevgeny-primakov-by-madeleine-albright-us-russia/.
34. Primakov, Yevgeny (2012) "Ochen' Blizhniy Vostok", Interviewed by Vladimir Snegirev, *Rossiyskaya gazeta*, Federal'nyy vypusk, 180 (5853), https://rg.ru/2012/08/08/vostok.html.
35. Primakov, Yevgeny (2015b) "Edinstvennoy al'ternativoy dlya Rossii yavlyayetsya opora v pervuyu ochered' na vnutrenniye rezervy i vozmozhnosti", 13 January, https://tpprf.ru/ru/news/v-tsentre-mezhdunarodnoy-torgovli-moskvy-sostoitsya-zasedanie-merkuriy-kluba-i61924/.
36. Chubais, Anatoliy (2003c) "Liberal'naya imperiya — eto oriyentir, daleko ukhodyashchiy za predely 2008 goda", November 24, https://profile.ru/archive/anatoliy-chubays-liberalnaya-imperiya-eto-orientir-daleko-uhodyaschiy-za-predely-2008-goda-102284/.
37. Chubais, Anatoliy (2003a) "Osnovnaya zadacha RF – postroyeniye liberal'noy imperii", September 25, https://www.rbc.ru/politics/25/09/2003/5703b59a9a7947783a5a4b6c.
38. Chubais, Anatoly (2003b) "Liberal'naya imperiya – eto zakhvat Ukrainy rossiyskim biznesom", November 13, https://www.pravda.com.ua/rus/news/2003/11/13/4375407/.
39. Chubais, Anatoliy (2003c) "Liberal'naya imperiya — eto oriyentir, daleko ukhodyashchiy za predely 2008 goda" …
40. Ibid.
41. Veretennikova, Kseniya (2003) "Liberal'naya imperiya vmesto banditskogo kapitalizma", *Vremya novostey*, 13 October 2003, https://www.yabloko.ru/Publ/2003/2003_10/031013_vrn_debaty.html.

42 Sakwa, Richard (2017) *Russia against the rest: the post-Cold War crisis of world order*, Cambridge: Cambridge University Press, p. 71.
43 Mid.ru (2016) "Foreign Minister Sergei Lavrov's remarks at the Primakov Readings International Forum", Moscow, November 30, http://www.mid.ru/en/foreign_policy/news/-/asset_publisher/cKNonkJE02Bw/content/id/2540893.
44 Kremlin.ru (2013) "Presidential Address to the Federal Assembly", Moscow: the Kremlin, 12 December 2013, http://eng.kremlin.ru/transcripts/6402, accessed 7 November 2019.
45 Korolev, Alexander (2016) "Russia's Reorientation to Asia: Causes and Strategic Implications". *Pacific Affairs*, Volume 89, Number 1, March 2016, p. 70, DOI: 10.5509/201689153.
46 Drobinin, Alexey (2022) "The lessons of history and vision for the future: Thoughts on Russia's foreign policy" August 4, https://en.interaffairs.ru/article/the-lessons-of-history-and-vision-for-the-future-thoughts-on-russias-foreign-policy/.
47 Stent, Angela E.(2015) *The limits of partnership: US-Russian relations in the twenty-first century*, Princeton and Oxford: Princeton University Press, p. 6.
48 Sakwa, Richard (2017) *Russia against the rest: the post-Cold War crisis of world order ...*, p. 70.
49 Lukyanov, Fyodor (2016) "A Failed New World Order and Beyond: Russian View" ..., p. 474.
50 Ibid.
51 Trenin, Dmitry (2019b) "20 Years of Vladimir Putin: How Russian Foreign Policy Has Changed", August 27, https://www.themoscowtimes.com/2019/08/27/20-years-of-vladimir-putin-how-russian-foreign-policy-has-changed-a67043.
52 Ibid.
53 Lukyanov, Fyodor (2018) "Konets piramidal'nogo mira s Soedinennymi Shtatami na vershine uzhe priznayut vse", January 17, *Pervyi Kanal*, https://otr-online.ru/programmy/bolshaya-strana/fedor-lukyanov-29951.html.
54 Surkov, Vladislav (2018) "Odinochestvo polukrovki", April 9, http://www.globalaffairs.ru/global-processes/Odinochestvo-polukrovki-14-19477.
55 Ibid.
56 Tsygankov, Andrei P. (2019) *Russia and America: the asymmetric rivalry*, Cambridge; Medford: Polity Press, p. 186.
57 Ibid.
58 Sakwa, Richard (2017) *Russia against the rest: the post-Cold War crisis of world order ...*, p. 134.
59 Such as size and the parameters of its nuclear potential; number of populations; the number of Moscow oriented states and weaknesses of Moscow lead alliances; the degree of support for Russian initiatives at the UN; roles of Russian language and culture today.
60 Trenin, Dmitry (2019a) "Konturnaya karta rossiyskoy geopolitiki: vozmozhnaya strategiya Moskvy v Bol'shoy Yevrazii", February 11, https://carnegie.ru/2019/02/11/ru-pub-78328.
61 Trenin, Dmitry (2019a) "Konturnaya karta rossiyskoy geopolitiki: vozmozhnaya strategiya Moskvy v Bol'shoy Yevrazii" ...
62 Topol, Sarah A. (2019) "What Does Putin Really Want?", *The New York Times,* June 25, https://www.nytimes.com/2019/06/25/magazine/russia-united-states-world-politics.html?fbclid=IwAR3xaKF1wchQwHrVvhc1jKufdpfTx0Gw840kaNxQxUQADWOEgCLdhw5WF2w.
63 Ibid.
64 Lavrov, Sergey (2019) "Mir na pereput'ye i sistema mezhdunarodnykh otnosheniy budushchego", *Rossiya v global'noy politike*, September 20, http://www.mid.ru/ru/foreign_policy/news/-/asset_publisher/cKNonkJE02Bw/content/id/3792556.
65 Lukyanov, Fyodor (2016) "A Failed New World Order and Beyond: Russian View" ..., pp. 482–483.

220  *Implementation of Russia's foreign policy*

66 Trenin, Dmitry (2019b) "20 Years of Vladimir Putin: How Russian Foreign Policy Has Changed", 27 August, https://www.themoscowtimes.com/2019/08/27/20-years-of-vladimir-putin-how-russian-foreign-policy-has-changed-a67043.
67 Ibid.
68 *Foreign Policy Concept of the Russian Federation* (2016) Approved by President of the Russian Federation Vladimir Putin, 30 November 2016, *Mid.ru*, December 1, https://www.mid.ru/en/foreign_policy/official_documents/-/asset_publisher/CptICkB6BZ29/content/id/2542248.
69 Ibid.
70 Ibid.
71 Lavrov, Sergey (2019) "Mir na pereput'ye i sistema mezhdunarodnykh otnosheniy budushchego" …
72 Ibid.
73 See: Malcolm, Neil (1989) "The 'Common European Home' and Soviet European Policy", *International Affairs*, Royal Institute of International Affairs, Vol. 65, No. 4 (Autumn, 1989), pp. 659–676; Strokan, Sergey; Reutov, Aleksandr and Tarasenko, Pavel (2009) "Bezopasnost' bez granits-Dmitriy Medvedev predlozhil novyy Dogovor o yevropeyskoy bezopasnosti", *Gazeta "Kommersant"*, 223, November 30, p. 8, https://www.kommersant.ru/doc/1283626; Petrov, Vitalii (2010) "Ot Lissabona do Vladivostoka – Vladimir Putin rasskazal o perspektivakh sotrudnichestva Rossii i Evropy", *Rossiiskoya Gazeta*, № 268(5347), November 26, https://rg.ru/2010/11/26/putin.html.
74 Trenin, Dmitry (2018a) "Zaglyadyvaya na pyat' let vpered. Kakovy osnovnye tseli rossiyskoi vneshnei politiki" …
75 Ibid.
76 Drobinin, Alexey (2022) "The lessons of history and vision for the future: Thoughts on Russia's foreign policy", August 4, https://en.interaffairs.ru/article/the-lessons-of-history-and-vision-for-the-future-thoughts-on-russias-foreign-policy/.
77 Putin, Vladimir (2022) "Vstrecha s rukovodstvom Gosdumy i glavami fraktsiy", July 7, http://kremlin.ru/events/president/news/68836, accessed 4 October 2022.
78 Drobinin, Alexey (2022) "The lessons of history and vision for the future: Thoughts on Russia's foreign policy" August 4, https://en.interaffairs.ru/article/the-lessons-of-history-and-vision-for-the-future-thoughts-on-russias-foreign-policy/.
79 Ibid.
80 Ibid.
81 Renz, Bettina (2016) "Russia and 'hybrid warfare'", *Contemporary Politics*, Vol. 22, No. 3, p. 294, DOI: 10.1080/13569775.2016.1201316.
82 Ibid., p. 297.
83 Topol, Sarah A. (2019) "What Does Putin Really Want?" …
84 Trenin, Dmitry (2019c) "Russia's Comeback Isn't Stopping With Syria", November 12, https://www.nytimes.com/2019/11/12/opinion/russias-comeback-isnt-stopping-with-syria.html.
85 Ng, Nicole and Rumer, Eugene (2019) "The West Fears Russia's Hybrid Warfare. They're Missing the Bigger Picture", July 3, https://carnegieendowment.org/2019/07/03/west-fears-russia-s-hybrid-warfare.-they-re-missing-bigger-picture-pub-79412.
86 Trenin, Dmitry (2019a) "Konturnaya karta rossiiskoi geopolitiki: vozmozhnaya strategiya Moskvy v Bol'shoi Evrazii" …
87 Miller, Christopher (2019) "In Ukraine, Foreign Minister And Others Fear Being 'Pushed' By West Into Bad Deal With Russia", September 16, https://www.rferl.org/a/ukraine-foreign-minister-and-others-fear-being-pushed-by-west-into-bad-deal-with-russia/30167312.html,; See also: Kommersant.ru (2019) "Ushakov ne isklyuchil vstrechi v 'normandskom formate' v Parizhe v oktyabre", September 13, https://www.kommersant.ru/doc/4093855.
88 Savina, Mariya (2022) "Lukyanov Fyodor: 'U nas mirovozzrencheskaya kolliziya, kotoraya ne predusmatrivayet kompromissa'", interview, June 24, https://nop-society.ru/interview/tpost/f6e5zojtz1-fedor-lukyanov-u-nas-mirovozzrencheskaya.

## Implementation of Russia's foreign policy 221

89 Trenin, Dmitry (2022a) "Politika i obstoyatel'stva. Sposobny li my sokhranit' stranu i razvivat' yeyo dal'she", May 20, https://globalaffairs.ru/articles/politika-i-obstoyatelstva/.
90 Ibid.
91 Kortunov, Andrey (2018) "Politics as Continuation of War by Other Means?", October 28, https://moderndiplomacy.eu/2018/10/28/politics-as-continuation-of-war-by-other-means/.
92 Ibid.
93 Tsygankov Andrei (2016) *Russia's foreign policy: change and continuity in national identity*, 4th ed., Lanham: Rowman & Littlefield, p. 214.
94 Ibid.
95 Ibid.
96 Ibid.
97 Keenan, Edward L. (1986) "Muscovite Political Folkways". *The Russian Review*, Vol. 45, No. 2 (April), pp. 119–120, http://www.jstor.org/stable/130423.
98 Trenin, Dmitry (2018b) "Zaglyadyvaya na pyat' let vpered. Kto budet opredelyat' vneshnyuyu politiku Rossii", April 2, https://carnegie.ru/commentary/75901.
99 The Kremlin (2022a) "Zasedaniye Soveta Bezopasnosti", February 21, http://kremlin.ru/events/president/news/67825.
100 Trenin, Dmitry (2018) "Zaglyadyvaya na pyat' let vpered. Kto budet opredelyat' vneshnyuyu politiku Rossii", April 2, https://carnegie.ru/commentary/75901.
101 Ibid.
102 Felgenhauer, Pavel (2018) "Russia Develops a New Ideology for a New Cold War", *Eurasia Daily Monitor*, Vol. 15, No. 52, April 5, https://jamestown.org/program/russia-develops-a-new-ideology-for-a-new-cold-war/.
103 Naryshkin, Sergei (2018) "Vystupleniye direktora Sluzhby vneshney razvedki RF S. Naryshkina na MCIS-2018", 4 April, https://www.youtube.com/watch?v=rOTPCf1uXWA; Translated in Felgenhauer, Pavel (2018) "Russia Develops a New Ideology for a New Cold War" ...
104 Ibid.
105 Naryshkin, Sergei (2019) "Vystupleniye direktora Sluzhby vneshney razvedki RF S. Naryshkina na MCIS-2019", April 30, https://www.youtube.com/watch?v=LtZu8m RyEtc.
106 Galeotti, Mark (2018) "Do the Western Balkans face a coming Russian storm?", Policy Brief, April 4, http://www.ecfr.eu/publications/summary/do_the_western_balkans_face_a_coming_russian_storm.
107 Grozev, Christo (2018) "The Kremlin's Balkan Gambit: Part I", *Bellingcat*, March 4, https://www.bellingcat.com/news/uk-and-europe/2017/03/04/kremlins-balkan-gambit-part/; See also Galeotti, Mark (2018) "Do the Western Balkans face a coming Russian storm?" ...
108 Galeotti, Mark (2018) "Do the Western Balkans face a coming Russian storm?" ...
109 Malsin, Jared and Thomas Grove (2021) "Researcher or Spy? Maxim Shugaley Saga Points to How Russia Now Builds Influence Abroad", *The Wall Street Journal*, October 5, https://www.wsj.com/articles/researcher-or-spy-maxim-shugaley-saga-points-to-how-russia-now-builds-influence-abroad-11633448407.
110 Schwirtz, Michael and Cora Engelbrecht (2021) *The New York Times*, September 21, https://www.nytimes.com/2021/09/21/world/europe/skripal-arrest.html.
111 Bellingcat Investigation Team (2020) "'V' For 'Vympel': FSB's Secretive Department "V" Behind Assassination of Georgian Asylum Seeker In Germany", February 17, https://www.bellingcat.com/news/uk-and-europe/2020/02/17/v-like-vympel-fsbs-secretive-department-v-behind-assassination-of-zelimkhan-khangoshvili/.
112 The Insider (2020) "Diplomat s 'Novichkom'. Ob"yavlennyy v rozysk Interpola GRUshnik-otravitel' okazalsya deystvuyushchim chlenom missii Rossii v VTO", February 25, https://theins.ru/politika/203460.
113 Lewis, Simon and Humeyra Pamuk (2022) "US warns that Russia will step up covert political influence to undermine sanctions", Reuters, September 13, https://www.

reuters.com/world/us-says-russia-spent-over-300-million-foreign-influence-efforts-since-2014-2022-09-13/.
114 Bertrand, Natasha and Jim Sciutto (2022) "Russia's Ukraine war effort running 'out of steam' as Putin's ability to spy in Europe cut in half, MI6 chief", *CNN*, July 21, https://edition.cnn.com/2022/07/21/politics/mi6-chief-russia-spying/index.html.
115 Uvarchev, Leonid (2022) "Putin napomnil razvedchikam o vazhnosti promyshlennogo shpionazha", June 30, https://www.kommersant.ru/doc/5436825.
116 Gurganus, Julia and Rumer Eugene (2019) "Russia's Global Ambitions in Perspective" 20 February 2019, https://carnegieendowment.org/2019/02/20/russia-s-global-ambitions-in-perspective-pub-78067.
117 Ibid.
118 Pukhov, Ruslan (2019) "A proving ground for the future", *Russia and the Middle East: viewpoints, policies, strategies*, Fyodor Lukyanov (ed.), Minneapolis: East View Press, p. 197.
119 Kortunov, Andrey (2016) "Seven Phantoms of the Russia's Policy Toward the European Union", April 6, https://russiancouncil.ru/en/analytics-and-comments/analytics/sem-fantomov-rossiyskoy-politiki-v-otnoshenii-es/.
120 Ibid.
121 Ibid.
122 Trenin, Dmitry (2019b) "20 Years of Vladimir Putin: How Russian Foreign Policy Has Changed" …
123 Kortunov, Andrey (2016) "Seven Phantoms of the Russia's Policy Toward the European Union" …
124 Popescu, Nicu (2019) "Familiarity breeds contempt: Why Russia makes mistakes on the world stage", March 14, https://ecfr.eu/article/commentary_familiarity_breeds_contempt_why_russia_makes_mistakes_on_the_wor/.
125 Walt, Stephen M. (1985) "Alliance Formation and the Balance of World Power", *International Security*, Spring 1985, Vol. 9, No. 4, p. 11.
126 Ibid.
127 Ibid.
128 Walt, Stephen M. (1985) "Alliance Formation and the Balance of World Power" …, p. 13.
129 Lukyanov, Fyodor (2019) "V shleyfe posledstviy", *Rossiyskaya gazeta*, Federal'nyy vypusk, 86(7844), April 17, https://rg.ru/2019/04/17/lukianov-irracionalnaia-politika-sozdaet-fenomen-mirovogo-rasstrojstva.html.
130 Ibid.
131 Trenin, Dmitriy (2022b) "Spetsial'naya voyennaya operatsiya na Ukraine kak perelomnaya tochka vneshney politiki sovremennoy", *Rossii, Rossiya v global'noy politike*, November 30, https://globalaffairs.ru/articles/perelomnaya-tochka/.
132 Ibid.
133 Vyrodova, Yuliya (2022) "Tokayev zayavil o nepriznanii «kvazigosudarstv» DNR i LNR", June 17, https://www.rbc.ru/politics/17/06/2022/62aca4ff9a7947d44a976f2e.
134 Radio Azattyk (2022) "Press-sluzhba Tokayeva zayavila o yego otkaze prinyat' orden za sotrudnichestvo s Rossiyey", June 18, https://rus.azattyq.org/a/31904054.html.
135 Meduza (2022) "Putin s'yezdil na sammit SHOS v Uzbekistan. Glavnaya novost'— on bol'she ne opazdyvayet na vstrechi (teper' opazdyvayut k nemu)", September 17, https://meduza.io/slides/putin-s-ezdil-na-sammit-shos-v-uzbekistan-glavnaya-novost-on-bolshe-ne-opazdyvaet-na-vstrechi-teper-opazdyvayut-k-nemu.
136 Umarov, Temur (2022) "Russia and Central Asia: Never Closer, or Drifting Apart?", *Carnegie Politika*, December 23, https://carnegieendowment.org/politika/88698.
137 The Ministry of Foreign Affairs Tajikistan (2022) Statement, *Telegram*, https://t.me/mfa_tj/1267.

138 Kurbanov, Murad (2022) "CHVK Vagner provodit mobilizatsiyu sredi zaklyuchennykh Turkmenistana!", September 17, https://graph.org/CHVK-VAGNER-PROVODIT-MOBILIZACIYU-SREDI-ZAKLYUCHENNYH-TURKMENISTANA-09-17.
139 Factcheck.kg (2022) "Kyrgyzstan eksportiroval v Rossiyu pritselov dlya oruzhiya na 10 mln somov", October, https://factcheck.kg/kyrgyzstan-eksportiroval-v-rossiyu-priczelov-dlya-oruzhiya-na-10-mln-somov/.
140 Nardelli, Alberto, Bryce Baschuk and Marc Champion (2022) "Putin Stirs European Worry on Home Appliance Imports Stripped for Arms", October 29, https://www.bloomberg.com/news/articles/2022-10-29/putin-stirs-european-worry-on-home-appliance-imports-stripped-for-arms?leadSource=uverify%20wall.
141 Umarov, Temur (2022) "Russia and Central Asia: Never Closer, or Drifting Apart?" …
142 Mamatkulov, Mukhammadsharif (2022) "India's Modi assails Putin over Ukraine war", *Reuters*, September 16, https://www.reuters.com/world/china/putin-xi-speak-summit-uzbekistan-2022-09-16/.
143 The Kremlin (2022b) "Vstrecha s Predsedatelem KNR Si TSzin'pinom", September 15, http://kremlin.ru/events/president/news/69356.

## Bibliography

Albright, Madeleine (2015) "Remembering Yevgeny Primakov", *Foreign Policy*, 29 June 2015, available at: https://foreignpolicy.com/2015/06/29/remembering-yevgeny-primakov-by-madeleine-albright-us-russia/, accessed 29 November 2021.

Bandeira, Moniz, and Luiz Alberto (2017) *The Second Cold War: Geopolitics and Strategic Dimension of the USA*, Berlin; Heidelberg: Springer.

Bellingcat Investigation Team (2020) "'V' For 'Vympel': FSB's Secretive Department "V" Behind Assassination Of Georgian Asylum Seeker In Germany", February 17, available at: https://www.bellingcat.com/news/uk-and-europe/2020/02/17/v-like-vympel-fsbs-secretive-department-v-behind-assassination-of-zelimkhan-khangoshvili/, accessed 11 October 2022.

Bertrand, Natasha, and Jim Sciutto (2022) "Russia's Ukraine war effort running 'out of steam' as Putin's ability to spy in Europe cut in half, MI6 chief", *CNN*, July 21, available at: https://edition.cnn.com/2022/07/21/politics/mi6-chief-russia-spying/index.html, accessed 11 October 2022.

Chubais, Anatoliy (2003a) "Osnovnaya zadacha RF – postroyeniye liberal'noy imperii", 25 September 2003, available at: https://www.rbc.ru/politics/25/09/2003/5703b59a9a7947783a5a4b6c, accessed 28 November 2019.

_____ (2003b) "Liberal'naya imperiya – eto zakhvat Ukrainy rossiyskim biznesom", November 13, available at: https://www.pravda.com.ua/rus/news/2003/11/13/4375407/, accessed 28 November 2019.

_____ (2003c) "Liberal'naya imperiya — eto oriyentir, daleko ukhodyashchiy za predely 2008 goda", November 24, available at: https://profile.ru/archive/anatoliy-chubays-liberalnaya-imperiya-eto-orientir-daleko-uhodyaschiy-za-predely-2008-goda-102284/, accessed 28 November 2019.

Drobinin, Alexey (2022) "The lessons of history and vision for the future: Thoughts on Russia's foreign policy", August 4, available at: https://en.interaffairs.ru/article/the-lessons-of-history-and-vision-for-the-future-thoughts-on-russias-foreign-policy/, accessed 4 October 2022.

Factcheck.kg (2022) "Kyrgyzstan eksportiroval v Rossiyu pritselov dlya oruzhiya na 10 mln somov", October, available at: https://factcheck.kg/kyrgyzstan-eksportiroval-v-rossiyu-priczelov-dlya-oruzhiya-na-10-mln-somov/ accessed 5 December 2022.

Felgenhauer, Pavel (2018) "Russia Develops a New Ideology for a New Cold War", *Eurasia Daily Monitor*, Vol. 15, No. 52, April 5, available at: https://jamestown.org/program/russia-develops-a-new-ideology-for-a-new-cold-war/, accessed 5 December 2019.

*Foreign Policy Concept of the Russian Federation* (2016) Approved by President of the Russian Federation Vladimir Putin 30 November 2016, Mid.ru, 1 December 2016, available at:https://beijing.mid.ru/ru/countries/rossiya/kontseptsiya_vneshney_politiki_rossii/, accessed 26 November 2019.

Galeotti, Mark (2018) "Do the Western Balkans face a coming Russian storm?", Policy Brief, April 4, available at: http://www.ecfr.eu/publications/summary/do_the_western_balkans_face_a_coming_russian_storm, accessed 5 December 2019.

Gorbachev, Mikhail Sergeevich (1987) *Perestroika: New Thinking for Our Country and the World*, New York: Harper & Row.

Grozev, Christo (2018) "The Kremlin's Balkan Gambit: Part I", *Bellingcat*, March 4, available at: https://www.bellingcat.com/news/uk-and-europe/2017/03/04/kremlins-balkan-gambit-part/, accessed 5 December 2019.

Gurganus, Julia, and Eugene Rumer (2019) "Russia's Global Ambitions in Perspective", *Carnegie Endowment*, 20 February 2019, available at: https://carnegieendowment.org/2019/02/20/russia-s-global-ambitions-in-perspective-pub-78067, accessed 21 September 2022.

Keenan, Edward L. (1986) "Muscovite Political Folkways". *The Russian Review*, Vol. 45, No. 2 (April), pp. 119–120, available at: http://www.jstor.org/stable/130423, accessed 5 February 2018.

Kissinger, Henry (2014) 'Do We Achieve World Order Through Chaos or Insight?', Interview conducted by Juliane von Mittelstaedt and Erich Follath, *Spiegel*, 13 November 2014, available at: http://www.spiegel.de/international/world/interview-with-henry-kissinger-on-state-of-global-politics-a-1002073.html, accessed 22 November 2021.

Korolev, Alexander (2016) "Russia's Reorientation to Asia: Causes and Strategic Implications", *Pacific Affairs*, Vol. 89, No. 1, pp. 53–73, DOI: 10.5509/201689153.

Kortunov, Andrey (2016) "Seven Phantoms of the Russia's Policy Toward the European Union", 6 April 2016, available at: https://russiancouncil.ru/en/analytics-and-comments/analytics/sem-fantomov-rossiyskoy-politiki-v-otnoshenii-es/, accessed 6 December 2019.

_____ (2018) "Politics as Continuation of War by Other Means?", October 28, available at: https://moderndiplomacy.eu/2018/10/28/politics-as-continuation-of-war-by-other-means/, accessed 4 October 2022.

Kommersant.ru (2019) "Ushakov ne isklyuchil vstrechi v 'normandskom formate' v Parizhe v oktyabre", September 13, available at: https://www.kommersant.ru/doc/4093855, accessed 27 November 2019.

Kremlin.ru (2013) "Presidential Address to the Federal Assembly", Moscow: the Kremlin, 12 December 2013, available at: http://eng.kremlin.ru/transcripts/6402, accessed 7 November 2019.

Lavrov, Sergey (2014) "V nedalekom budushchem istoriki sformuliruyut takoye ponyatiye, kak 'doktrina Primakova'", 28 October 2014, available at: https://tass.ru/politika/1537769, accessed 28 November 2019.

_____ (2019) "Mir na pereput'ye i sistema mezhdunarodnykh otnosheniy budushchego", *Rossiya v global'noy politike*, September 20, available at: http://www.mid.ru/ru/foreign_policy/news/-/asset_publisher/cKNonkJE02Bw/content/id/3792556, accessed 22 November 2021.

Lewis, Simon, and Pamuk Humeyra (2022) "U.S. warns that Russia will step up covert political influence to undermine sanctions", Reuters, September 13, available at: https://

www.reuters.com/world/us-says-russia-spent-over-300-million-foreign-influence-efforts-since-2014-2022-09-13/, accessed 11 October 2022.

Lukyanov, Fyodor (2016) "A Failed New World Order and Beyond: Russian View", *Strategic Analysis*, Vol. 40, No. 6 (Russia in Global Affairs), pp. 474–485, DOI: 10.1080/09700161.2016.1224064.

―――― (2018) "Konets piramidal'nogo mira s Soedinennymi Shtatami na vershine uzhe priznayut vse", Vypusk ot 17 January 2018, *Pervyi Kanal*, available at: https://otr-online.ru/programmy/bolshaya-strana/fedor-lukyanov-29951.html, accessed 2 December 2019.

―――― (2019) "V shleyfe posledstviy", *Rossiyskaya gazeta*, Federal'nyy vypusk, 86(7844), April 17, available at: https://rg.ru/2019/04/17/lukianov-irracionalnaia-politika-sozdaet-fenomen-mirovogo-rasstrojstva.html, accessed 10 December 2019.

Malsin, Jared, and Thomas Grove (2021) "Researcher or Spy? Maxim Shugaley Saga Points to How Russia Now Builds Influence Abroad", *The Wall Street Journal*, October 5, available at: https://www.wsj.com/articles/researcher-or-spy-maxim-shugaley-saga-points-to-how-russia-now-builds-influence-abroad-11633448407, accessed 11 October 2022.

Mamatkulov, Mukhammadsharif (2022) "India's Modi assails Putin over Ukraine war", *Reuters*, September 16, available at: https://www.reuters.com/world/china/putin-xi-speak-summit-uzbekistan-2022-09-16/, accessed 10 October 2022.

Marcus, Jonathan (2018) "Russia v the West: Is this a new Cold War?", 1 April 2018, available at: http://www.bbc.com/news/world-europe-43581449#, accessed 22 November 2021.

Mearsheimer, John J. (2019) "Bound to Fail: The Rise and Fall of the Liberal International Order", *International Security*, Vol. 43, No. 4, pp. 7–50, DOI: 10.1162/ISEC_a_00342.

Meduza (2022) "Putin s'yezdil na sammit SHOS v Uzbekistan. Glavnaya novost'—on bol'she ne opazdyvayet na vstrechi (teper' opazdyvayut k nemu)", September 17, available at: https://meduza.io/slides/putin-s-ezdil-na-sammit-shos-v-uzbekistan-glavnaya-novost-on-bolshe-ne-opazdyvaet-na-vstrechi-teper-opazdyvayut-k-nemu, accessed 10 October 2022.

Mid.ru (2016) "Foreign Minister Sergei Lavrov's remarks at the Primakov Readings International Forum", Moscow, November 30, available at: http://www.mid.ru/en/foreign_policy/news/-/asset_publisher/cKNonkJE02Bw/content/id/2540893, accessed 29 November 2019.

Miller, Christopher (2019) "In Ukraine, Foreign Minister And Others Fear Being 'Pushed' By West Into Bad Deal With Russia", September 16, available at: https://www.rferl.org/a/ukraine-foreign-minister-and-others-fear-being-pushed-by-west-into-bad-deal-with-russia/30167312.html, accessed 27 November 2019.

Ministry of Defence of the United Kingdom (2023) "Latest Defence Intelligence update on the situation in Ukraine – 20 January 2023", Twitter, available at: https://twitter.com/DefenceHQ/status/1616323761392812033?s=20&t=Ep1-yuQimoaoFqJzRLUOPA, accessed 20 January 2023.

Nardelli, Alberto, Bryce Baschuk, and Marc Champion (2022) "Putin Stirs European Worry on Home Appliance Imports Stripped for Arms", October 29, available at: https://www.bloomberg.com/news/articles/2022-10-29/putin-stirs-european-worry-on-home-appliance-imports-stripped-for-arms?leadSource=uverify%20wall, accessed 5 December 2022.

Naryshkin, Sergei (2018) "Vystupleniye direktora Sluzhby vneshney razvedki RF S. Naryshkina na MCIS-2018", 4 April, available at: https://www.youtube.com/watch?v=rOTPCf1uXWA, accessed 5 December 2019.

_____ (2019) "Vystupleniye direktora Sluzhby vneshney razvedki RF S. Naryshkina na MCIS-2019", April 30, available at: https://www.youtube.com/watch?v=LtZu8mRyEtc, accessed 5 December 2019.

Ng, Nicole, and Eugene Rumer (2019) "The West Fears Russia's Hybrid Warfare. They're Missing the Bigger Picture", July 3, available at: https://carnegieendowment.org/2019/07/03/west-fears-russia-s-hybrid-warfare.-they-re-missing-bigger-picture-pub-79412, accessed 29 November 2019.

Popescu, Nicu (2019) "Familiarity breeds contempt: Why Russia makes mistakes on the world stage", 14 March 2019, available at: https://ecfr.eu/article/commentary_familiarity_breeds_contempt_why_russia_makes_mistakes_on_the_wor/, accessed 6 December 2019.

Primakov, Yevgeny M. (2015a) *Vstrechi na perekrestkakh*. Moskva, "Tsentrpoligraf", (Nash XX vek), available at: https://history.wikireading.ru/82808, accessed 28 November 2019.

_____ (2015b) "Edinstvennoy al'ternativoy dlya Rossii yavlyayetsya opora v pervuyu ochered' na vnutrenniye rezervy i vozmozhnosti", 13 January, available at: https://tpprf.ru/ru/news/v-tsentre-mezhdunarodnoy-torgovli-moskvy-sostoitsya-zasedanie-merkuriy-kluba-i61924/, accessed 29 November 2019.

_____ (2015c) "Ne prosto rabotat', a znat' vo imya chego", *Rossiyskaya gazeta*, Stolichnyy vypusk, 3(6574), January 13, available at: https://rg.ru/2015/01/13/primakov-site.html, accessed 28 November 2019.

_____ (2009) *Mir bez Rossii? K chemu vedet politicheskaya blizorukost*, Moscow: IIK "Rossiyskaya gazeta", electron version, available at: http://yanko.lib.ru/books/politologiya/primakov.mir_bez_rossii.2-l.pdf, accessed 28 November 2019.

_____ (2012) "Ochen' Blizhniy Vostok", Interviewed by Vladimir Snegirev, *Rossiyskaya gazeta*, Federal'nyy vypusk, 180(5853), available at: https://rg.ru/2012/08/08/vostok.html, accessed 29 November 2019.

Putin, Vladimir (2022) "Vstrecha s rukovodstvom Gosdumy i glavami fraktsiy", July 7, available at: http://kremlin.ru/events/president/news/68836, accessed 4 October 2022.

Pukhov, Ruslan (2019) "A proving ground for the future", *Russia and the Middle East: viewpoints, policies, strategies*, Lukyanov, Fyodor (ed.), pp. 197–212, Minneapolis: East View Press.

Radio Azattyk (2022) "Press-sluzhba Tokayeva zayavila o yego otkaze prinyat' orden za sotrudnichestvo s Rossiyey", June 18, available at: https://rus.azattyq.org/a/31904054.html, accessed 10 October 2022.

Renz, Bettina (2016) "Russia and 'hybrid warfare'", *Contemporary Politics*, Vol. 22, No. 3, pp. 283–300, DOI: 10.1080/13569775.2016.1201316.

Safranchuk, Ivan (2014) "Rossiyskaya politika v Tsentral'noy Azii". *Strategicheskiy kontekst*. Zapiska Analiticheskogo tsentra Observo, CCI France Russie, No. 8, November.

Sakwa, Richard (2017) *Russia against the rest: the post-Cold War crisis of world order*, Cambridge: Cambridge University Press.

Savina, Mariya (2022) "Lukyanov Fyodor: 'U nas mirovozzrencheskaya kolliziya, kotoraya ne predusmatrivayet kompromissa'", interview, June 24, available at: https://nop-society.ru/interview/tpost/f6e5zojtz1-fedor-lukyanov-u-nas-mirovozzrencheskaya, accessed 7 October 2022.

Schwirtz, Michael, and Cora Engelbrecht (2021) *The New York Times*, September 21, available at: https://www.nytimes.com/2021/09/21/world/europe/skripal-arrest.html, accessed 11 October 2022.

Stent, Angela E. (2015) *The limits of partnership: U.S.-Russian relations in the twenty-first century*, Princeton and Oxford: Princeton University Press.

Surkov, Vladislav (2018) "Odinochestvo polukrovki", 9 April 2018, available at: http://www.globalaffairs.ru/global-processes/Odinochestvo-polukrovki-14-19477, accessed 2 October 2022.

The Insider (2020) "Diplomat s 'Novichkom'. Ob'yavlennyy v rozysk Interpola GRUshnik-otravitel' okazalsya deystvuyushchim chlenom missii Rossii v VTO", February 25, available at: https://theins.ru/politika/203460, accessed 11 October 2022.

The Kremlin (2022a) "Zasedaniye Soveta Bezopasnosti", February 21, available at: http://kremlin.ru/events/president/news/67825, accessed 4 October 2022.

―――― (2022b) "Vstrecha s Predsedatelem KNR Si TSzin'pinom", September 15, available at: http://kremlin.ru/events/president/news/69356, accessed 10 October 2022.

Trenin, Dmitry (2018) "Zaglyadyvaya na pyat' let vpered. Kto budet opredelyat' vneshnyuyu politiku Rossii", 2 April 2018, available at: https://carnegie.ru/commentary/75901, accessed 4 December 2019.

―――― (2019a) "Konturnaya karta rossiyskoy geopolitiki: vozmozhnaya strategiya Moskvy v Bol'shoy Yevrazii", February 11, available at: https://carnegie.ru/2019/02/11/ru-pub-78328, accessed 3 December 2019.

―――― (2019b) "20 Years of Vladimir Putin: How Russian Foreign Policy Has Changed", August 27, available at: https://www.themoscowtimes.com/2019/08/27/20-years-of-vladimir-putin-how-russian-foreign-policy-has-changed-a67043, accessed 25 November 2019.

―――― (2019c) "Russia's Comeback Isn't Stopping With Syria", November 12, available at: https://www.nytimes.com/2019/11/12/opinion/russias-comeback-isnt-stopping-with-syria.html, accesses 23 November 2021.

―――― (2022a) "Politika i obstoyatel'stva. Sposobny li my sokhranit' stranu i razvivat' yeyo dal'she", May 20, available at: https://globalaffairs.ru/articles/politika-i-obstoyatelstva/, accessed 7 October 2022.

―――― (2022b) "Spetsial'naya voyennaya operatsiya na Ukraine kak perelomnaya tochka vneshney politiki sovremennoy", Rossii, Rossiya v global'noy politike, November 30, https://globalaffairs.ru/articles/perelomnaya-tochka/.

The Ministry of Foreign Affairs Tajikistan (2022) Statement, Telegram, available at: https://t.me/mfa_tj/1267, accessed 21 December 2022.

Tsygankov, Andrei (2016) *Russia's foreign policy: change and continuity in national identity*, 4th ed., Lanham: Rowman & Littlefield.

―――― (2019) *Russia and America: the asymmetric rivalry*, Cambridge; Medford: Polity Press.

Topol, Sarah A. (2019) "What Does Putin Really Want?", *The New York Times*, June 25, available at: https://www.nytimes.com/2019/06/25/magazine/russia-united-states-world-politics.html?fbclid=IwAR3xaKF1wchQwHrVvhc1jKufdpfTx0Gw840kaNxQxUQADWOEgCLdhw5WF2w, accessed 3 December 2019.

Umarov, Temur (2022) "Russia and Central Asia: Never Closer, or Drifting Apart?", Carnegie Politika, December 23, available at: https://carnegieendowment.org/politika/88698, accessed 25 December 2022.

Uvarchev, Leonid (2022) "Putin napomnil razvedchikam o vazhnosti promyshlennogo shpionazha", June 30, available at: https://www.kommersant.ru/doc/5436825, accessed 11 October 2022.

Veretennikova, Kseniya (2003) "Liberal'naya imperiya vmesto banditskogo kapitalizma", *Vremya novostey*, October 13, available at: https://www.yabloko.ru/Publ/2003/2003_10/031013_vrn_debaty.html, accessed 29 November 2019.

Vyrodova, Yuliya (2022) "Tokayev zayavil o nepriznanii «kvazigosudarstv» DNR i LNR", June 17, available at: https://www.rbc.ru/politics/17/06/2022/62aca4ff9a7947d44a976f2e, accessed 10 October 2022.

Walt, Stephen M. (1985) "Alliance Formation and the Balance of World Power", *International Security*, Vol. 9, No. 4, pp. 3–43.

———— (2018) "I Knew the Cold War. This Is No Cold War", *Foreign Policy*, 12 March 2018, available at: http://foreignpolicy.com/2018/03/12/i-knew-the-cold-war-this-is-no-cold-war/, accessed 22 September 2022.

Zięba, Ryszard (2018) *The Euro-Atlantic Security System in the 21st Century: From Cooperation to Crisis*, Cham: Springer International Publishing.

# 7 Russia's security and foreign policy approaches
## Ukraine, star wars, and Afghanistan

### The war in Ukraine

*Strike first [Bei Pervym]?*

After Russian troops invaded Ukraine on February 24, 2022, the first question for many experts, politicians, scholars, and the public was: why did Russia invade? Other supplementary questions were: why didn't Putin consider the Soviet experience in Afghanistan or in Central Europe during the Cold War? Did the Russian elite not consider the patriotic mood and the power of nationalism in Ukraine which even Putin mentioned in his article of 2021?[1]

To answer any of those questions definitively, at least in the current environment, is a difficult task. However, based on the developments immediately before and during the war, we can briefly try to shed light on what happened and what directed Moscow to start its invasion. Now, after some hindsight, it is obvious that there were miscalculations in Moscow's war planning.

As far as an example of modern Russia's external security policy, this is not the first miscalculation. Similar miscalculations in analyzing Ukrainian society's preferences, support, and perception of Russia's policies happened in 2013–2014 as well. Although the final decision was based on the president's will, Putin's opinion on the Ukraine situation was formed by various departments whose actions were poorly coordinated, according to Vlast's reports in 2014.[2]

In 2014, many participants to the events mentioned a lack of coordination and presence of large apparatus conflicts. The government, which was engaged in integration negotiations with Kyiv, was not in contact with Putin's adviser Sergei Glazyev. At the same time, Glazyev did not communicate much with the government, or with the Foreign Ministry, or with his colleague in the Kremlin, Vladislav Surkov.[3]

Considering the developments before and during the second war in Ukraine, it can be argued that no essential changes in the decision-making or implementation process of the Russian Ukrainian policy happened. Moreover, the influence of the security institutions, which have their own maxims and conflicts of interests, including in Ukraine, and seem to be the main analytical information providers for top Russian decision-makers, must be noted.

DOI: 10.4324/9781003344391-8

A misunderstanding of Ukrainian society regarding the will of Ukrainians to resist an invasion, changes among the populations, and Russian leaders forgetting the Soviet past, might also explain why Moscow miscalculated. As the author of this book personally witnessed during field visits to Ukraine between 2009 and 2019, in several parts of the country including smaller villages, that despite the economic problems, corruption, grievances about local politicians and oligarchs, criticism of the West's lack of help, and even some language and societal contradictions between the regions, the majority did not support Russian-backed politicians or wish to have Russia as a patron or occupier.

There are several thoughts among scholars about the reasons for Moscow's decision to invade.

For instance, Anatol Lieven noted that it was not a simple miscalculation but a planned approach accepted and supported by the main group of the Russian elite—*Siloviki.*

According to Lieven, they have become impressed with the Chinese model: a tremendously dynamic economy, a disciplined society, and a growing military superpower ruled over with iron control by a hereditary elite that combines huge wealth with deep patriotism. They even promote the idea of China as a separate and superior civilization:

> They may well want the west to push Russia into the arms of China, despite the risk that this will turn Russia into a dependency of Beijing. And of course, they believe the war in Ukraine will consolidate patriotic feeling in Russia behind their rule, as well as permitting them to engage in intensified repression in the name of support for the war effort. This repression has already begun, with the closing of Russia's last remaining independent media and laws punishing as treason any criticism of the war.[4]

Another explanation of the Russian invasion of Ukraine by John Mearsheimer argues that it is the result of the great power competition between the United States and Russia and an expected outcome which fit well within the frame of offensive realism explanations.[5]

Samuel Charap and others suggested that Russia generally is most likely to intervene to prevent the erosion of its influence in its neighborhood, particularly following a shock that portends any such erosion occurring rapidly.[6]

Most probably the likelihood of a strengthened Ukrainian Army increasing its cooperation with NATO was also one of the causes of Putin's decision to attack. This is a result of the "strike first" thinking which has been stressed several times by Putin himself regarding multiple issues during interviews or speeches. Moreover, issues such as a regime security and the possibility that a successful and brief offensive would increase Putin's support among the public—as happened following the occupation of Crimea in 2014—also likely influenced Moscow's decision to invade Ukraine. A Washington Post report based on information shared by high-level political, military, and intelligence officials also confirms this. According to the report, by the late summer of 2021, analysts who advised the White House were increasingly convinced that the Russian leader saw a window of opportunity closing. They suggested that while not a member of NATO or the European Union, Ukraine was now moving steadily into the Western political, economic, and cultural orbit. The analysts concluded in the assessment that Putin, who was about to turn 69, understood that he was running out of time to cement his legacy as one of Russia's great leaders, "the one who had restored Russian preeminence on the Eurasian continent."[7]

Moreover, the analysts believed Putin calculated that any Western response to an attempt to reclaim Ukraine by force would be big on outrage but limited in actual punishment. The Russian leader, they said, believed that the Biden administration—after the humiliating US withdrawal from Afghanistan—wanted to avoid new wars especially as the United States and its allies in Europe were still struggling through the coronavirus pandemic. Moreover, German Chancellor Angela Merkel was leaving office and handing power to an untested successor, French President Emmanuel Macron was facing a re-election, and Britain was suffering from a post-Brexit economic downturn. Furthermore, as large parts of the EU depended on Russian oil and natural gas, Putin believed he could use energy as a wedge to split the Western alliance. Putin's government had built up hundreds of billions of dollars in cash reserves and was confident the Russian economy could weather the inevitable sanctions as it had in the past, the report says.[8]

Besides the mentioned miscalculations, two other issues prevented Russia from successfully following through on its plans for a quick victory: Ukraine's unexpectedly strong resistance and an over-reliance on the strength of the Russian Army. Russia, perhaps for the first time after Afghanistan and Chechnya, faced asymmetrical strategic approaches against itself at a large scale.

Russian military expert and a retired colonel with the Russian general staff, Mikhail Khodarenok, correctly predicted the main developments of the invasion three weeks before its start. Analyzing Russia's military power and Ukraine's resistance potential, he concluded that there will be no way to blitzkrieg Ukraine. He stressed that the statements of some experts that the Russian Army will defeat most of the units of Ukraine's armed forces in a short period of time in the event of a full-scale war, had no serious grounds. "No one will meet the Russian Army with bread, salt, and flowers in Ukraine ... it seems that the events in the southeast of Ukraine in 2014 did not teach anyone anything,"[9] Khodarenok wrote.

*At war as at war?*

Since the beginning of the war, Ukrainian forces tried to use different strategies than Russia. Thinking they were well-informed about the state and armament possibilities of Ukraine, Russia decided to use its heavy military power, with the aim of pressing Kyiv to accept Moscow's demands and if they didn't, to destroy the equipment of the weaker Ukrainian forces early on. To achieve the latter purpose, it was necessary to drive the main Ukrainian units into heavy clashes along the borders with Belarus, the already occupied Donbas, or in southern Ukraine but not to wage urban battles and to avoid dividing its ground forces in several directions.

Russia's military build-up around Ukraine increased since the spring of 2021. Until the start of the war, Russia had been gradually shifting troops, adding to an already robust and permanent military posture.[10] In January 2022, Russian forces surrounded Ukraine on three sides.[11]

On the eve of the invasion, it seemed obvious that Russia's military power was significantly stronger than Ukraine's. At least "on paper," the Russian Army's equipment and staff looked like one of the strongest armies in the world. In December 2021, Putin stated that in the Russian armed forces, the staffing of officer positions had exceeded 96% and an additional 13,000 officers had been sent to the troops. The number of army personnel under contract was double that of its conscripts. Sixty-seven percent of them had a secondary vocational education or higher. He emphasized that the demographic setback of the past had been overcome and the staffing of the armed forces had reached 91%. According to Putin, all ground troop commanders had combat experience, while that figure was 92% for pilots, 58% for air defense specialists, and 62% for those in the navy. The share of modern weapons in the country's nuclear triad had reached a historic high of 89.1%. Over 2,400 new and upgraded weapon systems were delivered to the army, and motorized and tank divisions and missile, as well as air defense brigades, were deployed at the end of 2021:

> Aviation and air defense missile brigades have been created in the Aerospace Forces. As many as 151 new and upgraded pieces of aviation equipment have been delivered. The air and missile defense forces have been equipped with over 30 new systems, including the S-400 Triumf and S-350 Vityaz air defense systems. A separate aviation regiment has been created and equipped with the MiG-31K interceptors armed with Kinzhal hypersonic missiles.[12]

Although, most probably, Putin exaggerated these numbers as is usually done in Russia's official statements—and those numbers were quietly questioned after February 24—Russia's air strike and high-precise missile capabilities gave it huge advantages over the Ukraine's weaker air defense and air strike systems.

It was obvious that a Russian large-scale multidomain operation[13] would be devastating for the Ukrainian military and population, and that Ukraine should work to prevent that. Dara Massicot noted that despite this Ukraine could also take steps to reduce the effects of the air and missile strikes that would likely begin such an operation. Kyiv and its supporters must urgently take such steps, she urged one month before the war.[14]

However, Ukraine had a natural advantage, its strategic depth. And the relative decentralization of its political management and military added to Ukraine's advantage especially in the first phase of the war.

Against Russian battle tactics, the Ukrainian forces did not fight under its adversary's conditions but on Ukraine's own terms. Specifically, they let the Russian forces enter deeper into the country and hit them with small, armored units not with heavy equipment. The mobility of the Ukrainian units against Russian convoys shows the strategic asymmetry conducted by the Ukrainians. In this regard, Moscow's miscalculations regarding the Ukrainian military and society's will to resist and about the state of its own (Russia's) ground forces played a mean trick on Russia.[15]

After several days, it was obvious that the war was not going well for Moscow, and it turned out to be a protracted one with elements of insurgency or guerrilla warfare. After the first month of war, Ukrainian civilians were already being brought into the protests and in several cases even began fighting against Russian occupation, and this tendency was even more important in the parts of Ukraine that were occupied by Russia. One can argue that civil resistance and insurgency would play a critical role if Russia were to occupy larger parts of Ukraine.

Ukraine already had historical experiences of insurgency and guerrilla warfare, most recently during WWII against both the Nazis and Soviets. Only the state sponsored extreme terror programs of the Germans and the Soviets prevented a popular uprising against the occupational forces between 1940 and 1950. Facing a stronger adversary, the best option for Ukraine was to use an asymmetric strategy against the relatively advanced Russian military machine. Co-ordination between the army, territorial defense, the police, and several other armed units of Ukraine's security services worked well. The use of different approaches along with asymmetric tactics, as well as using operational information obtained from civilians and the use of several other tools and methods in the defense of Kyiv and Sumy, stressed an asymmetric strategy. The hit-and-run tactics used by Ukrainian soldiers have had a stunning impact, tangibly affecting the Russian military machine:

> All that happened on February 24th was an increase in scale. Before then we had a front of 403 km and 232 strongpoints. And by February 24th that front grew to 2,500 km. And we were a relatively small force, but we engaged. Naturally, we understood that we were not strong enough. Our task was to distribute our smaller forces in such a way as to use unconventional tactics to stop the onslaught.[16]

The defense of Kyiv and Sumy are striking cases of how Ukraine largely used methods of asymmetric warfare. Armed with antitank weapons, small groups of the Ukrainian forces—in close cooperation with civilians—advanced to stop the Russians.[17]

> General Syrsky's command style emphasizes the elements of deception and surprise, using them to compensate for Ukraine's obvious disadvantage in firepower. In Kyiv, where at one-point Ukrainian forces were outnumbered by 12 to one, he cobbled together makeshift battalions from military-training institutes, and then used partisan groups to pick off a 64 km-long supply convoy as it attempted to steamroll its way towards Kyiv. It was a close-run thing, he says.[18]

Of course, the asymmetric methods were not the sole reason that Russia's attempt to take Kyiv and several other cities was defeated. Ukraine's cooperation with NATO created a group of professional officers that aspired to Western standards and helped build a decentralized, empowered, more agile way of warfare than the Russian model. After the war in Donbass, the United States, the United Kingdom, Canada, Poland, Lithuania, and other NATO allies opened training centers in western Ukraine, including for special operations forces. That training and battlefield experience against the Russians and their separatist proxies in Donbas allowed commanders of small, dispersed units to think for themselves, overturning the old Soviet model of top-down leadership that has paralyzed Russian units and forced top generals to venture to the front lines, where several have been killed.[19]

Moreover, Ukraine used asymmetric methods in the naval war in destroying several Russian military ships, including the flagship of the Black Sea Fleet, the cruiser Moska (the Project 1164). Benjamin Armstrong noted that the adoption of greater coastal defense measures, combined with a limited *guerre de razzia* strategy that might even put the facilities as Sevastopol at risk, offers a clear naval strategy that will both limit the advantages the Russians established in the early weeks of the war while at the same time giving Ukrainian naval forces the opportunity to impose costs on Russian forces.[20] *Guerre de razzia* or a war by raiding strategy is based on the theory that emphasizes guerre de course, or attacks on enemy commerce, and the use of what today would be termed asymmetric warfare at sea and irregular warfare.[21]

A combination of factors including the recent reforms in the Ukrainian armed forces, their training with the participation of NATO instructors, freedom of action for commanders of small groups, geography, experiences in Donbass since 2014, command and control, and shortcomings of the attackers added to Ukraine's advantages.

Several weaknesses of the Russian military personnel were revealed during the war. The main issue seemed to be that the Russian Army was not prepared for a large conventional war. And since the end of WWII, the Russian military only participated in small wars, such as in Afghanistan, Chechnya, and Georgia. Even in eastern Ukraine in 2014 and in Syria, the Russian military was only involved to a relatively small degree. While they certainly gained operations experience in Syria, their adversaries were primarily insurgents. Additionally, while Russia was competing against other regional powers such as Turkey in Syria, they fought against those powers mainly using proxies. Moreover, since the end of the Cold War, the Russian political and military elites have considered the possibility of large-scale land wars as unlikely—and probably only with NATO—and for that scenario, they mainly relied on their strategic forces as a deterrent.

One of the consequences of the military expeditionary campaigns of recent years in Georgia, and especially in Syria, was the increase in numbers of the airborne forces. They surpassed the ground forces in numbers and mobility but the airborne forces have worse manpower security and relatively lower firepower capabilities.

The navy that Russia had at the beginning of the war was overall of dubious combat capability and combat value. At the same time, the navy diverted huge manpower and material resources. Their personnel numbers at the beginning of 2021 were more than 50% of the ground forces, and the share in the state defense order in recent years was much higher than that of the ground and airborne forces combined.[22]

The key advantage for the Russian Army in such conditions was its modern and combat-ready aviation, which gained extensive combat experience in Syria. However, there were a limited number of modern operational-tactical and army aircraft in the Russian Aerospace Forces. In recent years, it was developed based on the targeted expeditionary campaigns in Syria. According to Russian scholar Vasilii Kashin, during the USSR there was a strong airfield network in Ukraine. Russia seems to have lacked the resources necessary to destroy the Ukrainian airfield network and Ukraine was able to use it to disperse their combat aircraft and drones.[23]

The main causes for the Russian Army's poor performance are command and control, such as the unpreparedness of especially low-level commanders to act independently in conditions of a full-scale war against a comparable adversary; the non-existence of a delegated authority; communication and the frequent necessary use of unsecured communication channels and violations in management; the quality of the supplied communications equipment; the use of different standards of communications equipment for different troops (the armed forces and the national guard), as well as the general low level of interagency interaction; and a lack of supply capacity. The lack of military equipment and arms and the insufficient number and quality of reconnaissance and attack UAVs; the lack of signals intelligence and an insufficient number of radar stations (RLS) for artillery reconnaissance; the range and quantity of high-precision weapons in the aviation and ground forces; a shortage of modern means of observation, primarily thermal imagers; the lack of new-generation armored vehicles and active protection of those armored vehicles, were all well documented by Russian experts.[24]

Russian experts observed that the Russian military had a shortage of manpower, especially in infantry as well as problems in establishing a partial mobilization force. Consequently, according to Michael Kofman and Rob Lee, the Russian Army was optimized for a short and sharp war and lacked the capacity to sustain a major conventional conflict at "peace time" manning levels.[25] Kofman and Lee stress that the Russian military is well-suited to short, high-intensity campaigns defined by a heavy use of artillery:

> By contrast, it is poorly designed for a sustained occupation, or a grinding war of attrition, that would require a large share of Russia's ground forces, which is exactly the conflict it has found itself in. The Russian military doesn't have the numbers available to easily adjust or to rotate forces if a substantial amount of combat power gets tied down in a war. Their big assumption was that in the event of a crisis with NATO, political leadership would authorize mobilization to raise manning levels and deploy staffed-up formations.[26]

The Russian military rolled back some reforms in 2013, not only because they proved deeply unpopular but also because the force was considered too small for a regional or large-scale war against a superior opponent. For instance, Russia stated that 12 new units and subunits would be created in the Western Military District by the end of 2022.[27]

Rob Lee reasons that Russia's failures in the first months of the invasion developed because the initial operation prioritized speed and secrecy above all other factors. Because Moscow expected little Ukrainian resistance, Russian forces made minimal attempts at executing a coherent combined-arms operation, which would have required careful coordination and planning between air, ground, and naval forces. Russian ground units simply drove toward cities, unprepared for a fight, Lee stresses. Moreover, Lee argues that Russian forces were given insufficient time to prepare for such a complex operation, "this decision was likely made at the political level, since the Russian military's doctrine, exercises, and previous conflicts all prioritized combined arms."[28]

Another striking problem observed during the war regarded Russian battalion tactical groups (BTG). This term was popularized with Russia's invasion of Ukraine in 2022 and is commonly used among the expert community and in the mass media as well. Throughout the Cold War, the USSR tried different combinations of forces to create an optimum battalion tactical group. After the breakup of the USSR, the idea to develop the BTG was strengthened by the Chechen campaigns and related counterterrorism operations. Nowadays, the BTG is a semi-permanent task force found in the maneuver (motorized rifle and tank) regiments and brigades of the Russian ground forces, naval infantry, and VDV. They are task-organized combat entities that can perform semi-independent combined arms combat missions.[29] They are designed to conduct deep raids, envelopments, and flanking maneuvers.[30] Lester W. Grau and Charles K. Bartles note that in the Russian system, the lowest echelon of combined arms command has traditionally been the maneuver regiment or brigade. Therefore, the Russians do not use terms like "Regimental Tactical Group" when referring to their maneuver formations, as these formations are inherently combined arms in nature. "The term 'battalion tactical group' is a special delineation of function which notes that this formation is combined arms in nature," they stressed.[31] Each regiment or brigade is to have two designated BTGs exclusively manned by contract soldiers and officers.[32]

In August 2021, Russian Defense Minister Shoigu stated that the Russian military had 168 BTGs.[33] Each BTG is meant to have between 700 and 900 servicemen, but as the official number of battalion tactical groups was rapidly increasing, the number of soldiers serving under contract plateaued, and the annual draft figure has remained largely unchanged over the past four years. "Consequently, contemporary depictions of the Russian battalion tactical group's typical size and composition were inaccurate," write Kofman and Lee.[34] Kofman and Lee note that the end result in Ukraine was that the Russian military deployed maneuver formations with few dismounted infantry available, but still brought many of their armored vehicles with them, "this situation begins to resemble the problems Russian forces faced in Grozny-1995: tons of metal, little manpower."[35]

### *The battle of Donbass*

Despite the failure of blitzkrieg in toppling the Ukrainian government shortly after the start of the intervention, Russian forces were slowly and tactically advancing in the east and the south of Ukraine. After the unsuccessful military offensive operations in the north, during the first phase of the war, the Russian offensive has focused on eastern Ukraine since the end of April 2022. The battle of Donbass reflected the classic Russian/Soviet military approach, a reliance on the indiscriminate use of fire power. The Russian Army are correctly characterized as an artillery army with tanks.[36] The popular belief among the Russian military elite is that artillery conquers and infantry occupies. As David E. Johnson put it, an artillery projectile does not need anything but an elevation and a deflection to go where you want it to go, "it does not care that it is not a precision munition or that it was fired by a conscript directed by inept sergeants and corrupt officers who do not exercise initiative. Nor does it care about the nature of the target. It just goes where sent and does its high explosive damage."[37]

Moreover, Russia performed preventative measures to maintain its advantage in artillery fire until the start of the invasion in 2022. Several official and media reports stressed that between 2014 and 2022, Russian intelligence agencies, mainly the GRU, conducted a clandestine campaign of bullying and sabotage, including bombings of key munitions depots across Eastern Europe. Additionally, in 2017–2018, several important Ukrainian ammunition storages were destroyed. It appears that Russia had spent years targeting Ukrainian and other Eastern European ammunition storage facilities and suppliers, and that Moscow took additional steps to acquire ammunition or otherwise prevent its sale to Ukraine before launching its full-scale invasion in February 2022. After the start of the second phase of the war, the Ukrainian lack of artillery rounds was badly felt. The problem is that most of Ukraine's artillery pieces date back to the Soviet Union, and they rely on the same 122 mm- and 152 mm-caliber rounds as Russia. Very little supply of those rounds exists outside of Russia in large part reportedly because Russia spent years targeting Ukrainian and other Eastern European ammunition storage facilities and suppliers before launching its invasion. In June 2022, Ukrainian Deputy Defense Minister Hanna Malyar said that Russia was firing more than 60,000 shells per day, ten times more than the Ukrainians. Malyar said that "even if everyone gives us this ammunition, it will still not be enough," adding that Ukraine uses more of the 152 mm shells than are produced globally in one day.[38]

Regarding atrocities committed in the occupied Ukrainian territories, we should remember that in the Russian forms of wars, issues of legal and illegal matter little. Similar uses of force against civilians were previously done in Afghanistan and Chechnya. Russia also cares less about casualties among its troops than the West.

From the start of the second phase, it is clear that Russia is waging a war of attrition, to which the traditional Russian approach on the reliance of fire power is highly suited. Aware of their tactical shortfalls and other problems revealed in the first phase of the war, Russia likely decided to change course rather than assume a crushing defeat in the north. Moreover, learning from their failures, Russia is, in some cases, mirroring the tactics of the Ukrainian forces. To avoid a huge number of casualties, Russia now uses small units during battles. In several cases, small units were used to identify the locations of adversary forces allowing artillery fire and air strikes to hit their positions.[39] But despite Russia's slowly developed tactical success in Donbass, the problems for the Russian military have not ended.

The battle of Donbass revealed Russian artillery problems. Russian military expert Ruslan Pukhov noted that the invasion of Ukraine once again confirmed the thesis that you can launch hundreds, thousands of unguided missiles, which seem to be cheap, but all this power is overcome by two precision-guided missiles that accurately hit a target. "Two missiles, for all their high cost, will solve more problems than thousands of unguided ones," notes Pukhov when describing the old conventional projectiles largely used by Russia.[40]

Even before the start of the invasion when analyzing Russian firepower, Russian expert Mikhail Khodarenok—previously a head of the Group of the Main Operational Directorate of the Russian General Staff—noted that although the strike will inflict heavy losses on a potential enemy, to expect it to crush the armed forces of an entire state with just one such blow shows unbridled optimism in the course of planning and conducting combat operations. Khodarenok stressed that in the course of operations on the war theater, a lot of fire strikes will have to be used. In this respect, the reserves of promising and high-precision weapons in the Russian armed forces are not unlimited. He noted that hypersonic missiles of the Zircon type are not yet in service and the number of Kalibr (sea-launched cruise missiles), Kinzhals, Kh-101 (air-launched cruise missiles) and Iskander missiles are limited. "This arsenal is absolutely not enough to wipe out a state the size of France and with a population of more than 40 million from the face of the Earth. Namely, Ukraine is characterized by such parameters," Khodarenok warned.[41]

However, after Russia's relative tactical success in Donbass since the end of June, more than a dozen major Russian supply depots, primarily used to store artillery ammunition, were attacked by long-range HIMARS rockets deployed by the United States. Once again, the Ukrainians, shifting away from the attritional fight they had been drawn into in Donbas, are re-adopting the asymmetric conventional tactics they used so successfully early in the war.[42] "They are attacking the Russian weak points once again—its railway centric logistics, its over talkative battlefield generals, and its over reliance on massed artillery to advance in the east," correctly observed Mick Ryan.[43]

The second phase of the war strikingly revealed how short Russia is on infantry. Recognizing Russia's shortcomings in its offensive operations, Russian military expert Ruslan Pukhov explained that the front is large, and the number of people involved in the special operation is not enough. "We have to break into the front with an insufficient number of soldiers and on vulnerable tanks and infantry fighting vehicles," he notes.[44] "Now in Donbass, the Russian forces are trying to solve this by using a large amount of artillery, but, as you can see, things are going very slowly," Pukhov stressed.[45] Pukhov pointed to the shortcomings of Russian artillery stating that the problem of Russia lagging behind the USSR in this regard has been obvious since the 1980s. He stressed that Western equipment supplies to Ukraine are growing and it will be a huge problem for Russia because during an artillery duel, Ukrainian systems will be able to destroy Russian batteries, and any return fire simply will not reach its target. "This issue is becoming particularly acute in connection with the commenced deliveries of HIMARS and MLRS missile systems to the armed forces of Ukraine, which fire high-precision GPS-guided GMLRS missiles with a range of up to 85 km," Pukhov warned.[46] Assessing the Ukrainian military staff, Pukhov recognized that "in fact, underestimating the enemy played a cruel joke on us."[47]

Russia's underestimation of the Ukrainian military and Western support and the overestimation of its own capabilities were once again confirmed by Ukraine's successes at the end of summer 2022. Around August, Ukrainian forces started to conduct offensive operations and succeeded to liberate several settlements in the Kherson and Kharkov regions as well as Donbass. Ukrainian manpower advantages since the beginning of the invasion, increase of western military equipment supply, particularly MLRS systems, and the exhaustion of the Russian forces on the other hand were the primary reasons for Ukraine's advancement between August and October. Amid these developments, Russia conducted a "partial mobilization" and began to receive Iran-produced drones (Sahid-136 and 131) and reportedly other Iranian equipment and ammunitions.[48] Moreover, at the beginning of October, just two days before the massive missile attacks on Ukraine, former Chief of the Russian Air and Space Force, Sergey Surovikin, was officially appointed as a commander of the United Grouping of Russian Troops in Ukraine. Russian sources described Surovikin as a supporter of massive missile strikes against Ukrainian infrastructure, including civilians.[49] Using mainly Iranian-produced drones, Russia restarted large air attacks on infrastructure and cities, and also targeted Ukraine's air defense and aviation. As of December 2022, the total amount of documented damage to Ukraine's infrastructure due to the invasion was $137.8 billion (at replacement cost), according to a Kyiv School of Economics estimation.[50]

Using similar tactics as in Syria—where General Surovikin also was in charge of the Russian force operations—Moscow aimed to force Kyiv to stop the advances of its forces and to accept Russian peace terms, that is, accept territorial losses in the Kherson and Donbass regions. But given the state of Russian manpower and the decreasing equipment and ammunition supply capabilities of the military industry as a result of sanctions, this signaled that a successful strategic advance for Russia was not a realistic target. Mobilization or arms supply from countries such as Iran may temporarily solve Russia's problems; however, they can't promise significant changes on the battlefield to Russia's benefit. In this respect, Gustav Gressel explains that mobilization cannot essentially solve Russian problems if the West would increase its military assistance to Ukraine. Such support allows Ukraine to further exploit the momentum of its successes and liberate more territories before large numbers of Russian forces arrive on the battlefield. "In the long term, it should enable Kyiv to transition to Western-designed systems in all weapons to increase the sustainability of the war effort and signal to Moscow it will not win a war of attrition," Gressel stressed.[51]

In November, Russian troops, under pressure from Ukrainian forces, withdrew from Kherson and from the right bank of the Dnieper. Although Ukraine succeeded in liberating Kherson, Russia could stabilize its defense along the whole frontline and weaken Ukrainian advances. Russia was changing tactics under new commander, Sergei Surovikin. According to the commander of the Ukrainian ground forces General Syrsky, Russian forces attacked using smaller, well-coordinated detachments on foot, "costly in terms of soldiers' lives, but that has never been Russia's highest priority."[52]

Ukraine continued to use asymmetric tactics. At the end of 2022, Ukraine reportedly used Soviet-made Tu-141 Strizh UAVs to hit the Engels Airfield in Rostov Oblast and an airport in the Ryazan Oblast deep inside Russia.[53] Moreover, a simple mobile phone app has been developed by Ukrainian volunteers to allow civilians to report sightings of incoming Russian drones and missiles and to increase the proportion that are shot down before they hit a target.[54]

On the other hand, Russia's use of cheap, Iranian-produced UAVs can be explained as an asymmetric warfare approach. Moscow aims to make Ukraine and the West's costs high in the war, that is, to hit Iranian drones which cost only several thousand dollars with air defense systems and ammunitions which cost hundreds of thousands—and in some cases even millions—of dollars.

After the frontline was stabilized, Ukrainian advances weakened and Russia gained control over several towns in Donbass under the command of Surovikin, chief of the Russian General Staff Gerasimov was appointed as a commander of troops in Ukraine. Most probably, Gerasimov's appointment and the change of commanders in the Western and Southern Military Districts in January 2023 were made to optimize troop management for the next offensive in Donbass. However, despite partially solving its manpower problems following the mobilization, since the autumn of 2022, Russia has been experiencing shortages in equipment and ammunition. As Michael Kofman put it "following mobilization, the Russian armed forces now have manpower but will find themselves constrained by availability of ammunition and equipment."[55] However, material capacity constraint is a problem for both sides.

At the end of 2022, Russian Defense Minister Shoygu announced the defense ministry's plans for the coming years. Among them are returning brigades to divisions; to gradually increase the age of conscription from 18 to 21 years, and raise the limit of the recruitment to 30 years; to ensure the possibility to enter military service under a contract from the first day of joining the service; to recreate the Leningrad Military District; to create two inter-group strategic territorial units of the armed forces—the Moscow and Leningrad Military Districts; to reorganize into motorized rifle divisions (seven motorized rifle brigades in the Western, Central, Eastern military districts and in the Northern Fleet); to additionally form two airborne assault divisions in the airborne forces; to increase the numbers of manpower of the armed forces to 1.5 million, including 695,000 contract servicemen; to increase the number of servicemen under contract, taking into account the replacement of mobilized citizens in the troop groupings and the recruitment of new formations—by the end of 2023—to 521 thousand people.[56] Despite the declaration to actually achieve such goals, especially increasing the number of serviceable manpower, will be problematic. Even if they succeeded in achieving the number of servicemen targeted, their preparation for combat duty would require more time. Moreover, Shoygu's announcement was mainly to stress the intention to fight with large units, just as the Soviets had. Despite Shoygu's statement, no cohesive vision was put forward to further Russia's aims of preparing for a large-scale war. Most probably the leadership of the Defense Ministry was taking into account the lessons learned in Ukraine when preparing the plans announced by Shoygu.

Moscow's likely goal—as of the beginning of 2023—is to occupy the whole Donbass region and maintain control over land access to Crimea while getting a break under the pretext of a truce. Several months after the start of the war, it has turned into a war of attrition with heavy battles for every inch of territory. Since the end of summer 2022, both sides have significant problems with fulfilling ammunition demands, especially in artillery. Providing the demanded number of armored vehicles and precision-strike capabilities for Ukraine by the West may speed up the end of the war to Ukraine's benefit. Otherwise, given Russia's preparation for a sustained war of attrition, it may take a long time until both sides feel an existential need for a truce.

Several issues including the establishment of the Coordination Council under the Russian government to meet the needs of military and law enforcement agencies during the war,[57] and the increase of spending for national defense and national security for the planned budgets of 2023–2025,[58] signal that Russia is preparing for a long war of attrition and that it is getting to be a kind of garrison state. In such a situation, developments in the war will primarily depend on Ukrainian resistance, and whether the West will continue to supply the weapons required by Ukraine or try to influence Kyiv to make the concessions demanded by Russia. Of course, internal developments in Russia, such as Putin being removed from power is another—albeit less likely—scenario for the war's end. However, it seems that both sides will try to advance along several parts of the frontline and from time to time will conduct offensive operations. It looks like that after a year of fighting, neither side is capable of gaining any strategic advance in the war.

*The "grain war"*

Russia also used non-conventional forms of war, such as a "grain war" and an energy war against not only Ukraine but also the West. This stems from the general understanding of the Russian elite that this war is not only with Ukraine but also with the West. A lot of significant works about Russia using the natural gas supply to the EU as a tool of political influence have been written since the 2000s. Therefore, here we are going to focus on the specific form of pressure Russia used during its invasion of Ukraine.

Since the beginning of the war, the Ukrainian agriculture area was heavily affected. Three months after Russia's invasion, the damage to Ukraine's agriculture reached $4.3 billion, or nearly 15% of its capital stock. The Center for Food and Land Use Research of Kyiv School of Economics reported that Russia targeted elevators and other storage facilities because damage to these would weaken Ukraine's agricultural capacity. Given that storage facilities are frequently located in open areas and provide an excellent sight of the surroundings, they suffer from direct military assaults to limit the enemy's situational awareness. The general number of damages due to the destruction of storage facilities is estimated at $272 million.[59]

The indirect war losses in Ukraine's agriculture are estimated at $23.3 billion. Reportedly, the most significant drop in the estimated 2022 harvest is for wheat (expected 33% drop compared to the baseline), sunflower (32%), and barley (31%) since a substantial share of these crops are produced in areas directly affected by the war. Compared to the previous year, a relatively less pronounced decrease in the 2022 harvest is expected for corn (18%). This is mainly because the corn belt of Ukraine is located in the country's center—above the occupied south and below the liberated north of Ukraine.[60]

Because of the port blockade by Russian naval forces, Ukraine could not export commodities through the Black Sea or the Sea of Azov. Before the invasion, more than 90% of the grain and vegetable oil exports were maritime export. Lacking opportunities to export through other modes of transport, Ukraine is suffering from a domestic supply shock—leading to a nearly 30% domestic price decrease—as reported by the Center for Food and Land Use Research.[61]

The total estimates for the combined value of losses of the top-four export-oriented crops (wheat, corn, barley, and sunflower) are at 11.9 billion US dollars.[62]

Ukraine is one of the world's largest grain exporters, and accessing Ukraine's stockpiled grain became urgent internationally because of the millions of tons that are exported annually to Africa and the Middle East. The UN subsequently sought to ease the Russian blockade of grain shipping to avert food shortages in those regions. The Wall Street Journal reported that United Nations Secretary-General António Guterres was pursuing a high stakes deal with Russia, Turkey, and other nations to open up Ukrainian food exports to world markets. Reportedly, he asked Moscow to permit some Ukrainian grain shipments in exchange for moves to ease Russian and Belarusian exports of potash fertilizer.[63] In response, the Russian President stated that "there is no problem with the export of grain from Ukraine" and offered five export directions, the first of which was through the Ukrainian ports, "but they need to be cleared," said Putin. Other export routes—as stated by Putin—were through Poland, along the Danube through Romania, through Russian-controlled ports in the Azov and Black Seas, and—"the easiest and cheapest way"—through Belarus, "but for this sanctions should be lifted from this country," he stated.[64]

The main affordable route for exports was through the Ukrainian ports but Russia said Ukraine must demine the waters off the Black Sea coast for export corridors to become operational. Such a scenario could be a huge threat to the Ukrainian coastal territories, including Odessa, and therefore, President Zelenskyy responded that Kyiv is negotiating with several states and the UN to unblock ports, but the main guarantor in this are the weapons that Ukraine will receive from partners.[65] However, a few days after Putin's statement, Russian missile strikes destroyed a large grain storage terminal in the southern port city of Mykolaiv. The European Union's High Representative, Josep Borrell, condemned the Russian missile strike saying that it was "another Russian missile strike contributing to the global food crisis."[66] Turkey was trying to broker a deal to create safe maritime corridors.[67] But even if an agreement was reached and Ukraine's ports were able to reopen, the danger from sea mines planted by Ukraine and Russia will hold up shipments, potentially for months, according to maritime officials.[68]

Moreover, the Ukrainian officials accused Russia of stealing about 600,000 tons of its grain and exporting some of it. Western countries accused Russia of creating a risk of global famine by shutting Ukraine's Black Sea ports.[69] The United States warned that Russia is trying to profit from their plunder by selling stolen wheat to drought-stricken countries in Africa, the New York Times reported. According to the report, the United States sent an alert to 14 countries, mostly in Africa, that Russian cargo vessels were leaving ports near Ukraine laden with, what a State Department cable described as "stolen Ukrainian grain."[70] Russia in return blamed Western sanctions for the food crisis and stated that Russia did not steal any grain.[71]

However, a separate investigation by BBC Russia and BBC Ukraine had shown that in some cases, the Russians are forcing Ukrainian farmers to sell grain at prices well below market rates, and sign documents to prove it was purchased "legally."[72]

According to the BBC investigation, while early reports were typically of outright theft by Russian forces, farmers suggest there had been a change in tactics as the Russians realize that if they pay nothing, future harvests could be sabotaged. The farmers said they must accept the low prices as they have no alternative and need to buy fuel and pay workers.[73] Moreover, the Russian-appointed head of the Russian-held areas in the Zaporizhzhia region, said grain had left the region on freight trains bound for Crimea and, from there, the Middle East. He told Russian state TV "Rossiya 24" that the main contracts are being concluded with Turkey.[74] Later, he stated that stocks of grain in the Zaporizhzhia region, which belonged to Ukraine, "were nationalized."[75] The arrival of grain wagons to Crimea from Melitopol (Zaporizhzhia) was also confirmed by the Russian official of occupied Crimea. This official also stated that grain was being transported from the occupied Kherson region.[76] Using data from Lloyd's List Intelligence, the BBC has tracked these ships on journeys between Crimea and ports in Turkey and Syria between April and June 2022.[77]

On the one hand, the blockading of the Ukrainian ports along the Black Sea can be explained by the needs of the Russian offensive operations to cut off sea routes capable of deploying military equipment and to minimize Ukraine's already weaker naval possibilities. On the other hand, Ukraine laid mines around its ports to challenge any possible Russian offensive operations from the sea. However, Russian air strikes on Ukraine's second biggest grain terminal at nearby Mykolaiv and the changing nature of Russia's strategy (from blitzkrieg in the first phase to the attrition of the second phase) might signal Moscow's intentions to use the existing situation to Russia's benefits in any negotiations with Ukraine and the West.

Statements from Russian officials about using Belarus for grain exports or discussing a lifting of the sea blockade in return for softening some of the sanctions on Russia, which were discussed above, are signs that Moscow used the Ukrainian grain export as a subject of the war and for negotiations. Yes, Russia's security policy will use any affordable method and opportunity for its benefit. As Margarita Simonyan, the head of the Russian propaganda outlet RT, mentioned, "the jokes discussed in Moscow … the famine will start now and they will lift the sanctions and be friends with us, because they will realize that it's impossible not to be friends with us." "Do you think this is realistic? I would not want it to be through hunger, but still," Simonyan asked Putin at the St. Petersburg Economic Forum.[78] Denying claims that Russia did indeed blockade Ukrainian grain exports intentionally, Putin stressed that he hopes "common sense will nevertheless prevail, that the situation in world affairs will calm down, everyone will begin to treat each other's interests with respect, and we will function normally."[79]

After some period of negotiations in July Russia, Ukraine, the UN, and Turkey signed a deal to resume Ukrainian grain exports from the Black Sea ports.[80] In return, Moscow and the UN agreed to lift any indirect effects of the sanctions on the export of Russian agricultural products and fertilizers.[81] After several months, Moscow declared that Russia would leave the agreement. Clearly, Moscow will use its naval blockade of the Ukrainian ports as a tool in the invasion until the end of the war or for as long as Russia is able to do so.

In deciding to use a blockade as a tool in the war and in negotiations with the West, Moscow's calculations were likely based on experiences of similar food crises and the public reaction in Western societies. Moreover, Moscow used the situation to pressure the West to soften some of the sanctions. Anatol Levin wrote that the Russian naval blockade of Ukraine and Western restrictions on international payments for Russian goods, combined with the impact of the climate crisis in India, threatened acute food shortages in many vulnerable countries. "As during the Arab Spring and the Syrian Civil War," Levin put it, "these shortages risk causing instability and local conflicts. The sooner this war can be brought to an end, the better for the entire world," Levin concluded.[82] As discussed in the previous chapters, influencing the public mood in Western societies—where governments are responsible to and dependent on the will of the people through elections—is one of the main tools of asymmetric warfare.

## Russia's anti-satellite program

### How Russia prepares for star wars

On November 15, 2021, the Russian Defense Ministry reported a successful test of an anti-satellite weapon (ASAT) and as a result the inoperative spacecraft Tselina-D, which had been in orbit since 1982, was destroyed. Reportedly, it may also have destroyed an old Soviet electronic intelligence satellite Kosmos-1408, launched in 1982. The statement stressed "the active development and testing by the Pentagon of strike-combat assets in space, including the latest modifications of the X-37B unmanned spacecraft."[83] US Secretary of State, Antony Blinken condemned the tests stating that "it will significantly increase the risk to astronauts and cosmonauts on the International Space Station and other human spaceflight activities."[84] Russian Foreign Minister Sergey Lavrov hit back and accused the United States of "hypocrisy" and added that "there are no facts." However, he mentioned negotiations and suggested a discussion about their (United States) concerns in connection with the "treaty that Russia and China are proposing to prevent this arms race in space."[85] The United States had previously raised concerns about Russian satellite activities. In 2018, the United States and the United Kingdom accused Russia of testing a weapon-like projectile in space that could be used to target satellites in orbit.

Russian military experts claim that the X-37B Orbital Test Vehicle is designed to conduct long-endurance surveillance of satellites and destroy them either by mechanical blow or by means of explosive energy.[86] In 2021, Almaz-Antey CEO said that "the American Boeing X-37B spacecraft" is capable of carrying up to six nuclear warheads and the United States will build eight such spacecrafts in the coming years, which "creates new challenges in terms of improving the means of aerospace defense."[87] Then the head of Roscosmos Dmitry Rogozin also stated that the corporation is concerned that "the United States and NATO are launching likely weapons carriers into space" and thus, he concluded that "Russia must have anti-satellite weapons."[88]

Mutual accusations between Moscow and Washington occurred after every Russian test of its anti-satellite capabilities in recent years and only added to the general blame game of the two powers. The situation is similar to the arms race in space of the 1980s when the USSR launched its "asymmetric response" program against the US Star Wars program.[89]

Since the 1990s, there has been a belief among the Russian military and political elite that the next generation of warfare between NATO and Russia will be waged in the aerospace domain, as high-precision weapons enabled by satellite targeting and navigation will be used to destroy the strategic forces and the political and economic centers of an adversary.[90] Moscow is concerned that, in a possible conflict with NATO, such high-precision weapons may be used against Russia in a satellite-coordinated strike to destroy its strategic and conventional forces. President Vladimir Putin also mentioned that such threats against Russia's security might be used by the United States and NATO. For instance, in 2015, he mentioned "the use of high-precision long-range non-nuclear weapons comparable in their effect to nuclear weapons."[91] Talking about future military conflicts, the Russian Chief of the General Staff General Valery Gerasimov stressed that the adversary's economic infrastructure and the system of state administration will be targeted for priority destruction and in addition to the traditional domains of battles, "the information domain and space will be actively involved."[92]

There are critics of such thinking. Stressing Russia's effective missile defense and other air defense capabilities, Russian scholar Major General Vladimir Dvorkin (retired)—who previously served as the director of the Russian Defense Ministry's Fourth Central Research Institute and was one of the main authors of program documents on Russia's strategic nuclear forces and strategic missile forces—noted that "it seems rather fantastical to suggest that the Pentagon could be planning a disarming conventional strike against Russia's strategic nuclear forces: such a measure would not only prove absolutely useless, but would trigger a devastating retaliatory nuclear strike." Dvorkin wrote that the imaginary concept of a conventional disarming strike comes not from American officials but rather Russian ones, and as an example, he points to the statements of Russian officials who coordinate the military industry and promote its interests.[93] He explained that such official statements from Russia's political leadership were most probably intended to instill a militaristic fervor among their citizens.[94]

In recent years, four countries, Russia, the United States, China, and India, have demonstrated anti-satellite capabilities. Russian leadership claims that their anti-satellite and counter-space programs are a pro rata response to US and NATO efforts to dominate and militarize space. They also repeatedly call for discussions regarding arms control in space. In 2019, Russian Chief of the General Staff Gerasimov stated that the Pentagon "repeatedly declared" its intention to use outer space for military purposes and that the US Space Force was created to enable continued American militarization of it. He stressed that Russia would have to respond to those military threats with "mirror and asymmetric measures."[95]

Knowing the technological backwardness of its industry and likely to avoid cost burdens, Russia, in its arms competition in space, once again prefers "asymmetric responses" as had the Soviet Union in the early 1980s. Even the basis of Russia's current anti-satellite weapon projects were established during the Soviet Union. Moreover, the fact that the United States uses its technological advantages in space for its own power projection capabilities means its satellites are attractive targets for Russia. The 2001 Rumsfeld Commission report called the United States an attractive candidate for a "Space Pearl Harbor." The report explained that with the growing commercial and national security uses of space, US assets in space and on the ground offer such targets.[96] This thought, which cannot be considered an ungrounded exaggeration, might not be just a concern of the United States but it can be a driver of Russian anti-satellite weapons and counter-space programs as well.

According to Jaganath Sankaran in direct response to American technological demonstrations, Russia appears to have restarted some of its Cold War anti-satellite and counter-space weapons programs to hedge against a technological surprise. "As a result, during the last ten years, Russia has demonstrated with increasing frequency a plethora of anti-satellite and other advanced counter-space weapons not seen since the heights of the Cold War," he notes.[97]

*Tools*

Since 2010, reports on the testing of Russian anti-satellite capabilities have appeared. According to the Global Counterspace Capabilities Report 2021, since 2010 Russia has been testing technologies for rendezvous and proximity operations (RPO) in both low earth orbit (LEO) and geosynchronous orbit (GEO) that could lead to or support a co-orbital anti-satellite weapons (ASAT) capability, and some of those efforts have links to a Cold War-era LEO co-orbital ASAT program.[98] The report suggested that Russia may have started a new co-orbital ASAT program called Burevestnik, potentially supported by a surveillance and tracking program called Nivelir. The technologies developed by these programs could also be used for nonaggressive applications, including surveilling, and inspecting foreign satellites, and most of the on-orbit RPO activities done to date match these missions. However, "Russia has deployed two 'sub-satellites' at high velocity, which suggests that at least some of their LEO RPO activities are of a weapons nature," stressed the report.[99]

Since 2013, Russia has launched several satellites with the ability to rendezvous with other space objects, and in some cases do so after periods of dormancy.[100]

According to the report, between June 2014 and October 2020 Russia conducted eight rendezvous and proximity operations.[101] Between December 24, 1991, and December 16, 2020, Russia conducted 13 ASAT tests in space.[102]

The Russian direct ascent ASAT (DA-ASAT) capabilities currently consist of three primary programs that have direct or indirect counterspace capabilities. All three projects are based on Soviet-era programs but have been revived or reconstituted in recent years:

> Nudol—a rapidly maturing ground-launched ballistic missile designed to intercept targets in LEO; Burevestnik—an air-launched rocket that could either be a new version of the Kontakt DA-ASAT or an SLV to place co-orbital ASATs into LEO orbit, on a several-year development timeline; and S-500—a next-generation exo-atmospheric ballistic missile defense system that may have capabilities against targets in low LEO orbits.[103]

The programs Nivelir, Burevestnik, and Numizmat are likely to be satellites with masses in the range of 50 to 100 kilograms, which are generally referred to as microsatellites.[104] Reportedly, the Russian main satellite construction facility is the Central Scientific Research Institute of Chemistry and Mechanics which is named after D.I. Mendeleyev (TsNIIKhM or in Cyrillic ЦНИИХМ).[105] Regarding the S-500, in 2020, the head of the Anti-Aircraft Missile Troops of the Russian Aerospace Forces stated that satellites and hypersonic weapons in near space could be hit by the new S-500 Prometheus air defense system.[106] In April 2022, the head of the production company said that Almaz-Antey is mass-producing S-500s.[107]

There are also several cases in recent years that signal Russia is testing rendezvous and proximity operations (RPO) in space.

Since 2013, as mentioned previously, Russia has launched several satellites into space (both LEO and GEO) that have demonstrated the ability to rendezvous with other space objects, and in some cases do so after periods of dormancy. The first publicly known event occurred on December 25, 2013, when a Russian rocket launch vehicle from Plesetsk Cosmodrome placed three small satellites into LEO in what appeared to be another routine launch to replenish the Rodnik constellation.[108] Shortly afterward, the Russian Defense Ministry announced that the three spacecraft (Kosmos 2488, 2013-076A, 39483; Kosmos 2489, 2013-076B, 39484; Kosmos 2490, 2013-076C, 39485) had successfully separated from the upper stage (Breeze-KM R/B, 20113-076D, 39486).[109] Soon after, US Strategic Command's (USSTRATCOM) Joint Space Operations Center (JSpOC) published its initial assessment which mentions a fourth payload from the launch (Kosmos 2491, 2013-076E, 39497). Reportedly, four out of the five objects from the December 2013 launch had maneuvered to change their orbits shortly after launch.[110]

However, Kosmoses' adventures in space continue. Several orbital experiments conducted by the Russian Kosmos satellites, in several classifications described as "Russian nesting doll satellites," seem to have exhibited some characteristics of a weapons system.[111] In October 2017, three Russian satellites, Kosmos-2519,

Kosmos-2521, and Kosmos-2523, conducted high-velocity orbital maneuvers. In January 2020, two Russian satellites, Kosmos-2542 and Kosmos-2543, performed coordinated, close-approach orbital maneuvers in the vicinity of a US military reconnaissance satellite, the KH-11. Six months later, in July 2020, the Kosmos-2543 satellite fired a high-velocity projectile into outer space.[112] Jaganath Sankaran notes that such a projectile could act as a potent ASAT weapon.[113]

Let's check how these Russian "nesting dolls" in space work. Then US Assistant Secretary of State for International Security and Nonproliferation, Christopher A. Ford, noted that once in orbit, Kosmos-2519 deployed a sub-satellite, Kosmos-2521, that displayed the ability to maneuver around another satellite in space after it launched an additional object into space, Kosmos-2523, at high relative speed of about 250 kilometers per hour, off into space, and that Kosmos-2521 demonstrated the ability to position itself near another satellite and fire a projectile.[114] Russian experts called Kosmos-2519 "a maneuvering military inspector satellite" capable of flying up to other satellites and inspecting them. Russian experts emphasized that such devices could determine the functionality of foreign spy satellites, and, if necessary, create space "fighter satellites." According to these experts, such satellites will become an important element of the Russian orbital constellation and will play the role of a deterrent in the space military race.[115]

Besides the mentioned tools, Russia has electronic warfare and laser systems in its anti-satellite arsenal.

In recent years, Russia has prioritized the use of electronic warfare (EW) systems in military operations and launched several programs for developing electronic jamming tools. Russia has a multitude of systems that can jam GPS receivers within a local area, potentially interfering with the guidance systems of unmanned aerial vehicles (UAVs), guided missiles, and precision-guided munitions. The Russian military has several types of mobile EW systems, some of which can jam specific satellite communication user terminals within tactical ranges. According to assessments, Russia can likely jam communication satellite uplinks over a wide area from fixed ground station facilities.[116] Russia has operational experience in the use of counterspace EW capabilities from its recent military campaigns in Syria and Ukraine (during the first invasion in 2014–2015 and to some extent in 2022).[117] They are also used in Russia to protect possible strategic targets.

As an example, we can focus on the GPS disruptions that Ben Gurion International Airport in Tel Aviv experienced in June 2019. The announcement by the Israel Airports Authority (IAA) followed a report by the International Federation of Air Line Pilots' Associations (IFALPA) that "many" pilots had lost satellite signals from the Global Positioning System around Tel Aviv's Ben Gurion Airport.[118] The Israeli Airline Pilots Association reported that the GPS problems were a "spoofing" attack that produced incorrect location data. It means receivers on planes sometimes reported their location as miles away from where they actually were. Israel suggested that the disruption was linked to "electronic warfare" systems that Russia used to protect its planes at the Hmeimim airbase in Syria—the military base is about 350 km (217 miles) north of Ben Gurion. Russia denied its involvement in the Israeli airport GPS jamming.[119]

However, some reports argued that Russia has a long history of involvement in GPS spoofing and jamming and that Russia was "pioneering" the technique to "protect and promote its strategic interests."[120] For instance, officials of Finland and Norway reported that pilots lost GPS navigation signals during NATO's large-scale Trident Juncture exercise near Russia's western border in 2018 and also during the previous year's Russian-Belarussian "Zapad-2017" drills.[121] Such GPS interruptions reportedly occur often in that region.[122]

Russia also used its EW capabilities in Ukraine in 2014 and 2015. It blocked drones, disabled warheads, and penetrated cellphone networks. Reportedly, some of the Russian EW systems, including those for jamming GPS (such as R-330Zh Zhitel, RB-341V Leer-3, and RB-301B Borisoglebsk-2) were deployed in Donbass and Crimea, several years before the start of the invasion in 2022.[123] In the spring of 2021, the Organization for Security and Co-operation in Europe, which was monitoring Moscow's military buildup, reported on the deployment of a large number of Russian electronic-warfare systems in Donbas, such as TORN and SB-636 Svet-KU signals-intelligence systems, R-934B Sinitsa radio-jammers, and Navodchik-2.[124] However, in the early days of the 2022 invasion, Russia's use of electronic warfare reportedly was less effective and less extensive than anticipated. This may have contributed to its failure to destroy enough Ukrainian radar and anti-aircraft units to gain air superiority. Some experts stressed that Russian commanders held back units fearing that those units would be captured. According to the AP's report, at least two were seized by early June, 2022.[125] One was a Krasukha-4, which a US Army database says is designed to jam satellite signals as well as surveillance radar and radar-guided weapons from more than 100 miles (160 kilometers) away—Russia claims 300 km.[126] The other was the more advanced Borisoglebsk-2,[127] which can jam drone guidance systems and radio-controlled land mines. Russia might have limited the use of electronic warfare early in the conflict because of concerns that its ill-trained or poorly motivated technicians might not operate it properly.[128]

Another case of the Russian 2022 invasion of Ukraine relates to Starlink's network satellites in low Earth orbit, which are designed to deliver high-speed Internet anywhere. Since the beginning of the war, SpaceX had been continuing to expand its Starlink satellite Internet network in besieged Ukraine, with a government official saying in May that about 150,000 people in the country used the service each day.[129] Reportedly, around 10,000 Starlink terminals were operational in the country. In March, SpaceX founder and CEO Elon Musk wrote on Twitter that some Starlink terminals near conflict areas were being jammed for several hours at a time but that the company's latest software update bypassed the jamming.[130] A US military official pointed to SpaceX's ability to swiftly stymie a Russian effort to jam its Starlink satellite broadband service, which was keeping Ukraine connected to the Internet. According to the official, Starlink had slung a line of code and fixed it.

Russia's EW experience in Ukraine shows how important it is to properly train the personnel assigned to carry out electromagnetic warfare operations and the degree of coordination and synchronization required for these types of operations. In April 2022, the Director of Electronic Warfare for the Office of the US Secretary of Defense said that the Pentagon expected a "much stronger" EW showing from Russia, but "cautioned that isn't to say all of Russia's efforts have failed."[131] Later, the situation changed. As Russian EW systems began to be deployed systematically, the Ukrainian military's problems such as the jamming of air-to-ground and air-to-air communications, suppressed navigation equipment, and radar knocking increased. The Russian Defense Ministry reported the use of the Palantin electronic warfare system in Ukraine. Reportedly, they are used against drones and jamming centers of cellular communications and Internet sources at Ukrainian command posts at a distance of up to 20 km. The system strikes devices pointwise, and not with a "directed beam," the ministry explained.[132] According to a RUSI report, with the concentration of effort on the Donbas, Russia set up to 10 EW complexes per 20 km of frontage. The report found that of all the UAVs Ukraine used, up until July 2022, around 90% were destroyed.[133]

Global Navigation Satellite Systems (GNSS) jamming, particularly of the US GPS network, is a specific technology and jammers are widely proliferated throughout the globe. Russia is assessed to be proficient in GPS jamming capabilities, having developed both fixed and mobile systems. The known systems are downlink jammers, which affect GPS receivers within a local area. However, according to the 2021 Global Counterspace Capabilities report, there is no known system that targets uplink jamming of the GPS satellites themselves.[134] There are reports suggesting that Russia uses jamming systems to protect fixed facilities.[135] Another category of Russian GPS jammers are mobile systems integrated within military EW units.[136]

Russia has capabilities for both downlink and uplink signal jamming of communications satellites as well.[137] For instance, R-330Zh: Zhitel is an automated jammer against the INMARSAT and IRIDIUM satellite communication systems, GSM and GPS, and was deployed during Russia's recent military campaigns.[138] For jamming of Synthetic Aperture Radar (SAR) satellites, Russia uses the Krashukha-4 mobile electronic warfare system.[139] There are reports detailing discussions on developing a new EW system called Divnomorye that will reportedly replace "Moskva-1," "Krasukha-2," and "Krasukha-4" and serve as an integrated electronic warfare system against air, space, and ground systems. In 2020, referring to "Defense Ministry sources," Izvestiya reported that the Divnomorye system was deployed to the Electronic Warfare Center of the Baltic Fleet near Kaliningrad.[140] Moreover, some reports suggest that Russia is working on space-based jamming systems and might be developing a new generation of nuclear reactors to power on-orbit jammers via a project called Ekipazh.[141]

In recent years, Russia developed other EW tools that can potentially target satellite communications, the Murmansk-BN and RB-109A Bylina EW weapon systems. The Murmansk-BN reportedly has a range of 5,000 km and can monitor activity on airwaves and intercept enemy signals with its broad jamming capability.[142] Russian officials reported about other projects currently under development such as Rudolfph, a mobile anti-satellite strike system, and Tirada-2S, a mobile system for the electronic destruction of communication satellites.[143]

In addition to these anti-satellite space weapons and ground-based EW systems, Russia also developed ground-based laser systems. Besides their dazzling or blinding optical sensors of satellites, lasers may also have the potential to physically destroy targets. The systems developed are named Kalina, Persvet, and Sokol-Eshelon (airborne system).[144] Kalina is the newest system and much of the information about it is classified; however, there is evidence to support that it has a counterspace role.[145]

Kalina is one of the three Russian laser dazzlers designed for use against satellites. Sokol-Eshelon has been under development since 2001, but it seems to have been on the verge of cancellation several times and its current status remains unclear.[146] The only system known to be operational is Peresvet.[147] In 2022, Yuri Borisov, then Russia's Deputy Prime Minister for the defense industry, stated it can "blind" all reconnaissance satellites of an adversary up to an altitude of 1,500 kilometers, thereby "disabling" them as they pass over Russian territory.[148]

According to Bart Hendrickx, a longtime researcher of the Russian space program, having designed three laser systems for similar purposes, Russia clearly attaches a great deal of importance to denying its enemies the opportunity to image its territory from space. "Among the targets of these systems could not only be government-owned reconnaissance satellites but also the numerous commercial optical imaging satellites that are currently in orbit," he stressed.[149] However, Yuri Borisov said that Russia is working on a more powerful laser system capable of physically destroying targets. He also mentioned Zadira, which is a mobile laser system for shooting down drones.[150] Later, he claimed that Zadira was being used by Russian forces in Ukraine, but that cannot be independently verified.[151]

## Russia's contemporary Afghan policy

Since the 19th century, Russia has been involved in Afghanistan. During the Great Game, a tense rivalry existed between the Russian and British Empires in Afghanistan and Central Asia. This continued through to the late 1900s as Britain sought to influence or control Central Asia to buffer British India while Russia sought to expand its territory toward India. Together with Persia and Tibet, Afghanistan was one of the front lines between these two rivals.[152] A similar rivalry developed between the Soviet Union and the United States during the Cold War and resulted in the Soviet military intervention in Afghanistan.

Despite the role of the Soviet Union in economic and educational development in Afghanistan, the military intervention of 1979–1989 dramatically affected Russia's image among the Afghan elite and public. This legacy plays against the perceived reliability of Russia to this day. On the other hand, casualties (the total human losses of the Soviet armed forces, together with the border and internal troops, amounted to 15,051 people[153]) and the legacy of an unsuccessful military intervention prevents the Russian political and military elite from trying to stage any similar involvement in Afghanistan. Moreover, one could not expect the Russian public to support such a military adventure.

Following the breakup of the Soviet Union, Moscow noticeably altered its involvement in Afghanistan. Following a complicated partnership, that lasted several years, with the United States since the mid-2010s Russia has been trying to gain a leading role in the Afghanistan settlement process and continue its preparation for a strong post-American presence there. Moscow's Afghan policy after 2014 has reflected the changes and corrections of Russia's foreign and security policy priorities, and is generally influenced by developments in the international system.

Since the early 1990s, Russia's Afghanistan policy has gone in spirals and zigzags. The end of the 2000s however, saw Russia's approaches to Afghanistan—previously balanced along intra-Afghan lines "north-south" and "north-national level"—began to gradually straighten.[154] The 2010s saw Russia's Afghan policy tend toward regionalization and since 2014 Moscow has been actively involved in peace negotiations and intensified their efforts in promoting their own interests within the peace settlement process. Since that time, Moscow has considered the Taliban as an internal actor with which it can negotiate. Following the US troop withdrawal and the Taliban takeover in 2021, Russia's opportunities and burdens increased in the region.

### *Moscow's interests, challenges, and strategic objectives in Afghanistan and the region*

Russia's interests in Afghanistan center on ensuring security and preventing the destabilization of the Afghan-Central Asian border area. Three of these Central Asia countries—Tajikistan, Kyrgyzstan, and Kazakhstan—are Russian allies within the framework of the Collective Security Treaty Organization (CSTO) and the Eurasian Economic Union. An additional goal is to keep Afghanistan a neutral state which cannot be used as a launching pad against Russia. Afghanistan's geographic location, already considered by China, India, Iran, and Pakistan as a site for several transport and energy projects, is attractive to Russia as well as it looks to play a major role in Eurasia. Although Russia's current economic participation is weak, it does try to ensure its economic interests in Afghanistan for whenever the situation stabilizes.[155] It should be noted that although a stable Afghanistan would align with Russia's interests, Moscow does not have vital interests (economic or otherwise) in the country.[156]

The export of radical ideology, terrorism, and narcotics, the penetration of Afghan military groups to Central Asia and the destabilization of those countries, the strengthening of the American military presence in Afghanistan, and its influences over the Central Asian states were perceived by the Russian leadership as the main threats emanating from Afghanistan over the past few years. However, while the export of terrorism and the penetration of military groups could have been perceived as real concerns previously, their current threat has been exaggerated.

It is possible to argue that Russia currently pursues two main strategic objectives in Afghanistan: to keep its influences in the region and prevent the United States from strengthening its own presence following their troop withdrawal. And more importantly, to challenge US power projection in Central Asia.

It should be noted that Russian resources in Afghanistan are quite limited. While Russia has historically had economic and cultural relations with the Central Asian countries and currently participates in alliances with some of them, there are several complicated issues limiting Moscow's resources and influence. The political leadership in these countries tries to balance between Russia, the United States, and China. The Russian military presence is relatively small and unable to project power across the whole region.[157]

Although Russia participates in controlling the Tajik-Afghan border, China's involvement has increased in recent years. A similar situation has also developed with Kyrgyzstan. Afghanistan's borders with Uzbekistan and Turkmenistan are controlled by those countries, and they are not bound by any allied obligations to Russia. However, there have been reports stating that Russia provides military advisors, and in some cases, even a small number of troops for the Turkmen border guards.[158] Moreover, on November 9, 2020, an agreement with Turkmenistan on security cooperation was ratified.[159] Although Russia's central and southern military districts have the capability to defeat challenges emanating from Afghanistan, they have troop mobility and deployment issues due to underdeveloped railway lines. Despite these difficulties, several Russian experts refuse to accept even the possibility that radical groups based on Afghanistan have the capability to penetrate Central Asia any time in the foreseeable future.[160]

However, Moscow does have opportunities to influence regional security via targeted diplomacy within Afghanistan and with regional powers, especially China, India, Iran, and Pakistan; Russian military bases in Tajikistan and Kyrgyzstan; regional institutions such as the CSTO (the Collective Rapid Reaction Forces of the CSTO totals some 18,000 servicemen and is the main instrument in emergency situations) and the Shanghai Cooperation Organization (SCO).[161]

*Diplomacy as Moscow's main tool in Afghanistan?*

Even though Moscow considered the permanent military bases of the United States in Afghanistan a threat to its interests in that region, it was at the same time concerned with what would happen if American troops left entirely. Moscow understood that if this occurred, Russia would need to share the burden of maintaining stability in Afghanistan. Russia did not and does not want a direct military presence there.

Russia remains more influentially limited in Afghanistan than any of the other regional powers (Pakistan, Iran, China, and India). Considering their historical experience, the understanding of the economic and military burdens of any direct military involvement, and their relative inability to influence internal groups, Moscow has, since the early 2010s, decided to seek diplomatic solutions to influence developments in Afghanistan. In doing so, they have turned themselves into one of the main actors in the peace process.

In the Moscow-initiated peace formats, which are out of the United States' control, Russia plays a leading role. In two of these formats, the Moscow format of regional peace consultations on Afghanistan and the informal inter-Afghan dialogue in Moscow, Russia acts either as the main organizer or as host and sponsor. A third format with the participation of Moscow is a joint initiative, the China-Russia-US,[162] that grew out of the US-Russian dialogue on Afghanistan, which in the summer of 2019 expanded to include Pakistan.[163] During this time, Moscow continued its dialogue with Washington and in 2019–2021, the US and Russian special envoys for Afghanistan met regularly.[164] Moscow also uses other diplomatic initiatives, such as the SCO-Afghanistan Contact Group, which was revived on October 11, 2017 when the deputy foreign ministers met in Moscow.[165]

Russia uses the Moscow format as a platform for consultations at the Eurasian level. It began in December 2016 in the form of trilateral consultations between Russia, China, and Pakistan.[166] On 14 April 2017, a third round was held, and the formally referred to "consultations" were upgraded to the "Moscow conference on the Afghan settlement." Diplomats from 11 states (Russia, Afghanistan, the regional powers—Pakistan, Iraq, China and India, as well as all five Central Asian countries) attended. The Moscow format—for the first time at a regional level—called on the Taliban to negotiate with the Afghan government. Delegations of the Taliban and the Afghan High Peace Council took part in the next meeting of the Moscow format in November 2018.[167]

Moscow officially supported negotiations between the United States and the Taliban while simultaneously being skeptical of any US-led peace initiative.[168] For instance, former Afghan President Ashraf Ghani initiated peace talks with the Taliban without preconditions in February 2018. These were quite skeptically received by Zamir Kabulov, Putin's envoy on Afghanistan.[169] According to Kabulov, Russia considered the Moscow format as the optimal platform for promoting national reconciliation in Afghanistan, since other initiatives did not look to involve the Taliban in the talks.[170] In 2020, Secretary Pompeo's visit to Central Asia and the new US Central Asia Strategy were negatively perceived by Moscow.[171] Moscow had no doubt that the United States plan was aimed at tearing the Central Asian states away from Russia and China by involving them directly in US-sponsored regional security and energy projects.[172]

The informal inter-Afghan dialog in Moscow was organized by Russia under the auspices of Afghan diaspora organizations in Russia. In February 2019, leaders of almost all the major movements and factions of the former Afghan Northern Alliance, various mujahedeen groups, and the Taliban met in Moscow to discuss the prospects for peace in Afghanistan.[173] These happened despite the fact that the Taliban's continued inclusion on Russia's official list of designated terrorist organizations.[174] The inter-Afghan dialogue in Moscow helped stress Russia's image as a neutral broker without a military presence and without preference toward any internal group in Afghanistan.

Most importantly, Russia organized a parallel dialog platform to Western-led initiatives which was intended to compete with the negotiation process launched by the United States.[175]

Ekaterina Stepanova notes that Russia pursues two interrelated strategies regarding negotiations over the settlement of the Afghan conflict.[176] The first strategy is the regionalization of Russian policy on Afghanistan aimed at intensifying dialog, coordination, and interaction with the main regional powers (Iran, China, India, and Pakistan). She argues that the regionalization of Russia's Afghan policy started long before 2014 and was a reaction to significant shifts at the regional level, including the growing role of those four countries in regional politics and security and their expanding influence on the situation in Afghanistan. She stresses that the decreasing presence of the United States and NATO by the mid-2010s, and the gradual decline of Western influence in the region, further contributed to strengthening the regionalization of Russian politics. The second strategy focuses on Russia's turn toward a more active diplomatic support for a negotiated Afghan settlement. Russia's foreign policy leadership gradually came to understand that none of the challenges to Russia and its allies' security emanating from Afghanistan could be dealt with so long as "the armed confrontation between Kabul/US/NATO and the Taliban, continued and escalated."[177] She notes that coming to an understanding of this reality became the main impetus for Moscow's policy shift toward favoring active diplomatic efforts to find a peaceful solution to the Afghan problem.[178]

In this regard, it should be noted that Russia's main goal in conducting parallel formats to the United States was to exert influence over the internal and external negotiations on Afghanistan, and that this happened amid increasing confrontations between Russia and the United States. It is possible to argue that Russia used the regionalization of international negotiations and Moscow-led intra-Afghan negotiations with the aim of conducting parallel negotiations to the US-led peace formats. With this approach, Moscow hopes to gain a leading role in the negotiations on Afghanistan and promote their own interests. By regionalizing the Afghan peace settlement, Russia might hope to handle regional issues without the involvement of NATO or the United States.

### *Complicated relations with the Taliban*

Moscow's attitudes toward the Taliban went from being an officially forbidden terrorist organization to seeing them as one of the important internal actors of the Afghan peace settlement.

According to Russian researcher Arkady Dubnov, contacts between Moscow and the Taliban existed since the 1990s. Attempts by the Taliban in the 90s to communicate with Moscow led to a single, closed meeting of Russian diplomats with Mullah Omar's representative in Ashgabat.[179] Even before the overthrow of the Taliban regime, Moscow was actively involved in the search for a future Afghan government, proposing to form a coalition government with the participation of all political and ethnic groups of the Afghan population. The goal of Russia's foreign policy was, as President Putin said in October 2001, that the new Afghan government "must be friendly towards its neighbors, including the Russian Federation."[180] At the same time, he categorically rejected the possibility of representation by moderate Taliban members participating in such a government (Ibid.). The recognition of the independence of the Chechen Republic (Ichkeria) by the Taliban in January 2000 and the opening of the Chechen embassy in Kabul further tightened Russia's position against this organization.[181]

However, by 2009, there was information in the Russian media that Russia was seeking to establish relations with some Taliban groups in Afghanistan. There were even calls from Russian experts about the importance of improving relations, not solely with government representatives but also with various Pashtun groups.[182] Additionally, a group of Afghans suspected of having ties with the Taliban took part in the Russian-Afghan Forum in Moscow.[183]

Initially, Moscow's main goal regarding its relations with the Taliban was to use its moderate groups against organizations such as Al-Qaeda and then ISIL or the Islamic State–Khorasan Province (ISKP) in Afghanistan. Taking advantage of the split between the Taliban militants that arose in the middle of 2015, following the news of Mullah Omar's death, Moscow wanted to partner with the Taliban group most hostile toward ISIL.[184] Moscow seemed to decide that there was little chance of the United States achieving anything remotely close to stability in Afghanistan, and that the Taliban were more than likely going to be a dominant force for the foreseeable future. The continued deterioration of relations between Russia and the United States after 2014 also influenced Moscow's Afghan policy in general and its relations with the Taliban in particular.

In early 2018, the head of US forces in Afghanistan, General John Nicholson stated that Russia was supporting and even supplying arms to the Taliban, but he could not say in what quantity.[185] Russia denied this, as it did the allegations regarding Taliban bounties for killed US troops.[186] In his commentary General Nicholson wrote that Russian assistance was calibrated.[187] Artemy M. Kalinovsky explained that Moscow's decision to open a channel with the Taliban, and ultimately supply the group with arms, reflected a desire to be on good terms with whoever ruled the country.[188]

*After August 2021*

Moscow has been slow in recognizing the Taliban-led government after the Taliban takeover in August 2021. Moreover, Russia's approaches on developments in Afghanistan's Panjshir province should be noted. There were reports that Tajikistan supports the Panjshir Valley.[189] Most probably, Dushanbe agreed on this with Moscow. It can also be a sign of Moscow's maneuverings between Afghan internal forces after August 2021. Such a dichotomy could also be explained by the frictions and preferences of different approaches between the Ministry of Foreign Affairs and the security institutions.

However, amid Russia's invasion of Ukraine and the real possibility of a global grain crisis, the Russian Foreign Ministry mentioned the possibility of recognizing the Taliban government in June 2022. The Special Representative of the Russian President for Afghanistan stated that the Taliban does not pose a threat to Central Asia, and it has well-established political and diplomatic relations with, at least, Uzbekistan and Turkmenistan.[190] These can be seen as signs of Moscow's decreasing uncertainties regarding perspective relations with the Taliban government.

Russia's cooperation with the regional states on Afghanistan and how it can maneuver between them, is also another interesting case. For instance, despite cooperation with China, it seems Moscow also wants to continue engagement with India on Afghanistan.[191] Since the 2010s, there have been several changes in Russia's approaches toward the United States, Pakistan, Iran, China, India, Saudi Arabia, Afghan internal actors, and the Taliban. Former enemies are current partners or former partners now lack importance and their place easily changed depending on Russia's given interests at a particular moment. Using any contradiction between partners and adversaries is the most important approach. And using these contradictions between the involved external and internal parties, with the aim of achieving its own goals in the region, is the main pillar of Russia's contemporary Afghan policy.

## Summary

After reviewing these three cases of Russia's external security and foreign policy, we can conclude that their similarities and differences depend on the given context, Russia's real and perceived opportunities, and Russia's willingness and ability to act.

Despite their shortcomings in the war, Western sanctions and the worsening economic prospects of Russia, it is likely that Putin and the elites will continue their offensive in Ukraine. Any predictions that Russia's worsening economic situation will push the Russian people into the streets and spark a massive protest movement against the Kremlin's current security policy in Ukraine have not been borne out. Several Russian experts and various public surveys signal a continuation of the mass obedience or acceptance of the current realities by a majority of the Russian people. This is driven both by a fear of punishment from the security institutions and the superpowered nostalgia being offered by the state's propaganda. Moreover, having such tight security controls over society lets the Kremlin continue its external security adventures including, and primarily, in Ukraine. Even if a truce between Ukraine and Russia is achieved, it is unlikely to be a permanent one.

Regarding the Russian military's performance during the 2022 invasion of Ukraine, it must be stressed that Russia gained relative success using its war of attrition during the second phase but relatively little when using its blitzkrieg strategy in the first phase. As discussed in the first chapter, attrition is one of the main pillars of asymmetric warfare. Ukraine used asymmetric approaches during the first phase and succeeded to some extent, whereas when Russia turned from blitzkrieg to attrition it relatively succeeded. However, the increase of Western armaments to Ukraine and the exhausting of Russian forces helped Ukraine advance by the end of the summer. Current developments signal a long war of attrition ahead, the outcome of which will mainly depend on the Ukrainian society and military's resistance and whether the West continues to increase its supply of weapons to Ukraine or instead tries to influence Kyiv to make the required concessions to Russia. Another possible end to the war may arise from internal developments in Russia, such as the toppling of Putin. However, this is a significantly less likely scenario.

Although a prolonged war was never in Russia's interests, it is also a concern for the West which militarily and financially supports Ukraine, and this may be one of the factors for Moscow's attrition approach. An axiom in democratic states says that governments should mainly obey public demands and sending huge amounts of financial support to another country in addition to increasing prices of energy, due to the sanctions placed on Russia, could create problems for Western governments. This is likely one of Moscow's calculations. Moreover, the blocking of the Ukrainian ports in the Black Sea which Ukraine used prior to the war as the main route for its agricultural exports, including grain, must be considered one of the tools of Moscow's non-conventional warfare strategy. Moscow seems willing to threaten the wider world's stability to achieve its goals, specifically a softening of sanctions or Kyiv's acceptance of peace on Moscow's terms.

As of this moment, it is difficult to say whether this was always Russia's plan B or if it was decided by the military and political leadership during the war based on lessons from earlier failures. However, it happened, the current state of Russia's military capabilities, its economy, and its weaknesses demands that Russian external security policy uses asymmetric strategies when it faces a closely matched adversary.

Based on developments in the Russian anti-satellite program, it is possible to see Russia's asymmetric approaches there as well. Facing the technologically sophisticated and high-cost programs of its adversaries, Russia tries to use "asymmetric responses" as the Soviet Union once tried to do in the early 1980s. To challenge its main adversary's military capabilities in space, such as its satellite surveillance systems, Russia sought to develop its anti-satellite capabilities to deny its enemies any opportunity to monitor its territory from space. Amid the sanctions and economic war with the West, Russia may potentially use its anti-satellite capabilities to challenge the commercial satellites of "non-friendly states."

Since 1989, Russia's Afghan policy has undergone several changes. Currently, it reflects Russia's traditional interests, such as maintaining its influence and preventing US military bases in the region, and its temporary interests, challenging the United States amid a worsening of relations between Moscow and Washington. Russia's intensified diplomatic efforts help Moscow not only prevent it from being on the sideline of any Afghan settlement but also to maintain its influence in Afghanistan and Central Asia, or at least this was true until their 2022 intervention in Ukraine. Their diplomatic efforts greatly contributed to the resumption of its dialog with the United States on Afghanistan despite the ongoing crisis in Russian-American relations. One of the unique opportunities for Russia in these negotiations is that amid the deterioration of relations between the United States, China, and Iran, Moscow has strategic relations with Beijing and Tehran.

Moreover, to engage in close cooperation with the regional powers, such as China, India, Pakistan, and Iran, Moscow tries to challenge US leadership in the peace settlement and limit its influence in Afghanistan and Central Asia. Up until now, Russia's contemporary Afghan policy can be seen as one of the few success stories of their contemporary foreign and external security policies.

However, it appears that the end of the contemporary "Great game" in that region is not on the horizon. Russia's behavior toward the former Soviet republics, especially its invasion of Ukraine, has only increased the concerns of the Central Asian elites and pushes them to look for further balancing. A demand for other great powers with which to balance is especially acute when the US presence in the region is diminishing. Therefore, China is currently, and likely for the foreseeable future, the main regional power through which to balance, and even potentially deter, Russian pressure and possible aggression. Such a situation may even result in conflicts of interest between Russia and China in the region, including in Afghanistan.

All three cases reflect several aspects of Russia's contemporary external security policy and emphasize its main facet, which is to use all possible and affordable approaches. As we see with the war in Ukraine and the anti-satellite program, using asymmetric strategies and approaches is the most important issue of Russia's security policy. But in the case of its strategy regarding Afghanistan, Russia mainly relies on diplomacy but is also supported by its security policy to some extent. However, while Moscow uses several approaches regarding Afghanistan, it is not possible to claim that these are asymmetric or that Russia has developed an entirely new approach in its contemporary Afghanistan policy.

**Notes**

1 Putin, Vladimir (2021a) "Ob istoricheskom yedinstve russkikh i ukraintsev" July 12, Kremlin.ru, http://kremlin.ru/events/president/news/66181.
2 Gabuyev, Aleksandr and Sidorenko, Sergey (2014) "Mnogoglavyy orel – Kto vliyal na ukrainskuyu politiku Kremlya", Vlast', № 8, 3 March, p. 9, https://www.kommersant.ru/doc/2416461?utm_source=pocket_mylist.
3 Gabuyev, Aleksandr and Sidorenko, Sergey (2014) "Mnogoglavyy orel – Kto vliyal na ukrainskuyu politiku Kremlya" …
4 Lieven, Anatol (2022a) "Inside Putin's circle — the real Russian elite", March 11, *The Financial Times*, https://www.ft.com/content/503fb110-f91e-4bed-b6dc-0d09582dd007?utm_source=pocket_mylist&fbclid=IwAR3m0epCqtnsQtAbma3GPtCwo8XB5rbm0DxBoDOvQ7F5cUlR38c-bb3Rjr4.
5 Professor Mearsheimer noted about this in several of his public speeches. For instance, "The causes and consequences of the Ukraine war – A lecture by John J. Mearsheimer", *The Robert Schuman Centre for Advanced Studies*, streamed on YouTube.com on June 16, 2022, https://www.youtube.com/watch?v=qciVozNtCDM.
6 Charap, Samuel, et al. (2021) "Russia's Military Interventions-Patterns, Drivers, and Signposts", *RAND Corporation*, DOI: 10.7249/RR-A444-3.
7 Harris, Shane, Karen DeYoung, Isabelle Khurshudyan, Ashley Parker and Liz Sly (2022) "Road to war: US struggled to convince allies, and Zelensky, of risk of invasion", The Washington Post, August 16 https://www.washingtonpost.com/national-security/interactive/2022/ukraine-road-to-war/?itid=ap_shaneharris.
8 Harris, Shane, Karen DeYoung, Isabelle Khurshudyan, Ashley Parker and Liz Sly (2022) "Road to war: US struggled to convince allies, and Zelensky, of risk of invasion" …
9 Khodarenok, Mikhail (2022) "Prognozy krovozhadnykh politologov", *Nezavisimoe Voennoe Obozrenie – Nezavisimoya Gazeta*, https://nvo.ng.ru/realty/2022-02-03/3_1175_donbass.html.
10 Gorenburg, Dmitry and Kofman, Michael (2022) "Here's what we know about Russia's military buildup near Ukraine", January 15, *The Washington Post*, https://www.washingtonpost.com/politics/2022/01/15/heres-what-we-know-about-russias-military-buildup-near-ukraine/.
11 Schwirtz, Michael and Reinhard, Scott (2022) "How Russia's Military Is Currently Positioned", The New York Times, January 7, https://www.nytimes.com/interactive/2022/01/07/world/europe/ukraine-maps.html.
12 Putin, Vladimir (2021b) "Expanded Meeting of the Defence Ministry Board", December 21, Kremlin.ru, http://en.kremlin.ru/events/president/news/67402.
13 Russian large-scale multidomain operation designed to encompasses multiple Military Districts (MDs) across the country. Since 2016 Russia has practised it in large exercises, They have involved multiple MDs and appear to have happened across many "strategic

directions" or large fronts simultaneously. For more about the Russian multidomain operations see: Samuel Charap, et al. (2021) "Russian Grand Strategy- Rhetoric and Reality", RAND Cooperation, pp. 101–104, https://www.rand.org/pubs/research_reports/RR4238.html.
14 Massicot, Dara (2022) "Ukraine Needs Help Surviving Airstrikes, Not Just Killing Tanks", *Defence One*, January 19, https://www.defenseone.com/ideas/2022/01/ukraine-needs-help-surviving-airstrikes-not-just-killing-tanks/360898/.
15 Visual Storytelling Team (2022) "How Russia's mistakes and Ukrainian resistance altered Putin's war", *The Financial Times*, March 18, https://ig.ft.com/russias-war-in-ukraine-mapped/?utm_source=pocket_mylist.
16 The Economist (2022a) "An interview with General Valery Zaluzhny, head of Ukraine's armed forces", December 15, https://www.economist.com/zaluzhny-transcript.
17 For more detail about how Ukrainians used asymmetric approaches see: Judah, Tim(2022) "How Kyiv was saved by Ukrainian ingenuity as well as Russian blunders", *The Financial Times*, April 10, https://www.ft.com/content/e87fdc60-0d5e-4d39-93c6-7cfd22f770e8?sharetype=blocked&fbclid=IwAR3vbE3D6dR1AU-SXp9rVXLm0PcssarcR5udGd-SVKw-zYq7ybFXxO9kQkw and Kirilenko, Ol'ga (2022) "Kak Sumshchina pervoy vstretila, a potom ostanovila vraga po doroge na Kiyev", Ukrainska Pravda, April 16, https://www.pravda.com.ua/rus/articles/2022/04/16/7339908/, see also Nazarov, Nikolay(2022) "Ukraine's Resilience: Theory meets practice", ICDS, May, https://lmc.icds.ee/ukraines-resilience-theory-meets-practice/?fbclid=IwAR38Tth5bxnMgv7aFHQiQhWLWWTSAtnw7uQ3X-r5Lrn-zcE90WGREJej62I.
18 The Economist (2022b) "Anyone who underestimates Russia is headed for defeat", December 15, https://www.economist.com/syrsky-interview.
19 Herszenhorn, David M. and Mcleary, Paul (2022) "Ukraine's 'iron general' is a hero, but he's no star", *Politico*, April 8, https://www.politico.com/news/2022/04/08/ukraines-iron-general-zaluzhnyy-00023901.
20 Armstrong, Benjamin (2022) "The Russo-Ukrainian War at Sea: Retrospect and Prospect", *War On The Rocks,* April 21, https://warontherocks.com/2022/04/THE-RUSSO-UKRAINIAN-WAR-AT-SEA-RETROSPECT-AND-PROSPECT/.
21 Armstrong, Benjamin F. (2019) *Small Boats and Daring Men: Maritime Raiding, Irregular Warfare, and the Early American Navy,* University of Oklahoma Press.
22 Kashin, Vasilii (2022) "Pervaya bol'shaya voyna XXI veka", June 22, *Rossiya v Global'noy Politike,* https://globalaffairs.ru/articles/pervaya-bolshaya-vojna-xxi-veka/.
23 Kashin, Vasilii (2022) "Pervaya bol'shaya voyna XXI veka" …
24 Kashin, Vasilii (2022) "Pervaya bol'shaya voyna XXI veka" …
25 Kofman, Michael and Lee, Rob (2022) "Not built for purpose: the Russian military's ill-fated force design", *War on The Rocks*, June 2, https://warontherocks.com/2022/06/not-built-for-purpose-the-russian-militarys-ill-fated-force-design/.
26 Ibid.
27 Interfax (2022a) "Rossiya sozdast 12 novykh voinskikh chastey v ZVO iz-za narastaniya ugroz u granits", May 20, https://www.interfax.ru/world/841930.
28 Lee, Rob (2022) "The tank is not obsolete, and other observations about the future of combat", *War On The Rocks,* September 6, https://warontherocks.com/2022/09/the-tank-is-not-obsolete-and-other-observations-about-the-future-of-combat/.
29 Grau, Lester W and Bartles, Charles K (2022) "Getting to Know the Russian Battalion Tactical Group", *RUSI*, April 14, https://rusi.org/explore-our-research/publications/commentary/getting-know-russian-battalion-tactical-group.
30 Sosnitskiy, Vladimir (2021) "Na yuzhnykh rubezhakh strany: sovershaya glubokiye reydy, okhvaty i obkhody", *Zvezda-Ezhenedelnik*, February 11, https://zvezdaweekly.ru/news/2021291350-Qy88G.html.
31 Grau, Lester W and Bartles, Charles K (2022) …
32 TASS (2016) "Kolichestvo batal'onnykh takticheskikh grupp v rossiyskoy armii vozrastet pochti vdvoye", September 14, https://tass.ru/armiya-i-opk/3620165.

33 TASS (2021) "Shoygu zayavil, chto v armii Rossii naschityvayetsya 168 batal'onno-takticheskikh grupp", August 10, https://tass.ru/armiya-i-opk/12099255.
34 Kofman, Michael and Lee, Rob (2022) "Not built for purpose: the Russian military's ill-fated force design", *War on The Rocks*, June 2, https://warontherocks.com/2022/06/not-built-for-purpose-the-russian-militarys-ill-fated-force-design/.
35 Ibid.
36 Grau, Lester W and Bartles, Charles K (2016) "Russian Way of War", Report, *Foreign Military Studies Office*, https://www.armyupress.army.mil/portals/7/hot%20spots/documents/russia/2017-07-the-russian-way-of-war-grau-bartles.pdf.
37 Johnson, David E. (2022) "This is What the Russians Do", *Lawfire*, May 3, https://sites.duke.edu/lawfire/2022/05/03/dr-dave-johnsons-warning-on-brute-force-in-the-ukraine-this-is-what-the-russians-do/.
38 Khurshudyan, Isabelle and Sonne, Paul (2022) "Russia targeted Ukrainian ammunition to weaken Kyiv on the battlefield", *The Washington Post*, June 24, https://www.washingtonpost.com/world/2022/06/24/ukraine-ammunition-russian-sabotage-artillery/.
39 Current Time (2022) "Bitva za Donbass", *YouTube*, minutes: 9:40-16:38, streamed live on May 24, https://www.youtube.com/watch?v=tWD43kwIx1A.
40 Skorobogatyy, Pëtr (2022) "Ukraina: gladiatorskiye boi", PRISP, August 4, 2022, http://www.prisp.ru/analitics/11005-skorobogatiy-ukraina-gladiatorskie-boi-0408.
41 Khodarenok, Mikhail (2022) "Prognozy krovozhadnykh politologov", *Nezavisimoe Voennoe Obozrenie – Nezavisimoya Gazeta*, https://nvo.ng.ru/realty/2022-02-03/3_1175_donbass.html.
42 Ryan, Mick (2022) "Why HIMARS may shift the battlefield balance in Ukraine", The Sydney Morning Herald, July 12, https://www.smh.com.au/world/europe/why-himars-may-shift-the-battlefield-balance-in-ukraine-20220712-p5b0x0.html.
43 Ibid.
44 Skorobogatyy, Pëtr (2022) "Ukraina: gladiatorskiye boi", *PRISP*, August 4, 2022, http://www.prisp.ru/analitics/11005-skorobogatiy-ukraina-gladiatorskie-boi-0408.
45 Ibid.
46 Ibid.
47 Ibid.
48 Trofimov, Yaroslav and Dion Nissenbaum (2022) "Russia's Use of Iranian Kamikaze Drones Creates New Dangers for Ukrainian Troops", *WSJ*, September 17, https://www.wsj.com/articles/russias-use-of-iranian-kamikaze-drones-creates-new-dangers-for-ukrainian-troops-11663415140; Georgy, Michael (2022) "Iran agrees to ship missiles, more drones to Russia", *Reuters*, October 18, https://www.reuters.com/world/exclusive-iran-agrees-ship-missiles-more-drones-russia-defying-west-sources-2022-10-18/.
49 Radio Svoboda (2022) "Chelovek-armageddon. Novyy komanduyushchiy rossiyskim vtorzheniyem", October 10, https://www.svoboda.org/a/chelovek-armageddon-novyy-komanduyuschiy-rossiysim-vtorzheniem/32073403.htm.
50 Kyiv School of Economics (2023) "The total amount of damage caused to Ukraine's infrastructure due to the war has increased to almost $138 billion", January 24, https://kse.ua/about-the-school/news/the-total-amount-of-damage-caused-to-ukraine-s-infrastructure-due-to-the-war-has-increased-to-almost-138-billion/.
51 Gressel, Gustav (2022) "Mob unhappy: Why Russia is unlikely to emerge victorious in Ukraine", *ECFR*, October 21, https://ecfr.eu/article/mob-unhappy-why-russia-is-unlikely-to-emerge-victorious-in-ukraine/.
52 The Economist (2022b) "Anyone who underestimates Russia is headed for defeat", December 15, https://www.economist.com/syrsky-interview.
53 Defense Express (2022) "What Kind of Weapon Could Hit the Engels Airfield In Saratov Oblast And an Airport In Ryazan Oblast", December 5, https://en.defence-ua.com/analysis/what_kind_of_weapon_could_hit_the_engels_airfield_in_saratov_oblast_and_an_airport_in_ryazan_oblast-5056.html.

54 Sabbagh, Dan (2022) "Ukrainians use phone app to spot deadly Russian drone attacks", The Guardian, October 29, https://www.theguardian.com/world/2022/oct/29/ukraine-phone-app-russia-drone-attacks-eppo.
55 Kofman, Michael (2022) "The Russo-Ukrainian war ten months in: taking stock", *Riddle*, December 28, https://ridl.io/the-russo-ukrainian-war-ten-months-in-taking-stock/.
56 Ministerstvo oborony Rossiyskoy Federatsii (2022) "V Moskve pod rukovodstvom Verkhovnogo Glavnokomanduyushchego Vooruzhennymi Silami Vladimira Putina proshlo rasshirennoye zasedaniye Kollegii Minoborony Rossii", December 21, https://function.mil.ru/news_page/country/more.htm?id=12449212@egNews.
57 Grobman, Yekaterina and Anastasiya Mayyer (2022) "Sovet voyennogo vremeni: v chem unikal'nost' novogo organa, kotoryy vozglavil", *Vedomosti*, October 21, https://www.vedomosti.ru/politics/articles/2022/10/21/946817-sovet-voennogo-vremeni.
58 Duma.gov.ru (2022) Russia's draft budget for 2023–2025, September 27, https://sozd.duma.gov.ru/bill/201614-8; See explanation by Kluge, Janis (2022), on Twitter, September 28, https://twitter.com/jakluge/status/1575187748520009728?s=20&t=WHT52JKVw_Y2HApu7njcxg.
59 KSE Agrocenter (2022) "The total war damages in Ukraine's agriculture reached $4.3 billion", June 15, https://kse.ua/about-the-school/news/the-total-war-damages-in-ukraine-s-agriculture-reached-4-3-billion-kse-agrocenter/.
60 Centre for Food and Land Use Research (2022) "Agricultural War Losses Review Ukraine. Rapid Loss Assessment", *Kyiv School of Economics,* June 9, p. 2, https://minagro.gov.ua/storage/app/sites/1/uploaded-files/Losses_report_issue1.pdf.
61 Ibid., p. 4.
62 Ibid.
63 Mauldin, William (2022) "U.N. Seeks to Ease Russian Blockade of Ukraine Grain Shipping to Avert Food Shortages", *The Wall Street Journal*, May 16, https://www.wsj.com/articles/u-n-seeks-to-ease-russian-blockade-of-ukraine-grain-shipping-to-avert-food-shortages-11652717161?mod=Searchresults_pos1&page=1.
64 Kolganova, Viktoriya (2022) "Putin nazval pyat' sposobov vyvoza zerna iz Ukrainy", *Kommersant*, June 3, https://www.kommersant.ru/doc/5391307.
65 President of Ukraine (2022) "Ukraine is negotiating with a number of countries on the export of grain from ports, but weapons remain the main guarantor in this matter", June 6, 8, https://www.president.gov.ua/en/news/ukrayina-vede-peregovori-z-nizkoyu-derzhav-shodo-vivezennya-75653.
66 Fylyppov, Sanyo and Lister, Tim (2022) "EU foreign policy chief condemns Russian missile strike on Ukrainian grain terminal", *CNN,* June 6, https://edition.cnn.com/europe/live-news/russia-ukraine-war-news-06-06-22/h_808efd3980120d4391454b32863490d4.
67 TRT Haber (2022) "Tahıl krizinin çözümü için 'kırmızı hat' kuruldu", June 15, https://www.trthaber.com/haber/gundem/tahil-krizinin-cozumu-icin-kirmizi-hat-kuruldu-688087.html?utm_source=pocket_mylist.
68 Saul, Jonathan (2022) "Analysis: The sea mines floating between Ukraine's grain stocks and the world", *Reuters,* June 10, https://www.reuters.com/markets/commodities/sea-mines-floating-between-ukraines-grain-stocks-world-2022-06-10/.
69 Reuters (2022) "Russia has stolen 600,000 tonnes of grain, Ukrainian producers say", June 8, https://www.reuters.com/article/ukraine-crisis-grain-theft-idAFL1N2XV0XT.
70 Walsh, Declan and Hopkins, Valerie (2022) "Russia Seeks Buyers for Plundered Ukraine Grain, US Warns", *The New York Times,* June 5, https://www.nytimes.com/2022/06/05/world/africa/ukraine-grain-russia-sales.html.
71 Askerova, Kseniya (2022) "Peskov: Rossiya ne krala nikakogo zerna", *Kommersant*, June 23, https://www.kommersant.ru/doc/5424353.
72 Zakharov, Andrey and Korenyuk, Mariya (2022) "Bylo ukrainskoye, stalo russkoye". *BBC Russian*, June 20, https://www.bbc.com/russian/news-61763999.

73 Beake, Nick, Maria Korenyuk and Reality Check team(2022) "Tracking where Russia is taking Ukraine's stolen grain", *BBC News,* June 27, https://www.bbc.com/news/61790625.
74 Interfax (2022b) "Zerno iz Zaporozh'ya nachali postavlyat' v strany Blizhnego Vostoka", June 8, https://www.interfax.ru/business/845268.
75 RIA Novosti (2022) "V Zaporozh'ye zayavili o natsionalizatsii ukrainskogo zerna v regione", June 15, https://ria.ru/20220615/zerno-1795445513.html.
76 Peter, Laurence (2022) "Is Russia exporting grain from Ukraine?", *BBC News,* June 8, https://www.bbc.com/news/world-europe-61736179.
77 Beake and Et. All (2022) "Tracking where Russia is taking Ukraine's stolen grain" …
78 Kremlin (2022) "Plenarnoye zasedaniye Peterburgskogo mezhdunarodnogo ekonomicheskogo foruma", June 17, http://kremlin.ru/events/president/transcripts/68669.
79 Ibid.
80 Anadolu Agency (2022) "Türkiye, UN, Russia, Ukraine sign deal to resume grain exports", July 22, https://www.aa.com.tr/en/russia-ukraine-war/turkiye-un-russia-ukraine-sign-deal-to-resume-grain-exports/2643586.
81 Tarasenko, Pavel, Kirill Krivosheyev, Anatoliy Kostyrev (2022) "Likvidatsiya global'nogo pogolodaniya", *Gazeta Kommersant,* № 132, July 23, p. 1, https://www.kommersant.ru/doc/5479252.
82 Lieven, Anatol (2022b) "A Peace Settlement in Ukraine", *The Nation,* June 22, https://www.thenation.com/article/world/peace-settlement-ukraine/?fbclid=IwAR3u0UaXmjHvS104LF3JPVZsDw-JwhsEo7Un4-DjDFQU_ieRZc8aTny_ePQ.
83 Arkad'yev, Andrey(2021) "V MO soobshchili o porazhenii nedeystvuyushchego sputnika «Tselina-D» v khode ispytaniy", *TV Zvezda,* https://tvzvezda.ru/news/202111161414-i6RqD.html.
84 Blinken, Antony J. (2021) "Russia Conducts Destructive Anti-Satellite Missile Test" Press Statement od Secretary of State, *US Department of State,* https://www.state.gov/russia-conducts-destructive-anti-satellite-missile-test/.
85 RIA Novosti (2021b) "Lavrov nazval obvineniya v adres Rossii v ugrozakh mirnomu kosmosu litsemeriyem", November 16, https://ria.ru/20211116/kosmos-1759281701.html.
86 Tuchkov, Vladimir (2018) "Zvezdnyye voyny: Naydet li Rossiya protivoyadiye protiv X-37", *Svobodnaya Pressa,* October 28, https://svpressa.ru/war21/article/214435/.
87 Yermolov, Andrey (2021) "'Mozhet nesti yadernyye boyegolovki': chem opasen amerikanskiy kosmolet X-37", *Gazeta.ru,* May 22, https://www.gazeta.ru/army/2021/05/22/13603490.shtml?updated.
88 Izvestiya ( 2021) "Rogozin rasskazal o nablyudenii za amerikanskim bespilotnikom X-37", November 21, https://iz.ru/1252943/2021-11-21/rogozin-rasskazal-o-nabliudenii-za-amerikanskim-bespilotnikom-x-37.
89 It is largely discussed in the third chapter.
90 It is largely discussed in the first chapter, *"The Evolution of the Russian security thought".*
91 Putin, Vladimir (2015) "Meeting of the Valdai International Discussion Club", *The Kremlin,* October 22, http://en.kremlin.ru/events/president/news/50548.
92 TASS (2018) "Genshtab: osobennost'yu konfliktov budushchego stanet primeneniye robotov i kosmicheskikh sredstv", March 24, https://tass.ru/armiya-i-opk/5062463.
93 Dvorkin, Vladimir (2016) "Risky Contradictions: Putin's Stance on Strategic Arms and Missile Defense", *the Carnegie Endowment for International Peace,* February 2, https://carnegiemoscow.org/commentary/62719.
94 Ibid.
95 Petrov, Ivan (2019) "Genshtab ulichil SSHA v razrabotke novoy strategii 'Troyanskiy kon'", *Rossiyskoia Gazeta,* March 3, https://rg.ru/2019/03/02/genshtab-ulichil-ssha-v-razrabotke-novoj-strategii-troianskij-kon.html.

96 Commission to Assess United States National Security Space Management and Organization (2001) *The Committee on Armed Services of The US House of Representatives*, The Report, January 11, p. xiii, https://aerospace.csis.org/wp-content/uploads/2018/09/RumsfeldCommission.pdf.
97 Sankaran, Jaganath (2022a) "Russia's anti-satellite weapons: A hedging and offsetting strategy to deter Western aerospace forces", *Contemporary Security Policy* (Online), p. 9, DOI: 10.1080/13523260.2022.2090070.
98 Global Counterspace Capabilities: An Open Source Assessment – Russia (2021) Report, *Secure World Foundation* Russia, pp. 2–2.
99 Ibid.
100 Ibid., pp. 2–5.
101 Ibid. pp. 2–12.
102 Ibid, Table 14, Historical Russian ASAT Tests in Space Continued, pp. 10–13 (184).
103 Global Counterspace Capabilities: An Open Source Assessment – Russia (2021) Report ..., pp. 2–15/p. 79.
104 Hendrickx, Bart (2019a) "Russia's secret satellite builder", May 6, *The Space Review*, https://www.thespacereview.com/article/3709/1.
105 Ibid.
106 TASS (2020) "ZRS S-500 'Prometey' planiruyut postavit' v voyska v blizhayshiye gody", July 7, https://tass.ru/armiya-i-opk/8908911.
107 Novikov, Yan (2022) "Bezuslovnyy prioritet – vypolneniye zadach gosudarstvennogo oboronnogo zakaza", Interviewed by the journal *"Natsional'naya oborona"*, https://oborona.ru/product/zhurnal-nacionalnaya-oborona/bezuslovnyj-prioritet-vypolnenie-zadach-gosudarstvennogo-oboronnogo-zakaza-43621.shtml.
108 TASS (2013) "Raketa-nositel' 'Rokot' vyvela sputniki Minoborony RF na tselevuyu orbitu", December 25, https://nauka.tass.ru/nauka/856345?utm_source=tass.ru&utm_medium=referral&utm_campaign=tass.ru&utm_referrer=tass.ru. See also Global Counterspace Capabilities: An Open Source Assessment – Russia (2021) Report ..., pp. 2–5/p. 69.
109 Weeden, Brian (2015) "Dancing in the dark redux: Recent Russian rendezvous and proximity operations in space", October 5, *The Space Review*, https://www.thespacereview.com/article/2839/1.
110 Ibid.
111 Hennigan, W.J. (202) "Exclusive: Strange Russian Spacecraft Shadowing US Spy Satellite, General Says", *Time*, February 10, https://time.com/5779315/russian-spacecraft-spy-satellite-space-force/.
112 Sankaran, Jaganath (2022b) "Russia's Anti-Satellite Weapons: An Asymmetric Response to US Aerospace Superiority", *Arms Control*, March 22, https://www.armscontrol.org/act/2022-03/features/russias-anti-satellite-weapons-asymmetric-response-us-aerospace-superiority. For more detailed information on the Russian rendezvous and proximity operations (RPO) see Global Counterspace Capabilities: An Open Source Assessment – Russia (2021) Report ..., pp. 2-5–2-14/pp. 69–78.
113 Ibid.
114 Ford, Christopher A. (2020) "Arms Control in Outer Space: History and Prospects", Arms control in outer space: History and prospects", *Arms Control and International Security Papers,* 1(12), pp. 1–10, p. 5 https://www.newparadigmsforum.com/p2696.
115 Val'chenko, Sergey, Nikolay Surkov and Aleksey Ramm (2017) "Rossiya poslala na orbitu inspektora Voyennyye oprobovali v deystvii unikal'nyy manevriruyushchiy sputnik opoznaniya i perekhvata", *Izvestiya*, October 26, https://iz.ru/662230/sergei-valchenko-nikolai-surkov-aleksei-ramm/rossiia-poslala-na-orbitu-inspektora.
116 Global Counterspace Capabilities: An Open Source Assessment – Russia (2021) Report ..., pp. 2–23/87.
117 More information on EW systems used by Russia in recent conflicts, from Chechnya in 1990s to Ukraine until 2016 can be find here: McDermott, Roger N. (2017) "Russia's

Electronic Warfare Capabilities to 2025," *International Centre for Defence and Security*, September, pp. 19–28, https://icds.ee/wp-content/uploads/2018/ICDS_Report_Russias_Electronic_Warfare_to_2025.pdf.
118 Reuters (2019) "Israel says GPS mysteriously disrupted in its airspace but planes secure" June 26, https://www.reuters.com/article/us-israel-aviation-idUSKCN1TR1O3.
119 BBC (2019) "Russia denies role in Israeli airport GPS jamming", June 27, https://www.bbc.com/news/technology-48786085.
120 For instance, C4ADS (2019) "Above Us Only Stars", Report, https://static1.squarespace.com/static/566ef8b4d8af107232d5358a/t/5c99488beb39314c45e782da/1553549492554/Above+Us+Only+Stars.pdf.
121 Deutsche Welle (DW) (2018) "Finland to probe reports of Russia disrupting GPS during NATO drill", November 11, https://www.dw.com/en/finland-to-probe-reports-of-russia-disrupting-gps-during-nato-drill/a-46253512, and AFP (2018) "Russia blocked GPS data during NATO exercises: Norway", November 13, https://www.france24.com/en/20181113-russia-blocked-gps-data-during-nato-exercises-norway.
122 Nilsen, Thomas (2019) "Construction workers frustrated with GPS jamming near border to Russia", The Barents Observer, February 10, https://thebarentsobserver.com/en/security/2019/02/construction-workers-frustrated-gps-jamming-near-russias-militarized-border.
123 McDermott, Roger N. (2017) "Russia's Electronic Warfare Capabilities to 2025" …, p. 24.
124 Axe, David (2021) "Russia's Jamming Force Could Isolate Ukrainian Troops—So Artillery Can Destroy Them", Forbes, November 23, https://www.forbes.com/sites/davidaxe/2021/11/23/russias-jamming-force-could-isolate-ukrainian-troops-so-artillery-can-destroy-them/?sh=5afe4bab2015.
125 Stashevskyi, Oleksandr and Frank Bajak (2022) "Deadly secret: Electronic warfare shapes Russia-Ukraine war", AP, June 4, 2022, https://apnews.com/article/russia-ukraine-kyiv-technology-90d760f01105b9aaf1886427dbfba917.
126 Rostec. "Krasukha", https://rostec.ru/tags/%D0%9A%D1%80%D0%B0%D1%81%D1%83%D1%85%D0%B0, see also TASS (2022b) "Minoborony RF pokazalo primeneniye noveyshego kompleksa R·EB "Krasukha-S4" na Ukraine" June 29, https://tass.ru/armiya-i-opk/15064573.
127 Rostec(2015) Voyennyye poluchili kompleksy R·EB "Borisoglebsk-2", April 20, https://rostec.ru/media/pressrelease/4516362/.
128 Stashevskyi, Oleksandr and Frank Bajak, "Deadly secret: Electronic warfare shapes Russia-Ukraine war" …
129 Sheetz, Michael (2022) "About 150,000 people in Ukraine are using SpaceX's Starlink internet service daily, government official says", *CNBC*, May 2, https://www.cnbc.com/2022/05/02/ukraine-official-150000-using-spacexs-starlink-daily.html.
130 Musk, Elon (2022) posted in Twitter, March 5, https://twitter.com/elonmusk/status/1500026380704178178?s=20&t=wT4v4XtKU52ZK7pzMEd0OA. See also: Malik, Tariq, "Elon Musk says SpaceX focusing on cyber defense after Starlink signals jammed near Ukraine conflict areas", March 05, https://www.space.com/elon-musk-spacex-starlink-cyber-defense-ukraine-invasion.
131 Losey, Stephen (2022) "SpaceX shut down a Russian electromagnetic warfare attack in Ukraine last month — and the Pentagon is taking notes", *Defence News*, April 20. https://www.defensenews.com/air/2022/04/20/spacex-shut-down-a-russian-electromagnetic-warfare-attack-in-ukraine-last-month-and-the-pentagon-is-taking-notes/.
132 TASS (2022a) "Minoborony RF vpervyye pokazalo rabotu kompleksa REB "Palantin" na Ukraine", June 4, available at: https://tass.ru/armiya-i-opk/14821593.
133 Zabrodskyi, Mykhaylo, Jack Watling, Oleksandr V Danylyuk and Nick Reynolds (2022) "Preliminary Lessons in Conventional Warfighting from Russia's Invasion of Ukraine: February–July 2022" Royal United Services Institute for Defence and

Security Studies – RUSI, November 30, p. 37, https://rusi.org/explore-our-research/publications/special-resources/preliminary-lessons-conventional-warfighting-russias-invasion-ukraine-february-july-2022.
134 Global Counterspace Capabilities: An Open Source Assessment – Russia (2021) …, pp. 2–24/88.
135 For instance, in 2016 media reported that Russia is deploying GPS jammers (Pole-21) on 250,000 cellphone towers to reduce enemy cruise missile and drone accuracy in the event of large scale conventional war: Brian Wang (2016) "Russia will place GPS jammers on 250,000 cellphone towers to reduce enemy cruise missile and drone accuracy in the event of large scale conventional war", October 18, https://www.nextbigfuture.com/2016/10/russia-will-place-gps-jammers-on-250000.html.
136 Lastochkin, Yuriy and Falichev, Oleg(2017) "Kupol nad Minoborony", *VPK,* April 24, https://vpk-news.ru/articles/36422.
137 Global Counterspace Capabilities: An Open Source Assessment – Russia (2021) …, pp. 2–26/90.
138 McDermott, Roger N. (2017) …, pp. 9 and 18–19.
139 Krasukha-4, Stantsiya 1RL257 RB-271A Krasukha-4, http://library.voenmeh.ru/jirbis2/files/materials/ifour/book2/book_on_main_page/14.13.htm.
140 Lavrov, Anton and Roman Kretsul (202) "Elektronnyy tuman: pod Kaliningradom razmestili novyy kompleks pomekh", *Izvestia,* November 15, https://iz.ru/1086911/anton-lavrov-roman-kretcul/elektronnyi-tuman-pod-kaliningradom-razmestili-novyi-kompleks-pomekh.
141 Hendrickx, Bart (2019b) "Ekipazh: Russia's top-secret nuclear-powered satellite", *The Space Review*, October 7, https://www.thespacereview.com/article/3809/1.
142 RIA Novosti (2016) "Novaya strategicheskaya sistema R·EB smozhet podavit' svyaz' voysk SSHA i NATO", November 14, https://ria.ru/20161114/1481278392.html.
143 Interfax (2017) "Rossiya nachala rabotu nad oruzhiyem dlya porazheniya sputnikov" November 30, https://www.interfax.ru/russia/589740.
144 More details on the Russian anti-satellite laser systems is in Hendrickx, Bart (2022) "Kalina: a Russian ground-based laser to dazzle imaging satellites" …
145 Hendrickx, Bart (2022) "Kalina: a Russian ground-based laser to dazzle imaging satellites", *The Space Review*, July 5, https://www.thespacereview.com/article/4416/1.
146 Ibid.
147 Ramm, Aleksey and Lavrov, Anton (2021) "Luchnaya rabota: chto izvestno o novom rossiyskom boyevom lazere 'Peresvet'", *Izvestiya,* December 2, https://iz.ru/1258024/anton-lavrov-aleksei-ramm/luchnaia-rabota-chto-izvestno-o-novom-rossiiskom-boevom-lazere-peresvet.
148 Borisov, Yuriy (2022) "Rol' OPK v razvitii strany i novyye istoricheskiye usloviya", *Rossiyskoye Obshchestvo Znaniye,* May 18, available at: https://znanierussia.ru/library/video/rol-opk-v-razvitii-strany-i-novye-istoricheskie-usloviya-1032.
149 Hendrickx, Bart (2022) "Kalina: a Russian ground-based laser to dazzle imaging satellites" …
150 Borisov, Yuriy (2022) "Rol' OPK v razvitii strany i novyye istoricheskiye usloviya" …
151 Hendrickx, Bart (2022) "Kalina: a Russian ground-based laser to dazzle imaging satellites" …
152 Fromkin, David(1980) "The Great Game in Asia", *Foreign Affairs*, Vol. 58, No. 4, pp. 36–951.
153 Krivosheyev G. F. (ed.) (2001) *Rossiya i SSSR v voynakh XX veka: Statisticheskoye issledovaniye*, Moskva: OLMA-PRESS, p. 536.
154 Stepanova, Ekaterina (2019) "Mirnyi protsess po Afganistanu i rol' Rossii", *Puti k miru i bezopasnosti. Pathways to Peace and Security,* Vol. 2, No. 57, pp. 21–33, p. 26, DOI:10.20542/2307-1494-2019-2-21-33.
155 Naderi, Asef (2017) "Vozvrashcheniye Rossii v Afganistan: perspektivy dvustoronnego ekonomicheskogo sotrudnichestva", *Vestnik RUDN, International Relations*, Vol. 17, No. 4, pp. 781–792, DOI:10.22363/2313-0660-2017-17-4-781-792.

156 Trenin, Dmitriy, Oleg Kulakov, Aleksey Malashenko and Petr Topychkanov (2014) "Afganistan posle vyvoda voysk mezhdunarodnoy koalitsii: ugrozy, riski i vyzovy dlya Rossiyskoy Federatsii", *Carnegie Endowment for International Peace and Carnegie Moscow Center*, p. 8, https://carnegieendowment.org/files/CP_Afganistan_web_Rus2014.pdf.
157 Aliyev, Nurlan (2020) "Central Asia in Russia's Afghan Strategy", *The Oxus Society for Central Asian Affairs*, 20 October, https://oxussociety.org/central-asia-in-russias-afghan-strategy/.
158 Pannier, Bruce (2020) "Kak rossiyskiye voyennyye pomogayut Turkmenistanu?", January 6, https://rus.azattyq.org/a/turkmenistan-russia-afganistan-border/30362388.html.
159 Pravo.gov.ru, 'Soglasheniye mezhdu Rossiyskoy Federatsiyey i Turkmenistanom o sotrudnichestve v oblasti bezopasnosti ot 10 aprelya 2003 g. (ratifitsirovano Federal'nym zakonom ot 9 noyabrya 2020 g. № 355-FZ, vstupilo v silu 20 noyabrya 2020 g.)', 9 November 2020, http://publication.pravo.gov.ru/Document/View/0001202011240034.
160 Nevex TV (2013) "Rossiya vozvrashchayetsya v Afganistan?", *Moskovskiy politklub Rosbalta*, 5 April 5, https://www.youtube.com/watch?v=mjW4kVAh6lM.
161 CSTO Joint Staff (2020) "Collective Rapid Reaction forces of the CSTO", https://jscsto.odkb-csto.org/en/voennaya-sostavlyauschaya-odkb/ksorodkb.php.
162 The Ministry of Foreign Affairs of the Russian Federation (2019b) 'Trekhstoronniy konsensus Rossii, Kitaya i SSHA po mirnomu protsessu v Afganistane (Prinyat po itogam vstrechi spetspredstaviteley Prezidenta Rossii, MID KNR i Gosudarstvennogo departamenta SSHA po Afganistanu', April 25, https://dushanbe.mid.ru/novosti-posolstva/-/asset_publisher/tKTpTrZaRYxl/content/trehstoronnij-konsensus-rossii-kitaa-i-ssa-po-mirnomu-processu-v-afganistane?inheritRedirect=true.
163 The Ministry of Foreign Affairs of the Russian Federation (2019c) 'Sovmestnoye zayavleniye Rossii, Kitaya, SSHA i Pakistana po afganskomu mirnomu protsessu', October 28, https://www.mid.ru/ru/foreign_policy/news/-/asset_publisher/cKNonkJE02Bw/content/id/3867739.
164 US Mission Russia (2019) 'O vizite spetspredstavitelya SSHA po afganskomu primireniyu Zalmaya Khalilzada v Moskvu', October 27, https://ru.usembassy.gov/ru/u-s-special-representative-for-afghanistan-reconciliation-ambassador-khalilzad-holds-consultations-in-moscow-ru/.
165 Warikoo, Kulbhushan(2019) "The Shanghai Cooperation Organization and Afghanistan", April 26, available at: http://infoshos.ru/en/?idn=21303#:~:text=The%20SCO%2DAfghanistan%20Contact%20Group,through%20political%20consultations%20and%20dialogue.
166 Stepanova, Ekaterina (2018) "Russia's Afghan Policy in the Regional and Russia-West Contexts", Russie.Nei.Reports', *Ifri*, no. 23, https://www.ifri.org/en/publications/etudes-de-lifri/russieneireports/russias-afghan-policy-regional-and-russia-west.
167 Nessar, Omar (2019) "Afganskiy mirnyy protsess: predvaritel'nyye rezul'taty i otsenki", *Mezhdunarodnaya Zhizn*, 5, 2019, https://interaffairs.ru/jauthor/material/2188.
168 Afganistan Segodnya (2020) "Lavrov otsenil deyatel'nost' SSHA i NATO v Afganistane", July 10, http://afghanistantoday.ru/hovosti/lavrov-ocenil-deyatelnost-ssha.
169 BBC.com (2018) "Taliban offer: Afghan President Ashraf Ghani seeks talks", February 28, https://www.bbc.com/news/world-asia-43227860, accessed 11 December 2021.
170 Ria.ru (2018) "V MID rasskazali ob optimal'noy ploshchadke peregovorov po Afganistanu", March 14, https://ria.ru/20180314/1516309769.html.
171 US Department of State (2020) 'Secretary Pompeo's Travel to the U.K., Ukraine, Belarus, Kazakhstan, and Uzbekistan', Press statement, Morgan Ortagus, Department spokesperson, 24 January, https://www.state.gov/secretary-pompeos-travel-to-the-uk-ukraine-belarus-kazakhstan-and-uzbekistan/.
172 Strokan', Sergey et al. (2020) "Rossiya v kol'tse vizitov-Gossekretar' Pompeo zayavil o pretenziyakh SSHA na postsovetskoye prostranstvo", *Kommersant*, February 3, https://www.kommersant.ru/doc/4241536.

173 The Ministry of Foreign Affairs of the Russian Federation (2019a) 'O provedenii vstrechi predstaviteley vedushchikh politicheskikh sil Afganistana pod egidoy afganskikh diaspor', Brifing ofitsial'nogo predstavitelya MID Rossii M.V. Zakharovoy", February 7, https://www.mid.ru/press_service/spokesman/briefings/-/asset_publisher/D2wHaWMCU6Od/content/id/3503377#12.
174 FSB, 'Edynyi federal'nyi spisok organizatsii, v tom chisle inostrannykh i mezhdunarodnykh organizatsii, priznannykh v sootvetstvii s zakonodatel'stvom Rossiyskoy Federatsii terroristicheskimi', http://www.fsb.ru/fsb/npd/terror.htm accessed 11 December 2021.
175 Subbotin, Igor' (2019) 'Taliby igrayut na protivorechiyakh Moskvy i Vashingtona', *Nezavismaya Gazeta*, 5 February, https://www.ng.ru/world/2019-02-05/6_7500_afgan.html.
176 Stepanova, Ekaterina (2019) "Mirnyi protsess po Afganistanu i rol' Rossii" …
177 Ibid., 27.
178 Ibid., 28.
179 Dubnov, Arkadii (2016) "Pochemu interesy Rossii i 'Talibana' 'ob"yektivno sovpali'", *Carnegie Moscow*, 14 January, available at: https://carnegie.ru/commentary/62459.
180 Korgun, Viktor (ed.) (2004) *Afganistan v nachale xxi veka. Moscow: Institut izucheniya Izrailya i Blizhnego Vostoka*, Moskva: Institut izucheniya Izrailya i Blizhnego Vostoka, p. 116.
181 Mehemmedi, Mesiaga [Məhəmmədi, Məsiağa] (2017) *Əfqanıstan: Sovet işğalından Amerika müdaxiləsinə*. Baki: Azərbaycan Respublikasının Prezidenti yanında Strateji Araşdırmalar Mərkəzi, p. 127.
182 Mendkovich, Nikita (2009) "Rossiya i 'pushtunskiy factor'", July 3, https://afghanistan.ru/doc/15038.html.
183 Serenko, Andrei (2009) "Na 'linii Dyuranda' poyavilis' 'russkiye taliby'", May 29, https://afghanistan.ru/doc/14815.html.
184 Dubnov, Arkadii (2016) …
185 Rowlatt, Justin (2018) "Russia 'arming the Afghan Taliban', says US", *BBC*, March 23, https://www.bbc.com/news/world-asia-43500299.
186 Galeotti, Mark (2020) 'The "Talibangate" Claims About Russian Bounties Still Don't Add Up', *The Moscow Times*, 3 July, https://www.themoscowtimes.com/2020/07/03/the-talibangate-claims-about-russian-bounties-still-dont-add-up-a70772; The Moscow Times (2020) "'100% Bullsh*t': Russia Blasts Reports of Taliban Bounties for Killed US Troops', 30 June, https://www.themoscowtimes.com/2020/06/30/100-bullsht-russia-blasts-reports-of-taliban-bounties-for-killed-us-troops-a70737.
187 Nicholson, John W. (2020) "The US must respond forcefully to Russia and the Taliban. Here's how", *The Washington Post*, July 13, https://www.washingtonpost.com/opinions/the-us-must-respond-forcefully-to-russia-and-the-taliban-heres-how/2020/07/13/df13ed6c-c529-11ea-b037-f9711f89ee46_story.html.
188 Kalinovsky, Artem (2020) "Russian Moves in Afghanistan Are About Regional Stability, Not Revenge on US", *Russia Matters*, July 22, https://www.russiamatters.org/analysis/russian-moves-afghanistan-are-about-regional-stability-not-revenge-us.
189 Sputnik Tajikistan (2021) "Nalazhen vozdushnyy most Tadzhikistan – Pandzhsher", *Tj. sputniknews.ru*, August 23, https://tj.sputniknews.ru/20210823/nalazhen-vozdushnyy-most-tajikistan-panjsher-1041831090.html.
190 Erozbek, Dar'ya (2022) "MID Rossii dopustil priznaniye pravitel'stva talibov v Afganistane", *Kommersant*, June 14, https://www.kommersant.ru/doc/5410080.
191 Sovet Bezopasnosti Rossiyskoy Federatsii (2021) "V N'yu-Deli Prem'yer-ministr Respubliki Indiya Narendra Modi prinyal Sekretarya Soveta Bezopasnosti Rossii Nikolaya Patrusheva", *Scrf.gov.ru*, 8 September, http://www.scrf.gov.ru/news/allnews/3066/. See also RIA Novosti (2021a) "Patrushev v N'yu-Deli vstretitsya s prem'yerom Indii", September 7, https://ria.ru/20210907/patrushev-1749020853.html.

## Bibliography

Afganistan Segodnya (2020) "Lavrov otsenil deyatel'nost' SSHA i NATO v Afganistane", July 10, available at: http://afghanistantoday.ru/hovosti/lavrov-ocenil-deyatelnost-ssha, accessed 11 December 2021.

AFP (2018) "Russia blocked GPS data during NATO 1exercises: Norway", November 13, available at: https://www.france24.com/en/20181113-russia-blocked-gps-data-during-nato-exercises-norway, accessed 11 July 2022.

Aliyev, Nurlan (2020) "Central Asia in Russia's Afghan Strategy", *The Oxus Society for Central Asian Affairs*, 20 October, available at: https://oxussociety.org/central-asia-in-russias-afghan-strategy/, accessed 11 August 2022.

Anadolu Agency (2022) "Türkiye, UN, Russia, Ukraine sign deal to resume grain exports", July 22, available at: https://www.aa.com.tr/en/russia-ukraine-war/turkiye-un-russia-ukraine-sign-deal-to-resume-grain-exports/2643586, accessed 29 July 2022.

Arkad'yev, Andrey (2021) "V MO soobshchili o porazhenii nedeystvuyushchego sputnika «Tselina-D» v khode ispytaniy", *TV Zvezda*, available at: https://tvzvezda.ru/news/202111161414-i6RqD.html, accessed 28 May 2022.

Armstrong, Benjamin F. (2019) *Small Boats and Daring Men: Maritime Raiding, Irregular Warfare, and the Early American Navy*, Norman, OK: University of Oklahoma Press.

――――― (2022) "The Russo-Ukrainian War at Sea: Retrospect and Prospect", *War On The Rocks,* April 21, available at: https://warontherocks.com/2022/04/THE-RUSSO-UKRAINIAN-WAR-AT-SEA-RETROSPECT-AND-PROSPECT/, accessed 31 May 2022.

Askerova, Kseniya (2022) "Peskov: Rossiya ne krala nikakogo zerna", *Kommersant,* June 23, available at: https://www.kommersant.ru/doc/5424353, accessed 25 June 2022.

Axe, David (2021) "Russia's Jamming Force Could Isolate Ukrainian Troops—So Artillery Can Destroy Them", *Forbes,* November 23, available at: https://www.forbes.com/sites/davidaxe/2021/11/23/russias-jamming-force-could-isolate-ukrainian-troops-so-artillery-can-destroy-them/?sh=5afe4bab2015, accessed 25 June 2022.

BBC.com (2018) "Taliban offer: Afghan President Ashraf Ghani seeks talks", February 28, available at: https://www.bbc.com/news/world-asia-43227860, accessed 11 December 2021.

――――― (2019) "Russia denies role in Israeli airport GPS jamming", June 27, available at: https://www.bbc.com/news/technology-48786085, accessed 11 July 2022.

Beake, Nick, and Maria Korenyuk and Reality Check team(2022) "Tracking where Russia is taking Ukraine's stolen grain", *BBC News*, June 27, available at: https://www.bbc.com/news/61790625, accessed 29 June 2022.

Blinken, Antony J. (2021) "Russia Conducts Destructive Anti-Satellite Missile Test" Press Statement od Secretary of State, *U.S. Department of State*, available at: https://www.state.gov/russia-conducts-destructive-anti-satellite-missile-test/, accessed 28 May 2022.

Brian Wang (2016) "Russia will place GPS jammers on 250,000 cellphone towers to reduce enemy cruise missile and drone accuracy in the event of large scale conventional war", October 18, available at: https://www.nextbigfuture.com/2016/10/russia-will-place-gps-jammers-on-250000.html, accessed 28 May 2022.

Borisov, Yuriy (2022) "Rol' OPK v razvitii strany i novyye istoricheskiye usloviya", *Rossiyskoye Obshchestvo Znaniye*, May 18, available at:https://znanierussia.ru/library/video/rol-opk-v-razvitii-strany-i-novye-istoricheskie-usloviya-1032, accessed 13 July 2022.

C4ADS (2019) "Above Us Only Stars", Report, available at: https://static1.squarespace.com/static/566ef8b4d8af107232d5358a/t/5c99488beb39314c45e782da/1553549492554/Above+Us+Only+Stars.pdf, accessed 11 July 2022.

Centre for Food and Land Use Research (2022) "Agricultural War Losses Review Ukraine. Rapid Loss Assessment", *Kyiv School of Economics*, June 9, p. 2, available at: https://minagro.gov.ua/storage/app/sites/1/uploaded-files/Losses_report_issue1.pdf, accessed 17 June 2022.

Charap, Samuel, et al. (2021a) *"Russia's Military Interventions-Patterns, Drivers, and Signposts"*, RAND Corporation, DOI: 10.7249/RR-A444-3.

Charap, Samuel, et al. (2021b) *"Russian Grand Strategy- Rhetoric and Reality"*, RAND Cooperation, available at: https://www.rand.org/pubs/research_reports/RR4238.html, accessed 1 May 2022.

Commission to Assess United States National Security Space Management and Organization (2001) *The Committee on Armed Services of The U.S. House of Representatives*, the Report, January 11, available at: https://aerospace.csis.org/wp-content/uploads/2018/09/RumsfeldCommission.pdf, accessed 1 July 2022.

CSTO Joint Staff (2020) "Collective Rapid Reaction forces of the CSTO", available at: https://jscsto.odkb-csto.org/en/voennaya-sostavlyauschaya-odkb/ksorodkb.php, accessed 11 December 2021.

Defense Express (2022) "What Kind of Weapon Could Hit the Engels Airfield In Saratov Oblast And an Airport In Ryazan Oblast", December 5, available at: https://en.defence-ua.com/analysis/what_kind_of_weapon_could_hit_the_engels_airfield_in_saratov_oblast_and_an_airport_in_ryazan_oblast-5056.html, accessed 24 January 2023.

Deutsche Welle (DW) (2018) "Finland to probe reports of Russia disrupting GPS during NATO drill", November 11, available at: https://www.dw.com/en/finland-to-probe-reports-of-russia-disrupting-gps-during-nato-drill/a-46253512, accessed 11 July 2022.

Dvorkin, Vladimir (2016) "Risky Contradictions: Putin's Stance on Strategic Arms and Missile Defense", *The Carnegie Endowment for International Peace*, February 2, available at: https://carnegiemoscow.org/commentary/62719, accessed 1 July 2022.

Dubnov, Arkadii (2016) "Pochemu interesy Rossii i 'Talibana' 'ob"yektivno sovpali'", *Carnegie Moscow*, January 14, available at: https://carnegie.ru/commentary/62459, accessed 21 December 2021.

Duma.gov.ru (2022) Russia's draft budget for 2023–2025, September 27, available at: https://sozd.duma.gov.ru/bill/201614-8, accessed 24 October 2022.

Erozbek, Dar'ya (2022) "MID Rossii dopustil priznaniye pravitel'stva talibov v Afganistane", *Kommersant*, June 14, available at: https://www.kommersant.ru/doc/5410080, accessed 21 July 2022.

Fromkin, David (1980) "The Great Game in Asia", *Foreign Affairs*, Vol. 58, No. 4, pp. 936–951.

FSB, 'Edynyi federal'nyi spisok organizatsii, v tom chisle inostrannykh i mezhdunarodnykh organizatsii, priznannykh v sootvetstvii s zakonodatel'stvom Rossiyskoy Federatsii terroristicheskimi', available at: http://www.fsb.ru/fsb/npd/terror.htm, accessed 11 December 2021.

Ford, Christopher A. (2020) "Arms Control in Outer Space: History and Prospects", Arms control in outer space: History and prospects", *Arms Control and International Security Papers*, Vol. 1, No. 12, pp. 1–10, p. 5, available at: https://www.newparadigmsforum.com/p2696, accessed 10 July 2022.

Fylyppov, Sanyo, and Tim Lister (2022) "EU foreign policy chief condemns Russian missile strike on Ukrainian grain terminal", *CNN*, June 6, available at: https://edition.cnn.com/europe/live-news/russia-ukraine-war-news-06-06-22/h_808efd3980120d4391454b32863490d4, accessed 10 June 2022.

Gabuyev, Aleksandr, and Sergey Sidorenko (2014) "Mnogoglavyy orel – Kto vliyal na ukrainskuyu politiku Kremlya", Vlast, № 8, 3 March, p. 9, available at: https://www.kommersant.ru/doc/2416461?utm_source=pocket_mylist, accessed 1 May 2022.

Galeotti, Mark (2020) 'The "Talibangate" Claims About Russian Bounties Still Don't Add Up', *The Moscow Times*, 3 July, available at: https://www.themoscowtimes.com/2020/07/03/the-talibangate-claims-about-russian-bounties-still-dont-add-up-a70772, accessed 21 December 2021.

Georgy, Michael (2022) "Iran agrees to ship missiles, more drones to Russia", *Reuters*, October 18, available at: https://www.reuters.com/world/exclusive-iran-agrees-ship-missiles-more-drones-russia-defying-west-sources-2022-10-18/. accessed 24 October 2022.

Global Counterspace Capabilities: An Open Source Assessment – Russia (2021) Report, *Secure World Foundation*.

Grau, Lester W., and Charles K. Bartles (2016) "Russian Way of War", Report, *Foreign Military Studies Office*, available at: https://www.armyupress.army.mil/portals/7/hot%20spots/documents/russia/2017-07-the-russian-way-of-war-grau-bartles.pdf, accessed 13 June 2022.

_____ (2022) "Getting to Know the Russian Battalion Tactical Group", *RUSI*, April 14, available at: https://rusi.org/explore-our-research/publications/commentary/getting-know-russian-battalion-tactical-group, accessed 13 June 2022.

Gressel, Gustav (2022) "Mob unhappy: Why Russia is unlikely to emerge victorious in Ukraine", *ECFR*, October 21, available at: https://ecfr.eu/article/mob-unhappy-why-russia-is-unlikely-to-emerge-victorious-in-ukraine/, accessed 24 October 2022.

Grobman, Yekaterina, and Anastasiya Mayyer (2022) "Sovet voyennogo vremeni: v chem unikal'nost' novogo organa, kotoryy vozglavil", *Vedomosti*, October 21, available at: https://www.vedomosti.ru/politics/articles/2022/10/21/946817-sovet-voennogo-vremeni, accessed 24 October 2022.

Gorenburg, Dmitry, and Michael Kofman (2022) "Here's what we know about Russia's military buildup near Ukraine", January 15, *The Washington Post*, available at: https://www.washingtonpost.com/politics/2022/01/15/heres-what-we-know-about-russias-military-buildup-near-ukraine/, accessed 1 June 2022.

Harris, Shane, Karen DeYoung, Isabelle Khurshudyan, Ashley Parker, and Liz Sly (2022) "Road to war: U.S. struggled to convince allies, and Zelensky, of risk of invasion", *The Washington Post*, August 16, available at: https://www.washingtonpost.com/national-security/interactive/2022/ukraine-road-to-war/?itid=ap_shaneharris, accessed 17 August 2022.

Herszenhorn, David M., and Paul Mcleary (2022) "Ukraine's 'iron general' is a hero, but he's no star", *Politico*, April 8, available at: https://www.politico.com/news/2022/04/08/ukraines-iron-general-zaluzhnyy-00023901, accessed 3 June 2022.

Hendrickx, Bart (2019a) "Russia's secret satellite builder", May 6, *The Space Review*, available at: https://www.thespacereview.com/article/3709/1, accessed 10 July 2022.

_____ (2019b) "Ekipazh: Russia's top-secret nuclear-powered satellite", *The Space Review*, October 7, available at: https://www.thespacereview.com/article/3809/1, accessed 13 July 2022.

_____ (2022) "Kalina: a Russian ground-based laser to dazzle imaging satellites", *The Space Review*, July 5, available at: https://www.thespacereview.com/article/4416/1, accessed 13 July 2022.

Hennigan, W.J. (2020) "Exclusive: Strange Russian Spacecraft Shadowing U.S. Spy Satellite, General Says", *Time*, February 10, available at: https://time.com/5779315/russian-spacecraft-spy-satellite-space-force/, accessed 10 July 2022.

Interfax (2017) "Rossiya nachala rabotu nad oruzhiyem dlya porazheniya sputnikov" November 30, available at: https://www.interfax.ru/russia/589740, accessed 11 July 2022.

_____ (2022a) "Rossiya sozdast 12 novykh voinskikh chastey v ZVO iz-za narastaniya ugroz u granits", May 20, available at: https://www.interfax.ru/world/841930, accessed 5 June 2022.

_____ (2022b) "Zerno iz Zaporozh'ya nachali postavlyat' v strany Blizhnego Vostoka", June 8, available at: https://www.interfax.ru/business/845268, accessed 29 June 2022.

Izvestiya (2021) "Rogozin rasskazal o nablyudenii za amerikanskim bespilotnikom X-37", November 21, available at: https://iz.ru/1252943/2021-11-21/rogozin-rasskazal-o-nabliudenii-za-amerikanskim-bespilotnikom-x-37, accessed 1 July 2022.

Johnson, David E. (2022) "This is What the Russians Do", *Lawfire*, May 3, available at: https://sites.duke.edu/lawfire/2022/05/03/dr-dave-johnsons-warning-on-brute-force-in-the-ukraine-this-is-what-the-russians-do/, accessed 13 June 2022.

Judah, Tim (2022) "How Kyiv was saved by Ukrainian ingenuity as well as Russian blunders", The Financial Times, April 10, available at: https://www.ft.com/content/e87fdc60-0d5e-4d39-93c6-7cfd22f770e8?sharetype=blocked&fbclid=IwAR3vbE3D6dR1AU-SXp9rVXLm0PcssarcR5udGd-SVKw-zYq7ybFXxO9kQkw, accessed 17 June 2022.

Kalinovsky, Artem (2020) "Russian Moves in Afghanistan Are About Regional Stability, Not Revenge on US", *Russia Matters*, July 22, available at: https://www.russiamatters.org/analysis/russian-moves-afghanistan-are-about-regional-stability-not-revenge-us, accessed 21 December 2021.

Kashin, Vasilii (2022) "Pervaya bol'shaya voyna XXI veka", June 22, *Rossiya v Global'noy Politike*, available at: https://globalaffairs.ru/articles/pervaya-bolshaya-vojna-xxi-veka/, accessed 23 June 2022.

Khodarenok, Mikhail (2022) "Prognozy krovozhadnykh politologov", *Nezavisimoe Voennoe Obozrenie – Nezavisimoya Gazeta*, available at: https://nvo.ng.ru/realty/2022-02-03/3_1175_donbass.html, accessed 1 May 2022.

Khurshudyan, Isabelle, and Paul Sonne (2022) "Russia targeted Ukrainian ammunition to weaken Kyiv on the battlefield", *The Washington Post*, June 24, available at: https://www.washingtonpost.com/world/2022/06/24/ukraine-ammunition-russian-sabotage-artillery/, accessed 24 June 2022.

Kirilenko, Ol'ga (2022) "Kak Sumshchina pervoy vstretila, a potom ostanovila vraga po doroge na Kiyev", Ukrainska Pravda, April 16, available at: https://www.pravda.com.ua/rus/articles/2022/04/16/7339908/, accessed 17 June 2022.

Kluge, Janis (2022), on Twitter, September 28, available at: https://twitter.com/jakluge/status/1575187748520009728?s=20&t=WHT52JKVw_Y2HApu7njcxg, accessed 24 October 2022.

Kofman, Michael (2022) "The Russo-Ukrainian war ten months in: taking stock", *Riddle*, December 28, available at: https://ridl.io/the-russo-ukrainian-war-ten-months-in-taking-stock/, accessed 24 January 2023.

Kofman, Michael, and Rob Lee (2022) "Not built for purpose: the Russian military's ill-fated force design", *War on The Rocks*, June 2, available at: https://warontherocks.com/2022/06/not-built-for-purpose-the-russian-militarys-ill-fated-force-design/, accessed 5 June 2022.

Kolganova, Viktoriya (2022) "Putin nazval pyat' sposobov vyvoza zerna iz Ukrainy", *Kommersant*, June 3, available at: https://www.kommersant.ru/doc/5391307, accessed 10 June 2022.

Korgun, Viktor (ed.) (2004) *Afganistan v nachale xxi veka. Moscow:Institut izucheniya Izrailya i Blizhnego Vostoka*, Moskva: Institut izucheniya Izrailya i Blizhnego Vostoka.

Krasukha-4, Stantsiya 1RL257 RB-271A Krasukha-4, available at: http://library.voenmeh.ru/jirbis2/files/materials/ifour/book2/book_on_main_page/14.13.htm, accessed 13 July 2022.

Kremlin (2022) "Plenarnoye zasedaniye Peterburgskogo mezhdunarodnogo ekonomicheskogo foruma", June 17, available at: http://kremlin.ru/events/president/transcripts/68669, accessed 29 June 2022.

Krivosheyev, G. F. (ed.) (2001) *Rossiya i SSSR v voynakh XX veka: Statisticheskoye issledovaniye*, Moskva: OLMA-PRESS.

KSE Agrocenter (2022) "The total war damages in Ukraine's agriculture reached $4.3 billion", June 15, available at: https://kse.ua/about-the-school/news/the-total-war-damages-in-ukraine-s-agriculture-reached-4-3-billion-kse-agrocenter/, accessed 17 June 2022.

Kyiv School of Economics (2023) "The total amount of damage caused to Ukraine's infrastructure due to the war has increased to almost $138 billion", January 24, available at: https://kse.ua/about-the-school/news/the-total-amount-of-damage-caused-to-ukraine-s-infrastructure-due-to-the-war-has-increased-to-almost-138-billion/, accessed 25 January 2023.

Lastochkin, Yuriy, and Oleg Falichev (2017) "Kupol nad Minoborony", *VPK*, April 24, available at: https://vpk-news.ru/articles/36422, accessed 13 July 2022.

Lavrov, Anton, and Roman Kretsul (202) "Elektronnyy tuman: pod Kaliningradom razmestili novyy kompleks pomekh", *Izvestia*, November 15, available at: https://iz.ru/1086911/anton-lavrov-roman-kretcul/elektronnyi-tuman-pod-kaliningradom-razmestili-novyi-kompleks-pomekh, accessed 13 July 2022.

Lee, Rob (2022) "The tank is not obsolete, and other observations about the future of combat", War On The Rocks, September 6, available at: https://warontherocks.com/2022/09/the-tank-is-not-obsolete-and-other-observations-about-the-future-of-combat/, accessed 24 October 2022.

Lieven, Anatol (2022a) "Inside Putin's circle—the real Russian elite", March 11, *The Financial Times*, available at: https://www.ft.com/content/503fb110-f91e-4bed-b6dc-0d09582dd007?utm_source=pocket_mylist&fbclid=IwAR3m0epCqtnsQtAbma3GPtCwo8XB5rbm0DxBoDOvQ7F5cUlR38c-bb3Rjr4, accessed 1 May 2022.

_____ (2022b) "A Peace Settlement in Ukraine", *The Nation*, June 22, available at: https://www.thenation.com/article/world/peace-settlement-ukraine/?fbclid=IwAR3u0UaXmjHvS104LF3JPVZsDw-JwhsEo7Un4-DjDFQU_ieRZc8aTny_ePQ, accessed 29 June 2022.

Losey, Stephen (2022) "SpaceX shut down a Russian electromagnetic warfare attack in Ukraine last month—and the Pentagon is taking notes", *Defence News*, April 20, available at: https://www.defensenews.com/air/2022/04/20/spacex-shut-down-a-russian-electromagnetic-warfare-attack-in-ukraine-last-month-and-the-pentagon-is-taking-notes/, accessed 12 July 2022.

Malik, Tariq, "Elon Musk says SpaceX focusing on cyber defense after Starlink signals jammed near Ukraine conflict areas", March 05, available at: https://www.space.com/elon-musk-spacex-starlink-cyber-defense-ukraine-invasion, accessed 12 July 2022.

Massicot, Dara (2022) "Ukraine Needs Help Surviving Airstrikes, Not Just Killing Tanks", *Defence One*, January 19, available at: https://www.defenseone.com/ideas/2022/01/ukraine-needs-help-surviving-airstrikes-not-just-killing-tanks/360898/, accessed 1 June 2022.

Mauldin, William (2022) "U.N. Seeks to Ease Russian Blockade of Ukraine Grain Shipping to Avert Food Shortages", *The Wall Street Journal*, May 16, available at: https://www.wsj.com/articles/u-n-seeks-to-ease-russian-blockade-of-ukraine-grain-shipping-to-avert-food-shortages-11652717161?mod=Searchresults_pos1&page=1, accessed 10 June 2022.

McDermott, Roger N. (2017) "Russia's Electronic Warfare Capabilities to 2025," *International Centre for Defence and Security*, September, pp. 19–28, available at: https://icds.ee/wp-content/uploads/2018/ICDS_Report_Russias_Electronic_Warfare_to_2025.pdf, accessed 13 July 2022.

Mearsheimer, John J. (2022) "The causes and consequences of the Ukraine war – A lecture by John J. Mearsheimer", *The Robert Schuman Centre for Advanced Studies*, streamed on YouTube.com on June 16, https://www.youtube.com/watch?v=qciVozNtCDM.

Mehemmedi, Mesiaga [Məhəmmədi, Məsiağa] (2017) *Əfqanıstan: Sovet işğalından Amerika müdaxiləsinə*, Baki: Azərbaycan Respublikasının Prezidenti yanında Strateji Araşdırmalar Mərkəzi.

Mendkovich, Nikita (2009) "Rossiya i 'pushtunskiy factor'", July 3, available at: https://afghanistan.ru/doc/15038.html, accessed 21 December 2021.

Ministerstvo oborony Rossiyskoy Federatsii (2022) "V Moskve pod rukovodstvom Verkhovnogo Glavnokomanduyushchego Vooruzhennymi Silami Vladimira Putina proshlo rasshirennoye zasedaniye Kollegii Minoborony Rossii", December 21, available at: https://function.mil.ru/news_page/country/more.htm?id=12449212@egNews, accessed 24 January 2023.

Musk, Elon (2022) posted in Twitter, March 5, available at: https://twitter.com/elonmusk/status/1500026380704178178?s=20&t=wT4v4XtKU52ZK7pzMEd0OA, accessed 12 July 2022.

Naderi, Asef (2017) "Vozvrashcheniye Rossii v Afganistan: perspektivy dvustoronnego ekonomicheskogo sotrudnichestva", Vestnik RUDN, *International Relations*, Vol. 17, No. 4, pp. 781–792, DOI: 10.22363/2313-0660-2017-17-4-781-792.

Nazarov, Nikolay (2022) "Ukraine's Resilience: Theory meets practice", ICDS, May, available at: https://lmc.icds.ee/ukraines-resilience-theory-meets-practice/?fbclid=IwAR38Tth5bxnMgv7aFHQiQhWLWWTSAtnw7uQ3X-r5Lrn-zcE90WGREJej62I, accessed 31 May 2022.

Nessar, Omar (2019) "Afganskiy mirnyy protsess: predvaritel'nyye rezul'taty i otsenki", *Mezhdunarodnaya Zhizn*, 5, available at: https://interaffairs.ru/jauthor/material/2188, accessed 11 December 2021.

Nevex TV (2013) "Rossiya vozvrashchayetsya v Afganistan?", *Moskovskiy politklub Rosbalta*, 5 April 5, available at: https://www.youtube.com/watch?v=mjW4kVAh6lM, accessed 11 December 2021.

Nicholson, John W. (2020) "The U.S. must respond forcefully to Russia and the Taliban. Here's how", *The Washington Post*, July 13, available at: https://www.washingtonpost.com/opinions/the-us-must-respond-forcefully-to-russia-and-the-taliban-heres-how/2020/07/13/df13ed6c-c529-11ea-b037-f9711f89ee46_story.html, accessed 21 December 2021.

Nilsen, Thomas (2019) "Construction workers frustrated with GPS jamming near border to Russia", *The Barents Observer*, February 10, available at: https://thebarentsobserver.com/en/security/2019/02/construction-workers-frustrated-gps-jamming-near-russias-militarized-border, accessed 11 July 2022.

Novikov, Yan (2022) "Bezuslovnyy prioritet – vypolneniye zadach gosudarstvennogo oboronnogo zakaza", Interviewed by the journal *"Natsional'naya oborona"*, available at: https://oborona.ru/product/zhurnal-nacionalnaya-oborona/bezuslovnyj-prioritet-vypolnenie-zadach-gosudarstvennogo-oboronnogo-zakaza-43621.shtml, accessed 10 July 2022.

Pannier, Bruce (2020) "Kak rossiyskiye voyennyye pomogayut Turkmenistanu?", January 6, available at: https://rus.azattyq.org/a/turkmenistan-russia-afganistan-border/30362388.html, accessed 11 December 2021.

Peter, Laurence (2022) "Is Russia exporting grain from Ukraine?", *BBC News*, June 8, available at: https://www.bbc.com/news/world-europe-61736179, accessed 29 June 2022.

Petrov, Ivan (2019) "Genshtab ulichil SSHA v razrabotke novoy strategii 'Troyanskiy kon'", *Rossiyskoia Gazeta*, March 3, available at: https://rg.ru/2019/03/02/genshtab-ulichil-ssha-v-razrabotke-novoj-strategii-troianskij-kon.html, accessed 1 July 2022.

Pravo.gov.ru, 'Soglasheniye mezhdu Rossiyskoy Federatsiyey i Turkmenistanom o sotrudnichestve v oblasti bezopasnosti ot 10 aprelya 2003 g. (ratifitsirovano Federal'nym zakonom ot 9 noyabrya 2020 g. № 355-FZ, vstupilo v silu 20 noyabrya 2020 g.)', 9 November

2020, available at: http://publication.pravo.gov.ru/Document/View/0001202011240034 accessed 11 December 2021.

President of Ukraine (2022) "Ukraine is negotiating with a number of countries on the export of grain from ports, but weapons remain the main guarantor in this matter", June 6, 8, available at: https://www.president.gov.ua/en/news/ukrayina-vede-peregovori-z-nizkoyu-derzhav-shodo-vivezennya-75653, accessed 10 June 2022.

Putin, Vladimir (2015) "Meeting of the Valdai International Discussion Club", *The Kremlin*, October 22, available at: http://en.kremlin.ru/events/president/news/50548, accessed 30 June 2022.

―――― (2021a) "Ob istoricheskom yedinstve russkikh i ukraintsev", July 12, *Kremlin.ru*, available at: http://kremlin.ru/events/president/news/66181, accessed 20 June 2022.

―――― (2021b) "Expanded Meeting of the Defence Ministry Board", December 21, *Kremlin.ru*, available at: http://en.kremlin.ru/events/president/news/67402, accessed 20 June 2022.

Radio Svoboda (2022) "Chelovek-armageddon. Novyy komanduyushchiy rossiyskim vtorzheniyem", October 10, available at: https://www.svoboda.org/a/chelovek-armageddon-novyy-komanduyuschiy-rossiysim-vtorzheniem/32073403.htm, accessed 24 October 2022.

Ramm, Aleksey, and Anton Lavrov (2021) "Luchnaya rabota: chto izvestno o novom rossiyskom boyevom lazere 'Peresvet'", *Izvestiya*, December 2, available at: https://iz.ru/1258024/anton-lavrov-aleksei-ramm/luchnaia-rabota-chto-izvestno-o-novom-rossiiskom-boevom-lazere-peresvet, accessed 13 July 2022.

Reuters (2019) "Israel says GPS mysteriously disrupted in its airspace but planes secure" June 26, available at: https://www.reuters.com/article/us-israel-aviation-idUSKCN1TR1O3, accessed 11 July 2022.

―――― (2022) "Russia has stolen 600,000 tonnes of grain, Ukrainian producers say", June 8, available at: https://www.reuters.com/article/ukraine-crisis-grain-theft-idAFL1N2XV0XT, accessed 10 June 2022.

RIA Novosti (2016) "Novaya strategicheskaya sistema R·EB smozhet podavit' svyaz' voysk SSHA i NATO", November 14, available at: https://ria.ru/20161114/1481278392.html, accessed 11 July 2022.

―――― (2018) "V MID rasskazali ob optimal'noy ploshchadke peregovorov po Afganistanu", March 14, available at: https://ria.ru/20180314/1516309769.html, accessed 11 December 2021.

―――― (2021a) "Patrushev v N'yu-Deli vstretitsya s prem'yerom Indii", September 7, available at: https://ria.ru/20210907/patrushev-1749020853.html, accessed 21 December 2021.

―――― (2021b) "Lavrov nazval obvineniya v adres Rossii v ugrozakh mirnomu kosmosu litsemeriyem", November 16, available at: https://ria.ru/20211116/kosmos-1759281701.html, accessed 30 June 2022.

―――― (2022) "V Zaporozh'ye zayavili o natsionalizatsii ukrainskogo zerna v regione", June 15, available at: https://ria.ru/20220615/zerno-1795445513.html, accessed 29 June 2022.

Rostec. "Krasukha", https://rostec.ru/tags/%D0%9A%D1%80%D0%B0%D1%81%D1%83%D1%85%D0%B0, accessed 11 July 2022.

―――― (2015) Voyennyye poluchili kompleksy R·EB "Borisoglebsk-2", April 20, available at: https://rostec.ru/media/pressrelease/4516362/, accessed 11 July 2022.

Rowlatt, Justin (2018) "Russia 'arming the Afghan Taliban', says US", *BBC*, March 23, available at: https://www.bbc.com/news/world-asia-43500299, accessed 21 December 2021.

Ryan, Mick (2022) "Why HIMARS may shift the battlefield balance in Ukraine", The Sydney Morning Herald, July 12, available at: https://www.smh.com.au/world/europe/why-himars-may-shift-the-battlefield-balance-in-ukraine-20220712-p5b0x0.html, accessed 17 July 2022.

Sabbagh, Dan (2022) "Ukrainians use phone app to spot deadly Russian drone attacks", The Guardian, October 29, available at: https://www.theguardian.com/world/2022/oct/29/ukraine-phone-app-russia-drone-attacks-eppo, accessed 24 January 2023.

Sankaran, Jaganath (2022a) "Russia's anti-satellite weapons: A hedging and offsetting strategy to deter Western aerospace forces", *Contemporary Security Policy* (Online), DOI: 10.1080/13523260.2022.2090070.

—— (2022b) "Russia's Anti-Satellite Weapons: An Asymmetric Response to U.S. Aerospace Superiority", *Arms Control*, March 22, available at: https://www.armscontrol.org/act/2022-03/features/russias-anti-satellite-weapons-asymmetric-response-us-aerospace-superiority, accessed 10 July 2022.

Saul, Jonathan (2022) "Analysis: The sea mines floating between Ukraine's grain stocks and the world", *Reuters*, June 10, available at: https://www.reuters.com/markets/commodities/sea-mines-floating-between-ukraines-grain-stocks-world-2022-06-10/, accessed 11 June 2022.

Schwirtz, Michael, and Scott Reinhard (2022) "How Russia's Military Is Currently Positioned", The New York Times, January 7, available at: https://www.nytimes.com/interactive/2022/01/07/world/europe/ukraine-maps.html, accessed June 2022.

Serenko, Andrei (2009) "Na 'linii Dyuranda' poyavilis' 'russkiye taliby'", May 29, available at: https://afghanistan.ru/doc/14815.html, accessed 21 December 2021.

Sheetz, Michael (2022) "About 150,000 people in Ukraine are using SpaceX's Starlink internet service daily, government official says", *CNBC*, May 2, available at: https://www.cnbc.com/2022/05/02/ukraine-official-150000-using-spacexs-starlink-daily.html, accessed 12 July 2022.

Skorobogatyy, Pëtr (2022) "Ukraina: gladiatorskiye boi", *PRISP*, August 4, 2022, available at: http://www.prisp.ru/analitics/11005-skorobogatiy-ukraina-gladiatorskie-boi-0408, accessed 8 August 2022.

Sosnitskiy, Vladimir (2021) "Na yuzhnykh rubezhakh strany: sovershaya glubokiye reydy, okhvaty i obkhody", *Zvezda-Ezhenedelnik*, February 11, available at: https://zvezdaweekly.ru/news/2021291350-Qy88G.html, accessed 13 June 2022.

Sovet Bezopasnosti Rossiyskoy Federatsii (2021) "V N'yu-Deli Prem'yer-ministr Respubliki Indiya Narendra Modi prinyal Sekretarya Soveta Bezopasnosti Rossii Nikolaya Patrusheva", *Scrf.gov.ru*, 8 September, available at: http://www.scrf.gov.ru/news/allnews/3066/, accessed 21 December 2021.

Sputnik Tajikistan (2021) "Nalazhen vozdushnyy most Tadzhikistan – Pandzhsher", *Tj.sputniknews.ru*, August 23, available at: https://tj.sputniknews.ru/20210823/nalazhen-vozdushnyy-most-tajikistan-panjsher-1041831090.html, accessed 21 December 2021.

Stashevskyi, Oleksandr, and Frank Bajak (2022) "Deadly secret: Electronic warfare shapes Russia-Ukraine war", AP, June 4, 2022, available at: https://apnews.com/article/russia-ukraine-kyiv-technology-90d760f01105b9aaf1886427dbfba917, accessed 11 July 2022.

Stepanova, Ekaterina (2018) "Russia's Afghan Policy in the Regional and Russia-West Contexts", Russie.Nei.Reports, *Ifri*, no. 23, available at: https://www.ifri.org/en/publications/etudes-de-lifri/russieneireports/russias-afghan-policy-regional-and-russia-west, accessed 11 December 2021.

_____ (2019) "Mirnyi protsess po Afganistanu i rol' Rossii", *Puti k miru i bezopasnosti. Pathways to Peace and Security*, Vol. 2, No. 57, pp. 21–33, DOI: 10.20542/2307-1494-2019-2-21-33, available at: https://www.imemo.ru/publications/periodical/pmb/archive/2019/2-57/articles/conflict-and-peace-process-in-afghanistan/peace-process-in-afghanistan-and-the-role-of-russia.

Strokan', Sergey, Yelena Chernenko, Kirill Krivosheyev, Aleksandr Konstantinov, and Dmitriy Kozlov (2020) "Rossiya v kol'tse vizitov-Gossekretar' Pompeo zayavil o pretenziyakh SSHA na postsovetskoye prostranstvo", *Kommersant*, February 3, available at: https://www.kommersant.ru/doc/4241536, accessed 11 December 2021.

Subbotin, Igor' (2019) 'Taliby igrayut na protivorechiyakh Moskvy i Vashingtona', *Nezavismaya Gazeta*, 5 February, available at: https://www.ng.ru/world/2019-02-05/6_7500_afgan.html, accessed 11 December 2021.

Tarasenko, Pavel, Kirill Krivosheyev, and Anatoliy Kostyrev (2022) "Likvidatsiya global'nogo pogolodaniya", *Gazeta Kommersant*, 132, July 23, p. 1, available at: https://www.kommersant.ru/doc/5479252, accessed 29 July 2022.

TASS (2013) "Raketa-nositel' "Rokot" vyvela sputniki Minoborony RF na tselevuyu orbitu", December 25, available at: https://nauka.tass.ru/nauka/856345?utm_source=tass.ru&utm_medium=referral&utm_campaign=tass.ru&utm_referrer=tass.ru, accessed 10 July 2022.

_____ (2016) "Kolichestvo batal'onnykh takticheskikh grupp v rossiyskoy armii vozrastet pochti vdvoye", September 14, available at: https://tass.ru/armiya-i-opk/3620165, accessed 13 June 2022.

_____ (2018) "Genshtab: osobennost'yu konfliktov budushchego stanet primeneniye robotov i kosmicheskikh sredstv", March 24, available at: https://tass.ru/armiya-i-opk/5062463, accessed 30 June 2022.

_____ (2020) "ZRS S-500 'Prometey' planiruyut postavit' v voyska v blizhayshiye gody", July 7, available at: https://tass.ru/armiya-i-opk/8908911, accessed 10 July 2022.

_____ (2021) "Shoygu zayavil, chto v armii Rossii naschityvayetsya 168 batal'onno-takticheskikh grupp", August 10, available at: https://tass.ru/armiya-i-opk/12099255, accessed 1 June 2022.

_____ (2022a) "Minoborony RF vpervyye pokazalo rabotu kompleksa REB "Palantin" na Ukraine", June 4, available at: https://tass.ru/armiya-i-opk/14821593, accessed 10 June 2022.

_____ (2022b) "Minoborony RF pokazalo primeneniye noveyshego kompleksa R·EB "Krasukha-S4" na Ukraine" June 29, available at: https://tass.ru/armiya-i-opk/15064573, accessed 11 July 2022.

The Economist (2022a) "An interview with General Valery Zaluzhny, head of Ukraine's armed forces", December 15, available at: https://www.economist.com/zaluzhny-transcript, accessed 24 January 2023.

_____ (2022b) "Anyone who underestimates Russia is headed for defeat", December 15, available at: https://www.economist.com/syrsky-interview, accessed 24 January 2023.

The Ministry of Foreign Affairs of the Russian Federation (2019a) 'O provedenii vstrechi predstaviteley vedushchikh politicheskikh sil Afganistana pod egidoy afganskikh diaspor', Brifing ofitsial'nogo predstavitelya MID Rossii M.V. Zakharovoy", February 7, available at: https://www.mid.ru/press_service/spokesman/briefings/-/asset_publisher/D2wHaWMCU6Od/content/id/3503377#12, accessed 11 December 2021.

_____ (2019b) 'Trekhstoronniy konsensus Rossii, Kitaya i SSHA po mirnomu protsessu v Afganistane (Prinyat po itogam vstrechi spetspredstaviteley Prezidenta Rossii, MID KNR i Gosudarstvennogo departamenta SSHA po Afganistanu', April 25, available at: https://dushanbe.mid.ru/novosti-posol-stva/-/asset_publisher/tKTpTrZaRYxl/content/

trehstoronnij-konsensus-rossii-kitaa-i-ssa-po-mirnomu-processu-v-afganistane? inheritRedirect=true, accessed 11 December 2021.

_____ (2019c) 'Sovmestnoye zayavleniye Rossii, Kitaya, SSHA i Pakistana po afganskomu mirnomu protsessu', October 28, available at: https://www.mid.ru/ru/foreign_policy/news/-/asset_publisher/cKNonkJE02Bw/content/id/3867739 accessed 11 December 2021.

The Moscow Times (2020) '"100% Bullsh*t': Russia Blasts Reports of Taliban Bounties for Killed U.S. Troops', 30 June, available at: https://www.themoscowtimes.com/2020/06/30/100-bullsht-russia-blasts-reports-of-taliban-bounties-for-killed-us-troops-a70737, accessed 21 December 2021.

Trofimov, Yaroslav, and Dion Nissenbaum (2022) "Russia's Use of Iranian Kamikaze Drones Creates New Dangers for Ukrainian Troops", *WSJ*, September 17, available at: https://www.wsj.com/articles/russias-use-of-iranian-kamikaze-drones-creates-new-dangers-for-ukrainian-troops-11663415140, accessed 20 September 2021.

Trenin, Dmitriy, Kulakov Oleg, Aleksey Malashenko, and Petr Topychkanov (2014) "Afganistan posle vyvoda voysk mezhdunarodnoy koalitsii: ugrozy, riski i vyzovy dlya Rossiyskoy Federatsii", *Carnegie Endowment for International Peace and Carnegie Moscow Center*, available at: https://carnegieendowment.org/files/CP_Afganistan_web_Rus2014.pdf, accessed 20 September 2021.

TRT Haber (2022) "Tahıl krizinin çözümü için 'kırmızı hat' kuruldu", June 15, available at: https://www.trthaber.com/haber/gundem/tahil-krizinin-cozumu-icin-kirmizi-hat-kuruldu-688087.html?utm_source=pocket_mylist, accessed 15 June 2022.

Tuchkov, Vladimir (2018) "Zvezdnyye voyny: Naydet li Rossiya protivoyadiye protiv X-37", *Svobodnaya Pressa*, October 28, available at: https://svpressa.ru/war21/article/214435/, accessed 1 July 2022.

U.S. Department of State (2020) 'Secretary Pompeo's Travel to the U.K., Ukraine, Belarus, Kazakhstan, and Uzbekistan', Press statement, Morgan Ortagus, Department spokesperson, 24 January, available at: https://www.state.gov/secretary-pompeos-travel-to-the-uk-ukraine-belarus-kazakhstan-and-uzbekistan/, accessed 11 December 2021.

U.S. Mission Russia (2019) 'O vizite spetspredstavitelya SSHA po afganskomu primireniyu Zalmaya Khalilzada v Moskvu', October 27, available at: https://ru.usembassy.gov/ru/u-s-special-representative-for-afghanistan-reconciliation-ambassador-khalilzad-holds-consultations-in-moscow-ru/, accessed 11 December 2021.

Val'chenko, Sergey, Nikolay Surkov, and Aleksey Ramm (2017) "Rossiya poslala na orbitu inspektora Voyennyye oprobovali v deystvii unikal'nyy manevriruyushchiy sputnik opoznaniya i perekhvata", *Izvestiya*, October 26, available at: https://iz.ru/662230/sergei-valchenko-nikolai-surkov-aleksei-ramm/rossiia-poslala-na-orbitu-inspektora, accessed 10 July 2022.

Visual Storytelling Team (2022) "How Russia's mistakes and Ukrainian resistance altered Putin's war", *The Financial Times*, March 18, available at: https://ig.ft.com/russias-war-in-ukraine-mapped/?utm_source=pocket_mylist, accessed 1 June 2022.

Walsh, Declan, and Valerie Hopkins (2022) "Russia Seeks Buyers for Plundered Ukraine Grain, U.S. Warns", *The New York Times*, June 5, available at: https://www.nytimes.com/2022/06/05/world/africa/ukraine-grain-russia-sales.html, accessed 10 June 2022.

Warikoo, Kulbhushan (2019) "The Shanghai Cooperation Organization and Afghanistan", April 26, available at: http://infoshos.ru/en/?idn=21303#:~:text=The%20SCO%2DAfghanistan%20Contact%20Group,through%20political%20consultations%20and%20dialogue, accessed 11 December 2021.

Weeden, Brian (2015) "Dancing in the dark redux: Recent Russian rendezvous and proximity operations in space", October 5, *The Space Review*, available at: https://www.thespacereview.com/article/2839/1, accessed 10 July 2022.

Yermolov, Andrey (2021) "'Mozhet nesti yadernyye boyegolovki': chem opasen amerikanskiy kosmolet X-37", *Gazeta.ru*, May 22, available at: https://www.gazeta.ru/army/2021/05/22/13603490.shtml?updated, accessed 1 July 2022.

Zabrodskyi, Mykhaylo, Jack Watling, Oleksandr V Danylyuk, and Nick Reynolds (2022) "Preliminary Lessons in Conventional Warfighting from Russia's Invasion of Ukraine: February–July 2022", *Royal United Services Institute for Defence and Security Studies – RUSI*, November 30, p. 37, available at: https://rusi.org/explore-our-research/publications/special-resources/preliminary-lessons-conventional-warfighting-russias-invasion-ukraine-february-july-2022, accessed 10 February 2023.

Zakharov, Andrey, and Mariya Korenyuk (2022) "Bylo ukrainskoye, stalo russkoye". *BBC Russian*, June 20, available at: https://www.bbc.com/russian/news-61763999, accessed 22 June 2022.

# Why does Russia prefer strategic asymmetry?

Most asymmetric approaches are not new but there are new possibilities offered by the developments in the hi-tech industry and Internet technologies in the current age. The history of conflict is filled with examples of "asymmetric" thought and a subsequent utilization of its methods. Centuries before the creation of the term "asymmetric warfare" Sun Tzu quiet clearly understood this warfare philosophy. He explained how the weak can defeat the strong, "Military tactics are like unto water; for water in its natural course runs away from high places and hastens downwards" or "water shapes its course according to the nature of the ground over which it flows; the soldier works out his victory in relation to the foe whom he is facing."[1] Another Chinese thinker Sun Bin wrote in the 2nd century BC that the good strategist will look to initiate surprise by acting in an unexpected way, "When conventional tactics are altered unexpectedly according to the situation, they take on the element of surprise and increase in strategic value."[2]

Its historical pedigree goes back at least as far as the Peloponnesian War, the conflict between Athens and Sparta in the 5th-century BC. During the conflict between Athens and Sparta, the latter recognized it needed to keep significant forces in Laconia and Messenia to prevent a revolt by the Helots, upon whose backs its agricultural and military systems rested.

Williamson Murray and Peter R. Mansoor note that, Athenian stratagems such as the move to build an expeditionary base at Pylos rested in part on the aim of creating the conditions for a Helot uprising, which would then add an irregular dimension to the conventional conflict:

> After Athenian forces fortified Pylos on the southwest coast of the Peloponnese in 425 BC, they garrisoned the outpost with Messenians of Naupactus, whose ancestors the Spartans had expelled from the area after the great Helot uprising of 464 BC. The Messenians began a series of incursions into Laconia, aided by their ability to speak the local dialect. Helots soon began to desert to Pylos, thereby creating a national emergency in Sparta. This insurgency represented a form of war for which the exceptional Spartan phalanxes were ill suited.[3]

According to the records of Athenian historian Thucydides, the Spartans, hitherto without experience of incursions or warfare of this kind, upon finding the

DOI: 10.4324/9781003344391-9

Helots deserting, and fearing the march of revolution in their country, became seriously uneasy and, in spite of their unwillingness to betray this to the Athenians, began to send envoys to Athens and tried to recover Pylos and the prisoners.[4]

Asymmetric warfare is an age-old feature of conflict of which many of the Western powers have a great deal of operational experience both before and during the Cold War.[5] Tim Benbow notes that it is by no means distinct from "regular" strategy but rather an application of such basic strategic and tactical principles as avoiding strength and attacking weakness. It has long been a fundamental element of conventional warfare at all levels.[6] According to Benbow, the term is generally used to explain a contrast to the modern Western style of warfare encompassing state-based, regular armed forces, using conventional strategy and tactics. "Asymmetric actors or methods," he writes, "therefore differ from these and an actor that has opted for an asymmetric approach has done so precisely because its opponent enjoys a significant advantage in another field, and this gap can be exploited."[7]

As a theoretical concept, it was designed in the 20th century. In 1975, Andrew J.R. Mack first used asymmetric warfare as a specific terminology.[8] He analyzed the wars after WWII and concluded that the American war in Vietnam provided the most obvious demonstration of the falsity of the assumptions that underlie the "capability" conception of power.[9] According to Mack, the Vietnam war demonstrated how, under certain conditions, the theater of war extends well beyond the battlefield to encompass the polity and social institutions of the external power.[10] Mack stressed the role of interests as well as psychological and political warfare tools in asymmetric conflicts. His main answer to the question, "how did they (weaker sides) win?" is the destruction of the strong external power's political capability to wage war.[11] He explains the relationship between powers in asymmetric conflicts as "the asymmetric relationship" or "a function of the asymmetry in 'resource power.'"[12]

If power implies victory in war, then weak actors should almost never win against stronger opponents, especially when the gap in relative power is huge. However, weak actors sometimes do win. What then explains both the defeat of strong actors in asymmetric wars and the trend toward weaker actors claiming more victories over time? Ivan Arreguín-Toft argues that opposite-approach interactions (direct-indirect or indirect-direct) imply victory for weak actors because the strong actor's power advantage is deflected or dodged. These interactions tend to be protracted, with time favoring the weak:[13]

> Direct approaches target an adversary's armed forces in order to destroy that adversary's capacity to fight. Indirect approaches seek to destroy an adversary's will to fight: Toward this end, a Guerrilla Warfare Strategy targets enemy soldiers, and barbarism targets enemy non-combatants. Same approach interactions (direct-direct or indirect-indirect) imply defeat for weak actors because there is nothing to mediate or defect a strong actor's power advantage. These interactions will therefore be resolved quickly. By contrast, opposite-approach interactions (direct-indirect or indirect-direct) imply victory for weak actors because the strong actor's power advantage is deflected or dodged. These therefore tend to be protracted, with time favoring the weak.[14]

Theoretically, Russia's preferences to use asymmetric methods in external security could be explained in frame of the strategic interaction. Faced with strong adversaries, it is appropriate for Russia to use an indirect security strategy.

According to Arreguín-Toft, the blitzkrieg model, which is mainly used by the West emphasizes direct strategic approaches, but the guerrilla warfare model stresses indirect strategic approaches. "When the two interact systematically, strong actors should lose more often. These patterns of socialization suggest that actors on the threshold of armed conflict are not entirely free to choose an ideal strategy for two reasons. First, forces, equipment, and training—all closely integrated—are not fungible."[15] Basically, there are three distinct and narrowly defined strategies: attrition, blitzkrieg, and limited aims strategy with each having different implications for deterrence.[16] The blitzkrieg and attrition strategies are invariably riskier because they are almost always employed in pursuit of a more ambitious objective and because they both involve directly engaging the defender's forces, but still, several factors reduce the attractiveness of the limited aims strategy.[17]

John Mearsheimer explains that the limited aims strategy is directly concerned with seizing a specific piece of territory stating "at the same time, the attacker seeks to limit contact with the main body of the opposition's forces. The key to success for the attacker is the achievement of strategic surprise, which means catching the defender unprepared. The attacker seeks to gain his territorial objectives when the defense is weakest, so that it is necessary to defeat only a portion of the defender's forces."[18] After achieving their objectives, the attacker turns from an offensive to a defensive posture and prepares for a possible counterattack, "at that point, the burden of starting a war of attrition is transferred to the defender. The assumption is that the defender would not start such a war and that therefore the conflict will remain limited," Mearsheimer notes.[19]

Russia's actions of purely military character in recent years, in Georgia and Ukraine in 2014–2015, could fit in the limited aims strategy, based on Mearsheimer's classification. It should be noted that in the cases of Georgia and Ukraine, Russia's main goal was to deter these countries from pursuing NATO or EU membership. It means that Moscow considered NATO and EU enlargements as the threats, not Georgia or Ukraine. Therefore, Russia's strategy considered activities not only against weaker states (Georgia and Ukraine) but also against stronger adversaries (NATO and the EU). When Russia chose to use a blitzkrieg strategy during its 2022 invasion of Ukraine, it encountered failure at the beginning of the war.

After trying to explain asymmetric warfare theoretically, it is possible to state that it is "fighting an opponent by using forces, tactics, or strategies that are dissimilar to his."[20] According to Rod Thornton, at its simplest, "asymmetric warfare is violent action undertaken by the 'have-nots' against the 'haves' whereby the have-nots, be they state or sub-state actors, seek to generate profound effects—at all levels of warfare (however defined), from the tactical to the strategic—by employing their own specific relative advantages against the vulnerabilities of much stronger opponents."[21] "Often this will," writes Thornton, "means that the weak will use methods that lie outside the 'norms' of warfare, methods that are radically different. It is this element of difference that lies at the heart of asymmetric approaches."[22]

For achieving its goals, an asymmetric adversary may use several methods and tools—conventional and non-conventional, military and non-military—any of which can be useful for implementation. They might be used separately or together. Tim Benbow, who analyzes the roles of asymmetric warfare methods in the age of revolutions in military affairs, emphasizes that it would be a serious mistake to assume that "asymmetric warfare" is necessarily low-technology.[23] He notes that modern technology has increased the capacity of rogue states or non-state actors, be they terrorist groups or disaffected individuals, to do harm. He stresses that the "aim of the opponent would not necessarily be the military defeat of the intervening states but would rather be to deter them from becoming involved in the first place or, failing that, to deny them their favored operational approaches, to complicate and frustrate their strategy, to foment and exploit political divisions (internally, among coalition allies, within the region, and in world opinion more generally) and to persuade them that the interests involved in the operation were simply not worth the risk and costs."[24]

## Who are the asymmetric actors in international security?

This leaves an important question: who can use asymmetric methods and therefore be classified as an asymmetric actor? Several scholars answer this question differently. Since Mack's aforementioned article, academic works have mainly emphasized that mostly non-state actors, such as terrorist groups and rebellious movements, prefer asymmetric approaches in confrontation with stronger adversaries. But no one denies the possibility that asymmetric methods and strategies can be used by a strong or declining power. Moreover, some scholars stress that in a confrontation with the United States and its allies, even relatively strong powers are inclined to use asymmetric strategies.

After the attacks of September 11, asymmetric warfare was primarily seen as a type of warfare utilized by terrorist groups, that is, non-state actors, but actors are a highly heterogeneous group and it would be a mistake to group them all together. As pointed out by Thornton, "asymmetric warfare is a broad church ... its exponents range from individual computer hackers, through terrorist and insurgent groups, criminal gangs, all the way up to states themselves. It can be practiced in land, sea, and air battle spaces. The tools used by the asymmetric warrior can include everything from box cutters to submarines, from Trojan horses to jammers, and from dummy tanks to satellite-destroyers."[25] An "asymmetric strategy" might be used by a rogue state that "seeks to avoid conventional war but pursues its objectives via other means."[26] Benbow notes that "asymmetric tactics" or "asymmetric actions" can be utilized by states or by non-state groups using conventional or unconventional forces, and could take place in the context of a regional conflict or separately.[27] Thornton stresses that asymmetric does not mean unequal, "Asymmetrical implies a relationship that cannot be considered to be alike. If one side in a conflict, for example, has a lot of tanks and his opponent far fewer, then the battle would still be symmetrical."[28] In this respect, Christopher Belamy notes:

> Whatever differences there may be in numbers and quality, conventional military forces still designed, trained, and equipped to fight near mirror images of themselves; forces are broadly similar infrastructures. A true asymmetric conflict is where the means are used are quite different.[29]

Roger Barnett argues in favor of this definition writing that "true asymmetry [involves] those actions that an adversary can exercise that you either cannot or will not."[30]

Thornton emphasizes that "it is useful to point out that asymmetric technics can also be applied by the stronger power,"[31] and argues that in the contemporary world overreaching global antagonisms "have a different hue." Thornton expands on this by writing that "the Cold War's painful dichotomy between Soviet Bloc and 'Free World' has been replaced by less defined animosities, but ones that are often very powerful, nonetheless. These have led to, and will yet spawn, an increased level of asymmetric thinking by possible foes of the West."[32] He explains that even strong powers beyond the West may use asymmetric lines rather than symmetric ones, stating that "these, seeing how powerful the US is, will be forced to think along asymmetric lines. China, for instance, is a rising power, but also one which will need to apply something other than symmetrical approaches if it is to emerge. As Robert Kaplan put it, 'in Iraq the insurgents have shown us the low end of asymmetry ... but the Chinese are poised to show us the high end of the art.'"[33]

Since the end of the Cold War, asymmetric warfare has become relatively more attractive. The military and economic strength of the United States and the West in general proves that there is no truly symmetric potential opponent. According to Benbow, powerful regional actors might wish to challenge the West but their clear inferiority in conventional military power would make asymmetric strategies and tactics all the more tempting. "The 1991 Gulf conflict demonstrated with brutal clarity the folly of confronting the US and its major allies with their ideal form of warfare."[34]

As General James N. Mattis and Frank Hoffman put it in 2005, the United States conventional superiority creates a compelling logic for states and non-state actors to move out of the traditional mode of war and seek some niche capability or some unexpected combination of technologies and tactics to gain an advantage.[35]

Nowadays, asymmetric warfare is a type of warfare that is receiving much of the focus of military thinkers, political and military decision-makers, and experts and will continue to do so for the foreseeable future, including for Russia. Unlike its Cold War predecessor, a new conflict situation between Russia and the West is asymmetrical. Since the 1960s, the Soviet Union was the United States' equal in terms of nuclear and conventional military power. But now, Russia is weaker than the USSR in terms of its conventional military capabilities, economy, and international partners as witnessed in the war in Ukraine. As asymmetries in power factors lead to asymmetric actions, Russia is increasingly inclined to use asymmetric tools. In these conditions, the use of mainly asymmetric methods might give Russia an advantage in a confrontation with a more powerful adversary. After the Gulf War and the NATO military operations in the former Yugoslavia in the 1990s, several Russian generals and military scholars concluded that no conventional, non-linear warfare strategies could be decisive in a future military operation and that NATO had more sophisticated conventional military capacities for utilizing non-linear strategies (i.e., high-precision weapons, high military technology, etc.). And regarding Russia's weaker economic and social conditions, it would be very difficult, if not impossible, to achieve a conventional deterrence balance with NATO. That is why it was, and is, attractive and appropriate for Russia to use asymmetric strategies rather than symmetric ones.

It should be noted that since the break-up of the Soviet Union, Russia has been using several warfare methods and strategies in its external security policies. This period has seen several prominent representatives of the military elite call out the importance of using several warfare methods in the country's military affairs. Russia's military operations and activities, over this time, hinted at the fact that they were using several methods based on several military theories. But, given the mentioned theoretical explanations, Russia's contemporary external security behavior can best be explained by using the asymmetric warfare theory since the main strategic approaches utilized by Russia, in the face of a stronger adversary, are asymmetric.

However, in its invasion of Ukraine in 2022, Russia faced a larger adversary, which received essential external support, unlike in the cases of Chechnya and Georgia, and which used asymmetric approaches. Moscow's misperceptions about the state of possibilities and international support of Ukraine and the overconfidence in its own military capabilities have wreaked havoc on Russia. However, the use of proper strategic asymmetry and asymmetric approaches by Ukraine has shown the effectiveness of asymmetric warfare approaches in contemporary military conflicts.

## Notes

1. Sun Tzu (2009) *The Art of War*, Lionel Giles (trans, ed), Seattle: Thrifty Books, http://classic.mit.edu/Tzu/artwar http://classics.mit.edu/Tzu/artwar.html.
2. Sun Bin, Lost Art of War, quoted in David L. Grange (2000) "Asymmetric warfare: old method, newconcern", *National Strategy Forum Review*, Winter 2000, p. 1, online available at: http://indianstrategicknowledgeonline.com/web/cam_grange.pdf.
3. Murray, Williamson and Mansoor, Peter R. (2012) *Hybrid Warfare-Fighting Complex Opponents from the Ancient World to the Present*, New York: Cambridge University Press, pp. 3–4.
4. Strassler, Robert B. (ed.) (1996) *The Landmark Thucydides*, New York: Free Press, pp. 245–246.
5. Benbow, Tim (2004) *The magic bullet?: understanding the 'revolution in military affairs'*, London: Brassey's, p. 156.
6. Ibid.
7. Ibid., p. 158.
8. Mack, Andrew J.R. (1975) "Why Big Nations Lose Small Wars: The Politics of Asymmetric Conflict", *World Politics*, Vol. 27, No. 2 (January 1975).
9. Ibid., p. 177.

10 Mack, Andrew J.R. (1975) "Why Big Nations Lose Small Wars" ..., pp. 177–178.
11 Ibid., p. 195.
12 Ibid., p. 182.
13 Arreguín-Toft, Ivan (2001) "How the Weak Win Wars A Theory of Asymmetric Conflict", *International Security*, Vol. 26, No. 1, pp. 93–128.
14 Ibid, p. 105.
15 Arreguín-Toft, Ivan (2001) "How the Weak Win Wars A Theory of Asymmetric Conflict" ..., p. 106.
16 Mearsheimer, John J. (1983) *Conventional deterrence*. London: Cornell University Press, p. 29.
17 Ibid. p. 30.
18 Ibid. p. 53.
19 Mearsheimer, John J. (1983) Conventional deterrence ..., p. 54.
20 Benbow, Tim (2004) *The magic bullet?: understanding the 'revolution in military affairs'* ..., p. 155.
21 Thornton, Rod (2007) *Asymmetric Warfare: Threat and Response in the 21st Century*, Cambridge: Polity Press, p. 1.
22 Ibid., p. 2.
23 Benbow, Tim (2004) *The magic bullet?: understanding the 'revolution in military affairs'*..., p. 164.
24 Ibid.
25 Thornton, Rod (2007) *Asymmetric Warfare: Threat and Response in the 21st Century* ..., p. 177.
26 Benbow (2004) *The magic bullet?: understanding the 'revolution in military affairs'* ..., p. 157.
27 Ibid., p. 185.
28 Thornton, Rod (2007) *Asymmetric Warfare: Threat and Response in the 21st Century* ..., p. 4.
29 Belamy, Christopher (2002) "The shifted conflict paradigm and reduced role of conventional military power", *Cambridge Review of International Affairs*, 15/1 (April. 2002), p. 152; Cited in Thornton, Rod (2007) *Asymmetric Warfare: Threat and Response in the 21st Century* ..., p. 4.
30 Barnett, Roger (2002) *Asymmetric Warfare: Today's challenges to US military Power*, Washington, DC: Brassey's, p. 15; Thornton, Rod (2007) *Asymmetric Warfare: Threat and Response in the 21st Century* ..., p. 4.
31 Thornton, Rod (2007) *Asymmetric Warfare: Threat and Response in the 21st Century* ..., p. 4
32 Ibid., p. 7.
33 Ibid.
34 Benbow, Tim (2004) *The magic bullet?: understanding the 'revolution in military affairs'* ..., p. 160.
35 Mattis, James N. and Hoffman, Frank (2005) 'Future Warfare: The Rise of Hybrid Wars', *Proceedings Magazine*. U.S. Naval Institute. Issue: November 2005, Vol. 132/11/1,233. https://www.usni.org/magazines/proceedings/2005-11/future-warfare-rise-hybrid-wars.

## Bibliography

Arreguín-Toft, Ivan (2001) "How the Weak Win Wars A Theory of Asymmetric Conflict", *International Security*', Vol. 26, No. 1, pp. 93–128. DOI: 10.1162/016228801753212868.

Barnett, Roger (2002) *Asymmetric Warfare: Today's Challenges to US military Power*, Washington, DC: Brassey's.

Benbow, Tim (2004) *The Magic Bullet?: Understanding the 'revolution in military affairs'*, London: Brassey's.

Bin, Sun, *Lost Art of War*, quoted in David L. Grange (2000) "Asymmetric warfare: old method, new concern", *National Strategy Forum Review*, Winter 2000, p. 1, online available at: http://indianstrategicknowledgeonline.com/web/cam_grange.pdf, accessed 1 November 2018.

Mack, Andrew J.R. (1975) "Why Big Nations Lose Small Wars: The Politics of Asymmetric Conflict", *World Politics'*, Vol. 27, No. 2 (January 1975), pp. 175–200.

Mattis, James N., and Frank Hoffman (2005) 'Future Warfare: The Rise of Hybrid Wars', *Proceedings Magazine*. U.S. Naval Institute. Issue: November 2005, Vol. 132/11/1, 233. https://www.usni.org/magazines/proceedings/2005-11/future-warfare-rise-hybrid-wars, accessed 30 November 2018.

Mearsheimer, John J. (1983) *Conventional deterrence*, London: Cornell University Press.

Murray, Williamson, and Peter R. Mansoor (2012) *Hybrid Warfare-Fighting Complex Opponents from the Ancient World to the Present*, New York: Cambridge University Press.

Strassler, Robert B. (ed.) (1996) *The Landmark Thucydides*, New York: Free Press.

Thornton, Rod (2007) *Asymmetric Warfare: Threat and Response in the 21st Century*, Cambridge: Polity Press.

Tzu, Sun (2009) *The Art of War*, Lionel Giles (trans, ed), Seattle: Thrifty Books, available at: http://classic.mit.edu/Tzu/artwar http://classics.mit.edu/Tzu/artwar.html, accessed 1 October 2018.

# Index

active defense strategy 129, 130
Afghanistan 251–257
Africa 95–96, 172–173
airborne forces 13, 234
anti-satellite capabilities 104, 245–246, 258
anti-satellite weapons (ASAT) 103, 244–246
Arbatov, A. 59
Arbatov, G. 102
Arreguín-Toft, I. 281–282
asymmetric actors 281, 283
asymmetric advantage 130
asymmetric approaches 26, 31–32, 81, 103, 122, 125–131, 150–152, 167–170, 207–208, 257–258, 280, 283, 285
asymmetric measures 29, 31, 130, 168–169
asymmetric response 101, 103–104, 245–246
asymmetric strategies 28–29, 32, 149, 152, 175, 284–285
asymmetric warfare 11–12, 16, 18, 24, 30–32, 122, 125, 167–168, 280–285
attrition war 8, 14, 65, 129, 169, 207, 235, 237, 239, 241

Baluev, D. 26
bandwagoning 214
Bartles, Ch. K. 148, 150, 236
Bartosh, A. 64–65
battalion tactical groups (BTG) 236
Baunov, A. 58
Benbow, T. 281, 283–284
Berzina, I. 64
Berzins, J. 122
"biological warfare laboratories" 156–159
biological weapons 156–160

Charap, S. 152, 230
Chechnya 55, 104–105
Chekinov, S. G. 167–169
China 41–43, 47, 100, 126–128, 159, 170–171, 193–195, 197, 206–208, 214, 216, 252–253, 258, 284
Civil War 9, 14, 52
code breaking 93–95
Cold War 11, 52, 82, 94–07, 192–195
color revolutions 59–66, 120, 125–126, 129
Connolly, R. 42–43, 127
cryptography 93–95
CSTO 204, 215, 253
cyber operations 161–167

Denisov, I. 126
Denisov, V. 55, 59
disinformation 28, 85–89, 91, 153
Dvorkin, V. 245

electronic warfare (EW) 31, 94–95, 248–250
Engels, F. 9
Erickson, J. 14–15
European Union 126, 168, 193, 213–215

Foreign Policy Concept 199–200, 204–205
Freedman, L. 152
Frunze, M. 10–11

Galeotti, M. 147, 152, 175, 210
Gareev, M.A. 26–31, 117–121
Gerasimov, V. 17, 24, 31, 65–66, 128–131, 245–246
Gorbachev, M.S. 54, 55, 91, 195
Gorbunov, Y. A. 86–87
Gorenburg, D. 171
"grain war" 241–244
Grau L.W. 16, 236

great power 68, 116, 192, 194–195, 198–205, 214
Gressel, G. 239
GRU 83, 94, 96, 163, 173, 211, 237
Gudkov, L. 135–136
Guerre de razzia 234
Guerrilla warfare 18, 20, 96, 171–172, 233, 281–282
Gulevich, A.A. 8
Gulin, V.P. 26

Hendrickx, B. 251
Hill, F. 134
Hoffman, F. 147, 284
hybrid war 24, 64–65, 147–149, 206
hypersonic weapons 43, 45, 99–101, 247

India 126, 196, 206, 216, 252–253, 256
indirect methods 11, 151, 167
information operation 30, 130, 151, 153–156, 160, 163
information warfare 19, 30, 129, 153–161
initial period of war 11, 52–53, 169
insurgency 18, 95–97, 172, 175, 233
Isserson, G. S. 13–14, 17
Ivanov, S. 62, 118–119

Kalinovskii, K.B. 13
Kartapolov, A. 30–31
Kashin, V. 235
Keenan, E. 49–51, 209
Kennan, G. 11, 51–52, 82–83, 147
KGB 83–91, 94–97, 137, 162, 165
"Khorovod" 89
Kofman, M. 42, 147, 149, 169, 235–236, 240
Kokoshin, A. 103–104
Kortunov, A. 208–209, 213
Kristensen, H. M. 43–44

Laruelle, M. 171, 173
Laser systems 250–251
Lavrov, S. 59, 195–196, 199, 203, 205, 244
Lee, R. 235–236
Levada Analytical Center 134
"Liberal Empire" 198–199
Lieven, A. 230
limited actions 130–131
Lukyanov, F. 122, 192, 195, 200–201, 203, 208, 215

Mackfarland, S. B. 15
Maritime Doctrine 127

Marxism 9–11
Marxism-Leninism 9, 11, 81, 194
Mattis, J. N. 284
McDermott, R. 130–131
Mearsheimer, J. 193, 230, 282
Messner, Y. 17–24
Middle East 94, 96–97, 104, 127, 194, 196, 203–204, 206–207, 242–243
Mikhnevich N. P. 8–9
military doctrine 10, 20, 23, 53, 119–122, 124, 126, 128–129, 131
military expenditures 41–43
military operation 10–11, 31, 55, 117, 147, 152, 167–170
Miliutin, D. 8
missile defense 44–45, 68, 101–104, 123–124, 170, 232, 245, 247
multi-vector foreign policy 196–197
mutiny warfare 17–24

National Center for the Management of Defense of the Russian Federation 152
National Security Strategy 123–126
NATO enlargement 54–59, 67–68, 118
New START Treaty 44, 47, 59, 170–171
Neznamov, A.A. 8
non-linear warfare 12–17
non-military methods 30, 129, 175
nuclear weapons 43–47, 59, 67, 101

Oliker, O. 124

Patrushev, N. 66, 158, 210–211
Petersen, M. B. 127
Pintner, W. 7–8
Pipes, R. 7, 49–51, 67, 84
PMC 170–174
Primakov, Y. 195–198
"Primakov Doctrine" 196
propaganda 15, 18–19, 22–23, 85–93, 103, 135–136, 153–156, 160
Pukhov, R. 238–239
Putin, V. 44–47, 57, 60, 101, 104, 133–134, 158, 170, 172, 199, 201, 205, 212, 229–232, 242, 244–245, 255
Pynnöniemi, K. 125

regime security 21, 59, 61, 68, 119–120, 126, 149, 230
Renz, B. 132–133, 147–149, 206
Rojansky, M. 149, 152–153, 175

Russian economy 48, 198, 231
Ryabkov, S. 58

Safranchuk, I. 196
Security Council of the Russian Federation 209
security documents 116–131
Shoigu, S. 44, 148, 158, 163, 236
Siloviki 132–133, 165, 199, 210, 230
Slipchenko, V. 25
Snetkov, A. 61, 119
Soviet military school 25
Stalin, I. V. 82, 151
strategic interaction 16, 281–282
Sukhankin S. 172
Surkov, V. 23, 61–64, 201
surprise attack 11, 52–53
Suvorov's legacy 7, 31
Svechin, A. 14
Syria 30, 130, 168, 172, 203–204, 207, 235

Taliban 254–256
The Academy of Military Sciences 27, 131
The battle of Donbas 236–241

The Department for Disinformation 87
The 6th-generation warfare 25
Thornton, R. 282–284
threat perception 51, 56, 61, 121, 131–137
Trenin, D. 46, 58, 195, 201–202, 204–205, 207–208, 213, 215
Triandafillov, V. K. 13
Trotsky, L. 9–10, 12
Tsygankov A. 201, 209
Tukhachevskii, N. M. 13–14

Ukraine 45–46, 57–59, 63–64, 133, 135, 152, 154–156, 165–167, 174, 215–216, 229–244, 248–250
Unified Military Doctrine 10

Wagner 172–174
Walt, S. 193–194, 214–215
Waltzman, R. 160–161
whole-country war 11, 15
world order 192–195, 201–202, 203–208

Zaluzhnyi, V. 233
Zimmerman, W. 56–57, 83

For Product Safety Concerns and Information please contact our EU representative GPSR@taylorandfrancis.com
Taylor & Francis Verlag GmbH, Kaufingerstraße 24, 80331 München, Germany